John Cameron West
Huntingdon College
Montgomery, Alabama
2012, October

The Redemptive Self

The Redemptive Self

STORIES AMERICANS LIVE BY

DAN P. McADAMS

2006

OXFORD
UNIVERSITY PRESS

Oxford University Press, Inc., publishes works that further
Oxford University's objective of excellence
in research, scholarship, and education.

Oxford   New York
Auckland   Cape Town   Dar es Salaam   Hong Kong   Karachi
Kuala Lumpur   Madrid   Melbourne   Mexico City   Nairobi
New Delhi   Shanghai   Taipei   Toronto

With offices in
Argentina   Austria   Brazil   Chile   Czech Republic   France   Greece
Guatemala   Hungary   Italy   Japan   Poland   Portugal   Singapore
South Korea   Switzerland   Thailand   Turkey   Ukraine   Vietnam

Published by Oxford University Press, Inc.
198 Madison Avenue, New York, New York 10016

www.oup.com

Oxford is a registered trademark of Oxford University Press

Library of Congress Cataloging-in-Publication Data
McAdams, Dan P.
The redemptive self : stories Americans live by / Dan P. McAdams
     p.   cm.
Includes bibliographical references (p.   ) and index.
ISBN-13 978-0-19-517693-3
     1. Self-perception—United States. 2. Redemption—Psychology—
     Miscellanea. 3. Success—United States—Psychological aspects.
     I. Title.
BF697.5.S43M33   2005
155.2′5—dc22   2004026514

9 8 7 6 5 4

Printed in the United States of America
on acid-free paper

To the memory of Jeanne M. Foley (1922–2001)

Acknowledgments

I am grateful to the many colleagues, students, friends, and family members who have made contributions to this book. Jon Adler, Michelle Green, Robert Hogan, five anonymous (and extraordinarily conscientious) reviewers, and my wife Rebecca Pallmeyer read the entire manuscript and provided me with many thoughtful comments and critiques. Jim Anderson, Nana Akua Anyidoho, Susan Arellano, John Barresi, Ed de St. Aubin, Alexandra Freund, Ruthellen Josselson, Alan Lepp, Dan Lewis, Gina Logan, Mary Anne Machado, Shadd Maruna, Tom McGovern, Arlin Meyer, Dan Ogilvie, Ken Paller, Jen Pals, Jefferson Singer, and Paul Wink read and commented on selected chapters. Although they did not always say what I wanted to hear, I benefited greatly from the wise counsel I received from all these astute readers. Thank you also to Catharine Carlin and Heather Hartman at Oxford University Press for their editorial advice and enthusiastic support.

What was to become the book's main thesis became clear to me in a wonderful conversation I had with Alan Lepp in the summer of 2000. David Winter, Jeff Smith, and Carl Smith made invaluable suggestions for books to read on the topic of redemption and American history. Peter Zeldow suggested the very cool idea of coding stories from *People* magazine for redemption imagery. Jim Egan gave me an original Horatio Alger book, along with good ideas about redemption and the American dream. Dick Anderson dug up the Cardinal George quote with which I begin chapter 6. My mother, Millie McAdams, helped me research the 1968 mayoral election in Gary, Indiana, as background for chapter 7. Between tennis sets, Greg Korak made a key suggestion regarding the role of atonement in redemption. My analysis of generativity among African American adults was strongly influenced by my stimulating collaboration and friendship with Phil Bowman. Other colleagues who have had a big impact on my thinking regarding generativity, redemption, and life narratives over the past few years include Don Browning, Bert

Cohler, Anne Colby, Bill Damon, Kai Erikson, Bert Hermans, Tae-Chang Kim, John Kotre, Amia Lieblich, Ron Manheimer, Bill Peterson, Michael Pratt, Peter Raggatt, Todd Schultz, Mark Snyder, Avril Thorne, Jerry Wakefield, and Barbara Woike.

I owe special thanks to the many undergraduate and graduate students and postdocs who have worked with me over the past few years on the research projects described in this book. All of the following have made major contributions to our efforts to understand generativity, redemption, and life narratives in adulthood: Jay Azarow, Dana Baerger, Jack Bauer, Reginald Blount, Irene Carvalho, Ann Diamond, Amanda Faniff, Jennifer Goldberg, Holly Hart, Bonnie Kaplan, Avi Kay, Amy Kegley, Erin Kennedy, Emily Kissel, Martha Lewis, Elizabeth Mansfield, David McConville, Derek McNeil, Nathania Montes, Allison Patten, Elizabeth Reyes, April Sakaeda, and Janet Shlaes. I owe enormous gratitude to the Spencer Foundation for funding my research between 1990 and 1997 and to the Foley Family Foundation for funding my research for the past eight years and establishing the Foley Center for the Study of Lives at Northwestern University. Without the support of Steve Fisher, Wendy Bosworth, and the late Jeanne M. Foley of the Foley Family Foundation, this book could not have been written.

Finally, I must thank again my wife, Rebecca Pallmeyer, who continues to be the most redemptive force in my life narrative.

Contents

The Redemptive Self

Prologue

A LIFE STORY

MADE IN AMERICA

Beginning September 11, 2001, William Langewiesche spent 9 months at the site of the World Trade Center disaster. He observed and interviewed firefighters, construction workers, engineers, police officers, and paid volunteers who cleared the debris and dug through the rubble in search of survivors. "Within hours of the collapse [of the towers], as rescuers rushed in and resources were marshaled," Langewiesche later wrote, "the disaster was smothered in an exuberant and *distinctively American* embrace." The workers were convinced that something good would arise from the carnage. "Despite the apocalyptic nature of the scene," Langewiesche suggested, "the response was unhesitant and almost childishly optimistic: *it was simply understood* that you would find survivors, and then that you would find the dead, and that this would help their families to get on with their lives, and that your resources were unlimited, and that you would work night and day to clean up the mess, and that this would allow the world's greatest city to rebuild quickly, and maybe even to make itself into something better than before."[1]

Put differently, it was simply understood that there would be *redemption.*

An "exuberant" and "distinctively American" response, "unhesitant," almost childish. The workers were convinced that the death and the destruction of September 11 would give way to new life, new growth, new power, and a new reality that, in some fundamental sense, would prove better than what came before. Their faith reflected the hopes of many American citizens— men and women who had never known a foreign attack on American soil

3

but who felt deep in their bones that bad things, even things this bad, ulti- mately lead to good outcomes, that suffering is ultimately redeemed.

Maybe there *is* something childish (and presumptuous) about this re- sponse, this expectation that we will be delivered from our pain and suffer- ing no matter what, that we will overcome in the long run, that we will rise from the depths of the present, that things will get better and that we will eventually grow and find fulfillment in the world. But I am not talking here about the naïveté of children. I am talking instead about mature men and women who, like many of the workers at the World Trade Center site, are committed to making a positive difference in the world. I am talking about productive and caring, socially responsible, hardworking adults who try to pay their bills and their taxes, try to provide for their families, and try to make something good out of their lives, even as they fail and get distracted along the way. I am talking about the kinds of people who support the insti- tutions that are necessary to create and sustain what the sociologist Robert Bellah calls a "good society."[2] Let us imagine that these are the people whom the framers of the U.S. Constitution had in mind when they identified the ultimate authors of their document as "we the people." For the framers, we the people aimed to "form a more perfect union, establish justice, insure do- mestic tranquility, provide for the common defense, promote the general welfare, and secure the blessings of liberty to ourselves and our posterity."[3]

From a psychological standpoint, who *are* "we the people"? What are we like? In considering this question, I turn first to the eminent psychoanalyst Erik H. Erikson, who, during much of the second half of the 20th century, wrote provocatively about mental health, maturity, and the human life span. Erikson depicted we the people as those members of a society who have worked through the psychological dilemmas of childhood, adolescence, and the very early years of adulthood and who have committed themselves to pat- terns of love and work aimed at leaving a positive legacy for the future. The Constitution suggests that we the people should strive to assure justice, peace, security, and freedom not just for us today—but also for our posterity, our children and our children's children. The good society must work to promote the well-being of future generations. Erikson claimed that responsible and mature men and women—especially in their middle-adult years—should do the same. Erikson even had a word for this. He called it *generativity*.

Generativity is the adult's concern for and commitment to promoting the welfare and development of future generations.[4] The most obvious and nat- ural expression of generativity is the care that parents provide for their chil- dren. But generativity can be expressed in many other ways, too, including teaching, mentoring, leadership, and even citizenship. Generative adults seek to give something back to society. They work to make their world a better place, not just for themselves but for future generations, as well. They try to take the long view. Whether they consciously think about it this way or not, generative adults work for the good of posterity. A good society depends on the generative efforts of adults. For this reason (among others), Erikson believed that generativity was more than simply a psychological standard for adult mental health. He also saw it as the prime virtue of adulthood.[5]

Different people have different virtues. Some people are more honest than others. Some may be more courageous, faithful, or self-disciplined.[6] And so it is with generativity, as Erikson well knew. Most adults are moderately generative on the average, focusing most of their generative inclinations on their families. A few adults show virtually no generativity in their lives. And some, on the other end of the spectrum, are extraordinarily generative in many different ways. Think of them as generativity superstars.

For many years now, I have been studying the superstars. Who are the especially generative people in our society? What are their lives like? In the summer of 2000, I was presenting some of this research at a scientific conference in the Netherlands when I received a comment from a woman in the audience that eventually gave birth to this book. The main point of my talk was that highly generative adults tend to tell a certain kind of story about their lives, a story that emphasizes the themes of suffering, redemption, and personal destiny. The comment I received went something like this: "Professor McAdams, this is very interesting, but these life stories you describe, they seem so, well, *American*." Initially, I heard this as a criticism of the work. After all, I had been assuming that my findings applied to very generative adults *in general*, regardless of their backgrounds. To say the life stories I described all sounded very "American" was to suggest that my research findings were too limited, that they were not "generalizable," as we social scientists often say.

After thinking longer about the woman's comment, however, I came to realize two things. First, she was probably right, at least in part. My results about Americans might *not* generalize completely to other societies. Second, I think I like the fact that she may have been right. Her comment suggests an important insight: The life stories of highly generative American adults may reveal as much about American society and culture as they do about the generative adults themselves. It is as if these well-meaning American people who dedicate their lives to promoting the well-being of the next generation are walking embodiments of some of the most cherished (and contested) ideas in our American heritage. Their lives personify and proclaim the stories that

FIGURE P.1 "We the people of the United States, in order to form a more perfect union, establish justice, insure domestic tranquility, provide for the common defense, promote the general welfare, and secure the blessings of liberty to ourselves and our posterity, do ordain and establish this Constitution for the United States of America." In aiming to address the needs and aspirations of "our posterity," the framers of the U.S. Constitution invoked a psychological idea underscored almost 200 years later by the psychologist Erik H. Erikson. Erikson defined *generativity* as the adult's concern for and commitment to promoting the well-being and development of future generations. Generativity is the central psychological issue and arguably the most important virtue of the middle adult years. Reprinted with the permission of the National Archives and Records Administration.

we all—we Americans—might like to tell about our own lives, stories that we indeed *do* often tell, though perhaps with less conviction, consistency, and gusto. The stories they live and tell are our stories, too—made in America.

What is the story that highly generative American adults tell? Everybody has a unique life story to tell. But if you listen to many life stories, as I and my students have over the past 20 years, you begin to recognize some common patterns.[7] The pattern that I will focus on in this book is the one that tends to distinguish the life stories told by highly generative American adults from those told by less generative American adults.[8] Research findings suggest that highly generative American adults are statistically more likely than their less generative counterparts to make sense of their own lives through an idealized story script that emphasizes, among other themes, the power of human redemption. In the most general sense, redemption is a deliverance from suffering to a better world. Religious conceptions of redemption imagine it as a divine intervention or sacred process, and the better world may mean heaven, a state of grace, or some other transcendent status. The general idea of redemption can be found in all of the world's major religions and many cultural traditions.

It is important to realize, however, that redemption carries many secular meanings that have nothing to do with religion. Everyday talk is filled with redemptive metaphors. People often speak of "putting the past behind" them in order to move away from something negative to a positive future. Adages such as "every dark cloud has a silver lining," "it's always darkest before dawn," and "no pain, no gain" suggest that suffering in life can often lead to growth or fulfillment. "When life gives you lemons, make lemonade," we are told. Try to transform the negative into some kind of positive. We all know expressions like these, and we can all probably find a few instances in our own lives when this general idea seemed to take hold. Furthermore, we are encouraged to think about our lives in redemptive terms. As just one example, many high school counselors in the United States today strongly urge their college-bound seniors to write personal essays that document the ways they have overcome adversity. College admissions officers appear to value these redemptive accounts quite highly, sometimes even assigning extra points to an applicant's file for especially compelling stories of resilience, recovery, defying the odds, and the like.

When they take stock of their own lives, highly generative American adults tend to *narrate* them around the theme of redemption. They are more likely than the rest of us to see redemptive patterns in their lives. Almost everybody can find some kind of redemption in his or her life story. But highly generative American adults tend to see more of it and to attribute more significance or meaning to the redemptive scenes and situations they do recall. They also expect more redemptive scenes for the future. In the prototypical life story told by the highly generative American adult, the protagonist encounters many setbacks and experiences a great deal of pain in life, but over time these negative scenes lead to especially positive outcomes, outcomes that might not have occurred had the suffering never happened in the first place. Thus, redemption helps to move the life story forward.

Let me say more about this story.

How does the story begin? In the beginning is a blessing, a special advantage, a sense of personal destiny. Highly generative adults are much more likely than less generative adults to emphasize in their autobiographies ways in which they felt lucky or advantaged early on in life. The advantage they think they enjoyed is typically not economic or material. Perhaps, instead, Mom liked them the best. Perhaps they had a special skill. Perhaps they had a teacher or an uncle who sought them out for special treatment. Whatever, they believe they were fortunate in some way. At the same time, the story suggests, certain other characters were *not* fortunate. Highly generative adults are much more likely than less generative adults to recall *scenes in early life in which they witnessed the suffering or disadvantage of other people.* "I remember the retarded kid on our street, how the boys used to pick on him," one highly generative adult recalls. "Our church bus was rerouted so it wouldn't pick up the Black kids," recalls another, as he remembers how it dawned on him as a young White boy that not all people in American society are treated equally.

The implicit message in the beginning of the story is clear: *I am blessed; others suffer.* This stark contrast sets up a moral challenge: Because I (the main character in the story) am advantaged in some way, I have the opportunity, or responsibility, to help improve the lives of those who may not be so blessed. I may even feel that I am *called* to do this, that it is my special fate or personal destiny to be of service to others. "I have some basic gifts," says one highly generative adult, "and I think the purpose of life is to take the gifts you're given and leave the world better for them." Asked what life's most important value is, another says, "Finding your own personal gift and utilizing it the best you can for your personal welfare and for the welfare of everybody else."

How does the plot develop? Early on (typically in adolescence), the protagonist in this story takes in (or develops) a system of beliefs, often rooted in a religious tradition, which serves to guide him or her for the rest of the story. Although the protagonist will go through many changes as the plot unfolds over the life course, the core of this belief system is not likely to change much at all. It is a steadfast foundation for the person's identity. What will change, though, are motivations—the wants and needs and strivings of the story's main character. During certain chapters of my life story, I may want to change the world in a powerful and positive way. At other times, I may want to be loved and cherished by others. Sometimes I want to stand out as different; after all, I am special, blessed. At other times, I want to be accepted as an equal in a community of caring people. I want to be strong, but I want to be loved. I want to be free, but I want to belong. The tension between individual self-expression and human belongingness is arguably a universal feature of social life.[9] But the tension is especially pronounced in the life stories of highly generative American adults. On the one hand, they have clear and compelling belief systems that have convinced them that they know what is right, what is true in life. On the other hand, they do not always know what they want, or they may want things that seem mutually incompatible—like power and love, perhaps, or freedom and community.

Guided by a clear personal belief system and striving to attain goals that express both power and love, the main character in this story encounters expected and unexpected obstacles and challenges as the plot unfolds. The protagonist will encounter friends and enemies, heroes and villains. There will be scenes of joy, excitement, sadness, fear, shame, and almost any other emotion that may be imagined. But a recurrent pattern will hold: Negative emotional scenes will often lead directly to positive outcomes. Suffering will consistently be redeemed. Redemptive sequences will help to move the plot forward and ultimately help give the story its *progressive* form. As one generative adult puts it, "When dealing with anything negative, I was taught to swing the door and make something positive out of it." Another highly generative adult sees his life mission as "confounding ignorance with good works." Many scenes in his life story begin with an expression of ignorance, but this gives way (is redeemed) by a positive action that proves to enlighten others. Despite many setbacks, things get better over time in these kinds of life stories. There is growth and improvement.

How does the story end? The stories people tell about their own lives are works in progress. Still, people can imagine what the future will hold and how, ultimately, things may or may not work out in the end. Highly generative adults see continued progress and growth in the story, even if they anticipate daunting obstacles ahead and even if they are pessimistic about the overall future of the world. They see their contributions to others as having enduring impact, even if only in small ways. Through their children, but often also through many other projects and endeavors in their lives, they see themselves as leaving a legacy for the future. The imagery of growth and progress is very common in these stories. The protagonist gives birth to many things and people, cares for them and provides for their well-being, and eventually lets them go so that they can move forward in life with the generative blessings they have received. One highly generative adult put it this way: "When I die, I guess the chemicals in my body, well, they'll go to fertilize some plants, you know, some ears of corn, and the good deeds I do will live through my children and through the people I love."

In sum, then, here is the general script of the life story I have described: *I learn in childhood that I have a special gift. At the same time, I see (and am moved by) suffering and injustice in my world. As a result, I come to believe that my personal destiny is to have some positive impact on others. In adolescence I internalize a belief system that sustains my commitment to improving the world. I will never abandon these core beliefs. Over the course of my adult life, I struggle to reconcile my strong needs for power and independence with my equally strong needs for love and community. Bad things happen to me, but good outcomes often follow. My suffering is usually redeemed, as I continue to progress, to learn, to improve. Looking to the future, I expect the things I have generated will continue to grow and flourish, even in a dangerous world.*

Do you see your life this way? Is this the kind of story you might tell if asked to tell the story of your life? Some people will say that their life fits the pattern pretty closely; others will claim that there is no resemblance at all. Most likely, though, there are parts of this story that seem like yours and others that do not. Highly generative American adults tend, on average, to construct life stories that resemble, sometimes quite closely, the pattern I have described. Like many of us, but perhaps a little more strongly than most of us, they tell life stories that affirm the power of human redemption. What does this life story mean? Why does this kind of redemptive story appear so often in the lives of very generative American adults? What is so great about this story? And what is wrong with it?

My central goal in this book is to explore the psychological and cultural meaning of redemptive stories in American lives. The great American novelist Robert Penn Warren has written that to be an American is not a matter of blood or birth; it is a matter of an idea.[10] That idea is large and "contains multitudes," as Walt Whitman wrote, but at the heart of it are stories that Americans have traditionally told about themselves and about their nation.[11] Highly generative American adults tell life stories that unconsciously rework deep and vexing issues in our cultural heritage. These same stories, furthermore, address thorny new problems we face as Americans living at the dawn of the 21st century. As I move back and forth in this book between

Box P.1. The Redemptive Self: A Plot Outline

Highly generative American adults tend to recount and imagine their own lives in ways that roughly correspond to the outline below. A key theme in the story is redemption.

How does the story begin?
The main character (protagonist, or "P") is favored in some way, enjoys a special blessing, advantage, gift, or status that distinguishes him or her from others. At the same time, P sees that others in the world are not so fortunate. P shows a precocious sensitivity to the suffering of others. By the time P enters young adulthood, he or she has established a firm and coherent belief system that will promote prosocial action and provide life guidance for the rest of the story.

How does the plot develop?
P encounters many obstacles and suffers many setbacks. But bad things often lead to positive outcomes, or else they teach positive lessons. P moves forward over time, makes progress, rises from adversity, recovers from setbacks, frees the self from oppressive forces, and/or develops toward some full actualization of an inner destiny. Along the way, however, P's strong needs for power and freedom often conflict with his or her equally strong needs for love and community.

How does the story end?
P works to promote the well-being of future generations. P leaves a positive legacy of the self. Even though his or her life will end someday, P expects to leave behind people and things that will continue to grow and prosper.

psychology and American culture, I will affirm and defend six key points. Taken together, these six points make up my book's essential argument:

1. Generativity is the central psychological and moral challenge adults face, especially in their 30s, 40s, and 50s.
2. Generative adults tend to see their lives as redemptive stories that emphasize related themes such as early advantage, the suffering of others, moral clarity, the conflict between power and love, and leaving a legacy of growth.
3. Redemptive life stories promote psychological health and maturity, and they provide narrative guidelines for living a responsible and caring life.
4. Redemptive life stories reflect and rework such quintessentially American ideas as *manifest destiny, the chosen people,* and the

ambivalence Americans have traditionally felt about our most cherished of all values—freedom. Expressions of these themes can be found not only in the life stories of highly generative American adults, but also in a wide range of American cultural texts, from Puritan conversion stories and the Gettysburg Address to contemporary self-help books and *People* magazine. And, indeed, you do not have to be a generativity superstar to see your life in redemptive terms. Many Americans see their lives this way, to some extent. The story, like our lives, is made in America.

5. Redemptive life stories in America are profoundly shaped by two American peculiarities: (a) that this is one of the most religious industrialized societies in the world and (b) that this society has been torn asunder, from its inception, by the issue of race. Some of the most redemptive texts in the American tradition may be found in the African American heritage and in the life stories of highly generative Black adults.

6. For all their psychological and moral strength, redemptive life stories sometimes fail, and they may reveal dangerous short-comings and blind spots in Americans' understandings of themselves and the world. After all, is it not presumptuous to expect deliverance from all suffering? Is it not an affront to those who have suffered the greatest calamities and heartaches to expect, even to suggest, that things will turn out nice and happy in the end? In this sense, there may indeed be something "almost childish" about the redemptive self—something a bit too naïve and Pollyanna for a world where tragedy often seems more common and compelling than redemption. And is it not arrogant to imagine one's life as the full manifestation of an inner destiny? You can sometimes detect an entitled, "true believer" quality in the life stories of many highly generative American adults—an assuredness regarding the goodness and the power of the individual self that may seem off-putting and can sometimes prove destructive. We will see, then, that redemptive narratives sometimes condone and reinforce social isolation and a kind of psychological *American exceptionalism*. Redemptive narratives may support, intentionally or unconsciously, a naïve optimism about the world, excessive moral fervor, and self-righteous aggression, even war, in the service of self-centered ends. The rhetoric of redemption makes it easy for us Americans to see ourselves as superior to the rest of the world and to identify our enemies as the "axis of evil."

While redemptive life narratives affirm hope and human progress, therefore, we must also face up to the dark side of American redemption.

Twenty years ago, the sociologist Robert Bellah and his colleagues published an influential book, *Habits of the Heart,* that examined the ways Americans have traditionally talked about their strivings for personal fulfillment and interpersonal community.[12] In the 18th and 19th centuries, figures like Thomas Jefferson and Abraham Lincoln personified uniquely American character types, the authors argued, who inspired Americans to live good lives. These types no longer work for us, however. *Habits of the Heart* showed that Americans today have a difficult time finding an appropriate language to express desires for living together in harmony, helping each other, and committing themselves to meaningful, long-term life projects beyond the self. It is not so much that we are selfish people as that we are incapable of expressing the desires we do have to go beyond self-interest. Bellah and his colleagues challenged their readers to imagine new character types that might inspire future generations of Americans to live caring and productive lives.

From a psychological standpoint, the authors of *Habits of the Heart* may have been asking for too much. Research in personality and developmental psychology suggests that most people are too complex to fit into the kind of neat character types that Bellah ascribed to American heroes like Jefferson and Lincoln. Human lives are messy and filled with contradictions. Each person shows a wide range of different traits; different traits get expressed in different situations; people change in important ways over time.[13] Nonetheless, Bellah and his colleagues were definitely onto something important in focusing so much attention on how Americans talk about their lives. When people talk about their lives, they tell *stories.* It is through stories that we often learn the greatest lessons for our lives—lessons about success and failure, good and evil, what makes a life worth living, and what makes a society good. It is through stories, furthermore, that we define who we are. Stories provide us with our identities.[14]

Highly generative American adults may not fit neatly into any single character type, but they do seem to have a type of *story* to tell about life. The redemptive stories that highly generative American adults tell recapture some of the ideas espoused in moral character types from long ago, but they also speak in the very contemporary language of 21st-century America. Redemptive stories provide images, scenes, plots, and themes that we might wish to borrow and rework into our own lives. I will never be just like my most admired hero from history or the movies, or my most beloved high school coach. But I may borrow pieces of their stories and work them into my own.

This book blends ideas from psychology, sociology, and American history and culture to explore the meanings and manifestations of redemption in American lives. While many popular books (and a good deal of research) look first at what is wrong with people (think: addictions, disorders, mental illness), I take the opposite tack in this book. I begin with the positive psychology of generativity and redemption, even though my analysis will eventually lead to a critique.[15] This book is grounded in social-scientific research, especially research published in the domains of personality, developmental, cognitive, and social psychology, and in sociology. I am a research scientist, not a clinician. Rather than offer armchair speculation or the kind of hysterical hand-wringing that many observers of American society love to present, I rely more on statistical studies, empirical data, and well-documented scientific findings. Having cast my lot with psychological science, I nonetheless acknowledge that most of the research I do does not involve sterile laboratories, brain scans, running rats in mazes, or most of the other accoutrements you may associate with the label *research psychologist*. Although some of the best research in psychology today connects to the brain sciences, what I study moves more in the direction of human personality and the self, culture, and humanities.[16]

My research is part of an emerging movement in the social sciences called the *narrative study of lives*. The central idea in this movement is that human lives are cultural texts that can be interpreted as stories.[17] People create stories to make sense of their lives. These evolving stories—or *narrative identities*—provide our lives with some semblance of meaning, unity, and purpose. Along with our dispositional traits and our motives and goals, internalized life stories make up important aspects of our personality. Our stories are implicated in determining what we do and how we make sense of what we do. As a *narrative psychologist*, I systematically analyze the texts of people's life stories to obtain a better understanding of both the people who tell the stories and the culture within which those stories (and those people) are born. "We tell ourselves stories in order to live," writes the American essayist Joan Didion.[18] By examining life stories, we may learn more about how Americans live, and how we might live better.

One

REDEMPTION
AND THE
AMERICAN SOUL

If asked to name a person who had a positive influence on you while you were growing up, you might pick a teacher. For more than a handful of graduates from a high school in one Chicago suburb, Mr. Washington would be their top choice.[1] A 53-year-old English teacher, Elliot Washington works hard to inspire in his students a passion for literature and the arts. But even if they reject Dickens and never once visit the Chicago Art Institute, Washington hopes that his students will learn something good from him about how to live.

For Washington, living well means finding a truth deep in your soul and participating productively as an enlightened citizen of the world. A teacher's job is to educate and guide the next generation—a role that captures the essential meaning of generativity. But Washington seems to be even more generative in his approach to his work and his life than most teachers you might meet, if indeed honors and recognition are any indication of generative accomplishment. Washington has won numerous awards for teaching excellence. His colleagues describe him as a gifted leader. Outside the classroom, Washington is a serious musician and a devotee of Taoist meditation. He believes that his music and his religious perspective on life are both instrumental in his making a positive difference in the world.

Elliot Washington is African American. He grew up poor on the south side of Chicago, in the "Black Belt," as he puts it. His mother was a member of the African-Methodist-Episcopal Church, but Elliot and a close cousin attended Catholic mass and became deeply involved with Catholicism. In high school Elliot began to play the clarinet and saxophone. He continued with music and the arts in college, and when he graduated he began working for the Chicago public school system. After struggling through 10 difficult years at his first school, he was transferred to the high school where he has taught ever since. Divorced in his early 20s, Elliot has been married to his second wife for more than 25 years. They are parents to two teenaged girls.

I have told you the basic facts. But what is the story?

As Elliot Washington tells it, his life is a story of redemption. The story begins with death. Elliot's father dies before Elliot is even born. Economically strapped to begin with, the family falls into deeper poverty. While his mother struggles to make a living as a seamstress, Elliot is bounced around from grandmother to aunt to older sister, with each trying to provide him the care and discipline a young boy needs. The apartments the young boy sleeps in are infested with rats and roaches. What will come of this? How will the young protagonist fare as the story's plot unfolds? We get a clue early on as Elliot describes how the tough times his family endured drew them all closer: "I enjoyed a protective, loving relationship; early childhood was extremely happy; very, very satisfying." In thinking back almost 50 years, Elliot construes his early childhood—fatherless and impoverished—as an *advantage*. "I knew that other kids were not so lucky, those with the unhappy childhoods." Elliot felt blessed, even as others suffered. But not only that. His blessing was born from death and suffering. As a middle-aged man today, and devoted father himself, Elliot would never claim that it was good for him to have grown up without a father. But he still sequences events and interpretations in his own life story as if to suggest that his father's death and the poverty his family suffered had redemptive meaning—both then and now. Bad things end up making good things happen in the long run.

The story Elliot Washington tells about his life today is filled with redemptive sequences. In each sequence, a very negative scene or chapter in the story is followed immediately by a positive outcome or by an interpretation suggesting a long-term benefit. One of only a handful of Black students attending a small rural college, Elliot sits alone and disconsolate in his dorm room on a Saturday night, as the White kids head for the fraternity parties. "I felt like I was in Babylon, you know, and how can you sing the praises of God in Babylon?" Well, you can, in a way. He takes out his saxophone and begins to play. Elliot's mood improves as the music flows. He learns that night to savor the loneliness, for it is life's tough experiences as much as anything else, Elliot says, that give his music texture and soul.

The toughest experience in Elliot's life may have been his first teaching job. As Elliot tells this chapter, he is the only Black teacher in a school where 90% of the children are White and the principal is a White woman, an autocrat, and a racist. Elliot consistently receives superior ratings for his teaching, but he cannot please the principal. They disagree on everything from dress codes to teaching philosophy. Many of their arguments are public and heated. In one scene Elliot is so enraged that he comes very close to hitting her. Ironically, one thing that seems to infuriate the principal as much as anything else is that Elliot is *not* "hitting on" the female teachers and students. He refuses to confirm her belief that Black men are out to seduce every cute woman in sight: "I just simply refused to buy into the stereotypes. I didn't jump on the females. You know what I'm saying? And I think that was my mistake in a way! You see what I'm saying? There's nothing wrong with their [White people's] perception in their minds. Something's wrong with me [they assume], because niggers are supposed to do this! I know it's funny, but it's sad at the same time."

The dismal first chapter in Elliot's teaching career ends when he takes a job at a new high school. There he finds redemption, for he is immediately loved and admired. As for the first principal, Elliot remarks, "Today, I am eternally grateful to her; I mean, she did what was in her nature, and hateful as it was, she didn't know any better." It all, he continues, "made me immeasurably stronger" and "helped me to evolve as a person."

The same pattern is reflected in Elliot's recollection of an incident of discrimination in his experience as a high school student. A White shop teacher refuses to let African American boys enroll in his course, for if they did they would receive the training that would enable them to get high-skilled blue-collar jobs when they graduate. The shop teacher wants to help keep Blacks out of the building trades. Elliot is enraged and deeply ashamed. He fights to get into the class, but he cannot break through. Looking back today, he is thankful he failed, for if he had been allowed to enroll he might never have gone to college, pursued music, or become a teacher.

Redemptive stories affirm hope for the future and a belief in human progress. No matter how bad the situation may seem, these stories suggest, there is always hope that things will get better. Redemption may come from the hard work and sacrifice of the story's hero. It may result from the kindness and good works of others. It may be due to fate, luck, or God. Or it may simply happen by virtue of time's passing. Elliot Washington is no Pollyanna. From an early age, he has keenly perceived injustice and suffering in the world. He believes that the United States promulgates a "pornographic caste system" in which "African-descended" citizens are forced to occupy society's bottom stratum. But Elliot still nurtures an abiding hope for the future. In his own life as a teacher, musician, and Taoist, Elliot has tried to blend traditions from around the globe—European classical music, Black American jazz, Eastern philosophy, African spirituality, and Roman Catholicism, to name the most important influences on his life and work. A man with such an integrative worldview wishes dearly that other citizens of the world might embrace so readily the diversity humankind has to offer. He urges his students to do and wish the same. Elliot worries about race relations in the United States, but mainly he is concerned with "the one race that really counts—the human race." We may not survive as a race, he acknowledges. But despite long odds, Elliot bets on redemption:

> I like to look at the larger picture. How are we going to survive as
> a race? I see this great, great challenge that can go in either direc-
> tion. But I'm saying I really can't help but feel that [hopeful] way,
> because I see so much beauty, so much creativity, so much produc-
> tivity. I just can't help but be hopeful for the future. It's something
> that I've cultivated. And I know that there are a lot of times, things
> that tend to want to set you back, setbacks in terms of what you see
> and so on. But I'm very, very hopeful that people are going to be able
> to get it together. I don't think I'll see it before I die, but I think that
> we have to. We've got to pull our stuff together. All of the negativity
> that we see, those are dramas which I think are necessary so that
> we can evolve.

From Religion to *People*

In *The Varieties of Religious Experience,* the great American psychologist and philosopher William James suggested that redemption is a core idea in all of the world's major religions. He wrote that different religious traditions promise a "certain uniform deliverance" *from* an initial "sense that there is *something wrong about us* as we naturally stand" *to* a subsequent "solution" whereby "*we are saved from the wrongness* by making proper connection with the higher powers."[2] Put simply, religions tell us that things are bad at the beginning (perhaps because we are bad) but that things will get better and we will be delivered to a better place. Examples of stories that encode the sequence of early suffering followed by a (promised or actual) deliverance to a better state are legion in the Judeo-Christian tradition: Abraham and Sarah suffer infertility into old age until God sends them Isaac, their son; the Israelites suffer through Egyptian captivity and 40 years of wandering until

God delivers them to the Promised Land; Christ is crucified but raised up on the third day. Today, personal stories of conversion—moving suddenly from a bad and sinful state to a good and Godly one—are a staple of many Christian communities, a traditional paragon of which is the New Testament's story of Paul's conversion on the road to Damascus. Redemption sequences are also prevalent in Islam. The Arabic term *Islam* means "surrender," as in surrendering to the ultimate will of Allah in order to be purified and redeemed. In Hinduism and Buddhism, redemption sequences take the form of liberation from perpetual reincarnation. The first and second of the Four Noble Truths of the Buddha explain how it is that human existence is *dukkha*—full of conflict, dissatisfaction, sorrow, and suffering. The third and fourth speak of the liberation and freedom for human beings that come from following the Noble Eightfold Path on the way to Nirvana.[3]

As a citizen of the world and a highly religious man, Elliot Washington finds inspiration for his redemptive story in a number of different faith traditions. As a young boy, he loved the Catholic rituals surrounding Lent and Easter. Fasting and self-discipline would give way to the communal joy and celebration that he experienced at the Easter mass. From Taoism Elliot borrows the concept of "evolutionary change," as he terms it. Through successive reincarnations, he believes, our "true selves evolve to higher and higher states." In Elliot's life story and in the minds of many people, the concept of redemption contains strong religious meanings. For many Christians, furthermore, it is also tied up with beliefs about *sin* and *repentance*. The general idea goes like this: While Jesus may have died to save people from their sins, people nonetheless continue sinning and need to atone for their sins by admitting their wrongdoing and receiving forgiveness, as through prayer, confession, and the like. When people repent, they move from a bad and sinful state to a good and purified, or forgiven, one, even if only for a moment.

Redemption is not just about religion, however.[4] Many of the sources for Elliot Washington's redemptive story come from family experiences, music, schooling, his African American heritage, his ideas about literature and art, current events, the media, and everyday talk. In our own everyday talk, it does not take long before we run across a redemptive metaphor or image. If we are talking medicine, we speak of healing, recovery, and wellness. If we are talking law, we speak of restitution, rehabilitation, and reform. In parenting, we talk of the growth and development of our children. Our implicit theories of development, mirrored in psychology textbooks and self-help manuals, tell us that children are simple and unsocialized beings. As parents, we make it our job to deliver them from this immature state. We must prepare them for a complex world; we must make them into socially responsible citizens; we must give them what they need to fulfill their inner potential and become successful, fully functioning adults.

Contemporary American society is suffused with the rhetoric of psychotherapy, and today many laypeople speak knowingly of personal transformation and growth, fulfillment and self-actualization, individuation and reintegration, and the development and perfection of the self—all variations on the redemption idea. The burgeoning popular literature on self-help offers a cornucopia of redemption tales, as do television talk shows and human-interest stories in the media. Politicians celebrate their own redemptive journeys: Ronald Reagan rose from a dysfunctional family; Bill Clinton (nicknamed the "Comeback Kid") recovered from childhood poverty (as well as many self-inflicted "wounds"); George W. Bush turned his life around in his early 40s, after years of drifting and drinking. In the words of one literary critic and observer of social life, "There is no public narrative more potent today—or throughout American history—than the one about redemption."[5]

To see just how potent and pervasive the redemption narrative is in contemporary American society, let us consider a source that, at least on its surface, has no direct connection to religion. I am thinking here about *People* magazine.[6] After my younger daughter left for school one morning, I rummaged through her bedroom looking for back issues of *People*. The cover page for the first issue I found appears in figure 1.1. As you can see, the September 16, 2002, issue featured stories related to the one-year anniversary of the September 11 terrorist attacks in the United States. Perhaps not surprisingly, these "stories of hope" told how an assortment of Americans whose lives had been touched by the tragedy of that day had recovered and responded in the intervening year. The editors wrote, "In the following pages, we've chosen to tell the stories of people who, whether devastated by the loss of a loved one or simply moved to help those around them, have shown courage, selflessness, and hope." The editors then introduced the redemptive stories to be featured:

> To honor her brother-in-law Terence Manning, who died at the
> World Trade Center, Carolyn Manning created an organization
> to help new immigrants to the U.S. Wounded in the attack, Silvion
> Ramsundar, 31, has become close friends and spends family holidays
> with Doug Brown, 55, who helped save his life. Katy Soulas, 36,
> mourns her husband, Tim, every day, yet, with help from relatives
> and neighbors, manages to raise six children with a strength and
> grace that we all wish we could equal if we were forced by circum-
> stances to become our best selves.[7]

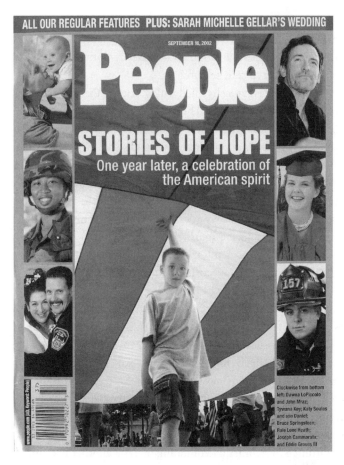

FIGURE 1.1 The September 16, 2002, issue of *People* featured redemptive stories about how Americans whose lives were altered by the terrorist attacks a year before had coped with crisis and turned their lives in a more positive direction. Reprinted with the permission of People Weekly, Time, Inc. All rights reserved.

The last expression in this quotation is fascinating, from a psychological point of view. The editors are saying that some "circumstances" in life are so trying—in the case of September 11, so horrific—that these circumstances "force" us to "become our best selves." It is only through suffering, they seem to suggest, that we can make ourselves into the best possible people we can be. Whether or not we agree with this psychological claim, it is clear that the stories of hope featured in this issue of *People* magazine capture as well as any discourse you may find the power of redemption in human lives. Coming on the one-year anniversary of a national trauma, however, it is not surprising that this issue of *People* should feature inspirational stories about how Americans have recovered and moved on. Perhaps, then, the September 16, 2002, issue of *People* is an anomaly—too redemptive to be typical. What does the magazine typically feature?

People magazine is typically filled with stories of the rich and glamorous, and sometimes the notorious. The typical issue describes lavish celebrity weddings, Hollywood divorces and scandals, fashion trends, new movies and television shows, trends in popular music, and so on. With glossy photos and chatty stories, *People* keeps you up to speed on what is happening in popular culture—which is why my daughter reads it (and why I have now started to read it, too). Even in the September 16, 2002, issue, the weekly poll asks the reader to weigh in on this heavy question: "Which of the boy-band standouts has the best shot at solo stardom?" (The results are 48% for Justin Timberlake of the band 'N Sync, and 52% for Nick Carter of the Backstreet Boys.) The magazine also contains stories of more ordinary people who in their daily lives do something odd or interesting or especially heroic.

To chart the extent to which redemptive narratives find their way into the pages of *People,* I went to the magazine's Web site—www.people.com—and looked for back issues in the site's archive. At the time of my search, the archive contained entries for each of the weekly issues, going back about a year and a half. In box 1.1, I have reproduced those entries for the two issues immediately preceding and following the September 16, 2002, issue of the magazine. As you can see, the four weeks' entries described 12 feature stories. Of those 12, 8 suggest some variation on redemption. For example, in one story a woman overcomes a debilitating disease; another tells how a young girl is kidnapped but then escapes; and another recounts how famous people caught in scandals eventually manage to turn their lives around.[8]

Continuing my informal analysis, I proceeded to classify every entry listed for the 4-month period of June–September 2002 and the 4-month period of May–August 2001 (the 4 months immediately *preceding* the September 11, 2001, attacks). In total, the archive provided capsule descriptions of 84 feature stories in *People* during the 8 months of my survey. For each, I made a conservative judgment as to whether or not the story was about redemption—that is, about people moving from suffering to an enhanced state or situation. Unless the evidence for redemption was obvious, I did not classify the entry as redemptive. Of the 84 stories in total, 44 (52%) suggested a clear theme of redemption. In other words, over half of the main stories featured on *People*'s Web site for 8 months during the years 2001 and 2002 were about redemptive changes in people's lives. And it did not matter whether I con-

sidered those stories written before September 11, 2001, or in the year after. The ratios were virtually identical for the two—52% for May–August 2001 and 53% for June–September 2002.

The Puritans and the Slaves

By the time the first Puritan settlers set sail for the Massachusetts Bay in 1630, they already knew that America would be a land of redemption. On board the flagship *Arbella,* Governor John Winthrop urged his fellow colonists to bind themselves together into a loving community so that they might do God's redeeming work. "We shall be as a city on a hill," Winthrop proclaimed, "and the eyes of all people shall be upon us."[9] The colonists believed that the whole world was watching them, for they had indeed embarked on a mission of cosmic significance. Their New World settlement was to be like a new Israel. Persecuted for their reformist beliefs in England, the Puritans had finally escaped their tormenters, as the Israelites had escaped the Egyptians. The Massachusetts forests would be like the "land flowing with milk and honey," long promised by their God to the chosen children of Abraham. With respect to the Christian church, the Puritans hoped (and expected) that their move to America would prove a victory for reform. Their city on a hill would serve as a model for all of Christendom—a model of a redemptive community made up of redemptive souls working together to redeem the world.[10]

As appallingly quaint as it seems to our modern ears, the Puritans had it all figured out. God's grand design would be equally manifest on a global level, on the level of the community, and in the holy tabernacle of each individual's heart. To that end, each man and woman's role in society—as a farmer, wife, preacher, tradesman, parent—should correspond in its redemptive end with the evolution of his or her soul. As the Puritans saw it, each man or woman was called to do the good work that God deemed necessary for the establishment, maintenance, and continuity of the good society. As that work contributed to the progressive good of the external community, the internal work of spiritual growth and development should move along at the same steady pace. Winthrop spelled out the awesome symmetry, and the deep generativity, of it all: "The end is to improve our lives, to do more service to the Lord, the comfort and increase of the body of Christ whereof we are members, that our selves and our posterity may be the better preserved from the common corruptions of this evil world, to serve the Lord and work out our salvation under the power and purity of his holy ordinances."[11]

If we were Puritans, how might we "improve our lives" and "work out our salvation"? The answers appear in the spiritual autobiographies that Puritans composed in their letters, memoirs, and published testimonials. In these documents, frequently addressed to their children and posterity, Puritans tried to tell the stories of their personal conversions. Some of these stories described sudden and dramatic changes in life, as modeled in the accounts of St. Paul and St. Augustine. Other stories described a more gradual process wherein the protagonist continues to advance in the faith over a long period of time. Whether change was sudden or gradual, though, the story followed a familiar redemptive course. The protagonist must depart from an old and bad life—full of sin, filth, indifference, selfishness, and so on—and move toward a good, purified, engaged, and generative life reflecting God's grace. The climax of the story would be the point of full repentance of sin and full acceptance of God's plan for one's life.[12] A signal theme in these stories, then, was confession—a full and honest disclosure of one's personal failings.

We may imagine the lone Puritan, tortured soul that he was, searching his heart and agonizing over his every thought and action, holed away in a tiny corner of his home or church, or cowering in some secluded spot of the great American wilderness, guilty, fearful, obsessing over the shortcomings in his own life, charting his own solitary Pilgrim's progress. The imagery is dark and brooding, and the Puritan is alone with his God. The picture dramatizes the fact that the Puritans did indeed believe that each man and woman faces God alone, with his or her own hoped for redemption story. The emphasis on a direct and accountable relationship between God and the individual came straight from the Protestant Reformation. The Puritans saw themselves as continuing the Reformation's work. But the picture is also misleading in suggesting that each Massachusetts colonist sought to work out his or her faith alone. Instead, the Puritans spent a great deal of time talking about their faith, comparing and contrasting their experiences to others' experiences, sharing stories, and working out their own viewpoints in a community of believers.[13]

The "Puritans were incessant talkers," wrote the historian Andrew Delbancho.[14] Ministers held private conferences with members of the flock, in which they tried to promote their congregants' spiritual development. Two hundred years before the birth of Freud, Puritan ministers engaged in a kind of talking therapy with their congregants. Delbancho calls them "soul physicians," suggesting that these conversations prefigure the modern forms of individual psychotherapy with which we are all familiar today.[15] Individual members would also give public testimonials of their own struggles with faith. Unlike the Puritans who stayed behind in Europe, the New England

FIGURE 1.2 John Winthrop, first governor of the Massachusetts Bay Colony, envisioned his Puritan settlement as a "city on a hill" in which God's redemptive work might be made manifest. New England Puritans charted their own spiritual journeys from sin to Godliness through personal narratives. Reprinted with the permission of Getty Images. Photo by Montage/Getty Images.

Puritans stipulated that before an adult could become a full member of the church he or she had to give a satisfactory life narrative of his or her development in faith.[16] Puritans would even debate the merits and limitations of different life-narrative accounts.

In their public works and in their personal stories, the New England Puritans developed a model for living that has had a profound effect on how Americans have seen themselves ever since. John Winthrop got it right when he imagined that the "eyes of all people shall be upon us." Of course, what the eyes have seen has not all been pleasant. Admired for their commitment to family and work, the Puritans have also been reviled for their own religious intolerance, their harsh and authoritarian values, their colonialist mentality vis-à-vis Native Americans, and a host of other failings that are captured in the less than complimentary adjective *Puritanical*. And did I mention the Salem witch trials? Anybody who has seen Arthur Miller's *The Crucible* or read *The Scarlet Letter* knows that the city on a hill fell well short of a utopian community. Still, the Puritans provided a language of redemption that has proven dear to the American soul. The language has been incorporated and reworked in many different ways over the past 350 years. Historians have noted, for example, that the Puritans' way of talking about themselves and their world provided a framework for the development of democracy and the belief in technological and civic progress in American life.[17] It also provided a way of narrating the redemptive move from slavery to freedom.

The Puritans' redemptive story found its most passionate expression, ironically enough, among the people who came to America as slaves. In the 18th century, African American slaves began to blend their indigenous folk beliefs with some of the central images and stories of the Christian tradition. By the early 19th century, many identified with the Old Testament Israelites in bondage to their Egyptian and Babylonian captors. Although the Puritans fled their persecutors in England, Black slaves were dragged—manacled and beaten—to the New World by theirs. Although the Puritans saw America as a potential heaven on earth, the slaves saw it as hell. Yet they both looked to the same grand redemptive narrative for sustenance and inspiration. In 1808, for example, a member of the African Society in Boston published a pamphlet, to be read by both Blacks and Whites, in which he analogized the condition of African American slaves to that of the Old Testament Israelites. To reassure Blacks that God would act for them in spite of their debased condition, the writer noted,

> It is not a real sign that a man is rejected of God because he is enslaved by man. The Israelites, after a long series of hardships by the oppressive hand of Pharaoh, were carried into captivity ten times. Although, perhaps, they did not experience slavery in that awful severity that their fathers did: yet they experienced it in such a manner, as in which, when they were delivered, it was so delightful a thing that their mouths were filled with laughter and their tongues broke forth in singing. . . . To know that the Lord reigneth, ought and will afford the slave that greatest consolation of anything in this world, if his heart is right with God.[18]

When slaves did manage to escape captivity and find freedom in the North, some wrote personal accounts of their harrowing journey. One historian has estimated that as many as 60,000 Black slaves may have escaped to freedom across the Ohio River and the Mason-Dixon Line before the onset of the American Civil War. Of these, over 100 wrote book-length slave narratives.[19] Like the spiritual autobiographies composed by the Puritans, the slave narratives were written to be examples for others. But whereas Puritan parents hoped to provide moral lessons for their children, the ex-slaves worked in concert with abolitionists to write stories that would awaken American readers to the horrors of slavery in the South. For the slaves, redemption meant much more than getting one's life right with God. It meant the flesh-and-blood freedom of real people whose brutal and complete bondage was something that the Puritans never had to worry about. Yet, like the Puritans in their stories, the ex-slaves usually identified themselves as God's chosen people, whose suffering and redemption followed a preordained and sacred plan.[20]

With their escape to the North, the ex-slaves finished one crucial step on the road to full liberation. But the story was not over, for their brothers and sisters were still in chains. Telling their stories to others was itself a redemptive act. Puritans might confess their own individual failings, whereas the ex-slaves bore witness to the trauma of their own people. In both cases, nonetheless, something very, very bad is first experienced and then (and this is critical) *it is told.* The telling is as much a redemptive act as are the acts that are told, for telling the story sets an example and provides an impetus for change. Sponsored by their abolitionist friends, the authors of the slave narratives traveled from town to town in the North, trying to rally American Whites to the cause of freedom. The redemptive stories they told were instrumental in ending slavery in the United States. Furthermore, their stories were used to inspire other American social movements. As one example, Harriet Jacobs's *Incidents in the Life of a Slave Girl,* published in 1861, tells of the sexual exploitation of slave women. Jacobs's readers, both men and women, recoiled at the notion that White masters routinely raped Black women in the South. But Jacobs also found a sympathetic audience among those White women who felt that they, in a sense, were like slaves to their husbands. Jacobs's redemptive narrative found meaning both in the abolitionist movement and, later, in efforts to secure equal rights for American women.

Personal Disclosure and Redemption

The Puritans and the ex-slaves shared their redemptive stories with others, hoping that their words would motivate others to act in a positive way. In both cases, the narrators and their audiences placed a premium on painful personal disclosure. The Puritans were to come clean regarding their many sins and shortcomings; the ex-slaves were to recount in detail the personal traumas they had experienced. In the 20th century, Americans began to share their personal stories of pain and suffering with therapists, counselors, social workers, support groups, and a host of other audiences, including those watching daytime talk shows and reality TV. According to many experts today, intimate self-disclosure has become a necessary ingredient for form-ing close personal relationships and leading an authentic and meaningful life. But what good does it really do? Are people better off for their confes-sions and disclosures? The Puritans and the ex-slaves put their bad experi-ences into words in order to help other people. Contemporary psychological research, however, suggests that through their painful personal disclosures they may indeed have helped themselves, as well.

Research psychologist James Pennebaker and his colleagues have over the past two decades conducted an impressive series of studies that document scientifically the positive effects of translating negative personal experiences into stories.[21] Participants in Pennebaker's studies—often college students—are typically asked to write about their most difficult life experiences, dis-closing their deepest thoughts and feelings about the experiences. The ac-counts run the gamut of negative emotional experiences, incorporating feelings of rage, fear, anxiety, sorrow, guilt, and shame. Pennebaker describes a few of his participants in one early study:

A female who has lived in fear for several weeks because of the physical and psychological harassment of a jealous woman who has apparently hired thugs.

A male who, in his high school years, was repeatedly beaten by his stepfather. After attempting suicide with his stepfather's gun, the stepfather humiliated the subject [participant] by laughing at his failed attempt.

A female who, in a fit of rage at her father, accused him of marital infidelity in front of her mother. The accusation, which apparently was true and unknown to the mother, led to the separation and divorce of the parents and overwhelming guilt on the part of the daughter.

A male who, at age 9, was calmly told by his father he was divorcing the boy's mother because their home life had been disrupted ever since the boy had been born.[22]

As many as one quarter of the participants in Pennebaker's studies cry during their disclosures, and many feel depressed for a time after the telling. Yet the respondents tend to rate the experience of disclosing the traumatic event to be especially valuable, and 98% say they would do the experiment

INCIDENTS

IN THE

LIFE OF A SLAVE GIRL.

WRITTEN BY HERSELF.

"Northerners know nothing at all about Slavery. They think it is perpetual bondage only. They have no conception of the depth of *degradation* involved in that word, SLAVERY; if they had, they would never cease their efforts until so horrible a system was overthrown."

A WOMAN OF NORTH CAROLINA.

"Rise up, ye women that are at ease! Hear my voice, ye careless daughters! Give ear unto my speech."

ISAIAH xxxii. 9.

EDITED BY L. MARIA CHILD.

BOSTON:
PUBLISHED FOR THE AUTHOR.
1861.

again. More important, the narrative act of translating personal trauma into words appears to have long-term health benefits. In one study healthy undergraduates were asked to write about either the most traumatic and stressful event in their lives, or a trivial topic for 4 consecutive days. Six months later the same students were asked to report on their health. Those who had disclosed the personal experiences 6 months before showed significantly fewer visits to the health center in the intervening period than did those students who wrote about trivial events. Evidence for the health-inducing effects of personal disclosure has been obtained in many other studies, too. For example, students who wrote about traumas over 4 consecutive days showed improved immune-system functioning by the 4th day, compared to those who wrote about trivial events. In another study, adult workers who wrote about traumas once a week for 4 consecutive weeks had fewer absentee days and improved liver enzyme function in the 2 months after writing, compared to a control group.

Why does disclosure of negative events improve health? Pennebaker argues that the process of actively inhibiting feelings and thoughts about bad experiences requires excessive physiological work, reflected in higher heart rate, skin conductance, and blood pressure. Over the long haul, the effects of physiological arousal accumulate, leading to stress-related illnesses such as infections, ulcers, and the like. Furthermore, research by other social psychologists has shown that the more that a person tries to inhibit thoughts and emotions, the more he or she is likely to think about that which is being inhibited.[23] But confiding and consciously confronting the perceptions and feelings associated with a traumatic event help the person to reorganize memory and thought in a more meaningful and coherent pattern. The narrative disclosure of the event enables the storyteller to "put it behind" him or her, to "close the book" on the problem. This leads to a reduction in physiological arousal, and it negates the need for further obsessing about the problem and inhibiting bad thoughts.

Psychologists of many different stripes have argued that the kinds of meanings people draw from negative events in their lives have profound im-

FIGURE 1.3 (Facing page) Title page from Harriet Jacobs's *Incidents in the Life of a Slave Girl.* Jacobs's account of her captivity and escape was published on the eve of the American Civil War. Expanding on some of the same themes apparent in Puritan autobiographies, the antebellum slave narratives were powerfully redemptive texts aimed at inciting moral outrage among Northern White readers, with the ultimate goal of ending slavery in the United States. Reprinted with the permission of Documenting the American South (http://docsouth.unc.edu), the University of North Carolina at Chapel Hill Libraries, North Carolina Collection.

plications for their mental and physical well-being. In one particularly important line of research, investigators have examined how people cope with naturally occurring negative events, including how people sometimes interpret negative events as leading to positive outcomes.[24] Anecdotal evidence and empirical research suggest that people frequently find silver linings in the dark clouds of illness, bereavement, and trauma. Although the negative turn of events may bring considerable pain and misfortune, many people will conclude that something good came or will come from the adversity. Recall that Elliot Washington came to believe that the racist school principal with whom he fought for 10 years helped him to evolve into a stronger person. People sometimes conclude that as a result of adversity they have developed greater courage, wisdom, patience, tolerance, empathy, or some other virtue. They may believe that their relationships with family and friends have improved. This kind of benefit-finding may prove to be useful in coping successfully with uncontrollable negative events, enabling the suffering person to exert a form of narrative control over daunting personal challenges.

The message from the scientific literature on benefit-finding is that people who perceive benefits in adversity tend to show better recovery from and adjustment to the negative events that brought them adversity in the first place. Positive adaptational outcomes of benefit-finding are evident in many indicators of psychological well-being. For example, evidence suggests that benefit-finding relates to less negative emotion among cancer patients.[25] It also suggests that benefit-finding effects superior psychological adjustment in women with breast cancer.[26] Likewise, there are fewer mood disturbances and intrusive thoughts in benefit-finding mothers of acutely ill newborns.[27] In one remarkable study, researchers found that 58% of men in one cohort of heart attack victims reported benefits from their heart attacks after 7 weeks of recovery. Some said the heart attack had made them appreciate life more. Others suggested that it brought them closer to their families or friends. Eight years later, those who construed some sort of benefit from the heart attack were in significantly better cardiac health and were less likely to have suffered a subsequent heart attack. The predictive relation between early benefit-finding and subsequent cardiac health remained significant even after statistically controlling for the patient's age, social class, and severity of the initial attack.[28] Believing that positive changes have resulted from negative events in life appears to exert a kind of self-fulfilling effect down the road. In the case of the heart attack victims, the long-term effect could be as significant as not having a second heart attack—indeed, as significant as living itself.

Although nobody wants to experience a trauma, we tend to believe that the deep suffering caused by such events as the loss of a loved one or a serious illness can sometimes bring out the best in us. Extremely negative experiences can sometimes turn our lives around in a positive direction. In their book *Trauma and Transformation: Growing in the Aftermath of Suffering,* psychologists Richard Tedeschi and Lawrence Calhoun review the scientific and clinical literatures on trauma and conclude that intense suffering often leads to increased self-reliance, enhanced intimacy in close relationships, better empathy for the difficulties of others, and an improved philosophy of life. Many people experience what Tedeschi and Calhoun call "posttraumatic growth." For example, studies of the physically disabled show that disabilities teach people how to fend for themselves in more effective ways and to build close relationships with others who suffer similar afflictions. One study of widows showed that the death of one's husband tends to improve a woman's relationships with her family and friends. Overall, 83% of widows said they realized through their bereavement that they had family and friends on whom they could depend, and 60% found themselves expressing emotion in a more open way than before.[29] In another study, 60% of women with breast cancer described positive changes in life priorities, such as taking life easier and enjoying it more.[30] People often report, furthermore, that loss and illness enrich their religious and spiritual beliefs. A woman whose fiancé died in an automobile accident describes her experience: "My beliefs are strengthened now, but I did go dead for a while. At first I doubted everything, but now my faith is even stronger than it was before."[31]

We may draw three conclusions from my brief review of research on disclosure, benefit-finding, and posttraumatic growth. First, disclosing emotionally painful experiences and traumas often has a positive effect on a person's health and well-being. Simply putting into words painful experiences can lessen the pain and lead to better psychological and physical health. Second, many people naturally come to construe their own negative experiences, such as loss and illness, in a redemptive manner, seeing ways in which the suffering they have experienced has led to positive changes in their lives. Posttraumatic growth does not happen for everybody, but it is a remarkably common occurrence among people who have suffered severe losses and illnesses in life. Third, the activity of perceiving positive outcomes in the wake of negative events in life—that is, the act of construing benefits in adversity—leads to even more benefits down the road. People who see (or imagine) good things coming from bad events in their lives tend to cope better with those bad events and find ways to grow and move forward in life. It would appear that translating trauma and adversity into redemptive life narratives may often benefit both the body and the soul.

Success Stories and the American Dream

Ben Franklin understood what it meant to rise from adversity. In the fall of 1723, this 17-year-old boy, dirty and poorly dressed, walked through the streets of Philadelphia carrying "three great puffy rolls" and less than a dollar to his name.[32] Through hard work and careful calculation, however, Franklin rose to become a successful printer in young adulthood. In his middle years, he conducted scientific experiments, established libraries, and promoted civic causes. He founded one of the world's great universities and helped to found a nation. In his advanced years, he became ambassador to France and an international celebrity. In his *Autobiography*, Franklin told the first and most famous "rags-to-riches" story in American letters. The story captured the boundless optimism of early America and became a model for how to live as the new American man. Like the Puritans, Benjamin Franklin hoped that future generations would find his story useful, as he told his son in 1771:

> From the poverty and obscurity in which I was born and in which
> I passed my earliest years, I have raised myself to a state of affluence
> and some degree of celebrity in the world. As constant good fortune
> has accompanied me even to an advanced period of life, my posterity
> will perhaps be desirous of learning the means which I employed,
> and which, thanks to Providence, so well succeeded with me. They
> may also deem them fit to be imitated, should any of them find
> themselves in similar circumstances.[33]

Franklin was a man of business, science, and government. Unlike the Puritans, he did not obsess over the vagaries of the spiritual life. He spent very little time scrutinizing his own consciousness for signs of divine election. Franklin wanted to get ahead in *this* life; he was not very concerned about the next one. Starting at the bottom of the social ladder, he aspired to raise himself up. Planning was an important part of it. You have to have a plan, Franklin counseled. You have to set goals. You have to organize your life, both in the long run and every day. Try to accomplish something important every day. Make a small step toward a bigger goal every day. And every day try to live out one important virtue, for virtues will pay dividends down the road.

In the *Autobiography*, Franklin listed 13 virtues—temperance, silence, order, resolution, frugality, industry, sincerity, justice, moderation, cleanliness, tranquility, chastity, and humility. With their roots in the Christian tradition, each virtue elevated a man's status in the eyes of God. What was so revolutionary about Franklin's message, however, was the idea that each virtue

FIGURE 1.4 Benjamin Franklin's *Autobiography* is the most famous rags-to-riches story in American history. Franklin told a story of secular redemption that served as a model throughout the 19th century for the optimistic, pragmatic, and expansive American identity. As an idealized myth about life, Franklin's story celebrated his move from poverty and obscurity to world fame and ignored many personal foibles and inconsistencies in his life. Reprinted with the permission of the National Portrait Gallery, Smithsonian Institution/Art Resource, New York.

could also work very well to elevate that same man in the eyes of society, and in the material world. Being chaste and humble might bring a payoff in the ever-after, but while we are here on this earth, isn't it nice to know that the same virtues might help us get that better job, nicer house, bigger yacht?

Of course, Franklin knew nothing of yachts. But he knew a tremendous amount about the American Dream for success. Indeed, he invented it, or at least helped to. That dream found its initial impetus in economic developments of the 17th and 18th centuries and in the moral and political ideals of the European Enlightenment. The Enlightenment philosophers celebrated the values of personal freedom, rationality, and human progress. They believed that individuals were endowed with natural rights that took priority over the rule of kings and sovereign nations. The free individual man enjoyed the opportunity to live fully and to make as much good of his life as might be possible in one lifetime. The free man enjoyed the opportunity to improve his life, to progress. The ideal of progress was both a moral and a material one. We should keep trying to improve our souls and the lives of our children and our neighbors, Franklin believed. But we can also improve our material lot. Franklin's Enlightenment view saw no contradiction between economic progress and moral progress, between living well and being good. It was all so wonderfully (and naïvely) American, as American as the answers my students often give me today, when I ask them what they really want to accomplish in life: "I want to make money, and I want to help people."

In the 18th and early 19th centuries, Americans increasingly saw themselves as living out a destiny of progress and improvement. The framers of the Constitution sought to craft a document that would assure the progressive improvement of human beings for generations to come. Some, like Thomas Jefferson, believed that independent farmer citizens, left pretty much to their own devices, could be trusted to improve their lives and to progress over time, so long as the government protected private contracts and property. Others, like Alexander Hamilton, believed that the citizenry needed to be taught to improve. Hamilton sought to establish institutions like a national bank and publicly chartered organizations for the promotion of economic enterprise.[34] Both Jefferson and Hamilton, nonetheless, imagined the new and idealized American citizen as the self-improving individual, the man on the move upward.

Restless upward mobility and the progressive realization of the individual self's full potential came to be seen, in the early 19th century, as distinctively American strivings. "Let us go on elevating our people, perfecting our institutions, until democracy shall reach such a point of perfection that we can acclaim with truth that the voice of the people is the voice of God," proclaimed Andrew Jackson.[35] In a famous visit to America during Jackson's presidency, the French nobleman Alexis de Tocqueville was struck by Americans' relentless drive to improve their lives and live out their personal hopes and dreams. In 1835 he wrote that Americans seemed to be true believers in "the Idea of the Indefinite Perfectibility of Man."[36] In 1857 Abraham Lincoln wrote, "I had thought the Declaration [of Independence] contemplated the progressive improvement of all men everywhere."[37]

Throughout the first half of the 19th century, Americans reveled in the redemptive rhetoric of economic progress, moral uplift, and the emancipation of the self. In the national mythology of the day, we became the chosen people whose manifest destiny was to grow and improve, to move ever upward and westward, to raise ourselves up by our bootstraps, to go from rags to riches, from adversity to enhancement, from oppression and ignorance to enlightened freedom. Most White Americans, moreover, were probably blind to the arrogance and the sense of privilege upon which these ideas rested. They lost little sleep worrying about the destruction of Native American cultures, for example, or the crass materialism of the emerging American Dream. Successful ends could justify ruthless means, many might have said. Indeed, nothing seems quite so soothing for the potentially ambivalent soul as success.

From Benjamin Franklin to the present day, the success story has enjoyed a privileged status in the anthology of American myths, even as it seems so tawdry and materialistic. As the Industrial Revolution transformed American society in the 19th and early 20th centuries, stories of success and upward mobility moved from the farmers and tradesmen of Franklin's day to the tougher work settings produced by capitalist industry. During America's Gilded Age, entrepreneurs like John D. Rockefeller and Andrew Carnegie amassed astounding fortunes while great numbers of industrial laborers toiled long and hard just to get by. Great sums of money were made and lost in land speculation and the stock market. Wages and profits fluctuated wildly, linked inexorably to unpredictable cycles of economic boom and bust. In this harsh environment of robber barons and frustrated labor, Americans still embraced stories of economic uplift and the triumph of the little man. In the long run, the most prolific and influential shaper of these success stories was Horatio Alger, Jr., a lapsed Unitarian minister who, if truth be told, wrote pretty bad books that did not sell very well in his lifetime. Nevertheless, history has been kind to him.[38]

Alger had served only 15 months as minister for the First Unitarian Church and Society of Brewster, Massachusetts, when in 1865 he was accused of sexual improprieties with boys. Alger admitted he had been "imprudent," and the church dismissed him. Disgraced and humiliated, Alger may have contemplated suicide, but he apparently experienced an epiphany that convinced him to atone for his sin through a new life of service. One of Alger's biographers suggests that Alger expressed his crisis and redemption in a poem entitled "Father Anselmo's Sin." It begins this way:

> Father Anselmo (God's grace may he win!)
> Committed one sad day a deadly sin;
> Which being done he drew back, self-abhorred,
> From the rebuking presence of the Lord.
> And kneeling down, besought with bitter cry,
> Since life was worthless grown, that he might die.

Resolved to die, Father Anselmo encounters a man in distress, and he comes to the man's aid. Then, an angel visits Father Anselmo and counsels him to take

> "Courage, Anselmo, though thy sin be great,
> God grants thee life that thou may'st expiate.
> Thy guilty stains shall be washed white again,
> By noble service done thy fellow-men.
> His soul draws nearest unto God above,
> Who to his brother ministers in love."[39]

Thankfully, Alger did not launch a second career as a poet to make amends with God. Instead, he resolved to write didactic success stories for young boys. Over the next 30 years, Alger wrote 103 juvenile books. Most of them followed a standard plot outline: An innocent teenaged boy finds he must earn his livelihood in the harsh world of American industry or business. He moves to the city, where he encounters temptations and con-men, but he keeps himself pure and good, and he makes friends. He struggles for economic independence and social respectability. When others falsely accuse him or an ally of impropriety, he strives to clear his or his friend's name. The hero confronts a greedy antagonist who aspires without principle to easy wealth and exalted social standing. The young and virtuous hero works tirelessly and keeps the faith, and he eventually wins out (and his nemesis fails). Success comes via a lucky break or through the benevolence shown him by a successful and virtuous businessman. At the end, the hero begins to enjoy the trappings of his success. He buys a new watch and business suit. (Not exactly rags to *riches*, you may say, but still a narrative of ascent as the protagonist moves upward in the direction of middle-class American respectability.)

Lampooned as hackneyed even in their own day (Mark Twain found them utterly laughable), Alger's books enjoyed only modest sales during his lifetime. But shortly after his death (1899), they became wildly popular and continued to sell well through the early 1920s. Over one million volumes were sold in the year 1910 alone. Alger's books exerted their greatest influence during a period of extensive immigration to the United States, especially from southern Europe. New immigrants looked to Alger's stories for inspiration in their economic and social struggles. Like Alger's young boys, they wanted desperately to assimilate into the mainstream of successful American society. The watch and business suit were symbols of the middle-class respectability they hoped to achieve. Historians of the mid-20th century hailed Alger as one of the most influential American figures of all time. In 1937 Henry Steele Commager contended that Alger influenced American culture more than any other writer except Mark Twain, and in 1955 another historian hailed Alger as one of "the great mythmakers of the modern world."[40] Since 1947 and up to the present day, the U.S. president presents Horatio Alger Awards to select citizens who have shown determination in overcoming obstacles and attaining success in America.

Living the American Dream has always been about self-made success, whether it is the success of the family farm, the entrepreneur, or the celebrity athlete. Over the course of the 20th century, success stories have expanded dramatically to encompass women, immigrants, people of color, people with disabilities, and other individuals who were essentially written out of the narratives that Franklin and Alger had to offer. With this greater inclusiveness has

FIGURE 1.5 Between 1866 and 1899, Horatio Alger, Jr., wrote 103 short novels about disadvantaged teenaged boys who overcame adversity to achieve success in industry and business. These less-than-stellar literary efforts were widely read by immigrants and other aspiring young men (and boys) in the 25 years after Alger's death. Today the term *Horatio Alger story* is still used, though sometimes ironically or satirically, to denote a tale of hard work, perseverance, and upward economic mobility. Reprinted with the permission of the Horatio Alger Association.

come an expanded and more complex understanding of the means to and meaning of success in America. The protagonists in Franklin's and Alger's success stories relied on strong character and will, whereas more contemporary versions also extol social and managerial skills, effective personality traits, and the strategic presentation of the self through image and appearance.[41] Advice manuals and motivational speakers of the 20th century taught aspiring men and women advantages such as "how to win friends and influence others" and how to cultivate "the seven habits of highly effective people."[42] Like Franklin and Alger, these hands-on lessons in American success rely heavily on inspirational stories of American men and women who have "made it."

Of course, not everybody makes it in American society. And many who do attain success attain it through lies and cheating, by exploiting the system or exploiting people, by sleeping with the boss's daughter or the Hollywood producer, through crime (or the stock market), and sometimes by sheer dumb luck. Whether you are talking about the robber barons of Alger's day or the corporate and accounting scandals of the year 2002, success in America has always had its seamy side. Not even Ben Franklin was consistently the virtuous man he claimed to be, as modern biographies have shown.[43]

Academics and social critics love to make fun of American myths of success. These stories are shallow, smug, simplistic, tawdry, hypocritical, contradictory, exclusionary, or downright false, it is often said.[44] At minimum, we should approach these narratives with strong ambivalence and a sense of irony. I find a great deal of merit in the skeptical view. Indeed, I largely share that view, if truth be told.[45] But I also know that these stories are alive and well, and that many, many people really like them, even as they maintain a critical eye. The most sociologically sophisticated critic of the American Dream will still go all teary-eyed when he recalls how his grandparents came over "on the boat," how they started with nothing but struggled and eventually managed to make a good living in their new American home. Immigrants, legal and otherwise, still stream to the United States with the hope of making a better life. The odds may be long, but the stories never seem to die.

Languages of Redemption

Most of the people who participate in the research studies I do have never read Ben Franklin's *Autobiography,* Horatio Alger's short novels, a Puritan conversion account, or any of the slave narratives published before the onset of the American Civil War. However, like Elliot Washington, they often employ a language of redemption—sometimes religious, more often secular—that sounds much like these canonical American texts. They say things like the following:

> My philosophy has always been to be positive instead of negative with the bad circumstances you deal with. If you get positive ideas, you'll progress. If you get involved with the negative, you'll sink.
> We started with nothing—I mean nothing. It was really, really terrible. It was all rigged against us. But we kept going, and we overcame.
> I don't think you appreciate the light unless you experience the dark.
> Salvation is what helps me to grow and to rise above. The negativeness and the badness and the things I had to overcome emotionally—dealing with lies and the different things he [an ex-husband] said about me—it made me a better person, it made me a stronger person, it toughened me up. . . . My life theme is Christ—He's helped me turn the bad into good.
> When she [a dear friend] died, I found a lot of strength inside myself that I didn't know was there. I would gladly give every bit of that

up to have her back, but she's gone, you know, she's gone, and I
have what is left.

My husband and I have grown—we've been to hell and back, to be
frank.

If it hadn't been for my divorce, I would have never gone back to
school. I put my life back together. I learned new skills. I left my
old life behind, thank God. I am happy today, because it all turned
out for the best.

I was nearly dead before I met her. She saved me—it's as simple as that.

My [Master's] degree has escalated me to do even greater things and
accomplish greater feats by overcoming obstacles created by
White people.

I was high all the time in those days—drugs mainly, but I drank
a lot, too. I was headed way down, you know what I mean?
Way down. And then one day . . .

Americans talk in many different ways about the redemptive moves in
their lives. In table 1.1, I have sketched out six different languages of redemption—that is, six different sets of images and ideas that people routinely draw
upon when they are trying to make sense of the moves in their lives from negativity and suffering, on the one hand, to positivity and enhancement, on the
other. From religious sources, we often borrow the language of *atonement*
and salvation, a way of talking that was enshrined in American cultural history by the Massachusetts Bay Puritans. Adopting the rhetoric of *emancipation*, we may speak of freeing ourselves from bondage and oppression, indeed
from forms of slavery itself, as told most powerfully and authentically in the
African American slave narratives of the 19th century. Ever since Franklin, we
have loved the rags-to-riches stories of *upward mobility*, even when we recognize that success may not come often and then often comes with a price. Stories of healing and *recovery* are among the most compelling for Americans
today, as almost any issue of *People* magazine will show. Self-help books and
parenting manuals provide us with an endless supply of *developmental* stories
showing us how to cope with problems and to promote the development of
ourselves and our children, while urging us all to move boldly in the direction
of self-fulfillment, self-actualization, personal integration, full inner awareness, and on and on. From education, science, and other sources, we learn *enlightenment* stories, charting the move from ignorance to knowledge. There
are other ways of talking about it, too. We all borrow and blend when we
make sense of our lives. When it comes to narrating our redemptive moments
and moves, we are probably never going to lack for words.

TABLE 1.1. *Six Languages of Redemption*

Type	Source Domains	Redemptive Move	Examples
Atonement	Religion	Sin → forgiveness, salvation	Puritan spiritual autobiographies Christian conversion experiences and confession
Emancipation	Political system	Slavery → freedom	African American slave narratives Stories of escaping abuse, liberation from oppression
Upward mobility	Economy	Poverty → wealth, social standing	Benjamin Franklin's *Autobiography* Horatio Alger stories, rags-to-riches immigrant success stories Motivational speakers, business testimonials
Recovery	Medicine, psychology	Sickness → health, wholeness	Stories of healing Psychotherapy narratives 12-step programs
Enlightenment	Education, science	Ignorance → knowledge	Stories of the growth of mind Stories of insight, discovery
Development	Parenting, psychology	Immaturity → actualization	Stories of psychological growth Stories of moral development and character-building

Common stories, images, and metaphors for redemption include religious atonement, political emancipation, upward economic mobility, the recovery of health and well-being, enlightenment and insight, and the many ways in which people talk about positive psychological and moral development. In making narrative sense of our own lives, we may borrow from and blend many different discourses to capture the idea of moving from suffering to a positive life outcome.

Still, some people use these kinds of words more than others do. Some of us speak the languages of redemption freely and often; others find other ways to tell the stories of our lives. We have already seen that people who have experienced severe losses and illnesses tend to cope better with those adversities and to show better health down the road if they are able to find some redemptive meaning in their trauma. But what about the more general case of a person's overall autobiography? What about the overall story of your life? If you had the opportunity that Franklin had to write your own life story, how much redemption would you put into it?

In a recent study examining the relationships between autobiographical memory and the quality of life, I obtained life-story accounts from two different samples of participants. The first consisted of 74 midlife adults, between the ages of 35 and 65 years.[46] Each adult was individually interviewed and asked to tell the story of his or her life. The relevant section of the interview for our purposes here contains 8 accounts of key *scenes* that stand out in the person's past. These include high-point scenes in life (the greatest thing that ever happened in my life), low-point scenes (the worst thing that every happened in my life), turning-point scenes (an event that marked a significant change in my life), and an earliest memory. For each of the 8 scenes, then, the participant described in detail what happened, who was there, what he or she was thinking and feeling in the event, and what the event may say about the meaning of his or her life. The interviews were tape recorded and transcribed. The second sample consisted of 125 college students. Each student wrote detailed accounts of 10 key scenes in his or her life story, following the same kind of instructions used in the adult interview. The participants in both samples also completed standard objective measures of psychological well-being, which included questionnaires assessing depression, life satisfaction, self-esteem, and life coherence.

The purpose of the study was to see whether or not the way in which a person narrates the most important events in his or her life is related to psychological health and well-being. My students and I analyzed all of the interviews and written accounts for themes of redemption, employing a content analysis procedure that has been used successfully in other scientific studies. The procedure involves examining each story to detect explicit examples of a move on the part of the main character from suffering to enhancement.[47] The adults and the students in our study provided many examples of redemptive sequences in their accounts, covering all six languages of redemption, as well as other ways of saying the same general thing. Yet participants differed dramatically with respect to the amount and strength of the redemptive imagery in their stories. Some, like Elliot Washington, provided many rich examples of redemption, telling many different stories of atonement, emancipation, upward mobility, recovery, enlightenment, or development. Others showed almost no redemptive imagery anywhere in the interview or written account. Not surprisingly, most participants fell somewhere in between these two extremes.

The main results of the study showed that, for both the adults and the students, the more redemptive the life story, the better a person's overall psychological well-being. In the parlance of researchers in social and personality psychology, we obtained positive correlations between redemption scores in the life narratives and independent indices of self-esteem, life satisfaction, and life coherence. People who told life stories containing many redemption sequences tended to be more satisfied with their lives, enjoyed higher self-esteem, and felt that their lives were more meaningful and coherent, compared to people who told life stories with fewer redemption sequences. Depression, by contrast, was negatively correlated with redemption, meaning simply that people who had fewer instances of redemption imagery in their life stories tended to be more depressed than people who had more redemption imagery. The same findings have been obtained in studies done in other psychological laboratories.[48]

Redemptive narratives are not simply happy stories. Rather, they are stories of suffering and negativity that turn positive in the end. Without the negative emotions, there can be no redemption in the story. In the same study, we analyzed the overall positivity of life story accounts, as well as the redemption theme. Many stories have happy endings; only some of them are redemptive. We found that simply telling or writing emotionally positive, upbeat, optimistic stories about life was *not* very strongly related to measures of life satisfaction, self-esteem, and life coherence. Instead, the redemption theme predicted psychological well-being much more strongly than did the measure of how "positive" and "happy" the person's story was.[49] Put simply, people who feel good about themselves and their lives do not necessarily tell life stories that are filled with positive emotions. Sometimes they do; sometimes they do not. But they often tell life stories that are filled with redemption themes. Life stories of atonement, emancipation, recovery, enlightenment, development, and upward mobility are the kinds of life stories that especially happy and well-functioning American students and adults tend to tell. Reflecting for sure the sensibilities of our current age, they are nonetheless reminiscent of the kinds of life stories that have captured some of the brightest and most hopeful aspects of American identity for over 300 years.

Two

THE GENERATIVE ADULT

In the beginning, it was no different than it is today. From the moment life first appeared, life demanded continuity from one generation to the next. The task has always been, and always will be, to pass it on. To pass *life* on. To pass life on *in our own image:* "Let the earth put forth vegetation, plants yielding seed and fruit trees bearing fruit in which is their seed, each according to its kind, upon the earth."[1] The plants and the fruit trees came equipped with their own seeds in the book of Genesis, promising continuity from one generation to the next. "Let the earth bring forth living creatures according to their kinds," moreover, "cattle and creeping things and beasts of the earth according to their kinds."[2] In the biblical story, the beasts and the creeping things were to reproduce their own kind. Serpents give birth to serpents, not sea monsters. Our children are our own kind, genome from our own genome. And let them all—all living things, from microbes to Eve—be fruitful and multiply. Let them all pass on their double-helixed essence to the next generation, and let that generation continue the process of passing it on to yet the next generation, and on and on.

Generativity is fundamentally about passing it on. Darwin did not know that organisms pass on *genes* to their progeny. But he knew they passed on something. He also knew that the opportunity to pass it on was not evenly distributed in any population of organisms. In the cold competition of natural and sexual selection, there were big winners and many losers. The winners were those who most successfully met the challenge to be fruitful and multiply. In the long course of evolution, winners (by definition) consistently displayed adaptations that gave them advantages over losers. It eventually had to come to pass, then, that those characteristics that were so wonderfully instrumental in winning would become so "selected," as it were, that virtually all descendant organisms, many generations down the road, would find themselves endowed with them—endowed with adaptational advantages like acute night vision for owls, or a very large brain for humans. Darwin suspected, furthermore, that some advantages were behavioral—like not eating feces, not having sex with close biological relatives, tending to love and protect offspring, tending to love and protect oneself. In sorting out the winning and the losing, evolutionary biologists today use the term *inclusive fitness*.[3] An organism's inclusive fitness is its overall (total, inclusive) ability to maximize the replication of the genes that designed it. Put another way, inclusive fitness specifies what it takes to be able to pass it on. What does it take?

For the last 2 million years or so, the organisms that we know today as human beings have mainly lived in small groups as hunters and foragers. Long before the advent of cities and even agriculture, human life was organized into nomadic communities through which food was obtained and shared, and protection was assured. To provide the calories necessary for life, our ancestors gathered fruits and other edible plants, hunted down or trapped the occasional meat source, and, if fortunate enough to live near large bodies of water, obtained their protein from fish. Survival depended on social cooperation. Our nonhuman competitors were often stronger and faster than we. But none were smarter, or better able to work together to devise flexible plans and strategies for meeting the challenges of their environment (in other words, *smarter*). Evolutionary biologists and psychologists use the term *environment of evolutionary adaptedness* (EEA) to refer to the physical and social conditions that enveloped human life and shaped human evolution during our 2-million-year stint as nomadic gatherers and hunters.[4] Most of us no longer live in the EEA, even if we occasionally hunt deer in Wisconsin or gather wild berries in Michigan or Maine. But we evolved to live (and to pass it on) in the EEA. Human nature was forged there and then.

What was life like in the EEA? It was intensely social. Human beings were never equipped to go it alone. In the struggles to survive the harsh elements, escape the predators, mate and reproduce, care for the young, hunt the prey, gather the berries, distribute the food, defeat the competitors, and form the alliances necessary to accomplish all of the above, our ancestors faced two huge social challenges. The first was to win *acceptance* in the group. Without the group, you were dead in the EEA. (And it is impossible to reproduce alone.) Inclusive fitness, then, depended on one's integration within the social community. The second main challenge was to obtain *status* in the group. Contrary to some romantic notions (natives cavorting on beaches, free love, "getting back to nature"), group life in the EEA was probably not innocent, peaceful, or egalitarian. Resources were always limited, and those individuals who achieved a higher status within the group—be it through hunting prowess, leadership skills, physical attractiveness, a good sense of humor, or whatever—were more likely than those whose status was lower to have better access to those resources (e.g., food, mates). In the words of personality psychologist Robert Hogan, successful adaptation in the EEA required "getting along and getting ahead" in everyday social life.[5] According to Hogan, we have evolved to care deeply about getting along and getting ahead, for those human organisms who were predisposed to care little about these goals in the EEA ended up losers in the long run. They obtained fewer resources on the average and were ultimately less successful in passing "their" genes down to subsequent generations. In evolution as in history, the winners write the story.

A key ingredient in the recipe for winning may be a *moral* sentiment. Ethologist Frans de Waal argues that the origins of human morality can be traced back to three conditions of group life in the EEA.[6] First is the condition of *group value:* Individual human beings depended on the group for finding food, and defense against enemies and predators. Second is *mutual aid:* Individuals cooperated with one another in group activities and engaged in reciprocal exchanges within the group. Third is *internal conflict:* Individual members had disparate interests and competed with one another for resources, status, and so on. Effective group life required that these conflicts be resolved, either face-to-face (as when disputants decide to forgive and forget), or through higher level social processes, such as mediation, peacemaking, and rule enforcement. In that the individual's very survival and reproductive success depended on the effective functioning of the social group, human beings evolved as inherently moral animals. Among the evolutionarily adaptive tendencies that de Waal argues are now part and parcel of human nature are empathy for others in distress, group allegiance and commitment, an appreciation for social order and rules, moral indignation about rule violations, and a tendency toward altruism.

Altruism is an especially interesting case, for it seems counterintuitive that helping others, especially at the expense of one's own immediate well-being, should contribute to inclusive fitness. Yet there are two strong examples of how this counterintuitive claim seems to hold great truth. First, it is well recognized that human beings, as well as many other animals, will en-

gage in altruistic behaviors that are aimed at benefiting their own kin, especially their children. This is called *kin selection*. Through kin selection, parents may even sacrifice their own lives to save their children and thereby increase the likelihood of passing down their genes, through their offspring, to
subsequent generations. Siblings are inclined to help each other, even sacrifice themselves for each other under certain conditions, for to promote the
survival and reproductive success of a sibling is to increase the chances of
passing down the genes siblings have in common. In general, the closer the
blood relation, the greater the likelihood of altruism.

But altruism can also happen among strangers. Even biologically unre-
lated members of the same species may be motivated to help each other if
the helping is likely to result in selective advantages for both—a phenomenon that is called *reciprocal altruism*.[7] For instance, rhesus monkeys, ba-
boons, and anthropoid apes are known to form coalitions based on mutual
assistance, while chimpanzees, gibbons, African wild dogs, and wolves beg
for food for each other reciprocally.[8] In the EEA, helping another member of
the social community might enhance the helper's chances of being helped
later, when he or she is the one in distress. Building a reputation as one who
helps others—a good person who acts for the good of others and the
group—is likely to accrue many advantages in group life, making it more
likely that the altruistic person should find success in getting along and getting ahead. At the same time, extreme selfishness and the lack of warm sentiment for other human beings may exact a price. The most low-down and
heartless villains may have been, on the average, among the biggest losers in
the EEA. They may have often ended up on the bottom of the resource totem
pole, even ostracized from the group, or been punished so severely that their
efforts to pass their genes down to the next generation were severely compromised. In the most fundamental evolutionary sense, then, it may be true
that it has often paid to be good, or at least to display social behaviors that
are appreciated as helpful and useful by other members of the group.

Of all the behaviors that human beings since the EEA have deemed to be
good and helpful, perhaps no other receives such consistent and unambiva-
lent praise as caring for our young. Making a baby is a good start, but it is
not enough for inclusive fitness. You may sire or give birth to a dozen offspring, but if none survive to childbearing age themselves, then what
progress have you made in passing it on? Human infants are born amazingly
dependent (compared to other species) and require years of care, support,
and training before they have any chance whatsoever of getting along and
getting ahead. As a result, human beings are endowed with powerful behavioral and emotional systems that predispose them to want to care for and

support their offspring. The most obvious manifestation of such a system is what psychologists call the *attachment* bond between the caregiver and the infant. In all human societies, caregivers (usually mothers) develop extremely strong bonds of love and care for their infants in the first year of each infant's life. Ever since the EEA, the most basic way in which we provide for the next generation is in the loving care we give to our babies. But a great deal more of what we do, and what we did in the EEA, directly and indirectly promotes the well-being of our children and our neighbor's children, and contributes in a more general way to the continuity of the social group and the social institutions upon which the future generation depends. Passing it on involves a wide range of activities—from mating, to raising children, to altruism, to supporting the social good—which stem from adaptations that became part of human nature over the past 2 million years of human evolution. It is, therefore, both natural and good—today as it was in the EEA—to be a *generative* adult.

Generativity and Human Development

Generativity is an adult's concern for and commitment to promoting the well-being of future generations. There is no gene for generativity—that is, no single gene that all by itself makes us generative people. Rather, human beings have been designed by evolution to act and feel in certain ways that, when filtered through culture, function to promote the growth and well-being of future generations. Procreation, child care, kin selection, certain acts of altruism, and commitments to moral codes and societal continuity, as well as a wide range of strivings and behaviors aimed ultimately at promoting the social good from one generation to the next, especially as displayed by mature, socially integrated adults, can be seen as expressions of generativity. In contemporary social life, generativity may be expressed in parenting, teaching, mentoring, volunteer work, leadership, charitable activities, religious involvements, political activities, and even paying one's taxes. It may be expressed in activities that aim to preserve social institutions, as well as activities aimed at progressive social change. Generativity, therefore, is a broad category that includes many things we adults do and feel as we strive, consciously and unconsciously, to pass on to posterity some aspect of our selves. As psychologist John Kotre writes, generativity involves "the desire to invest one's substance in forms of life and work that will outlive the self."[9] Through our genes, through our families, through our ideas, through our legacies of care and commitment, we do manage, in a sense, to live on, even after we are gone.

As a psychological term, *generativity* was born in the 1940s when Erik Erikson, with the assistance of his wife Joan, formulated a famous theory of human development. The Eriksons believed that each person moves through life, from birth to death, in a complex and changing social context. At every point in the life course, then, the person faces a set of developmental challenges that are shaped and addressed according to the resources and the meanings provided by family, society, and culture. Ultimately, the person confronts eight major challenges in life, and each is associated with a particular *psychosocial* stage. In infancy we move through the first stage, wherein the main task is to establish a trusting bond between the caregiver and the infant. In a sense, the infant and the family face the challenge of trust together. Basic trust can be established only in a relationship between the developing infant and the social context, the social context personified mainly

FIGURE 2.1 With the assistance of Joan Erikson, the psychoanalyst Erik Erikson formulated a famous theory that charted an eight-stage sequence for psychosocial development across the human life course. The central issue for Erikson's seventh stage—the long period in life between young adulthood and old age—is generativity, the adult's concern for and commitment to promoting the well-being of future generations. Reprinted with the permission of Getty Images. Photo by Sarah Putnam/New York Times Company/Getty Images.

as the primary caregivers in the infant's life. With each successive stage in the eight-stage scheme, the social context for development broadens somewhat, and the developing person moves forward to address issues whose resolution depends in part on how the preceding issues and stages have been resolved.

The Eriksons framed each stage in terms of a stark contrast. For Stage 1, the contrast is between the basic *trust* experienced in a secure attachment relationship between caregiver and infant and the *mistrust* experienced in insecure attachment relationships and other relationships outside the attachment realm (e.g., relationships with strangers or unfamiliar people). It is normal and good that infants experience *both* trust and mistrust in the first year of life, but the balance should ideally be tilted in the direction of basic trust. The same is true for all the stages. The good outcome is preferred to the bad, but both good and bad will be experienced in the course of healthy psychosocial development. Serious and long-term problems typically occur when the bad alternatives of each stage overwhelm the good. Therefore, the infant whose first year of life is contaminated by relentlessly negative and insecure experiences may come to apprehend the world in a mistrustful way, and this legacy of mistrust may make it difficult to achieve positive developmental outcomes in later stages. Still, development is never set in stone in the Erikson model. Early failures and mishaps can sometimes be overcome down the road. Even infants who experience high levels of mistrust can bounce back later on, in childhood, adolescence, or even later, if the social-cultural conditions change for the better, or if—and this is always mysterious but inspiring—they find within themselves a deep reservoir of psychological strength and resilience.

Here is how the rest of the stages go: As they begin to talk and walk, toddlers seek (and their social environments provide) greater levels of independence, marking the second stage of *autonomy* versus *shame and doubt.* For the third stage, the preschool years bring forth bolder developmental urges—the unconscious drives for power and lust depicted by Freud in the Oedipus complex, for example. The Eriksons clean it all up a bit and focus mainly on the social dimensions of this third stage, captured in the polarity of *initiative* versus *guilt.* Next is the mid-childhood period of *industry* versus *inferiority*—the school years up to puberty, wherein we learn to read and write and do other good things that socialize us into the broader contexts of school and peer group. With the eruption of puberty and a host of new challenges in adolescence, we move into the especially consequential fifth stage in the Erikson scheme—*identity* versus *role confusion.* It would take a book to do justice to this stage alone, but let us settle for now on the idea that identity involves figuring out who we are and how we may fit into the adult world.[10] Central tasks for identity include formulating a personal belief system and making substantial progress in the area of work and career. The Eriksons identified *intimacy* versus *isolation* as the prime psychosocial challenge of the sixth stage, encompassing the young-adult years. For many people, Stage 6 focuses mainly on marriage and romantic partnership.

Which gets us to *generativity* versus *stagnation*. Erik and Joan Erikson puzzled long and hard about how to characterize that extended period of life between young adulthood and old age. So much happens over such a long time frame that it is very difficult to come up with a neat label to capture the main psychosocial thrust. Adults in their 30s, 40s, 50s, and 60s assume many different roles and pursue many different goals. Their psychosocially important activities span work, family, community involvements, and leisure. The Eriksons decided that the most important actions adults typically accomplish during this period involve being *productive* and being *caring*. As breadwinners, homemakers, caregivers, taxpayers, group leaders, and the like, mature and well-functioning adults find themselves engaged in a broad assortment of activities—some glamorous, most not—that boil down to taking care of matters that people care about.

Taking care of business. Taking care of people. There is no common word that denotes all of this. So the Eriksons coined a very uncommon one—*generativity*. Unless you learned about Erik Erikson in college, you may never have heard of this word. But most adults have no trouble understanding what it means once they have been told, for generativity is often what their lives, or significant aspects of their lives, are all about. And it is problems in generativity (stagnation) that can give adults some of their toughest sorrows and frustrations. Infertility is an obvious example. Anxiety about the kids. Ungrateful kids. ("How sharper than a serpent's tooth it is to have a thankless child," cried King Lear.) Feeling stuck in your job. Feeling that you are making no contribution, or that nobody appreciates your contribution. Feeling that you have done nothing consequential in your life. Even when generativity is going great guns, we are never far from stagnation.

Although it has evolutionary roots, generativity is expressed and shaped through culture. For example, different societies set up different expectations regarding generativity. In any given society or cultural group, generativity may be strongly contoured along the lines of social class and gender. With regard to gender, many traditional societies mandate that women's generative expressions focus mainly on the family, whereas men are expected to direct their generative inclinations outward, toward society as a whole. In some other societies, gender roles may be more fluid and flexible. All societies hold expectations regarding the *timing* of generativity. As people move through young adulthood and toward midlife, their peers and their community typically hold greater and greater expectations regarding generative action and commitment. We expect men and women in their 40s to be generative in some way. By contrast, we expect less by way of generativity from young people. Most societies do not typically set forth high expectations for generativity among the very young and the very old. Still, societies differ dramatically with respect to what potentially generative actions they deem appropriate at given times in the life course. In the middle-class and professional strata of the United States, for example, young women today are typically expected to put off childbearing until well into their 20s and beyond. Yet in many cultural contexts (working-class families, agricultural communities, many traditional societies), beginning a family in the teenaged years may be viewed very favorably, and even encouraged.[11]

The forces of culture shape the meanings of generativity in many interesting ways. In traditional societies, generativity may take the form of passing on the eternal truths and wisdom of the ages that are embedded in religious and tribal traditions. The well-being of future generations may be tied explicitly to expectations about continuity of the past. By contrast, many modern societies tend to emphasize scientific progress, the questioning of convention, and an optimistic belief that the future can be better than the past. Under conditions of swift cultural change, generativity becomes a balancing act between tradition and innovation. In many modern societies today, youth may no longer value the wisdom of their elders, for that wisdom may be seen as specific to a bygone world. An older generation may seek to be generative by passing on traditional values of life, but the targets of their efforts—the younger generation—may want and need guidance and resources that better address new challenges in the future. Parents are not always able to give children what they need, and children do not always value what parents have to offer. Although generativity mismatches may go back even to the EEA, they appear to be especially vexing under conditions of rapid social and cultural change, as we witness in many modern and developing societies at the beginning of the 21st century.[12]

According to the Eriksons, generativity gradually fades in importance as people move into their advanced years. The last stage in their model is *ego integrity* versus *despair*. In this last stage, the older person looks back on his or her life and struggles to accept it as having been good and worthwhile. Ego integrity is essentially that feeling that "my life has been worthwhile and I can now accept it as a gift." Despair is the opposite: "My life was bad; it is too late to do anything about it; I regret it all." The Eriksons were never clear about when the generativity stage ends and this last stage begins. Some empirical

TABLE 2.1. *Erikson's Eight Stages of Psychosocial Development*

Stage	Age	Psychosocial Issue	Central Question	Associated Virtue
1	Infancy	Trust versus mistrust	How can I be secure?	Hope
2	Toddler	Autonomy versus shame and doubt	How can I be independent?	Will
3	Early childhood	Initiative versus guilt	How can I be powerful?	Purpose
4	Middle childhood	Industry versus inferiority	How can I be good?	Competence
5	Adolescence	Identity versus role confusion	Who am I?	Fidelity
6	Young adulthood	Intimacy versus isolation	How can I love?	Love
7	*Middle adulthood*	*Generativity versus stagnation*	*How can I fashion a "gift" (a legacy)?*	*Care*
8	Old age	Ego integrity versus despair	How can I accept a gift (the gift of life)?	Wisdom

Each stage contains a central issue or polarity that can also be posed as an experiential question the person must answer. Each stage also has its corresponding virtue, which Erikson assumed would become deeply internalized once the particular stage's issue was successfully resolved. For Stage 7, the central issue is generativity versus stagnation, and the question confronting the mature adult is how to contribute something of value to the next generation—that is, how to fashion a gift of the self that will outlive the self. Through parenting, teaching, mentoring, leadership, creative endeavors, and many other activities, adults find ways to be generative and to make a caring contribution to future generations.

research suggests that generativity inclinations increase as people move from young adulthood toward midlife and that generativity may decrease slightly in the retirement years.[13] But many people continue to engage in highly generative activities well into their 70s, 80s, and even beyond. Furthermore, many young adults, and even teenagers, engage in behaviors and express attitudes and feelings that indicate generativity to some extent. Therefore, it is probably not a good idea to think of the eight stages in a rigid, fixed way. What seems to be the case instead is that *on the average* people may become gradually more concerned with generativity issues as they move from young to middle adulthood and that there may be something of a decrease in generativity for some people as they move into old age. What also seems to be very much the case is that some people, even at the same age and "stage" in the life course, are much more generative than others.

Who are the especially generative people you know? For me, a few professors I had when I was an undergraduate come immediately to mind. Professor Arlin Meyer, for example, teaches English literature at a midwestern university. He has served in many leadership posts there, including dean of the Honors College. In the mid-1970s when I attended, he was the coordinator for the overseas studies program in England. Twenty-two of us lived for half a year in Cambridge, where Doc Meyer taught two of our literature classes: Modern British Fiction and Romantic Poetry. He led field trips to literary sites, joined us at pubs and clubs, repaired our bicycles and played soccer and cricket with us, and, along with his wife and two children, spent hours of time with us every week just hanging out, listening to our stories, and giving us advice on where to travel and what to read. His passion for literature and for the English countryside was infectious. But his passion for knowing and liking young people, his curiosity about our lives, his ability to be there for us as both a friend and a father figure, his studious attention to matching every name with every face before he ever met us and to learning so much about each of our unique lives before the first day of class, his enthusiasm for hosting reunions for our group 25 years later—it is in all *these* areas where his skills and commitment in generativity come through the best. Some people are masters of generativity, I think. You watch them in action and you marvel, just as you do when you gaze upon a Picasso or watch video clips of Michael Jordan in his prime.

But I digress. Let me be more objective and scientific about this. As is our wont, research psychologists have devised ways to measure individual differences in generativity. We use rating schemes, self-report questionnaires, behavioral checklists, and other relatively simple and objective methods for assigning overall scores on generativity, in order to differentiate between people who are relatively high, relatively low, or generally in the middle of a generativity continuum.[14] Although no single measure is perfect and each measure probably oversimplifies matters quite a bit, these measures have still proven very useful for testing hypotheses about individual differences in generativity in large samples of adults. To give you a sense of what these measures are like, I have reproduced in box 2.1 some of the items from my own self-report scale of generativity, which has been extensively validated and used in many studies. The items are designed to tap the extent to which a person expresses a strong conscious concern for generativity and feels that he or she is capable of acting in a generative way. A person taking the scale

Box 2.1. *Items From a Self-Report Scale Measuring*
Individual Differences in Generativity

I try to pass along knowledge I have gained from my experiences.
I have made and created things that have had a positive impact on other people.
I have important skills that I try to teach others.
If I were unable to have children of my own, I would like to adopt children.
I have a responsibility to improve the neighborhood in which I live.
I feel as though my contributions will exist after I die.

For each of the items like these on the scale, the person marks a "0" "if the statement *never* applies to you," a "1" "if the statement *sometimes* applies to you," a "2" "if the statement *often* applies to you," or a "3" "if the statement *always* applies to you." The researcher adds up the item scores to arrive at a total estimate of the person's overall generativity concern. The scale from which these items are taken contains 20 items in all. Other measures focus on such things as generativity goals, behaviors, and motivations.

simply rates the extent to which each of the items applies to his or her life. Scores are summed up at the end to arrive at an overall generativity rating.

What does psychological research on generativity show? Over the past 15 years, behavioral and social scientists have learned a lot about individual differences in generativity. Here is some of what the research shows:

- Parents who score high on generativity measures are more involved in their children's education than parents who score lower on generativity measures. For example, highly generative parents help their children with their homework more, attend school meetings more often, and have a fuller understanding of what their children do at school every day, compared to parents lower in generativity.[15]
- Parents high in generativity tend to adopt an *authoritative* style of parenting to a greater extent than do parents low in generativity. Authoritative parenting combines high standards and discipline with a caring and child-centered approach to family life. Research has shown that authoritative parenting leads to higher levels of autonomy, moral development, and emotional maturity in children.[16]
- Parents high in generativity are more likely to pass on values to their children and to emphasize the attainment of wisdom and insight in the family stories they tell their children, compared to parents low in generativity.[17]

- Adults high in generativity have broader friendship networks and perceive that they are more closely tied to other people in their communities, compared to adults low in generativity.[18]
- Adults high in generativity are more involved in religious, political, and civic ventures, compared to those lower in generativity. They attend religious services and engage in religious activities more often. They vote more often in local and national elections. They show greater interest in political issues and current events. They do more volunteer work in their communities. They give more money and time to charities.[19]
- Adults high in generativity show more social responsibility and higher levels of moral development, compared to adults low in generativity.[20]
- Highly generative adults report higher levels of happiness and life satisfaction and lower levels of depression and anxiety, compared to less generative adults.[21]
- Highly generative adults express strong, unconscious needs for both power and intimacy. Like most of us since the EEA, they are concerned with getting ahead and getting along, but their motivations in these areas seem to be even stronger than the average. They want to have a strong and positive impact on others, and they want to be accepted by others in warm and loving relationships, to a greater extent than less generative adults.[22]
- More than less generative adults, highly generative adults report that as children their families were especially religious.[23]

In sum, the empirical research suggests that generativity is good for others and good for the self. Motivated by strong needs to have a positive impact and to connect to others in loving ways, highly generative adults appear to be more effective and involved as parents, community members, and citizens, and they enjoy wider social networks and generally better mental health, compared to adults who score lower on psychological measures of generativity.[24]

Deborah Feldman: The Story of a Highly Generative Adult

Age 39, married with children, and employed as a public health administrator, Deborah Feldman is an especially generative woman. She is raising three children and hopes for a fourth. When the kids were in preschool and her husband was in medical school, she stayed home to be a full-time mother.

Given her husband's impossible schedule, she really had no choice but to stay home, but her "decision" to do so also fits nicely with her philosophy of life. "There is no crime as great as breaking the spirit of a child, and there is nothing as wonderful as molding a child," she says. "The early years are the most important." Trained as a nurse, Deborah recently took a position as head of an early intervention program. Her agency provides medical, educational, and psychological services for inner-city families. Raised in the Jewish traditions, she rejects the rigid hierarchies of organized religion but still gets together regularly with a small group of friends to worship and pray. Deborah always votes in local and national elections, and she frequently volunteers her time to work for political candidates and social causes. She knows everybody on her street. Deborah scored near the top of the distribution on the generativity questionnaires my students and I administered in 1995–1996. She scored so high that we asked her to come back for an interview. We wanted to know the story of her life.

Deborah divides her life into chapters according to the different homes where she has lived. Growing up in a suburb of Chicago, she was a "dreamy, happy kid" in a Jewish family where religion and politics were both very important. Her father carried her on his shoulders as he went door-to-door in 1960 campaigning for John F. Kennedy. Both parents were staunch political liberals who marched for civil rights and for peace. "My parents were very involved in social action, and so my brother and I grew up sort of like we had a social responsibility to the world, not just to ourselves and to our family, and so social consciousness became real important." The most vivid early memory for Deborah is the day John Kennedy was assassinated.

Deborah moved to Boston for college, where she regularly checked in with her grandparents, aunts, and cousins, who lived in the Boston area. She stayed at her grandmother's house for holidays and Shabbat. She fell in love with an older boy from a nearby college, and they decided to get married after her sophomore year. Struggling in her classes and dissatisfied with her English major anyway, Deborah dropped out of college, moved to Denver with her fiancé, and eventually enrolled in a nursing program. She completed the program and began work as a nurse. For the next few years, her husband combined duties in the Air Force reserves with medical school, so she followed him around to various military and medical settings. They spent three years in Spain. In every setting, Deborah made close friends and became involved in social and community groups. Desperately lonely when she arrived in Spain and knowing only a handful of Spanish words, she befriended the maid that the Air Force provided for the couple. This intense friendship was her entrée into the tight-knit local culture. "The Spaniards were really loving people," she says, "and they love children particularly."

After several miscarriages, the couple began to produce children. Deborah quit her job as a nurse. At the same time, her husband's work routine intensified. He spent less and less time at home, as his medical duties became almost overwhelming. Deborah relied on the social support provided by friends and family, but over time her husband distanced himself from these same friends and his own family and became increasingly depressed. The couple moved back to the Chicago suburb where Deborah grew up. She developed a very close relationship with a woman named Ramona. Ramona was a cancer survivor. After extensive surgery and a long period of recuperation, Ramona had received a clean bill of health from her doctors. In an effort to shake his depression, meanwhile, Deborah's husband entered therapy. At her husband's insistence, the family became more strictly observant with respect to Orthodox Judaism. They became integrated into a tight community of Orthodox families, which included Ramona's family as well. Then, Ramona learned that she had a spot on her lungs. The cancer had returned. She would be dead within a year. Upon Ramona's diagnosis, Deborah found that she needed to return to nursing:

> Ramona went to see her oncologist. I had not thought of myself as a nurse for years and years. At that point, I hadn't worked or anything like that. And it turned out that she was going to need some kind of injections every day. And she said, well, "my best friend is a nurse, and she'll give them to me." And she told me that. And I was like, oh, and I told my husband what I had to do, and he brought home some saline and a bunch of needles and let me give him shots in his leg. I gave him 24 shots in his leg so that I could feel comfortable doing it. I was terrified. I mean, because that was always the hardest thing for me [as a nurse] — giving injections. I hated it so much, but I told myself I was going to do anything it took for her. At that point, I thought we could still care for her and that she would get better, so I started giving her the shots. I remember the first one, and I thought I was going to die. I almost passed out afterwards, but she said it didn't hurt at all. She was in really good physical shape then. So I kept giving them. By the end of her course, her blood count was so crappy that I'd just look at her and she'd bruise, you know what I mean? But I'm still having to give her these shots in her legs, which now looked like tomatoes. *But, all of a sudden I became a nurse*

again. And I also took a lot of responsibility for her two children. I just said, I could do anything she needed. And then, oh my God, when she had her first chemo and her hair started falling out, she asked me to take her hair out. And we did it in her sink, and that was the most strange thing I've ever done in my life, I think. I mean to stand with someone who you *love!* I mean, she, I just loved her. And to pull handfuls of hair out of her head into a colander over the sink! I went with her to get her wig, and all this stuff, you know. And she lasted for ten months.

Ramona's death was the single greatest turning point in Deborah's life story. Shortly after the funeral, Deborah's husband began to experience relief from the depression that had plagued him for years. The therapy was working. Their marriage improved dramatically as his mood lifted. The family moved to a bigger house in a nicer neighborhood. The children seemed to be doing better in school. Deborah herself was devastated by Ramona's death. The funeral was the worst day of Deborah's life. But Deborah also began to feel a new level of confidence and competence, which she believes came directly from her efforts to minister to her dying friend:

> Ramona's becoming ill helped me regain my profession. It made me realize I can work with people outside my family. When she died, I found a lot of strength inside myself that I didn't know was there. I would gladly give every bit of that up to have her back, but she's gone, you know, she's gone, and I have what is left. . . . Oh, my life is changed. I'm a different person than I was then. I see myself as somebody who is very competent [now] and capable of doing big things. I mean, I know that I can really tackle big things because, man, if I could make it through that year and that funeral, I can do almost anything.

With her newfound strength and her third child's entry into elementary school, Deborah went back to work full time. After a short spell as a public health nurse, she turned to administration, for which it appears she has considerable skill. She has discontinued her involvement in Orthodox Judaism, but she has retained the spirituality that has always been part of her faith life. She and her husband now belong to a group "of people who get together to pray, and we're very, very loving, very accepting of different approaches, very experiential and sort of mystical, I guess you could say." Deborah wants a fourth child, but she thinks she will probably not be able to get pregnant. Her goals for the future include "watching my children grow, marry, and have children." "Professionally, I'd like to continue work for children in general, not just my own children." In her family and community activities, in her political views, and in her growing professional role as an administrator of a public health agency, Deborah sees herself as an advocate for the rights of poor children and other underrepresented groups. She is committed to "the rights of children, the rights of undocumented workers, the rights of the handicapped, because they're the people, they're my clients." She cares deeply about "the rights of all oppressed people right here in Chicago, in America."

Interpreting Deborah's Story

Deborah Feldman was one of more than 150 adults whom my students and I interviewed between the years 1991 and 1997 in two intensive studies of how people differing in generativity tell the stories of their lives.[25] Approximately half of the participants in the two studies were chosen for interviews because, like Deborah Feldman, they scored extremely *high* on questionnaire measures of generativity—that is, approximately in the top 25% of the distribution of generativity scores. The other half were chosen for interviews because they scored especially *low* on the same generativity measures—typically in the bottom 25%. The two groups—high and low—were matched on a number of demographic variables, such as income, education, and family backgrounds. Each of the participants in these two groups was given the same face-to-face interview. Each interview required about 2 hours to complete. All the interviews were tape recorded and later transcribed by a typist. A number of researchers then examined the transcriptions carefully, identifying key themes, applying various rating and scoring procedures, and generally trying to compare and contrast the experiences of the two different groups. Over many years of coding and repeated statistical tests, we found a pattern of themes that consistently differentiated the stories told by highly generative adults from those told by their less generative counterparts. No story follows the pattern exactly, but in terms of overall averages, the life stories told by high-generativity adults like Deborah Feldman tend to differ from life stories told by low-generativity adults in six important ways.[26]

Theme 1: Early Advantage

"My aunt once told me that my brother and I were the only people she knew who really had happy childhoods," said Deborah Feldman in an early segment of her interview. Highly generative adults do not always claim that their childhood experiences were especially happy, but they are statistically much more likely than less generative adults to identify a way in which they enjoyed a special advantage early on in their lives. The advantage might have to do with family, school, appearance, talent, or even luck. One highly generative woman told how she was fortunate to be chosen the "queen" of her first-grade class. Another said that, although her parents were abusive, she was the favorite of her maternal grandmother, who protected her and gave her special treats when she was little. A highly generative man pointed to his name—David—as the source of his advantage. Going back generations in his family, when a boy was named "David" he was expected to accomplish great things in his life. The name was a blessing for sure, but it also brought with it awesome expectations and burdens.

Sitting with my younger daughter in the doctor's waiting room one afternoon, I had no choice but to watch the kids' show *Barney* on the TV. To a catchy little tune, some character on the show was singing, "Every one is special, special, special—in his or her own way."[27] The sentiment, even in its insipid forms, is appealing to many of us, for it suggests that everybody has something good to offer, everybody has a skill or a talent or a calling that is worth celebrating. That special goodness, that uniqueness resides deeply within us, we often believe—a good, core, inner self. Barney's efforts to build up the self-esteem of young children, while celebrating human diversity, betokens a cultural preoccupation with "specialness" that many have suggested is peculiarly American.[28] Every child is gifted, we would like to believe. Anybody can grow up to be president. The Puritans were, after all, *the chosen people,* and we are the nation, our folklore says, that God chose for greatness. Historians speak of the doctrine of *American exceptionalism.* Individually and collectively, Americans have always believed that they are the good exceptions to all the rules.[29] There is no shortage of hubris in this characteristically American sentiment, and naïveté, as well. Not to "diss" a well-meaning dinosaur, but Barney might have to plead guilty to aiding and abetting preschool narcissism. Some parents might wish that their 3-year-olds sometimes thought a little less of themselves. Nonetheless, the life stories of many highly generative adults seem to reflect, unconsciously I am sure, a folk belief that is deeply ingrained in American mythology, psychology, education, and everyday talk—the belief that *I am blessed.*

Theme 2: The Suffering of Others

The most vivid early scene in Deborah Feldman's life story is the assassination of President Kennedy. Many people who are Deborah's age have vivid memories of this event.[30] But Deborah is the only participant we have ever interviewed who spontaneously imported this event into her life story, the only one to deem it important enough to be considered a self-defining memory in her life. I do not know exactly why she chose it, but the Kennedy assassination is similar in quality to something that comes up in many life stories told by highly generative adults (and comes up rarely in stories told by less generative adults). That something is an expressed childhood awareness that other people suffer pain or sickness, that other people die, are discriminated against, or experience things that are especially negative, and typically much more negative than what the author himself or herself experienced as a child. Research by developmental psychologists consistently shows that children who tend to help others and engage in prosocial behaviors of various kinds tend also to be especially empathic.[31] They are especially sensitive to the pain of others. The life stories of highly generative adults often seem to be expressing this same kind of empathy.

A century before Deborah Feldman began her work with poor children and families in Chicago, Jane Addams (1860–1935) championed the protection of poor immigrants, pushed for child labor laws, and established social-service agencies in that same city. Known in her prime as "the Mother of the World," Addams opened Hull House to serve the immigrants in Chicago's 19th ward. This settlement house offered the people of the surrounding neighborhood hot lunches, child care services, tutoring in English, and even parties. As an advocate for poor families, a social reformer, and a committed pacifist, Addams became a leader of the Progressive movement in America. Reaching its height in the early 20th century, the movement sought to overcome the often dehumanizing effects of rapid industrialization through a variety of political, economic, and social reforms. In 1931 Jane Addams was awarded the Nobel Peace Prize. Like Deborah Feldman, Addams was strongly influenced by her parents' social activism and their religious (Quaker) faith. Like Feldman, furthermore, Addams singled out a memory of death as a key early scene in her life story. She recalled a vivid memory of marching as a tiny child to the cemetery where a schoolmate's mother was being laid to rest. In tracing her evolution as a reformer, moreover, Addams identified as especially formative a trip she took to Europe when she was a young woman. There, she was deeply moved by the dismal living conditions she observed among the poor. Her preoccupation with death and the empathy she felt for the suffering of others may have left something of a morbid streak in Addams's personality. She was not one for levity and relaxation. But these factors also served as strong motivators for generativity throughout Jane Addams's life.

FIGURE 2.2 In September 1889, Jane Addams opened Hull House in an effort to promote the social welfare of children and families in an immigrant neighborhood of Chicago. Throughout her life, a strong empathy for the suffering of others was a prime motivation for Addams in her many projects to improve social life in America and to promote the well-being of the next generation. Reprinted with the permission of Getty Images. Photo by Hulton Archives/Getty Images.

Theme 3: Moral Depth and Steadfastness

By the time she was an adolescent, Deborah Feldman internalized a core set of religious and political values exemplified by her parents. As Deborah put it, the values center on "family, commitment to family, commitment to children, commitment to justice." The values have retained their power as guidelines for her community and professional life, even as she has come to reject certain features of her Jewish heritage. "I appreciate the social justice and the family values of Judaism," she says, but I "really reject the patriarchal parts of it and the hierarchy." "We don't belong to a synagogue anymore because I have a real hard time with corporate structure, just corporations masquerading around in this religious tradition." Through the prayer group they have joined and in other practices and rituals of everyday life, she and her husband enact a more spiritual and privatized faith.

My research assistants and I have rated life-story interviews for the depth, clarity, and continuity of the author's religious/political/ethical beliefs and values—what psychologists call *personal ideologies*.[32] On the average, highly generative adults receive higher ratings on these narrative dimensions than less generative adults. Highly generative adults tend to tell life stories in which the main character establishes a strong and well-developed religious or social/political belief system early in life, typically by adolescence, and then tends to carry that system forward intact through the subsequent chapters of the story. The beliefs may deepen and broaden over time, but they do not change much in terms of their essential character and meanings. These findings mirror those from other studies showing that moral and political commitment in adolescence and adulthood is often associated with religious upbringing, strong religious belief, or a significant spiritual dimension to personality.[33]

Former U.S. president Jimmy Carter always maintained that his public service and humanitarian work were motivated by a deep religious faith. Carter's detractors argue that he was too religious and too moralistic to be a strong president. His admirers see strength in his values and beliefs. What is beyond dispute are the following facts: As president, Carter brokered the 1978 Camp David accords that ended formal hostilities between Egypt and Israel. In the years following his defeat in the 1980 Presidential election, he has campaigned for world peace and human rights. In 1982 he founded the Carter Research Center at Emory University, with a mandate to resolve conflicts, foster democracy, and fight hunger and disease. Since 1984 he and his wife Rosalynn have volunteered one week of work per year renovating apartment buildings and constructing affordable housing with Habitat for Humanity. Carter has helped to end armed hostilities in Ethiopia, Bosnia, Haiti, and Uganda and monitored democratic elections in Liberia, Panama, Mexico, Peru, Paraguay, Nicaragua, Venezuela, Jamaica, and East Timor. When informed that he had won the 2002 Nobel Peace Prize, Carter responded that he would accept the honor on behalf "of suffering people around the world."[34] Even when he held high political offices, Carter continued to teach Sunday school at the Baptist church. For some people, a steadfast religious faith serves as a foundation for building a generative life.

Theme 4: Redemption

The most important and pervasive theme in the life stories of highly generative adults is redemption. Their stories often contain many instances in which very negative scenes and events give way, sometimes suddenly, to positive life outcomes. In Deborah Feldman's story, the most dramatic redemption sequence lies in her account of the sickness and death of her best friend, Ramona, and the way in which Ramona's dying was followed by a host of positive developments in Deborah's own life. By caring for Ramona during the terrible 10 months before she died, Deborah regained her nursing identity, and she came to feel empowered as a woman who can make a positive difference in the world outside her family circle. "When she died, I found a lot of strength inside myself that I didn't know was there." At the same time, her husband's depression subsided and their relationship improved, the family moved to a better house, and even the children's schoolwork improved. Deborah does not see the improvements in her family life as being directly related to Ramona's death. But the entire narrative sequence fits one large redemptive pattern. Out of suffering and death came a better life.

As we saw in chapter 1, the language of redemption can take many forms. American adults may narrate the moves from suffering to positive outcomes in their lives in terms of atonement, emancipation, upward mobility, recovery, enlightenment, psychological development, or some combination of these. For Deborah Feldman, redemption is typically a matter of recovery (as in the case of her husband's recovery from depression) or enlightenment. In what she identifies as a significant childhood scene, Deborah learns that her inability to perform a simple task in gym class is due to a deficiency in depth perception. The same deficiency turns out to be the reason for her bad handwriting, as well. "I wasn't a total idiot after all," she realizes. Once she learns the reason behind her problems, Deborah is able to make the necessary adjustments to move ahead. In adolescence, she is shocked when her politically liberal rabbi refuses to sign the antiwar petition she is circulating in the synagogue. She had never thought to read the petition, which apparently contained inflammatory language and bold claims that even many liberals found too extreme. The event was an important lesson, teaching her that she needs to study things carefully and think through her beliefs and values. Her last days with Ramona teach Deborah that she has the inner strength to make important contributions to the world. The strength was inside her all along, her story claims; she just needed to realize it was there. Again, the redemptive move in the story is from ignorance (not knowing) to enlightenment.

Theme 5: Power Versus Love

Highly generative adults often construct life stories in which strong needs for power conflict with strong needs for love. The main characters in these stories seem to want it all. They want to exert a strong positive impact on the world, and they want to be accepted by others in warm and caring relationships. In some stories, both of these needs can be fulfilled. In other stories, however, the protagonist experiences frustration at his or her inability to live out a script of strong, assertive, and independent action, on the one hand, and gentle, caring, and accepting relationships, on the other. You can readily imagine how these two motivational tendencies might indeed conflict in stories and in lives. If you exert power, others may find it difficult to accept you as a loving equal. If you are strong, you may not be seen as vulnerable enough for true intimacy. If you are gentle and self-effacing in your relationships with others, you may not be taken seriously as an agentic force. The freedom and power of the individual agent compete with the desires for belonging and community in many of the great stories in American literature, and this same conflict tends to be featured prominently in the life stories told by some highly generative American adults.

Interestingly, the conflict between power and love does *not* feature prominently in Deborah Feldman's story. For most of Deborah's story, the protagonist opts for love over power. She chooses to stay home with her children and support her husband as he strives to be a successful physician. It is not until her children are old enough for full-day school that she decides to take up again her nursing career. Deborah's decisions were likely determined by many forces, including social norms, gender roles, and the difficulty of running a two-career household when the male member of the couple is virtually never home. There is also some indication that, until Ramona's death, Deborah never felt empowered enough to push her ambitions beyond the family realm. It would be interesting to know where the story goes from here, now that Deborah seems to have found an inner strength and developed a more prominent professional role. Perhaps power and love will compete in the chapters to come. But to this point, her story has lacked the tension between power and love that we have observed in a number of other stories told by highly generative adults.

Some sort of tension between powerful self-strivings, on the one hand, and gentler communal desires, on the other, may be a natural outgrowth of generativity in some adult lives. Being a generative adult involves *generating* things, creating things (and people), making things happen, and making people do things that you want them to do. Like many generative adults, Jane Addams and Jimmy Carter offered strong agendas for social action and social change. Even (perhaps especially) at the level of parenting, we seek to have a strong, positive impact on our worlds. We want our children to do certain things and not do others. We intervene in their lives, sometimes in heavy-handed ways, to make things happen the way we believe they should happen. Even (perhaps especially) in the book of Genesis, the creating God made Adam and Eve "in his own image"—extensions of the powerful and controlling *self*. My children are *mine,* not yours. My generative efforts reflect *my* own powerful agenda.

At the same time, generativity challenges adults to care for that which they create and, eventually, to *let it go.* In the creation story, the Old Testament God gave humankind free will. He let them do what they wanted to do, as foolish as that may seem. And so it often is for the generative adult. We work hard to raise children, to contribute to society, to make the world a better place. But kids will often disappoint us. Things will not work out the way we want them to. Our best efforts may be misinterpreted, may compromise our dearest relationships, may prove destructive even when we thought we were helping out. If generativity were simple, selfless action, then this would all be much easier. But generativity involves the investment of the *self* in the lives of *others*—generating *and* caring, contributing *and* letting go, having a strong impact on others *and* seeking to connect with them in warm, caring, and egalitarian relationships. We should not be surprised, then, to see conflict.

Theme 6: Future Growth

When people tell their life stories, they not only recount the past. They also project their lives into the future. When highly generative adults do this, they tend to imagine the future as bringing continued growth for those things they have generated. They also foresee the realization of broader, prosocial goals. Highly generative adults expect that the things and people they have generated will continue to develop, advance, and flourish. They imagine and expect this even if they are pessimistic about the future of the world in general. They also expect to broaden their generative influence in the future. If their generativity has focused mainly on their families, they hope to expand their sphere to their community or professional life. If they have worked in local arenas, they may hope to effect change on a broader, societal level.

FIGURE 2.3 God creating Adam. The generative adult creates (generates) people and products in his or her own image—extensions of the powerful self. But then he or she must eventually care for those offspring and, finally, let them go. The conflict between the powerful, creating aspects and the caring, self-surrendering parts of generativity appears even in the creation story from the book of Genesis. Reprinted with the permission of Art Resource, Scala/Art Resource, New York.

Deborah Feldman sets forth a variety of goals for the future. On a material level, she hopes that she and her husband will be able to purchase a summer cottage someday. With respect to her family, she hopes to see her children continue to develop, to marry eventually, and to have children of their own. Many adults—regardless of their levels of generativity—hold out these kinds of personal and family goals. What differentiates especially generative adults from the rest, however, is their expectations for growth and development *outside the family*. Deborah hopes to improve the lives of children and families in Chicago. And her most encompassing goal is to spread her own

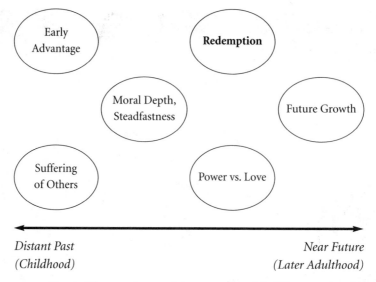

FIGURE 2.4 The six life-story themes of the generative adult. Taken together, these six themes make up a general story type that I call "the redemptive self."

generativity message. That message, which she repeats as if it were a life mantra, is this: "The early years are the most important." As a mother, she feels she has *lived* the message. Now, she wants to *spread* the message to many others, so that they can make better contributions of their own to the next generation. As much as her own children, the message is her legacy.

An American Text

It is as if the most generative adults among us personify, in their life stories, a set of ideas about life that Americans have always held dear. Early advantage, the suffering of others, moral depth and steadfastness, redemption, power versus love, and future growth are all narrative themes that enjoy a rich American pedigree. Deborah Feldman's life story is a psychological and literary *text* that affirms generativity and celebrates themes that have been articulated and reworked in some of the most significant texts in American cultural history, from American autobiographies, to fiction, to speeches. Let me conclude this chapter with one of the greatest of those texts.

"Four score and seven years ago our fathers brought forth on this continent a new nation, conceived in liberty and dedicated to the proposition that all men are created equal." The opening words of Lincoln's Gettysburg Address tell us that this will be a text about generativity. The founding fathers gave birth to ("brought forth") a fresh, "new nation." They "conceived" it, and they nurtured it along, perhaps, like Deborah Feldman, in the belief that "the early years are the most important." And no ordinary nation was this special offspring of their generative work. It was a chosen, a gifted, nation. *Conceived in liberty,* it was, and *under God*—the ultimate early advantage. This was a nation dedicated to a proposition—a nation morally steadfast, committed for all time to a value system centered on human equality and freedom. Like the protagonist in the life story of a highly generative adult, this nation believed from its youth in a few simple truths. And that is not going to change, Lincoln implies, no matter how long the story continues. Lincoln's is a text of generativity that underscores the narrative themes of early advantage and moral steadfastness.

Like the life stories told by highly generative adults, furthermore, Lincoln's oration gives voice to suffering and redemption, and the promise of future growth. "We are engaged in a great civil war," Lincoln says. Millions of people on both sides of the conflict have suffered immensely, and hundreds

FIGURE 2.5 Abraham Lincoln. His Gettysburg Address, delivered in November 1863 at the height of the American Civil War, is a quintessentially American cultural text that celebrates generativity and affirms a set of themes that appear frequently in the life stories of highly generative adults. The themes include early advantage, the suffering of others, moral steadfastness, redemption, and the promise of future growth. Reprinted with the permission of the Library of Congress, Prints and Photograph Division.

of thousands have died. In Deborah Feldman's life story, the death of her best friend ultimately results in Deborah's enhanced happiness and fulfillment in life. In the most redemptive of narrative moves, death generates new life. Lincoln says, "We have come to dedicate a portion [of the battlefield], as a final resting place for those who here *gave their lives that the nation might live*" (emphasis added). Lincoln urges the gathering at Gettysburg to "resolve that these dead shall not have died in vain—that this nation, under God, shall have a new birth of freedom." Redolent with the imagery of generativity and redemption, Lincoln's words tell a story that brought hope and light to a traumatized people in the dark days of the American Civil War.

Let me not get too carried away. The 272 words that comprise Lincoln's great American address were carefully chosen to commemorate a battle. Lincoln drew from classical and biblical sources, the Declaration of Independence, previous speeches used to mark the burial of soldiers, naturalistic and romantic imagery in 19th-century literature, his own personal struggles, and the particularities of the Battle of Gettysburg itself to craft what is essentially a political document.[35] Deborah Feldman's narrative account of her own life is a very different kind of text, a psychological and biographical text, with its own unique sources, meanings, and audience. Deborah may never have read the Gettysburg Address. And though I believe that Abraham Lincoln was a highly generative man, the famous address he gave in November 1863 does not prove that. Nor does it really say much about Lincoln's own life story.

What the Gettysburg Address and Deborah Feldman's life story have in common is their articulation of generativity and their affirmation of a set of quintessentially American life themes. Chief among these themes is redemption. Generative adults see their lives in redemptive terms. They tell *stories* that express how atonement, emancipation, upward mobility, recovery, enlightenment, and development often follow the pain and suffering that human life inevitably brings. Generative adults tell the stories, and they live the stories. Like Lincoln's text, their stories sustain optimism in the face of adversity and anticipate a future day when all good things will grow, when we will all be fruitful and multiply. These stories are hopeful even as they are presumptuous; and inspiring even when they seem cloying, naïve, or fanciful. Generativity and redemption are conveyed in the stories—the personal stories, the cultural stories, the prototypical American stories that many of us know.

But what is it about stories? Why are *stories* so special?

Three

LIFE STORIES

When I was a teenager, my favorite pro basketball player was Bob Love. Before Michael Jordan came along, Love was the leading scorer in Chicago Bulls history, with 12,623 career points during his seven seasons as a Bull (1969–1976). A three-time National Basketball Association (NBA) All-Star, Love was known for his silky-smooth moves and his dead-accurate shooting from the floor. What many fans outside Chicago did not know, however, was that Love was literally unable to speak. He had a stuttering problem so severe that he often could not get a single word out of his mouth. I found out about it one night when Jack Brickhouse, a legendary Chicago sports announcer, interviewed Love on local television after one of the games. In response to Jack's first question, Love stammered and sputtered for what seemed an eternity of television time and finally spit out one or two unintelligible words. Jack explained to the audience that Love had a speech impediment and that we all needed to be patient. He tried another question, but it just got worse. It was horrible to watch. The station terminated the interview, and I slammed off the set, with tears welling up in my eyes.

A serious back injury ended Love's basketball career in 1977. Following surgery, doctors told Love that he might never walk normally again. Returning home one evening, on crutches, Love found his wife had skipped town with their furniture, jewelry, and bank accounts. She left him only a short note, which read, "I don't want to be married to a stutterer and a cripple." Over the next few years, Love moved from one menial job to another. He finally found steady employment as a dishwasher and busboy at Nordstrom's department store in Seattle, Washington. He made $4.45 an hour. Patrons occasionally recognized him: "Hey, that's Bob Love," they would whisper. "He used to be a great basketball player. What a shame." Love was an all-star at Nordstrom's: "I decided that if I was going to be a dishwasher or busboy, I'd be the best one there was." He never missed a day of work. John Nordstrom, the store's head, told Love that if he could only speak more effectively, he would be promoted. Nordstrom offered to pay for speech therapy. For the next year, Love worked with therapist Susan Hamilton, focusing on breathing, pronouncing consonants, and the basic mechanics of speech. He improved dramatically. Nordstrom promoted him to manager in charge of health and sanitation for the store's 150 restaurants nationwide. Love eventually became a corporate *spokesman*.

Love's first opportunity for public speaking came in 1986, when he was invited to give an address at a high school sports banquet in Rockford, Illinois. Over 800 people were in attendance. Love told his life story—growing up poor in rural Louisiana; surviving his earliest years with an abusive stepfather; running away from home at age 8; spending his teenage years with a loving grandmother and 16 relatives in a two-bedroom shanty; being ridiculed in school for stuttering; becoming a football and basketball star in high school and college; enjoying his glory years with the Bulls; enduring his divorce, his menial jobs, and his humiliation; and working out his redemption. The speech "went smoother than I expected, and when I was finished there was a standing ovation," he remarked "It made me feel so good. It was the *turning point* in my life." Love returned to the Bulls organization in 1992 and since then has served as director of community relations. He gives hundreds of speeches a year. Friends and community leaders recently convinced him to try his luck in politics. At age 59, Bob Love ran for city alderman in Chicago.[1]

In a famous quote, F. Scott Fitzgerald once remarked, "There are no second acts in American lives." With all due respect to a great writer, I argue Fitzgerald could not have been more wrong. Ever since Benjamin Franklin, Americans have been reinventing themselves in astonishing ways and producing second, third, and even fourth acts. We see it in Bob Love. We see it in American fiction, biography, and folklore. We see it on talk shows and in the magazines.

The September 30, 2002, issue of *People* magazine ran an article entitled "Second Acts," featuring accounts of people who were caught in scandals or experienced substantial disgrace only to reinvent themselves in a second, redemptive "act." Rita Jenrette's story is the article's lead. The year after Bob Love's back surgery, South Carolina Representative John Jenrette was indicted in a bribery scandal and sentenced to 13 months of prison. Capitalizing on their notoriety, his wife Rita quickly wrote a best-selling memoir in which she described having sex with the congressman on the Capitol steps. Then she posed nude for *Playboy* and turned up in an especially tacky episode of *Fantasy Island*. Yes, they did divorce. Rita reemerged in the 1990s as a highly successful, commercial real estate broker who regularly attends seminars at Harvard Business School and works with charities in New York. Regarding her first act, Jenrette today says, "I made some choices that were not so judicious, and I have to live with them." Regarding her opportunism in the wake of the scandal, Jenrette resolved, "I will not let this incident be my epitaph." *People* concludes: "Her long, strange trip to respectability 'has been an intriguing journey,' says Jenrette, who lives in Manhattan with her fiancé, an architect she declines to name. 'It's painful, but it makes you stronger.' And she knows her past is never too far away. 'It'll crop up at the most inopportune times,' she says. 'But now I've made it a footnote.'"[2]

Notice the language Bob Love and Rita Jenrette use to describe the scenes and acts in their very different lives. Love says the speech he gave in Rockford, Illinois, was "the turning point in my life." Jenrette is determined that her first act be seen as a "footnote" rather than an "epitaph." In both cases, the actors see their lives as *extended narratives in time.* To say that an event marks a "turning point" in one's life is to suggest that one's life is like a story whose plot changes direction as a result of a particular scene. Like most of us, Bob

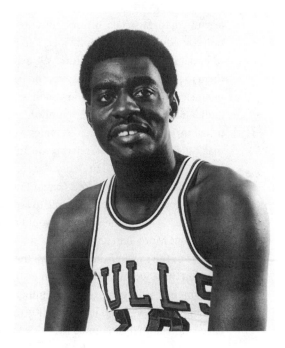

FIGURE 3.1 A professional basketball star in the 1970s, Bob Love had a severe stuttering problem that made it impossible for him to obtain gainful employment when he retired from the game. After a year of speech therapy, however, Love improved dramatically, and he now gives hundreds of motivational speeches a year across the United States. Love identifies the "turning point" in his life as the first public speech he ever gave, to a group of 800 people in Rockford, Illinois. Identifying "turning points" in life is one way that people indicate they understand their lives to be *stories* enacted over time. Reprinted with the permission of Getty Images. Photo by NBA Photo Library/Getty Images.

Love sees his life as a story. The story has a beginning (in rural Louisiana), a middle, and an anticipated ending. It contains heroes (his speech therapist) and villains (his first wife). There are chapters of triumph (the Bulls) and humiliation (the busboy). There is a challenge or obstacle that the hero must confront (stuttering). The challenge gives the story tension and direction. There is suspense, for we do not know how the story will turn out.

Rita Jenrette works to write her life as a narrative that portrays the full scope of her individuality as it has evolved over time. She wants to relegate a few disgraceful years to the footnotes. She is determined that her story will not end with *Playboy* and *Fantasy Island*. Her epitaph will not say that she was but a gold digger, a dumb blonde with a good body. Of course, you can never fully escape the past. A classmate at Harvard sheepishly asks if she is the same woman who posed nude for *Playboy* 20 years ago. (Bob Love still stutters a little bit, too.) Nonetheless, Rita decides that her life plot will take a different direction as the heroine transforms herself over time. Like Bob Love, she will rework the story, reauthor her life. And she will live the new story for as long as it seems to be the right story to live. And then she may rewrite it again.

The Storytelling Mind

Human beings are storytellers by nature. In a multitude of guises, as folktale, legend, myth, fairy tale, history, epic, opera, motion picture, television situation comedy, novel, biography, joke, and personal anecdote, the story appears in every known human culture. We expect much from stories. We expect them to entertain, educate, inspire, and persuade us; to keep us awake and put us to sleep; to make us feel joy, sadness, anger, excitement, horror, shame, guilt, and virtually any other emotion we can name. We also expect stories to tell us who we are. When it comes to human lives, storytelling is sense-making. I cannot understand who you are and what your life might mean unless I have some sense of the story you are working on—the way you see your life as a plot enacted over time. I cannot understand who I am if my life forms no narrative for me, if I am unable to see my own life as an intelligible story that makes sense to me now and would make sense if I were to tell it to you tomorrow. More than anything else, stories give us our identities.[3]

One of the cardinal authorities on the use of stories in human lives is the eminent psychologist Jerome Bruner. Bruner distinguishes between two fundamentally different forms of human knowing.[4] *Paradigmatic* knowing is mainly what we learn in school. It is the knowing of cause and effect, science, and rational discourse. If I wish to devise a mathematical proof, if I wish to test a scientific hypothesis, or if I wish to explain how something in the material world works (why the sun comes up in the east, why my car's engine will not run well on diesel fuel, or why my body will not run well if I drink a pint of vodka), I must try to formulate a logical argument that is *true*. Paradigmatic knowing aims to find the single, logical, causal truth.

By contrast, *narrative* knowing is what we learn from stories. We use stories, Bruner says, to convey and explain *human conduct*. When we seek to understand why a person does something, we look to narrative. If I want to know why Bob Love goes around the country giving motivational speeches, I have to understand his story. If I want to know why my daughter refuses to speak to me this morning, I need a story there, too. Perhaps it has to do with my asking her to clean her room 2 days ago. She said okay but then simply threw all her clothes in the closet. All was fine till my wife opened the closet door yesterday and was crushed by a virtual avalanche. After that, my daughter returned home with a friend, and I made a snide remark, which may have embarrassed her. And after that . . .

As Bruner puts it, stories are fundamentally about "the vicissitudes of human intention" organized in time.[5] In English, this means that stories are

FIGURE 3.2 A pioneer in narrative psychology, Jerome Bruner argues that the most natural and effective way to understand human behavior and human lives is through stories. Human beings are storytellers by nature. Photograph courtesy of Jerome Bruner.

about what characters want, what they intend to do, and how they go about trying to get what they want or avoid what they do not want, over time. To have a story, you need a motivated character whose efforts to achieve some end are blocked in some way. Little Red Riding Hood wants to get to Grandma's house with the cakes, but her efforts are thwarted by the Big Bad Wolf, who wants to eat Little Red Riding Hood and her grandma. If the Big Bad Wolf had never shown up, however, we would have no story, or at least nothing interesting to tell as a story. Bruner points out that stories are typically told when there is a "deviation from a culture's canonical pattern."[6] In English, this means that, unless something unexpected or out of the ordinary happens (something that deviates from a culture's canon of expectations), there is nothing really interesting to tell. The necessary deviation that creates the story is often some form of challenge, threat, or danger.

Bruner believes that the human brain is specially designed for storytelling. We have evolved to be storytellers, Bruner suggests, because being able to think about the world in storied terms and relate stories to each other proved adaptive for social life in our ancestral past. For example, the ability to imagine through hypothetical scenarios what another person—an enemy, for instance—might be thinking in a given situation might have been a wonderful survival skill in the environment of evolutionary adaptedness and might help explain why the tendency to tell stories seems to appear in all cultures.

Although neuroscientists have not pinpointed a particular brain region or mechanism that is exclusively linked to telling stories, they have begun to identify brain correlates of one particular component of storytelling in humans. The component is called *episodic memory*. Episodic memory is the ability to recall specific events (episodes) from the past. Your memories of your wedding day, your first day in school, and yesterday's argument with your partner exist in your mind as scenes from your past that you can recall and, in a sense, relive. Contrast these to another class of memory: Recall, for example, the moment you learned that Sacramento was the capital of California. I will make it easier (and harder): Recall the day you learned your name. You probably do remember (but maybe you do not—that is okay) that Sacramento is the capital of California, and I am sure you remember your name. But in both cases you probably do not associate a particular event with this knowledge. These are examples of *semantic* memory. We remember lots of things—birth dates, facts and figures, where our house is located, the rules of baseball, and on and on—but we do not necessarily remember episodes that go with them. Nor do we need to. Imagine how cumbersome and inefficient the human mind would be if for everything we knew we had to recall also the exact moment and setting in which we came to know it! Some cognitive scientists believe that semantic memory is more basic than episodic and probably goes back much further in human evolution. They suggest that episodic memory may have evolved out of semantic, as a kind of specialized skill that only humans have. It is a skill that enables us to travel backward in subjective time and to link remembered events to imagined future episodes.[7]

Episodic memory provides the personal experience of time that we draw upon when we tell stories. If we could not travel back in time to recall particular scenes from our own lives, then we would probably be unable to think in a storied way. We would not be able, for example, to construct narratives in which motivated characters enact their desires over time, from one scene to the next. Storytelling is so natural and so easy for most of us that it is almost impossible to imagine not being able to do it. But there are examples of people whose episodic memory abilities are so compromised that they seem unable to think about life in storied terms.

Consider the case of K. C.[8] Born in 1951, K. C. lived a normal and unremarkable life until he was 30 years old, when he sustained a serious head injury in a motorcycle accident. As a result, K. C. suffers today from a form of amnesia whereby he is unable to recall any personal experiences from the past. Much like the lead character in the 2000 movie *Memento,* K. C. is completely unable to remember any events, circumstances, or situations from his whole life—any episode whatsoever, from birth to the present day. The only exception is that he can recall events that have occurred in the last minute or two. Furthermore, K. C. is unable to predict what he may do in the future. When asked, he cannot tell what he plans to do later the same day, or the day after, or at any time for the rest of his life. He lives completely in the present, with no narrative sense of life's passing moments and scenes. Amazingly, K. C. shows *few* deficits in other areas of cognitive functioning. For example, he scores in the normal range of most measures that make up intelligence tests. And he does remember many facts and procedures that he learned before his motorcycle accident. He knows many things about his early life—when he was born, where he lived, the names of some of the schools he attended. But he does not remember the events themselves—cannot remember actually living in a particular house or going to a particular school. He knows mathematics, geography, history, and other subjects he learned in school, though of course he does not remember learning them. He plays chess. It is clear that although K. C. has lost all episodic memory, certain aspects of his semantic memory remain intact.[9]

The injury that caused K. C.'s particular form of amnesia involved severe damage to parts of the brain that appear to be implicated in episodic memory. Research with amnesiacs has shown that lesions to what is called the brain's medial temporal lobes are often implicated in the loss of episodic memory abilities. These regions lie in the lower area of the brain's cerebral cortex, which itself is the brain's large outer layer. Within the temporal lobes, furthermore, lies an inner brain structure called the *hippocampus.* The hippocampus plays an important role in the storage of new memories. It seems to do this by creating new interconnections with the cerebral cortex as each to-be-remembered experience takes place. Damage to the hippocampus can result in loss of episodic memory in that the brain loses the ability to lay down the elements of the event so that they can be retrieved later. Finally, the brain's prefrontal cortex—at the top and front of the brain—also appears to be involved in the processing of episodic information. New studies of brain imaging show that the prefrontal cortex may be involved in the effort of retrieving or recalling the event once it has been stored in memory (figure 3.3).

In sum, the uniquely human tendency to construe life in narrative terms is dependent on episodic memory. Although a great deal of what we do remember is not directly connected in our minds to particular occasions and events (semantic memory), humans are nonetheless able to travel back in time to recall particular scenes or episodes that have happened in their lives. Our brains are hardwired to recall past events and connect them to imagined future scenarios. Episodic memory, then, provides us with the feeling that

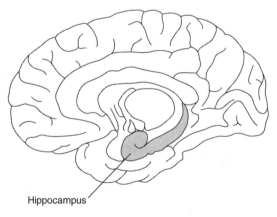

Hippocampus

FIGURE 3.3 Episodic memory—the ability to travel back in time to recall and relive autobiographical events—is a skill that may be unique to human beings. Neuroscience research has begun to identify parts of the brain that may be involved in taking in episodic information (*encoding*), storing the information, and recalling it later (*retrieval*). These areas include the hippocampus (especially involved in making new memories), parts of the temporal lobes, and parts of the prefrontal cortex.

our lives are set in time—the remembered past, the experienced present, and the anticipated future. This temporal sense is likewise essential for story-telling, for we relate in narratives the thoughts and actions of motivated char-acters as they move from episode to episode, from beginning to middle to end. Episodic memory provides the foundation for autobiography and iden-tity—for our narrative sense of self-in-time.

The Developmental Psychology of Life Stories

If you think you remember your first year of life, you are probably mistaken. Earliest episodic memories typically go back no further than age 3 or 4. Al-most 100 years ago, Sigmund Freud called this universal memory deficit *in-fantile amnesia*. Freud believed that our earliest years are so filled with dark and threatening impulses that we end up repressing them.[10] They are too scary to remember. But a much more reasonable and developmentally inter-esting explanation is this: *We simply were not conscious.* Even when they are awake, alert, and smiling straight into your eyes, 6-month-old babies are not experiencing life the way you and I typically do. They are not aware of them-selves as, well, *selves.* It is not simply that they do not know who they are. They do not even know *that* they are! To use a metaphor from the neurosci-entist Antonio Damasio, infants have yet to "step into the light" of "extended consciousness."[11] They are psychologically in the dark because they do not yet sense that the things that happen to them are *their own* experiences ex-tending *over time.* Six-month-old Sarah smiles at her daddy, but Sarah does not know that it is *she* who is smiling and does not sense that this entire 2-minute scenario of smiling and playing with daddy is *her own experience.*

"Consciousness begins," Damasio writes, "when brains acquire the power, the simple power I must add, of telling a story without words, the story that there is life ticking away in an organism."[12] What Damasio is saying here is that human consciousness is a matter of mentally taking on the position of a *narrator.*[13] A narrator is a teller. Consciousness involves a continual telling of lived experience, a kind of online stream of narration that flows through the minds of most sentient human beings much of the time. The telling does not require words, but the eventual development of language certainly in-fluences the quality of our consciousness. Research suggests that by the age of 2 years most children have stepped into the light of extended conscious-ness. Relatedly, most 2-year-olds have developed a primitive *autobiographi-cal self.*[14] As a 2-year-old, I now know that my lived experiences—the things I do and feel and think—belong to me, that they are part of *my* life evolving over time. In a self-conscious manner, I can now observe my own experi-ence. *I* can think about *me.* I can feel pride when I do something good, and shame when I fail.[15] In a primitive and halting way, I have begun to narrate my own personal experiences as if they were stories.

I will not narrate a very good story, however, if I am clueless about the basics of human motivation. What motivates people to do what they do? By the time children are 3 years of age, most have acquired the first principle of motivational psychology: People do things because *they want to*. Desires lead to behavior. Jessica eats the cookie because she wants to eat it. She is hungry, and she likes cookies. By the time children are 4 years of age, most have acquired the second principle: People do things because of *what they believe*. Jason looks for his shoes in the closet because he believes that is where he left them. An extensive body of research in developmental psychology shows that in their preschool years children develop a basic *theory of mind*.[16] They come to understand that people have desires and beliefs in their minds and that they act upon these desires and beliefs.

Understanding why people do what they do is essential, you can imagine, for social life. It also marks a monumental step forward for storytelling. Remember that Bruner said stories are about "the vicissitudes of human intention" organized in time—about what characters want (and believe) and how they go about acting upon those wants (and beliefs). By the time they enter kindergarten, most children can connect human desire and belief to subsequent human action. They understand the temporal sequence: First, a person wants (or believes) something, and then that person acts on the want (or belief). Most kindergartners have what it takes cognitively to recognize, to understand, and to tell a pretty good story. In addition, they have heard stories from their parents and friends, and have enjoyed opportunities to practice their storytelling in everyday talk and play. And they have begun to learn some of the ground rules and guidelines about stories in their own culture.[17] How boys and girls tell different stories, for example. How some stories are especially valued and others ignored. Like most interesting features of human psychological development, storytelling, therefore, evolves as a complex interaction of nature and nurture, mind and society, individual and culture.

Let me fast-forward about 12 years. I am talking now about 17-year-olds. In the United States, people of this age are usually approaching the end of their high school careers. Many will soon enroll in college. Many others will end formal schooling and search for full-time employment. Some will enter the military. Many will leave their childhood homes to live in dormitories or apartments, and those who stay home with parents will most likely feel a new sense of independence. It is customary to think of 17- and 18-year-olds as "adolescents," but this label is misleading when we lump them together with 6th graders and junior high kids, who are ages 12–14. Because older adolescents face many of the same challenges that people face in their early 20s, one psychologist has recently coined a new term, *emerging adulthood,* to demarcate the period between about age 17 and the mid-20s as it is played out in modern societies like ours.[18] What is the main psychological challenge of emerging adulthood in a modern society? It is the challenge of *narrative identity.*

By the time we hit our late teens, we are expected to have made some psychological headway on most or all of the following questions: What do I want to do when I grow up? What do I truly believe in? Where is my life headed? Where has my life been? What is the relation between where I have been and where I am going? How am I going to get there? What is the meaning of my life? What gives my life purpose and coherence? I said we are likely to have made *some* headway—I did not say that we have it all figured out by the time we hit 21. Indeed, these are questions that few of us will ever fully answer to complete satisfaction. The point is that we *begin* to ask these kinds of questions about life—identity questions—in the emerging adulthood years. (These questions make little realistic sense to children.) We begin, consciously and unconsciously, to ask these questions, because the cultural conditions and expectations of modern society are such that *we have to ask them.*

Modern societies offer a daunting range of life possibilities: There is no single, one-size-fits all, "correct" way to live in a society like ours. There are many things we can do and be, many choices we can make. And we have to make them. We cannot do everything and believe everything. One person cannot be a corporate lawyer and a concert pianist and a professional wrestler all at the same time. One person cannot be a full-fledged Catholic, a devout Jew, and a practicing Buddhist monk in the same body and mind. And if an individual does manage to do and believe many different things—say she is a corporate lawyer, a devoted mom, a marathoner, a born-again Baptist, a political liberal, and the person among her college friends who always provides the marital counseling—she is likely to wonder what it is that ties these different things together. What makes her life coherent? The answer is the story she lives by—that is, narrative identity.[19]

People begin to put their lives together into personalized life stories in their adolescent and young-adult years. Long before this time, they are able to narrate their own experiences in a storied manner. It is not until the period of emerging adulthood, however, that people begin to arrange their entire lives—the past as they remember it, the present as they perceive it, and the future as they imagine it—into broad and self-defining life narratives that provide their lives with some semblance of unity, purpose, and meaning. *Narrative identity is the internalized and changing story of your life that you begin to work on in the emerging adult years.* The story ties together the many different aspirations you have and roles you play into a meaningful narrative framework. The story spells out how you believe you have developed over time and where you think your life is going. The story suggests what you believe to be true and good, and how you expect to live up (or not) to those standards. The story serves as a flexible guide for the future and an historical archive for making sense of your past. The story is unfinished, complex, contradictory at times, and subject to considerable revision. It may contain many different plots, scenes, characters, and themes. The story situates you in an adult world where other people have their own stories, some of which may be similar to yours. The story is in you, in your mind, even if you rarely focus consciously on it. You carry the story around with you, and you share aspects of it with other people, especially when they share aspects of their stories with you.

There is no cultural or social need to put your life together into a narrative identity before you reach emerging adulthood. In modern societies, we do not expect children to make occupational choices, to decide on what their deep beliefs are, or to formulate plans for living a purposeful and meaningful life. Even if we were foolish enough to expect all this from children, they would not be able to do it. Research suggests that children and many early adolescents do not have the cognitive skills that are necessary for full life-story making. For example, children tend to see the world in highly concrete and specific terms. Questions about the meaning and purpose of life are too abstract to be appreciated and fully understood. Constructing a meaningful narrative identity involves weighing different hypothetical possibilities in life, choosing and mixing among alternative abstractions in a way that requires the full powers of abstract thought. The ability to weigh and balance hypotheticals—what some psychologists call *formal operational thinking*—is not usually seen before the teenage years.[20]

Life span psychologists Tilman Habermas and Susan Bluck have argued that people have to be able to exercise at least four different mental skills in order to construct a coherent life story.[21] First and most basic, they have to be able to construct little, goal-directed stories about single episodes in their life. Habermas and Bluck call this *temporal coherence,* because it shows that a person can narrate in a coherent way a sequence of actions that take place over time. Most children can do this by the time they enter kindergarten, and they get better at it as they grow older. Second, people have to be able to conform their autobiographical understanding to society's expectations of the life course, what Habermas and Bluck call *biographical coherence.* They have to learn what typically happens in their society over the full life span—how it is that for the middle class in modern societies like ours, for example, you go to school through age 18 or so, you probably leave home after that, you get a job, you probably get married as a young adult, you probably have children after that, you ideally move forward (make progress, get better) in a career or line of work, you reach "middle age" in your 40s or so, you probably retire around age 65, you are not likely to live much beyond 90, and so on. In kindergarten, we are only dimly aware of all this, but by the time we are in junior high school we have probably read enough biographies (or, more likely, seen them on TV), or had enough cultural experience to have internalized a basic sequence of milestones and events that comprise the typical life.

Once older children and young adolescents begin to understand the possibilities of biography, they may develop grand life fantasies for themselves. As for me, I was going to pitch for the Chicago Cubs. I had my entire career worked out in my mind by the time I was 11. I would win 22 games in my rookie season, suffer the "sophomore slump" in my second year and lose more games than I won, and then go on to pitch brilliantly for 15 more years, amassing Hall of Fame stats. I would end my career as a relief pitcher, coming out of the bullpen to close out the extra-inning victory in the final game of the World Series against the Yankees. In my imagined baseball career, I developed what psychologist David Elkind calls a *personal fable* for my life.[22] Personal fables are fantastical self-narratives that some children and adolescents formulate in their minds and sometimes express in diaries or, as in my case, notebooks filled with earned-run averages and won/loss percentages. These early drafts of narrative identity, filled with passionate fantasies and heroic feats, are often completely unrealistic (my Little League career was less than stellar) and suggestive of a kind of adolescent egocentrism that seems embarrassing even at the time. (I never showed my notebooks to anybody.) Still, there is nothing wrong with having personal fables at this time in the life course. They are like rough drafts of a narrative identity. Most of us tear them up and throw them away, but we do not forget them.

What Habermas and Bluck identify as *causal coherence* begins to emerge in the adolescent years, as people become increasingly able to link different life scenes into extended and realistic causal narratives. A mother asks her high school daughter, Samantha, why she has suddenly acquired a liking for rap music. Of course, Samantha will tell her mother nothing. But were she to give the full story of why she now likes rap, she might say something like this: Last year she hated rap music because her best friend Kristin hated it, and ever since junior high she looked up to Kristin and thought her best friend knew everything. But Kristin and she had a big fight last month when it became known that Kristin was flirting with Will, even though Will and

Samantha were supposedly "going out." Kristin and Samantha patched up their differences, once they both realized that Will was a loser anyway. But Samantha feels she can no longer fully trust Kristin, and now she enjoys challenging Kristin's views on lots of different things—like clothes and music. In a contrarian mood last week, Samantha bought a rap CD and she switched radio stations, and now that she has been listening to this stuff, well, it is pretty good, and it is also good that Kristin does not like it.

Okay, it is a weird story, but it shows how a person might link one event to another and to yet another in an extended sequence of causation. Should Samantha go on to conclude that this entire sequence illustrates what she believes to be an important tendency in her life—her tendency to rebel against convention, perhaps, or her newfound cynicism about friendships—then she would also begin to show what Habermas and Bluck call *thematic coherence* in life-story telling. In thematic coherence, a person is able to derive a general theme or principle about the self based on a narrated sequence of events. For example, a businessman may explain the origins of his politically conservative values by appealing to a series of events and realizations that transpired in his early 20s, after he graduated with liberal views and a humanities major but could not find a job—and then his liberal girlfriend dumped him, and then he enrolled in business school and was impressed with a politically conservative economics professor, and then he started up a small business but he really had to struggle because of oppressive tax laws and regulations, and then he married a woman who was pretty conservative herself and helped to reinforce his views, and then he became disillusioned with the Clinton administration and the impeachment scandal and decided he would never vote for a Democrat again, and then his business grew and he became pretty successful, and now he and his wife have two young children and worry a great deal about safety in their suburban community, and on the story goes. Habermas and Bluck have argued that both causal and thematic coherence are rare before adolescence but increase in prominence as a person moves toward emerging adulthood. By the time, then, that modern society expects us to begin work on our narrative identity, we have acquired the cognitive skills necessary for doing so.

Narrative identity links together episodic memories and future goals to define an adult life in time and social context. The story tells us who we are, even if in its details and scenes it is not exactly "true." This is perhaps the key point about the stories we live by: They are not objective replays of the past. Research in cognitive psychology shows conclusively that episodic memory is highly selective.[23] We cannot remember everything. Much of what we do remember is likely to be fuzzy and less than perfectly accurate on all the de-

TABLE 3.1. *Developmental Milestones in Narrative Identity: From Early Childhood to Young Adulthood*

Approximate Age	Stage	Milestones	Significance for Narrative Identity
1–2 years	Infant/ toddler	Extended consciousness Autobiograph-ical self	The emergence of an on-line stream of subjective narration; the consolidation of a sense of "I" as a narrator/actor extending over time
4–5 years	Preschool/ kindergarten	Theory of mind	Understanding that human actions are motivated by desires and beliefs in the minds of actors/characters Children are now able to understand and tell simple stories with *temporal coherence*
10–14 years	Early adolescence	Personal fable	Older children and young adolescents develop biograph-ical fantasies that serve as grandiose first drafts of narrative identity, now that *autobiographical coherence* has developed
17–25 years	Emerging adulthood	Full life stories	With the development of skills related to *causal* and *thematic coherence*, young people in modern societies begin to construct internal life stories—narrative identities—to provide their lives with meaning and purpose. The stories link the reconstructed past, experienced present, and imagined future.

tails. Furthermore, much of what we remember relates to our *current* situation and *future* goals. If I plan to become a physician, I may have very clear memories of learning science and helping people when I was a child. If I am about to get a divorce, I may find the most vivid memories from my distant past to be those related to loss and sadness. If my father suddenly dies, I may forget all the bad things he did and revamp my history to make him the hero

I never knew. Unconsciously and unwittingly, we reconstruct the past in light of what we see today and imagine the future to be. Of course, our life stories are based on the reality of our lives—there are real facts, no doubt about that. Bob Love *did* play for the Bulls. You can check the record books. He really *did* stutter badly—I saw it on television, I swear. But much of what is interesting in narrative identity flows from the dramatic license we employ in shaping our memories and goals into a compelling narrative form. To a certain extent, we *make* our stories. Within limits, we *decide* who we are, who we were, and who we may become.[24]

The Role of the Audience in Life Stories

In composing his biography of the late Ronald Reagan, Edmund Morris struggled to find the right narrative form. How do you tell the story of this inscrutable man? How do you convey an understanding of who Ronald Reagan really was? After 13 years of exhaustive research, Morris still had a big problem, for virtually nobody, Reagan included, has ever professed a deep understanding of the 40th president of the United States. And how could anybody explain how a B-grade Hollywood actor could ascend to the most powerful office in the world? Reagan was always an actor, Morris notes. Even before his Hollywood days, he lived as if he were perpetually on stage, moving nimbly and dreamily from one performance to the next. "As a teenager," Morris writes, Reagan "had taken no personal interest in people." They were, and remained," he continues, "a faceless audience to his perpetual performance."[25] He enacted the role of president as well as it has ever been played out, some would say. It should not be surprising, then, that nobody really knew him, for he was acting, always acting, from beginning to end. Morris writes,

> Screen actors are adept at moving from one production to another—
> sometimes between different productions, shot simultaneously on
> neighboring sound stages. Hence, I suppose, the fabled shortness of
> Dutch's [Reagan's] attention span, which an exasperated aide would
> compare to that of a fruit fly. Both the fable and the simile strike me
> as unjust: He was generally a serious, even dogged study. Yet Ronald
> Reagan remained all his life an actor, a man of exits and entrances,
> whether the "production" that engaged him was as short as a conver-
> sation or as long as the presidency. When he stepped onto the set, he
> knew exactly what to do and how to fill the space allotted him. And
> when he left it, it was with the word *CUT* sounding in his ears. On
> to the next cast of characters!

I remember greeting him one morning, having entertained him at home the night before. Not only did he fail to mention our dinner, it was obvious from his smiling and distant demeanor that he did not recall it.

To those readers who will seize on this as evidence of the incipient dementia in the White House, I reply: *You do not understand that actors remember forward, not backward.* Yesterday's take is in the can; today is already rolling; tomorrow's lines must be got by heart.[26]

How do you tell the life story of an actor? You do it with an audience. In a literary move that has been both praised and criticized, Morris decided to create an admiring (and fictional) audience for Reagan's early life. Essentially, he invented a person, whom Morris identified as himself—a person who followed Reagan around during his teenage and early adult years. Morris even invented biographical details for this fictional person. He was born on August 9, 1912. His father died in 1923. He attended Eureka College, which is where Reagan was also a student. By inventing a character that watches the developing hero from afar, Morris attempts to convey the very vivid and profound sense in which Reagan moved through life as if he were constantly performing in front of an admiring audience. The effect is surprising and unsettling, at least for this reader. On one level, the biographer is lying to you, even as he suggests obliquely that he is employing a literary device, for he did not and could not have known Reagan as a young man. (For one thing, Morris is much younger, and he grew up in Kenya.) However, the biographical strategy Morris employs helps him convey vividly what he believes to be a central truth in Ronald Reagan's life. The truth is this: Beyond all the roles he played, behind all the performances, when you get right down to the core of it all, Ronald Reagan was really and truly an *actor,* a graceful and powerful actor who played a truly noble role on an international stage, an amazing actor whom this skeptical biographer cannot help but admire from afar, always from afar because one can never really get close to an actor who is this good.

Morris's unusual strategy for telling the story of Ronald Reagan hints at a more general truth about life stories. Although few of us are actors in the senses that Ronald Reagan may have been, we each compose and live out our life stories with certain audiences in mind. Stories exist to be told. If each of us is a teller, there must be somebody at whom, or something at which, our tellings are aimed. Like Ronald Reagan, we all want applause and positive reviews. We want the critics to rave: "Great story! Nice performance! Really like that narrative identity you're working on!" Ever since Shakespeare declared

that "all the world's a stage," social behavior has been analogized to role performance. Sociologists and social psychologists have long emphasized the
ways in which social behaviors are scripted by social audiences and shaped
by social forces that are often beyond the actor's control.[27] Beyond mere
behavior, furthermore, the narrative identities that we begin to construct in
the emerging adult years—the internal stories we make, revise, and live
by—are oriented toward important observers, listeners, audiences, critics,
and the like.

There are two different senses in which life stories are made and told with
respect to audiences. First, many forms of social communication involve
sharing stories about the self. At parties, in the barbershop, in job interviews,
at the dinner table, in bed, at a bar, on the therapist's couch, over the phone,
in online chats, while waiting in line, while walking the dog, or you name it—
there are thousands of places and situations in which people tell stories about
themselves. Our identities are made and remade through conversation. As
people react to our stories and share their stories with us, we continue to edit
our own evolving accounts. We receive feedback and advice. We notice that
some tellings seem to go over very well whereas others receive poor reviews.
Sometimes it seems as if the audience members are very attentive; other
times, it seems as if they are distracted and that we are boring them.

FIGURE 3.4 Ronald Reagan,
as a young man. The 40th
president of the United States
and champion of American
conservatism was a Holly-
wood actor for many years.
In his controversial biography
of Reagan, Edmund Morris
attempted to convey just how
central the acting role was
throughout Reagan's life by
inventing a fictional character
who functions as an admiring
audience. Stories are made to
tell, and people construct
their own self-defining life
stories with particular audiences or listeners in mind.
Reprinted with the permission of Getty Images. Photo
by Hulton Archive/Getty
Images.

In an interesting set of studies, social psychologist Monisha Pasupathi arranged interviews between best friends in which one friend was a listener and the other a teller. The experimenter randomly assigned each listener to one of two different conditions. In one condition, the listener was told by the experimenter to listen attentively to the personal account that his or her friend was to tell. In the other, the listener was asked to focus his or her mind on a particular distracting task while trying to listen to the friend's account. (The task was to keep track in one's head of how many times the friend said any word that began with a "th.") The listeners were also told not to tell their friends about their instructions but simply to play out one of the two very different listening roles. The results showed that tellers find it a bit annoying and even depressing when their friends seem to be distracted during such conversation. Those tellers whose friends listened attentively rated the conversation more pleasant and rewarding than did those tellers whose friends were secretly counting "th" words. More interesting was what happened weeks later, when the tellers came back to the laboratory and were asked to recall the conversations they originally had. Those tellers whose friends had been distracted had a much more difficult time remembering the personal accounts they shared, compared to those whose friends were listening to them attentively. The quality of the conversation impacted subsequent episodic memory. The bottom line conclusion is that, when audiences do not focus on our personal stories, we tend to dismiss or even forget those stories.[28]

Fortunately for many of us, our audiences do often listen attentively, especially when we are sharing stories we consider to be especially significant for our lives. Personality psychologist Avril Thorne has studied the extent to which people find attentive listeners for memories of trauma and other highly emotional events. Her research shows that a surprisingly large number of people tell stories of highly personal experiences soon after those experiences occur. The practice of sharing stories with intimate others is so common that Thorne uses the term *intimate memories* to refer to the most salient and self-defining episodes in a person's life. Audiences serve many purposes in life-story telling. Like therapists and counselors, good listeners can provide empathy and encouragement for the teller of a sad or traumatic tale. Sharing stories also builds warmth and intimacy between friends. In addition, Thorne argues that people articulate and clarify the meanings and the nature of their episodic memories with each new telling. Audiences help us figure out what our stories mean, and they subtly work to shape and change our stories over time.[29]

Although we are accustomed to thinking of an audience as separate from the actor or teller, there is also a sense in which the audience is within. People watch themselves; they listen to the stories they tell; they sometimes serve as their own worst critics. In addition, there is a sense in which some psychologically important audiences are both *separate* from the self and observing the self *from within*. This is the second way in which audiences are related to narrative identity. Freud proposed that within the mind of every mature individual is a *superego*—an internalized audience that passes judgment on the self. He argued that as young children we internalize images of our parents, who then set up shop in our minds as harsh authority figures. Even after our parents are gone, we carry them around (unconsciously) in our minds, and they continue to boo and (sometimes) cheer.[30] Other thinkers have developed similar ideas. The renowned sociologist George Herbert Mead proposed that well-socialized people regulate their own behavior by making continual reference to a *generalized other*.[31] He meant that mature people can imagine how their behaviors will be viewed by society in general. For Mead, an internalized image of society functioned as the prime audience for the self. We seek to construct a self that will meet the audience's approval.

My own view is that we all have our own internalized audiences for our life stories and that these audiences indicate as much about who we are as the stories themselves. Indeed, I believe that the audiences cannot be separated from the stories, because it is for these very audiences that the stories are ultimately made. Who are your internalized audiences? Your parents? Your spouse? A former lover? A professor you once knew? The kids who once made fun of you in school because you stuttered so badly? Your children? The people you imagine may be talking about you 100 years from now? God? Our narrative identities are made, performed, and reviewed in everyday social life. A great deal of identity construction takes place with friends, with therapists, with family members, through conversation, and in culture. But a great deal happens inside, too, I think, on a private stage in front of a very exclusive audience. The story is told and retold, revised and affirmed in the presence of a cherished, venerated, and maybe even feared *inner Other*. The inner audience can be harsh and unforgiving, as Freud knew. But in our darkest and loneliest moments, a supportive and affirming inner audience can see us through to redemption.[32]

The Life-Story Interview: Rob McGowan

In my role as a narrative psychologist, I am an audience for the stories people tell. To be more accurate, my research assistants (who do most of the interviews) and I function as audiences, and what we hear in the interviews is not nearly as comprehensive and nuanced as a person's full narrative identity.

What we hear, instead, is a partial account—a narration of select aspects of a person's internalized and evolving life story. Because storytelling involves a relationship between a particular teller and a particular audience, what we hear is surely influenced by the participant's feelings about the encounter and his or her expectations regarding what is appropriate or tellable at this moment and in this setting. Feeding into those feelings and expectations are what we tell the participant about the interview process itself: "This is not a clinical interview. We are not therapists. We are not here to figure out what is wrong with you. Instead, this is research—biographical research. In our research, we collect people's life-story accounts. We tape and transcribe them, and later we read over the transcripts carefully and repeatedly, and we analyze them in various ways."

It has been within only the last 15 years or so that research psychologists have begun to examine the stories people live by. In many subfields of psychology, researchers today are turning their attention to the development and expression of stories in human lives.[33] Therapists and counselors have been listening to life stories for many years, but their main aims have been to help people and to understand psychopathology. From a scientific standpoint, narrative psychology aims instead to understand the role of stories and storytelling in "normal" human life, in interpersonal relationships, and in society. There are many different approaches to narrative psychology. Some researchers focus on the performance of narratives, as in conversations and other social interactions. Others look at the development of narrative understanding in children. Others emphasize the ways in which stories convey knowledge, while yet others examine stories as vehicles for emotional expression. Still others emphasize the shifting and indeterminate quality of life narration—how stories change unpredictably over time and through social discourse, how their meanings are difficult to pin down. My own approach emphasizes how life stories give us identity, providing adult lives with some sense of meaning and purpose. I am also interested in what these same stories say about culture, so I focus on the differences between people in the kinds of stories they tell, categorizing and classifying aspects of their stories as if the narrative accounts themselves were pieces of fine literature (which they are).

The life-story interview that my students and I use is designed for people who are in the middle years of their lives—roughly the years between ages 35 and 65. In modern societies, that large middle chunk of time following young adulthood but preceding the retirement years offers some of life's biggest rewards and disappointments. On the positive side, midlife adults are often at the top of their game with respect to professional achievement and influence. They may be leaders in their communities. They may wield considerable influence and power. The roles of spouse, parent, and grandparent may prove to be very rewarding. Midlife adults are old enough to have won some degree of maturity out of life but young enough still to have big goals for the future. Their lives may be centered on strong and caring generativity. On the negative side, midlife adults are no longer young—no way to get around that. Their parents, if still living, are even older (and maybe sick), and eventually they will die. Midlife adults worry about their own health and mortality, too. No matter how well they do professionally, they may feel unappreciated and frustrated in their work. The responsibilities and pressures of family life and parenting may be too much to handle. After all, it is not called "the midlife crisis" for nothing (even if psychological research shows that midlife adults are no more likely to have "crises" in life than anybody else).[34] Midlife adults may fail in generativity, experiencing stagnation and disillusionment.

Age 45, Rob McGowan is my midlife storyteller. Rob works as a screenwriter for television and movies. For about 8 years, he was an actor, as well. He is married and has two children. On self-report measures of an adult's concern for and commitment to the next generation (generativity), Rob scores near the top, which is why we are interviewing him. After a general description of the interview format, the interviewer begins as follows: "Imagine that your life were like a book, with chapters. Please divide your life story into its main chapters. Give each chapter a name and provide a brief plot summary for each."[35]

With the humor and dramatic flair you might expect from a screenwriter, Rob first describes the setting for the childhood chapters in his life. He grows up in a mining town in West Virginia: "If you give the world an enema, the syringe goes straight into this town." The town is a "shit hole," he says. Because it has flooded many times, the town's nickname is "the city that God keeps trying to flush." His father is a gambler and a rogue; his mother, histrionic and suicidal. Rob recalls her grabbing a handful of pills and threatening to swallow them as "her five little kids kept tugging at her dressing gown, trying to get her to stop it." On another occasion, she draws an outline of their father on the laundry room door and throws a bread knife through it. They live in a run-down neighborhood, yet they are not nearly the poorest family there. Rob vividly remembers his friends' poverty. The five kids are eventually farmed out to an orphanage, but Rob is lucky enough to spend considerable time with a loving and stable foster family. In another incident in which he is singled out for special advantage, a teacher recognizes and en-

courages Rob's writing talent. He becomes editor of his high school newspaper, and upon graduation takes a job as a "copy boy" for the local "rag."
After a woman declines his proposal of marriage, Rob moves to New York to
bus tables in his uncle's restaurant. Like many of the relatives on his father's
side, this uncle is a mobster.

Rob's tumultuous New York chapter runs through his emerging adult
years. It is the late 1960s and early 1970s, and Rob becomes a player on the
drug scene. But he also manages to take classes in acting and writing at a
local college. He works for an ad agency, writes scripts for commercials, and
stars in a few bit parts in off-off-Broadway productions. His life's tempo increases dramatically when he meets a major television star who invites him
to interview for a popular show. Rob thinks the producers want a writer, but
it turns out that they hire him to be an actor on the show. He stars on the
show for 3 wildly exciting but exhausting years. During the same time, he is
also writing movie scripts. "It was a very, very hard time, a very hard show;
creatively it took a lot out of me, so much that I ended up on a psychiatrist's
couch for a year." Rob's friends see that the show is killing him, and they encourage him to quit. The decision to leave television is clinched when he falls
in love with an artist (painter), and they decide to marry. They move to the
southwestern part of the United States, where she continues to paint and he
focuses on screenwriting. With a successful career, a loving wife, and many
close friends, he tries to balance strivings for power and love. Complications
from a failed pregnancy, however, almost end his wife's life. But she recovers.
The couple desperately wants children. They feel they have so much to offer
the next generation. Finally, they adopt a girl and a boy. Today the kids are in
elementary school.

The interviewer continues: "Now that you have provided me with a chapter outline and plot summary, I would like you to focus on particular scenes
or moments that stand out in the story. We will focus on eight key scenes. For
each, please tell in detail what happened in the scene, when and where it happened, what you were thinking and feeling, and what, if anything, you think
the scene means for your overall life story."

The interview asks for detailed accounts of (a) a life-story high point,
(b) low point, (c) turning point, (d) earliest memory, (e) significant childhood scene, (f) significant adolescent scene, (g) significant adult scene, and
(h) one other significant scene of the narrator's choosing. For Rob Mc-
Gowan, the high point is the day after his wife almost dies in the hospital.
Her recovery brings him the greatest joy he has ever known. His low point
is the 3 terrible days during which he and his wife believe that their son is

irrevocably brain damaged. At age 2, the boy rants and screams and still cannot talk. At first, doctors think he is fine, but both parents are convinced otherwise. Later, he is diagnosed as autistic. The worst 3 days follow the doctor's showing them new brain scans that suggest the child is very seriously impaired and likely never to live a normal life. But a different doctor diagnoses a seizure disorder, which is readily treated with medication. The boy improves, begins to speak, and now seems normal: "We still call him our miracle baby." For other scenes, Rob provides colorful and moving accounts of family experiences, his mother's death, travel, and friendships. Six of the eight scenes he describes are redemptive, each moving from suffering to reward.

Subsequent sections of the interview ask Rob to identify "the greatest life challenge" in the life story (his son's seizure disorder) and the "characters" in the story who have the most positive and the most negative influence. Among the positive characters, he identifies the grade-school teacher who recognizes his writing talent; as the most negative character, he identifies his father: "He was consistently a shit." Next, the interview moves to the future. What will happen next? Rob looks forward to his children's growing up. He hopes to enjoy continued success in screenwriting. He also would love to move to Ireland and perhaps settle there. It is his family's homeland, and though he feels tremendous ambivalence toward his family of origin, Rob holds a romantic vision of raising his children in a quiet pastoral setting where life seems less hectic and more balanced.

The interview moves to beliefs, values, and philosophy of life—the ideological setting or backdrop for a life story. Rob is articulate in describing his political views, mixing traditional liberal values regarding government support of the poor with conservative viewpoints on certain other social issues. When it comes to religion, he says he does not believe in God, even though the foster family he loved so much tried to raise him Catholic. However, he respects people with a "quiet, inner faith." If he had another life, he might like to come back to earth as a Jew. He admires what he sees as a Jewish take on generativity: "And if you lead your life as best you can and as lovingly and with as much charity and time for others, and repay those good favors and keep sowing good will, it will come back to you tenfold. You will have a bountiful life. And giving your children the chance to understand this too— that is the way this love, this religion is passed on."

The interview ends with the life theme: "Looking back on the entire story, do you see a central theme?" Rob responds, "Um, I guess for me, if you had to distill it into a nutshell, it would be redemption." In Rob's story, redemption happens because people are often unexpectedly and even strangely kind and caring to each other. Returning to his son's seizure disorder, he says,

There are so many good people that were helpful to us, as damnable as it was, and no matter how many brick walls we hit with the medical industry, there were people along the way whose kindnesses and generosity were overwhelming and humbling. . . . It made us aware that there are angels that walk on this earth. It made us a whole lot less cynical about life and the world we live in, about the place that we live. As awful as the experience was, in retrospect we gained more from it, learned more about life and human nature and how many good people there are in the world. Forget the bad stuff that happened. These wonderful things that people did for us make us better and happier as human beings, delighted to be alive, and [knowing now that there is] hope for planet earth and for the human race.

The redemptive self is a particular kind of story to live by—a narrative identity that highly generative American adults, like Rob McGowan, tend to make and tend to tell. Even before the interview's last lines, when Rob explicitly identifies "redemption" as the story's central theme, it is clear that he

---

Box 3.1. An Outline of the Life-Story Interview

Life chapters

Key scenes

    High point (peak experience)

    Low point (nadir experience)

    Turning point

    Beginning point (earliest memory)

    Significant childhood scene

    Significant adolescent scene

    Significant adult scene

    One other significant scene

Life challenge

Positive and negative characters

Future script

Personal beliefs and values

Life theme

The respondent, typically between the ages of 35 and 65 years, gives an account of his or her life story by responding to a series of questions in a one-on-one interview. Used for research purposes rather than therapy or counseling, the 2-hour session is taped and transcribed, and later the transcription is analyzed for various psychological and literary themes.

has constructed a narrative identity that celebrates those life episodes wherein we are delivered from suffering to a better place. The redemption occurs because of human kindness and caring. Like the life stories of many other highly generative adults, furthermore, Rob's underscores the sense of an early advantage, the childhood awareness of others' suffering, the tension between power and love, and a vision of future growth. Rob feels grateful for the positive turns his life has seen. Indeed, Rob has been blessed in many ways.

But Rob has also known great pain and deprivation. According to his account, his mother routinely tried to kill herself. His father was "a shit." Family members were criminals and derelicts. Rob spent at least one year in therapy. He may have had a drug problem for a time. It is tempting to say that Rob McGowan narrates a redemptive life story today because that is objectively how his life has gone. Our narrations of the past basically tell it how it was—objective history, instant replays. Anybody with the same experiences he had would tell the same story, the same way. But would they?

I believe that Rob might narrate his life in many different ways. And though I do not doubt that Rob's memories of the past are at least moderately accurate, we have seen in this chapter that episodic memory is highly selective and serves current concerns and future goals. It may indeed be true that one of the reasons Rob McGowan is a generative man today is the fact that he really has benefited from many events in his life in which bad things *really* did turn good. Perhaps, when these kinds of events occur in people's lives, they end up wanting to make good things happen for others. But I believe it to be equally true—and psychologically way more interesting—that Rob tells the life story he tells *because he is generative.* He needs to tell this kind of story; he needs to fashion his life into a narrative pattern that reinforces his generativity. The redemptive self is a kind of life story that provides sustenance and support for generativity at midlife. It is the kind of narrative identity that provides the midlife adult with the confidence and commitment required to make sustained and positive contributions to the next generation. Believing that you are blessed (whether you really are or not) and that many others suffer (whether they really do or not) sets up a stark contrast in life narrative and issues a kind of moral challenge: You are called because you are special; it is your destiny to be of good use to others. Seeing life in redemptive terms provides the faith that when future suffering occurs, good results may still obtain. The hard work of caring for the next generation will ultimately pay off. Things will grow. The future will be good.

Narrative identities are stories we live by. We make them and remake them, we tell them and revise them not so much to arrive at an accurate record of the past as to create a coherent self that moves us forward in life with energy and purpose. Our stories are partly determined by the real circumstances of our lives—by family, class, gender, culture, and the historical moment into which we are thrown. But we also make choices, narrative choices. The challenge of narrative identity calls upon our deepest sources of imagination and creativity. Living life well, with meaning and purpose, is as much an act of imagination and artistry as anything we ever attempt. Life-story telling is an art. You have the material; now what story are you going to make?

four

THE CHOSEN PEOPLE

In 1850 Herman Melville wrote about being an American:

> We Americans are the peculiar, chosen people—the Israel of our
> time; we bear the ark of the liberties of the world. Seventy years
> ago we escaped from thrall; and, besides our first birth-right—
> embracing one continent of earth—God has given to us, for a
> future inheritance, the broad domains of political pagans, that shall
> yet come and lie down under the shade of our ark, without bloody
> hands being lifted. God has predestinated, mankind expects, great
> things from our race; and great things we feel in our souls.[1]

Melville expressed a feeling about America that was over 200 years old
when he expressed it—a feeling that, in ways exalted and perverse, remains
with us today. It has only been within the last two decades that the United
States has come to be seen as the world's single superpower. But America had
a special power in the minds of Europeans even before they settled it. A century *before* the Pilgrims landed, Europeans imagined that the New World
lying beyond the western ocean might turn out to be an enchanted place of
utopian designs.[2] For some Protestants in England, taught from childhood
that God would work through the English faithful to effect the ultimate redemption of humankind, America represented a promised land where the
Reformation's next great victories might be realized.[3] Inspired by this Protestant dream, the Puritans who set sail for America in the first half of the 17th

century identified themselves as God's chosen people, called to achieve a special destiny in the New World.

The Massachusetts Bay Puritans truly believed that their "city on a hill" would become a New Jerusalem. Their belief was embedded in what historians have called the *Puritan Myth*—a sacred story that provided the New England settlers with a collective identity, as well as a model for personal meaning and purpose in the individual's life.[4] Central to the myth was the Puritans' strong identification with the ancient Hebrews. As the Old Testament Israelites had suffered through generations of bondage to their Egyptian captors, so too, the Puritans believed, had they suffered religious persecution back home in England. As the Old Testament Israelites had wandered 40 years in the wilderness before they could enter the land of Canaan, so too had the Puritans made a long and dangerous journey across the Atlantic to settle in their new home. A rich and complex symbol for the Puritans, the Atlantic crossing also represented personal conversion: the redemptive move in Christianity from sinfulness to salvation. Their leader, John Winthrop, was a latter-day Moses-Joshua, for he had both led them out of the wilderness and accompanied them into the Promised Land. The primeval forests of Massachusetts were as great and dark a wilderness as anything the Israelites ever faced, vast and dangerous, but also oddly tempting, like the desert where Christ was tempted by the Devil. And in the narrowed eyes of the Puritans, the Devil's children themselves were surely the Indians—savages just as menacing as the Old Testament Hittites, Jebusites, and Amorites. From the Puritans' point of view, the Native Americans may have been here first, but this could *not* be their land: It was promised to the chosen people.

As the Massachusetts Bay settlements grew and prospered in the 17th century, the Puritans' religious ardor cooled, and they became less focused on the original ideals that animated the sermons of John Winthrop. In the latter half of the century, Anglican preachers were already looking back in longing to the 1630s as the golden age of the Puritan mission, chastising their congregants for their lapsed convictions and compromised ideals. As Germans, Scots, Irish, Dutch, Scandinavians, and other European groups settled the colonies, they brought the competing conceptions and traditions espoused by Lutherans, Presbyterians, Methodists, Baptists, Quakers, Catholics, and others. The Puritan Myth seemed to fade across the decades of the late 17th and early 18th centuries, but it experienced a strong revival in the 1740s during what became known as America's Great Awakening. The most forceful spokesman for this movement, Jonathan Edwards, proclaimed again that the New World could be the place where God's greatest work might be done. Edwards and his fellow preachers inspired an upsurge in religious vitality and

Box 4.1. *The Puritan Myth*

A model for both collective and individual identity for the Massachusetts Bay settlers, the Puritan Myth blended sacred narratives from Jewish and Christian traditions. The Puritans identified themselves as God's chosen people, like the Old Testament Israelites.

The English Puritans	= The Israelites (God's chosen people)
Religious persecution back home	= Bondage in Egypt
Setting sail for the New World	= Exodus out of Egypt
Crossing the Atlantic Ocean	= Israelites' 40-year trek through the wilderness; the individual's personal conversion journey
Landing in America	= Arriving in the Promised Land
The "city on a hill"	= New Jerusalem; Godly society
John Winthrop	= Moses, Joshua
Massachusetts forests	= Wilderness; Christ's temptations in desert
The Indians (Native Americans)	= Israel's enemies (e.g., Philistines, Hittites); the Devil's children
Success, good harvests	= Proof of divine election, God's favor
Failure, hardships	= The Devil's temptations; proof of falling from God's favor

a renewal and strengthening of the idea that America was the place where God was breaking forth new light for the world at large.

The same idea became part of the founding narrative for the new republic. With victory in the Revolutionary War and the establishment of a constitutional government, many citizens of the new nation came to view themselves in a way not unlike that of the Massachusetts Bay settlers 150 years before. The hard-earned victory over the British became proof of God's blessing on American tasks. The achievement of a government by law was seen as the first step in a bold program to assure basic human freedoms. The new nation was to be a light unto the Old World, an inspiring model for democracy and freedom.

As John Winthrop hoped New England would pave the way for worldwide religious reformation, so too the Founding Fathers imagined that the United States would lead the way in political reform and the progressive development of democracy across the world. Benjamin Franklin, Thomas Jefferson, and James Madison were inspired more by the rationalistic and progressive social and political doctrines of the European Enlightenment than they were by the Puritans' old-fashioned religion. But they still saw God as part of the plan. The historian Conrad Cherry writes that "the American Founding Fathers were as vigorous in their pronouncements on America's providential destiny as any clergyman."[5] They viewed God as intimately involved in the events of American history. In a diary entry for February 1765, John Adams wrote, "I always consider the settlement of America with reverence and wonder, as the opening grand scene and design in Providence for the illumination of the ignorant and the emancipation of the slavish part of mankind all over the earth."[6] Adams used the redemptive discourses of enlightenment and emancipation to describe America's providential destiny. For Adams, Americans were the chosen people whose heroic accomplishments were imagined as the first victory in a worldwide narrative of political redemption.

There are two ways to be the redeemer nation.[7] The first is passive: Let the eyes of the world be upon you, and they will learn from your example. Both Winthrop and Adams imagined that their New World societies would serve as models for change in Europe. All the Europeans had to do was to observe the goodness and the success of the New World experiments, both Winthrop and Adams reasoned, and they would surely come to realize that their own souls and societies should be changed accordingly. The second way is more active: You intervene; you campaign for your viewpoint; you expand your domain; you go to war to fulfill your manifest destiny. The journalist John L. O'Sullivan coined the term *manifest destiny* in the 1840s to justify the westward expansion of the United States. Sullivan shamelessly asserted that it was part of a natural, God-given plan for the United States to expand its civilization and institutions across the breadth of North America. Expansion meant ruthless territorial aggrandizement, as well as the spread of democratic ideals and individual economic opportunity. The concept was originally applied to the annexation of Texas, and was later taken up by those wishing to secure the Oregon Territory, California, Mexican land in the Southwest, and even Cuba. By the end of the century, manifest destiny had come to assume explicitly racist and social-Darwinian connotations. The chosen people were Anglo-Saxon Americans. Their cultural imperialism and political hegemony might readily be justified as a brutal "survival of the fittest."

In the 20th century, Americans became increasingly ambivalent about their self-proclaimed status as the chosen people. America was the land of golden economic opportunity, yet the Great Depression wiped out countless fortunes and plunged millions into abject poverty. America was the land of freedom and equality, yet African Americans continued to suffer rampant discrimination in nearly every segment of social life. As the champion of liberty, America could spread democratic ideals and individual freedoms to the far corners of the globe, yet the effort to do so in Vietnam proved to be arguably the most crushing indictment of American purpose and destiny in the 20th century. Not only did the United States lose the war, but also the war's ultimate purposes came to be questioned. Were we really trying to spread freedom and democracy? Or were we killing Vietnamese, as well as suffering our own horrendous losses, for selfish and misguided ends?

Of course, my framing the Vietnam issue as an either-or question is over-simplified, for the Vietnam War had many meanings and purposes and may be viewed from many competing perspectives. Indeed, this complexity itself undermines the idea that Americans are embarked on a special destiny in the world, a destiny whose goals are pure and noble. Throughout history and surely even today, different groups and nations have claimed that their selfish agendas are really pure and noble, and blessed by higher powers or grand principles. History has shown that the rhetoric of chosen-ness can be very dangerous, as the example of Nazi Germany makes grotesquely clear. In the United States today, this way of talking and thinking about one's own people is easily hijacked by White supremacists and other hate groups to promote viewpoints that most Americans find deeply repugnant. And indeed many people the world over charge that Americans themselves, or at least U.S. governments, are guilty of a similarly arrogant and insensitive view. The ugly American was once caricatured as boorish and crude. Today, he or she is more likely to be seen as naïve, selfish, entitled, moralistic, and disdainful of other worldviews. In an increasingly pluralistic society and amid an increasingly interconnected world, claims of American exclusivity and superiority are more offensive today than perhaps they have ever been.

Nonetheless, milder and more inclusive rhetoric of this kind still has the power to draw us in. Woodrow Wilson may have been more than a little naïve when he envisioned the Great War of 1914–1918 as the "war to end all wars," but his belief that the United States could help create a safer and more democratic world was sincere and inspiring, even if he and much of the world were overtaken by events beyond anyone's control. In Wilson's words, "America had the infinite privilege of fulfilling her destiny and saving the world."[8] For Wilson, America's special status as redeemer nation came with considerable responsibility. He envisioned the United States as a moral leader, willing (in theory) to compromise national self-interest for the global good. The United States and other nations should be ready, in Wilson's view, to give up a modicum of national sovereignty in the interest of maintaining world peace.

Wilson campaigned hard for the creation of a League of Nations, through which human rights might be safeguarded and international conflicts might be reduced. His efforts failed in the short term, for the United States never ratified the treaty establishing the League. But Wilson's ideas laid the groundwork for the creation of the United Nations following the Second World War. His high-minded idealism not only won Wilson the 1919 Nobel Peace Prize, but it also helped advance a rhetoric of constructive American engagement in the world. Of course, this rhetoric has been as often criticized as praised. On the negative side, it summons up associations such as "noblesse oblige," "White man's burden," and other expressions of condescension and arrogance. In its most exalted and least imperialistic forms, however, it has continued to motivate Americans to take on the moral responsibilities that come with a sense of national calling—from the Marshall Plan following World War II, to the Kennedy Peace Corps of the 1960s, to the many American-sponsored organizations in existence today and aimed at making a positive difference in the world.

Although Wilson packaged the Puritan Myth and ideas about manifest destiny into a more conciliatory and ecumenical version of the American calling, some of the best-known and hotly contested versions of this kind of rhetoric mark a stark contrast between America-the-good and her enemies. At the center of Ronald Reagan's understanding of America, for example, was what one political scientist has called a "sacramental vision" of a redeemer nation in a perilous world.[9] Years before he was elected president, Reagan said, "I believe that God in shedding his grace on this country has always in this divine scheme of things kept an eye on our land and guided it as a promised land." For Reagan, the United States was "the last best hope of man on earth"—the champion of freedom locked in combat with the forces of tyranny and oppression.[10] Top on the list of enemies, of course, was communism. The Soviet Union and the United States did not differ just in political philosophy, in Reagan's view. The difference was more stark—the difference between good and evil. In one of his most famous lines, Reagan called the Soviet Union an "evil empire." Years later, George W. Bush would identify Iran, Iraq, and North Korea as an "axis of evil," again asserting the moral superiority of a chosen people.

In the 1830s Alexis de Tocqueville observed that Americans believe themselves to be "the only religious, enlightened, and free people." "They have an immensely high opinion of themselves," he wrote, "and are not far from believing that they form a species apart from the rest of the human race."[11] Yet Americans are not unique in deeming themselves to be special, and especially good.[12] Other nations have found sustenance in the idea that God or fate or historical circumstances have elected them to a preeminent position in history. The tendency to find special destiny in one's people may be as

FIGURE 4.1 During World War I, Woodrow Wilson's version of American destiny underscored the moral responsibility facing a people who enjoyed a special advantage in the world. Unlike proponents of manifest destiny in the 19th century, Wilson seemed willing to compromise American self-interests for the sake of international cooperation and world peace. Although he has been criticized, even ridiculed, for being overly idealistic and unable to effect political compromise, Wilson gave voice to an important strand of American political discourse—a way of talking about being American that both affirms an American special destiny and underscores a constructive engagement with people around the world. Reprinted with the permission of the Library of Congress.

old as nationalism itself, and it may ultimately spring from general social-psychological tendencies to favor one's own group over others.[13] But the interlocking ideas of chosen people, promised land, manifest destiny, and redeemer nation form a unique constellation with an especially powerful pedigree in American cultural history—going all the way back to the Puritan Myth. Variations on these ideas have sustained the American people since the colonial period. These ideas are almost always summoned forth during times of national crisis, as well as national celebration. They have been invoked again and again to justify important American projects, even as they are continually modified and reformulated to meet ever-changing cultural demands and moral challenges. Over the past few centuries, the Puritan Myth has morphed into a number of different forms, shedding certain features that seem worn and out-of-date and incorporating new ideas that give the sense of American identity new resonance and relevance. We are no longer Puritans, but their story, for good and for ill, has been absorbed into our own.

The American sense of being the chosen people combines easily with Americans' traditional belief in individualism. "One's self I sing, a simple separate person," proclaimed Walt Whitman.[14] Since the time of de Tocqueville, Americans have perceived themselves, and have been perceived by others, as the champions of the individual self. As much as national destiny, as much as the American institutions that distinguish this land from all others, the *individual* American man or woman has traditionally been held up by Americans as worthy of praise and affirmation. "Is not a man better than a town?" asked Ralph Waldo Emerson.[15] Even as Americans have seen themselves as the chosen people, Americans have traditionally believed that each person is chosen for a special destiny. Each individual person answers an inner calling. About 100 years ago, the sociologist Max Weber described how the concept of *the calling* linked Protestant Christianity with the rise of Western capitalism.[16] For Weber, *the calling* refers to the idea, introduced in the Reformation, that each individual has a moral obligation to fulfill a predestined duty in worldly affairs. Each man or woman is chosen to live out his or her own calling. In a similar sense, each Puritan man or woman was duty-bound to scrutinize his or her soul for evidence of divine election. After all, it was not the community that was destined for heaven (or hell); it was the individual person. Each person, therefore, needed to establish his or her own unique relationship with God.

Correspondingly, Americans have typically understood their destiny on two parallel levels, both of which may be traced back to the Puritan Myth. On the collective level, we are part of a great enterprise, a people chosen for an exalted destiny, but on the individual level, each person is chosen, too—called to a unique and special endeavor in life, *gifted* with an inner *specialness* that distinguishes him or her from every other person who has ever lived: I am chosen. I am special. I am gifted. I have a deep advantage. I am a unique self with unique talents, and I am here to do something unique and good, to be something extraordinary and wonderful, to fulfill an inner calling and actualize a vast inner potential, to manifest my own personal destiny and leave my own indelible mark, my personal signature, upon posterity.

"I Was Chosen": Individual Life Stories

Psychological research into the life stories of highly generative American adults reveals that it is among those midlife men and women who are most committed to promoting the well-being of future generations that we hear most clearly the rhetoric of chosen-ness. To a much greater extent than is the case with their less generative peers, highly generative American adults tend to believe that they were blessed early on in life with some special advantage or gift. In their life stories, they will often identify an incident from childhood as symbolic of their special status, as if to suggest that they have known that they were special, that they were chosen, for a very long time.[17] At the same time, they are significantly more likely than less generative adults to recall early events from childhood in which they felt empathy for the suffering of others, or in which they witnessed injustice or misfortune in other people's lives.[18] In their life stories, highly generative adults are the chosen people, called to do good work in a difficult world. They are the redeemers. Their special destiny is to make a positive difference in the lives of others, especially those of future generations.

How does the story begin? For America, the Eurocentric histories that many of us learned while we were growing up emphasize the "discovery" of the New World by Columbus and the subsequent settlement by Europeans. The Puritan Myth is a key feature of this origin narrative, for it spells out one way in which some Euro-Americans felt that they were a special, chosen people from the very beginning. For many American adults today, especially those who see themselves as productive and generative citizens working to make a positive difference for the next generation, their personal life stories begin in a strikingly similar way. Early on in their lives, there is a discovery. In childhood, they discover that they have a special advantage of some kind—a blessing, a gift, a skill, a unique status, a special friend or guardian, an especially positive situation that most other people do not have, an inner something that sets them apart, in a positive way, from almost everybody else. Reinforcing their special status is an early sensitivity to the misfortune of others. I am favored; others suffer.

A central component of American myth and folklore is the belief that Americans are an especially favored people and that other people do not enjoy the benefits Americans have. At times, this sense of special status—coupled as it is with an awareness or belief that other people may be less favored—has reinforced American arrogance and imperialism. At other times, it has promoted constructive and even humanitarian American projects. In a parallel fashion, a personal life story that features the protagonist's early realization of a special advantage over others can reinforce selfishness and promote a condescending or even disdainful attitude towards other people, but, as narrative research also shows, this kind of personal life story may, alternatively, promote a highly generative, productive, and caring approach to adult life. And, in some cases, it appears to do both. Arrogance is not necessarily an impediment to generativity. Holding yourself in extraordinarily high regard may fuel the confidence needed to see your generativity projects through.

Many highly generative adults say that they wish to "give something back" to society for the blessings they believe they have received. In the stories they construct to make sense of their lives, the sense of early advantage and an early awareness of the suffering of others may function to set up a long-term moral challenge: Because I have been blessed in some way (and because I perceive that other people have *not* been so fortunate), I now feel some sense of responsibility to be of service to others and to my social world. I am especially likely to aim my benevolence toward the young, toward the future generations who will carry on after I am gone, for when I was young somebody or something aimed such benevolence toward me, chose me, gave me a special destiny. As shown in examples to follow, in the case of many highly generative American adults, therefore, enjoying an early advantage in life is coupled with a responsibility to bring advantages to others.

Diane Chadwick

The first daughter of a Methodist minister, Diane Chadwick was the only baby in her father's tiny Iowa parish, and all the adults adored her. "I was everybody's favorite," says Diane. When Diane was still a young child, her father was called to serve a wealthier congregation, where Diane befriended "many famous people" who, she says, "gave me a different feeling about who I was and who I could be in life." Yet her childhood years were not completely happy, for when she was 9 years old her younger brother was run over by a car. She was grief-stricken, but her parents seemed even more devastated by the loss of their only son. The opening chapter in Diane's life story sets up a stark contrast: The heroine is blessed, even though her family suffers greatly. Indeed, Diane still blames herself for her brother's death. She was supposed to be watching him more closely that afternoon. Today, at age 49, Diane is a very popular and successful elementary school teacher and mother of three grown children. Her goals for the future include becoming a grandmother, moving to Kentucky to be near her daughters when she retires, writing a book on teaching, and "working for the betterment of the educational system," because, she explains, "I'd like to give something back" to society. Her most important value in life is "to grow and help other people grow."

Maria Lopez

Maria Lopez also grew up in the church. A devout Catholic who disagrees with the church's stand on abortion and birth control, Maria raised six children in her 20s, 30s, and 40s, and now (at age 50) she works as a school librarian. Her job is boring these days, but she finds rewards outside work. Maria tutors disadvantaged children and is involved in a number of other volunteer activities. As Maria tells it, she grew up in a large and loving family:

> I have been very blessed; I was born into an extremely loving family, parents who loved each other, stayed together—my parents were married for 49 years before my father died last year. I was gifted to have three brothers and a sister. We had great stability and security, but we never had wealth. When we were small, we asked my father, "Daddy, are you rich?" And he said, "Of course, I am; I have five children." That was a great memory for me. We were also fortunate to have and to know many aunts and uncles and 31 cousins. So, I have always felt supported and nourished and appreciated by a number of people.

Maria believes that everybody has a special gift to offer, everybody is chosen for some special destiny: "I guess I believe that all people are created for a purpose and that each person has potential, has gifts, has a contribution to make."

David Krantz

A 38-year-old class action attorney, David Krantz wants "to make the world a better place for somebody or some people." Modeling his career after that of the great American lawyer Clarence Darrow, David represents clients who feel they have been cheated or abused by industry or government. He also volunteers time at a local food pantry under the belief that "you have to make an effort, big or small, to leave the world a better place than you found it." David admits that his steadfast values and his zeal sometime make him a difficult person to live with. His marriage has been rocky. David's early advantage was his *name*. As he tells it, the name *David* brings with it special privileges and responsibilities in his family, going back generations. In David's family history, if one is given the name *David,* one is expected to be a scholar or a leader in society. Unlike Diane and Maria, David says that his family blessing did not necessarily bring him warmth and happiness as a child. Feeling that one is chosen is not necessarily the same thing as enjoying a greater level of love or happiness in early life. "I spent a lot of my childhood alone," he says, "and my companions were books more than they were other kids." As far back as David can remember, his mother taught him that the world is filled with injustice, and she instilled in him a desire to do something positive in response.

Tamara Jones

Like David, Tamara Jones was asked to assume special responsibilities early in life. The eldest child in an impoverished and chaotic family, Tamara functioned as a mother to her younger siblings. Even when Tamara was in elementary school, her sisters called her "the mommy." Their real mother was strung out on drugs. Their father once pulled a gun on the family. Tamara witnessed suffering all around—in her family, among her friends, and on the mean streets of her neighborhood. Yet she persevered, even through a series of disastrous relationships with men in her 20s and 30s. At age 43 today, Tamara focuses her generativity on her daughter and her business. Her top priority in life is to "lay a secure foundation for my daughter." As a business consultant, she believes she exerts a positive impact on other people through the assistance she provides in "growing their businesses." She also sees herself as a role model for younger Black women who are entering the business world.

Rosemary Brattle

Like Tamara, Rosemary Brattle also grew up in an abusive, dysfunctional family. According to her story, Rosemary's biological parents were alcoholics, and she herself has struggled with substance abuse and eating problems all her life. Her sister died of a drug overdose. Overcoming tremendous obstacles, Rosemary has managed to stay married to the same man for 39 years, and they have raised four children. A high-point scene in her story was a surprise "Mother's Day party" that her four children threw for her a few years back. Still, her grown children criticize her often, and they blame her for some of the problems they now have. "I was not a perfect mother, but I improved," Rosemary says. Today at age 57, Rosemary is employed as a secretary. Her most rewarding and generative experiences come through her role as an "elder" in her community. The young people in her neighborhood look up to her as a source of inspiration and wisdom, even if her own children do not. They marvel at how she has overcome so many hardships in her life. Why has she been able to overcome so much? Rosemary believes it is because of the many older women who have loved and taken care of her. The most important of these was the woman who adopted her when she was 8 years old, after Rosemary's biological parents proved unable to provide adequate care. "My adoptive mother saved me," she says. And since then, she continues, "I've always been loved. I've always been cared for. And I've always had women in my life. I've always had older women—elders. And they've always told me that I was gonna be okay. And I was okay. And I am okay. And now look at me! I'm an elder."

John Meredith

For John Meredith, a 48-year-old professor of education, the early advantage was musical talent. "I started taking piano lessons and music lessons very, very early," he explains, "and music has always been an interest in my life." In John's story, music won him his parents' affection, good friends in school, and a scholarship to a university. Because of opportunities that were opened up through music, John was able to avoid many of the pitfalls that the kids in his neighborhood encountered. He stayed out of gangs. He stayed away from drugs. John and his wife of 28 years have raised two children, one of whom became a musician and the other of whom became an educator. John expresses generativity today in his family life and in his role as a college instructor. At times, though, he questions his effectiveness as a teacher:

> I sometimes think: "What good am I doing teaching at a university? Teaching them research and statistics courses, how is that going to change people's lives?" But I often get comments from my students, the way I work with people and interact with people, my style, my teaching, it helps make them a different teacher. Then, if these teachers that I have as students go out as teachers and work with kids in their classrooms, maybe each one of those can influence 20 to 25 kids. Then you multiply that by the number of students you have each year, and before you know it you've had a really big impact.

In the story that John constructs as his personal identity, the positive, multiplying influence he is able to exert today on future generations has its origins in the gift for music he enjoyed as a child. He believes that if he had not been blessed with this special advantage early in life his life story would have taken a very different form.

Rita Jacobson

A 61-year-old lawyer and community activist who has devoted considerable effort to providing affordable housing, Rita Jacobson once served as mayor of the small town where she resides. Commenting on her highly generative approach to life, Rita says, "I have some basic gifts, and I think the purpose of life is to take the gifts you're given and leave the world better for them. And leave other people with whatever you can leave them to help them or just to make the world a better place to live in." Rita's life story highlights a number of ways in which she felt especially advantaged as a child. Indeed, she was literally "chosen" to be "the queen of the first grade." But the greatest gift she experienced when she was young was the special relationship she had with her father:

> I must have been about 3½ or 4. I remember it clearly; I can still feel it and see it. My father was a relatively big man, well not really big, but he was probably 5'9" or 5'10" and about 175 pounds, which isn't all that big, but, hey, I was a little kid. He had large muscular hands and he was muscular. He did physical work. He was a newspaper pressman and lifted heavy things. He was just the ideal of strong for me, and he doted on me. I can feel the feeling of walking down the street, holding his middle finger, and reaching up for it. And we'd talk. And I think I was the only little girl who got little metal cars and trucks. He'd take me to the dime store—oh, I was very fortunate, because he was so nice. My father would sleep in the mornings and get up and we'd have some afternoon time together, which most kids didn't have. And most little girls didn't have a father to buddy around with the way I did. He was a great guy for a little kid. He could make up stories, and he loved to teach me about things like how to throw a ball, even if I never really got good at it. . . . He was a very warm, loving father. I was extremely, extremely fortunate.

Cultural Sources for Individual Stories

Please understand me: I am not claiming that productive and caring American adults really *were* blessed with especially loving families, special skills and talents, and other important advantages when they were children. I am not saying that they actually received more benefits and were more favored when they were young than less generative adults. I am not claiming that highly generative adults were especially sensitive and empathic when they were children. I am not talking as a developmental psychologist might talk—not talking about how real childhood events, such as being chosen queen of the first grade class, predictably lead to real adult outcomes like being a generative person. Okay, I admit it: I do not know for sure what my research participants' childhoods *really* were like. How could I? I was not there, and I am not them. Instead, I am saying that highly generative American adults tend to tell these kinds of life stories—stories that begin with early personal advantage and with an early recognition of the suffering of others. More precisely, they tend to tell these kinds of life stories more often than less generative American adults.

As a *narrative* psychologist, I contend that highly generative American adults implicitly and unconsciously choose to tell stories that begin this way—they choose to tell stories of being chosen. They tend to reconstruct the past and anticipate the future through a narrative that begins with a sense that they are blessed and special, and that there is suffering in the world. This kind of life story recaptures in personal form certain ideas regarding "the chosen people" and "manifest destiny" that have enjoyed a most cherished and highly contested status in America ever since the days of the Puritan Myth. As we saw in chapter 3, narrative identity is an imaginative reconstruction of the personal past linked to an imaginative anticipation of the future. Narrative identity is based on reality—that is doubtlessly true. People do not usually make their life stories up out of the blue. But their life stories are still, well, stories—powerful and integrative stories for sure, deeply internalized and cherished stories that justify life decisions, shape future expectations, and provide adults with life meaning and purpose. For highly generative adults, the memory of and elaboration upon early life scenes that give the main character a special advantage in a troubled world can readily set up the kind of narrative in which the hero or heroine eventually feels called or destined to give something back, to make the world a better place for generations to come. Generative adults in America tend to tell these kinds of life stories to justify, reinforce, sustain, and extend their generativity. Put simply, it is not so much that people are generative because their lives have "really" followed a certain kind of story. It is rather that they construct and believe in these kinds of life stories because they are generative adults.

But why is it that a highly generative American adult—or anybody, for that matter—ever thinks to tell a life story in this way? Where does anybody ever get the idea that early childhood should be narrated to emphasize the hero's or heroine's early advantage in a dangerous world? Why does anybody ever think that he or she was endowed with a special blessing, gift, or sense of destiny as a young child? One answer—the wrong one, in my view—is that the story I have been describing in this chapter (and in this book) captures something that is (or should be) *universal* about human development itself. Variations on a universalistic argument might contend that childhood is or should be a time in life when one feels specially chosen or advantaged over and against others, that children in all cultures are viewed to have unique gifts or propensities that differentiate them from each other, or that the pathways to and narratives for generativity are the same in all cultures. However, anthropological studies and cross-cultural work in psychology suggest strongly that these kinds of statements are just not true.[19] There are indeed certain universals in human development, but they do not generally extend to the kinds of life stories that people tell to provide their lives with identity. In fact, it is in the realm of life narrative where some of the most interesting differences in cultures can be observed.

The kind of life story that research suggests is strongly associated with generativity among American adults, therefore, is a cultural invention, or what I call a *psychosocial construction.*[20] A person constructs his or her own story in a social context; that story is strongly shaped by culture. The kind of life story that I find so often among highly generative adults is a way of thinking about the life course that reflects the kind of society in which we live, the kind of history we have experienced, and the kinds of stories about life and about the world we have learned, consciously and unconsciously, by virtue of growing up and living in America today. The sources for this story are too numerous to list, but they include the ideas of a chosen people, manifest destiny, and the like, which have been absorbed unconsciously into American social life and talk.

Now, it is true that you do not need to know much about the Puritans or about Woodrow Wilson to feel that you have been chosen for a special destiny in life. But the fact that the Puritan Myth and related ideas are so deeply embedded in American folklore has helped render especially congenial the psychological notion that each person is a special, unique, and essentially gifted individual, called to do something important and good in life. The fact that ideas derived from the Puritan Myth and manifest destiny have been elaborated upon and worked through in so many different ways in American cultural history—from Benjamin Franklin's autobiography to the novels of Toni Morrison and Philip Roth; from Herman Melville to Maya Angelou; from the sermons of Jonathan Edwards to the latest episodes of TV talk shows—has contributed to our belief that early development is fundamentally about consolidating an early advantage and then moving forward in life through a tough world.

FIGURE 4.2 Times of national crisis, transition, and celebration provide occasions in American civic life for expressions of faith in and affirmation of America's special destiny. At President Bill Clinton's first inauguration, the poet Maya Angelou recited "On the Pulse of Morning." Representing America as a rock, a river, and a tree, the poem offered a dramatically inclusive vision of a grand and generous nation that welcomes all individuals, regardless of their races and backgrounds, as its chosen people. Reprinted with the permission of Getty Images. Photo by Brad Markel/Laison/Getty Images.

As the life stories of highly generative adults show, narrators are able to identify many different kinds of early advantages in life. Some advantages are internal. They include a unique talent, skill, attitude, or personal attribute. A narrator may take personal credit for an internal advantage, or he or she may attribute credit for the internal advantage to something or somebody else, such as God, good genes, or luck. Other advantages are external. Especially prominent here are special relationships that some children enjoy—an especially warm and caring family, a supportive teacher, an involved neighbor or friend. Whether the advantage is internal or external and whether the protagonist in the story actively "earns" the advantage or is the beneficiary of events beyond his or her control, the early advantage exerts a long-term positive impact. Good fortune continues to smile on the chosen people.

How does an early advantage confer a long-term positive benefit? Life-story tellers often suggest or imply that highly positive events or experiences in early life instilled, awakened, activated, consolidated, or solidified something deep and good inside of them. Even when the source of the advantage is an external factor, such as a positive relationship with another person, the storyteller will typically suggest that the external event or relationship had a long-term benefit in life because of its impact on the *inner self*. Rita Jacobson, for example, suggests that the special relationship she had with her father when she was very young instilled in her a deep sense of confidence that she could accomplish almost anything she wanted. Maria Lopez experienced the loving family environment of her childhood as a "gift" she is able to keep inside of her for the rest of her life.

In many life stories, early advantages are seen by the storytellers themselves as creating or sustaining an inner sense of self that the protagonist will take with him or her for the rest of life's journey. No matter how many things change over the long course of life, this *good inner core* will continue to provide benefits to its owner. Once I have been chosen, I keep within me the resultant good self as an everlasting gift. And how wonderful it is that I do! For what early experience also tells me is that the world through which I will travel— from birth to death—is a very dangerous place. I know that others suffer, that there is injustice and pain. Thank God (or luck, or my genes) that I am blessed!

Oh, to be one of the chosen. To receive the *gift* at the beginning of it all, before all the bad stuff happens, before we enter a threatening and unredeemed world. If I believe I am special, one of the fortunate ones, I can withstand any suffering that comes my way, and I can relieve the suffering of others, in gratitude for the great favor bestowed upon me. I long to be, in Melville's words, one of "the peculiar, chosen people." If I were so blessed, so gifted, then God or nature or good early experience would have "predestinated" and "mankind [would] expect, great things" from me, and great things I would feel in my soul.

Five

MY GOOD INNER SELF:
FROM EMERSON TO OPRAH

What is your problem? Substance abuse? A broken relationship? A failed business? You are not rich enough? Or free enough? Or happy enough? You feel your life lacks meaning? You are not getting the love and the success that you want and deserve? You do not like yourself?

It sounds as if you need professional help. You need to see an expert. But therapists and consultants are way too expensive. And besides, your problem is, well, not all *that* bad. I mean, you are not crazy or anything. You just have a problem. Everybody has problems. So what can you do? I suggest you drive over to the local bookstore. For less than $20 you can purchase a self-help book, and you may even have enough left over to buy a skim latte. Read the book carefully. Follow the directions the expert provides. You may be on your way to a happier, richer, more fulfilling, and more meaningful life.

But what book should you choose? In the sections marked "Popular Psychology," "Self-Help," "Addictions," "Recovery," "Relationships," "Spirituality," "New Age," and the like, your full-service bookstore stocks hundreds of titles. Some skeptics might say, "It doesn't matter which one you pick; those books are all the same." But a cursory review of, say, 10 or 20 suggests that there are some noteworthy differences.[1] If nothing else, some of the books have proven much more successful—in terms of sales—than others. Some—like M. Scott Peck's *The Road Less Traveled* (over 6 million copies in print) and Stephen Covey's *The Seven Habits of Highly Effective People* (over

10 million)—are among the best-selling American books of all time. I suggest you look over a few of the classics before you lay your money down.

To get an historical perspective, you might begin with Norman Vincent Peale's *The Power of Positive Thinking* (over 5 million copies sold).[2] Addressed to the anxious company man in postwar America, this classic from the 1950s "is written with the sole objective of helping the reader achieve a happy, satisfying, and worthwhile life."[3] Peale offers a "simple, workable philosophy of living" to "break the worry habit," "get other people to like you," and enable you to accomplish your most cherished goals.[4] As the book's title suggests, the key is to keep a positive mental attitude (PMA) about life. "Believe in your God-released powers," Peale exhorts.[5] Unabashedly Christian in his point of view, Peale urges self-doubting men to take Philippians 4:3 to heart: "I can do all things through Christ which strengthened me."[6] PMA, says Peale, stems ultimately from faith in Jesus, or at least some deep connection to a transcendent force:

> Every great personality I have known, and I have known many, who
> has demonstrated the capacity for prodigious work has been a person in tune with the Infinite. Every such person seems in harmony
> with nature and in contact with Divine energy. They have not necessarily been pious people, but invariably they have been extraordinarily well organized from an emotional and psychological point of
> view. It is fear, resentment, the projection of parental faults upon
> people when they are children, inner conflicts and obsessions that
> throw off balance the finely equated nature, thus causing undue
> expenditure of natural force.[7]

One of the most famous devotees of PMA was W. Clement Stone (1902–2002), a self-made billionaire who parlayed $100 in savings into an insurance empire. Stone also made prodigious contributions to conservative political causes and to many charities. It is said that Stone began each day, and demanded that his employees follow suit, by exclaiming, "I feel happy! I feel healthy! I feel ter-r-r-ific!" Inspired by Peale, by Napoleon Hill's (1936) *Think and Grow Rich,* and by the Horatio Alger stories he read as a kid, Stone personified a can-do, upbeat, and wildly successful version of the American entrepreneur-turned-philanthropist in the mid-20th century. His PMA and belief in human redemption were legendary. Struck by how enthusiastically a young man cut the grass in front of his office, Stone hired him for his company and eventually made him executive vice president. A longtime admirer and supporter of Richard M. Nixon, Stone saw a silver lining even in the

Watergate scandal, calling it "a wonderful thing" in a 1985 speech. "Because of Watergate," he explained, "attorney generals and state's attorneys now will press charges against public officials if they're warranted. Before President Nixon's time, they'd sweep those charges under the rug."[8] Stone could probably find redemption in anything.

Self-help books around the time of Watergate reflected the upsurge of interest among Americans in higher states of consciousness, meditation, spirituality, and a range of alternative lifestyles and conceptions associated with the human-potential movement. Humanistic theories of personality—such as those developed by Carl Rogers and Abraham Maslow—provided an intellectual framework for many of the popular psychology books of the day. Rogers revolutionized American psychotherapy by suggesting that therapists should relate to their clients in empathic ways designed to build self-worth. According to Rogers, people need to experience *unconditional positive regard* if they are to grow and realize their inner potential.[9] Maslow argued that psychologists were too concerned about deficits and deficiencies in human life, failing to see how human beings strive for *self-actualization* once their more basic needs for food, belonging, and esteem are met.[10] Both Rogers and Maslow prioritized conscious human experience and prosocial life values, and both asserted that personal development is fundamentally a matter of fully actualizing the inner, growing self.

Bringing humanistic ideas to the masses, Wayne Dyer sold millions of self-help books in the 1970s and 1980s under such titles as *Your Sacred Self* and *Manifest Your Destiny*. In his most popular book, *Your Erroneous Zones,* Dyer tells readers to trust and to love their inner selves and to ignore the norms of society. The inner self is good and sacred, and it is your sacred duty to actualize it, to give it its full expression. Writes Dyer, "Using yourself as a guide and not needing the approval of an outside force is the most religious experience you can have." Additionally, he says, "A careful look at Jesus Christ will reveal an extremely self-actualized person, an individual who preached *self*-reliance."[11] Okay, Dyer's theology may not be profound, but people still buy his books, and they like the message of personal freedom. To set the self free, Dyer urges every reader to sit down and compose a personal "declaration of independence."

An especially influential self-help book from the 1970s is Peck's *The Road Less Traveled*. Written with more style and balance than is common in the self-help genre, this classic begins with the problem of suffering. "Life is difficult," Peck asserts, but "with total discipline, we can solve all problems."[12] By *discipline,* Peck means strategies for transforming suffering and frustration into growth and actualization—in other words, strategies for accomplishing redemption in life: "Believing that the growth of the human spirit [inner self] is the end of human existence, I am obviously dedicated to the notion of progress. It is right and proper that as human beings we should grow and progress as rapidly as possible."[13] Peck even defines love in terms of growth, as "the will to extend one's self for the purpose of nurturing one's own or another's spiritual growth."[14] The four growth strategies Peck identifies are delay of gratification, acceptance of personal responsibility, dedication to truth, and balancing. Behind each of these, however, is a fundamental sense of feeling chosen, special, and good—a deep belief that one's inner self is valued: "The feeling of being valuable—'I am a valuable person'—is essential for mental health and a cornerstone of self-discipline. It is a direct product of parental love. Such a conviction must be gained in childhood; it is extremely difficult to acquire it during adulthood. Conversely, when children have learned through the love of their parents to feel valuable, it is almost impossible for the vicissitudes of adulthood to destroy their spirit.[15]

The 1980s and 1990s saw a proliferation of self-help books in two very different arenas. Success gurus—mainly men—provided formulas for striking it rich and finding personal meaning in America's "new economy." Personal counselors—increasingly women—addressed the problems of addiction, physical and sexual abuse, personal trauma, and other means whereby Americans felt themselves to be victims. A few cultural observers have suggested, somewhat sardonically, that among the biggest heroes in American culture in the 1990s were dot-com millionaires and recovering victims.

Written a few years before the economic boom of the Clinton presidency, Stephen Covey's (1989) *The Seven Habits of Highly Effective People* became something of a holy text for a generation of managers, business executives, entrepreneurs, and consultants. Readers of *Chief Executive Magazine* voted Covey's book "the most influential business book of the 20th century," and *Time* nominated Covey himself as one of the 25 most influential Americans in the 1990s.[16] Covey's is a book that Benjamin Franklin would have loved—or maybe written. Inspired by Franklin's *Autobiography* and by the American success literature of the 19th century, Covey argues that effective living must begin with the kind of "self-evident" truths or principles that inspired the American Declaration of Independence.[17] Covey holds this truth to be self-evident: that effective living is guided by "lighthouse principles that govern human growth and happiness—natural laws that are woven into the fabric of every civilized society throughout history and comprise the roots of every family and institution that has endured and prospered."[18] (Self-help writers are rarely guilty of understatement.) Forget PMA and superficial strategies for winning friends and influencing people, Covey says. Instead, effective living must proceed from the inside out: "'Inside-out' means to start first with self; even more fundamentally, to start with the most *inside* part of self—with your paradigms, your character, and your motives. . . . Inside-out is a process—a continuing process of renewal based on the natural laws that govern human growth and progress. It's an upward spiral of growth that leads to progressively higher forms of responsible independence and effective interdependence."[19]

Covey offers something like a business plan for leading an effective life—both in business and in the personal sphere. You must begin, says Covey, by writing a personal mission statement for life. The mission statement should lay out your fundamental core values—the innermost qualities of that good inner self. "You could call a personal mission statement a personal constitution," Covey writes. "Like the U.S. Constitution," the personal constitution is "fundamentally changeless," rarely to be amended and meant to endure for life.[20] As you begin to live out your self-proclaimed constitution, you must learn how to engage others in the kind of "win/win" interactions that result in "creative" and "synergistic" leaps forward in life (as well as improved profit margins). You move from independence to mature interdependence over time; your own successes and advances end up creating successes and advances for others, as well. Ultimately effective living becomes generativity, for "the highest and most powerful motivation" in living is not living "for ourselves only, but for our posterity, for the posterity of all mankind."[21]

For readers of Melody Beattie's (1992) *Co-Dependent No More* (over 4 million copies sold), the problem is that too many of us live for other people, rather than for ourselves. Covey goes to great lengths to show how interdependence and synergy with others ultimately enhance the self, whereas Beattie seeks to disentangle your codependent life from those to whom you feel irrationally committed. Often the children of abusive or alcoholic families, codependent people become caregivers and enablers for others who are addicted, abusive, or dysfunctional. As a result, codependent people end up as *victims,* for they become so obsessed with ministering to others that they are unable to care for themselves. Eventually, they lose control of their lives.

"This book is dedicated *to me,*" Beattie writes at the outset.[22] Drawing on her own personal experiences (a standard practice in almost all self-help books) and the stories of others she has known, Beattie shows how a codependent person can escape the cycle of exploitation and regain control of life. While her readers are likely to feel that they are in far greater pain than the aspiring entrepreneurs reading Covey's book, the model of healing she provides is similar to Covey's in at least one fundamental way. Like Covey, Beattie urges you to begin the redemptive process by focusing unswervingly on the inner self. Covey asks you to set forth your deep principles, but Beattie gets even more fundamental by telling you that you must first identify and work to relieve the deep pain at your very core. Disentangle the self from its entrapments and then "have a love affair with yourself," so that you can "set yourself free." Only then (in the last chapter of her book), can you reorient yourself to others, "learning to live and love again."[23]

From Dale Carnegie to today's highest paid motivational speakers, from success gurus to spiritual counselors, across the literatures of entrepreneurship, spiritual development, and recovery, the self-help tradition presents a characteristic viewpoint about the self and about self-development that is as American as manifest destiny and apple pie. Self-help books push forward ideas that rarely enjoy any research support from psychological science but that are popular with American readers anyway, because they affirm American cultural values. As a psychological scientist myself, I cringe almost every time I read through a self-help book. It is difficult for me to take in the many unfounded assumptions and the grandiose claims without experiencing a rise in blood pressure. But my topic here is not scientific fact for the moment, nor even well-reasoned argument. Instead, I want to focus on cultural values. I see self-help books as invaluable *cultural texts*. Like Puritan spiritual autobiographies, African American slave narratives, Horatio Alger stories, the U.S. Constitution, and the Gettysburg Address, these expressions reflect ideals about living that Americans often consider to be self-evident. These self-evident truths, furthermore, sometimes find their way into the redemptive self.

Were you to read through many of the classic American self-help books that I have introduced in the preceding pages, you might see five themes that self-help authors tend to reinforce again and again. And having read this deeply into my book, you may note that these five themes resonate with certain features of the redemptive self, certain aspects of the life stories that highly generative—productive and caring—American adults tend to tell.

First and most important is the belief that *the inner self is good, true, and innocent.* It is the essential, most authentic, "real" you. "Your life's work is similar to a calling," writes one self-help author. "You can find it by listening to the inner voice that urges you to do a certain thing in order to gain the utmost satisfaction."[24] Writes another, my book "will eventually release your inner strength, the self that's been hiding all these years, the unique and loving person you were meant to be."[25] "Believe in your God-released powers," proclaims Norman Vincent Peale. You must love your true, inner, good self before you can truly love anybody else. Call it the "inner child," the core of your being, your deepest principle or value, the inner self does not change much over time, though it can be lost, disguised, forgotten, or abused. "Inner

children are always good—innocent and pure—like the most sentimental-
ized Dickens characters, which means that people are essentially good and,
most of all, redeemable," writes Wendy Kaminer, a critic of the self-help tradition.[26] Like many of Dickens's characters, furthermore, inner selves remain steady and unchanging; they are sources for deep continuity across the
life course. "People can't live with change if there's not a changeless core inside them," writes Stephen Covey. "The key to the ability to change is a
changeless sense of who you are, what you are about and what you value."[27]

Second, the self-help tradition asserts, *the outer world cannot be trusted.*
The social environment is fundamentally alien to the self and filled with
temptations, constraints, threats, and dangers. Although love and collaboration with others are essential to growth, the norms and strictures of society
typically work to inhibit your growth and suppress the self. Unless you have
a Rogerian therapist or fabulous parents, you cannot count on unconditional
positive regard. Instead, you may learn to earn your love and respect by con-
forming to the status quo, "selling out" your soul in the process. Furthermore, some of the outside forces that seem most benevolent on first blush may
end up hurting you—the "toxic parents" who destroy your childhood, the
addicts and abusers who lure you into codependency, the friendly coworkers
who urge you to go along with the crowd.[28] "Self-worth cannot be verified
by others," writes Wayne Dyer. "You are worthy because you say it is so. If you
depend on others for your value it is other worth"—and worthless.[29]

Third, *redemption is the actualization of the self.* Your life moves from suffering to enhancement only when you are able to reconnect with the most elemental and natural aspects of selfhood, many authors assert. Growth and
development are a function of rediscovering the good and true inner self and
manifesting its potential destiny. Peale, Dyer, Peck, Covey, and Beattie all
place their faith in a general humanistic model of development, of the sort
championed by Rogers and Maslow. Material success, personal growth, spiritual enlightenment, recovery from abuse, and the like all depend on putting
into life practice what is already there in some sense, buried as it may be in
the inner self. Spiritual counselor Iyanla Vanzant "lectures and facilitates
workshops nationally with a mission to support and assist every individual
in realizing the truth in their authentic self."[30] Or as another self-help author
puts it: "I believe every person is born with a life purpose. That purpose is
sometimes hidden, but it can be discovered if you allow yourself to become
aware of it, to touch it with your mind's eye, and if you permit yourself to entertain the thought of making your dreams a reality.[31]

Fourth, in order to be redeemed, *you must follow a step-by-step plan.* Most
self-help books are as formulaic as chemistry texts. Whether you are consid-

ering Peale's "workable philosophy of living," Covey's 7-stage sequence, or the kind of 12-step recovery programs espoused in the codependency literature, self-help authors typically offer simple guidelines and linear programs to move you systematically upward and onward in life.[32] Reflecting a pragmatic, can-do approach to life (identified as characteristically American since the time of de Tocqueville), self-help books suggest that, no matter how bad and complicated life is, it is always possible to reduce things down to simple maxims and linear plans. Keep it simple; stay focused; move forward; continue to progress.[33]

Finally, it is difficult to ignore, even as it grates on the skeptical mind, the guileless optimism of most American self-help books. If you follow the plan and stay true to the inner self, *you can have, be, or do almost anything.* The American Dream suggests that anybody can grow up to be rich, or president. Of course, virtually nobody with half a brain believes such a statement to be literally true. But healthy skepticism is nowhere to be found in the self-help literature, even if M. Scott Peck insists that life is difficult. Indeed, it is the difficulties of life from which self-help authors promise to deliver us. If self-help authors had any doubts about their own powers in this regard, perhaps we would not buy their books or attend their weekend retreats. For sure, they have little doubt regarding the powers of the individual self. You can have it all—autonomy and attachments, money and sex, power and love—whatever your inner nature, so good and true, proclaims to be your destiny.

Ralph Waldo Emerson's "Self-Reliance"

Were he living today, Ralph Waldo Emerson might be running workshops on personal growth and fulfillment. Indeed, Emerson (1803–1882) may have been the most influential motivational speaker and self-help guru in America during the 19th century, long before Americans called themselves motivational speakers, or gurus. The son of a Unitarian minister whose male ancestors served as churchmen as far back as the Puritan days, the young Emerson knew early in life that his calling would be the ministry. When the boy was but 8 years old, his father died. His aunt took over the responsibilities of educating the young Emerson. She recognized and encouraged her nephew's literary gifts while emphasizing his disciplined study of the classics. At age 14, Emerson entered Harvard College. Upon graduation, he served as a teacher and studied part time for a degree at Harvard Divinity School. Illness slowed him down in his early 20s, but in 1829 he was ordained as Unitarian minister at the Second Church, Boston. In the same year, he married Ellen Louisa Tucker. Two years later, she died of tuberculosis. Emerson's grief drove him to question his religious beliefs and his profession. Despite his considerable success as a preacher, he resigned from the ministry in 1832 and began a new career as a poet, essayist, and public lecturer.

Emerson struggled with a fundamental religious question: *Where* is God? The Unitarian Church taught that God could be found in history. From the Old Testament to the present day, Unitarians believed, God manifested Himself through a series of miracles on earth. With his wife's death, however, Emerson came to find historical evidence for God to be less than compelling. Relatedly, he was unable to reconcile the idea of God's working in history with the growing consensus among scientists that the world's events could be fully explained according to natural laws. Emerson was deeply unsettled by some of what he learned and read at Harvard—for example, Isaac Newton's mechanistic conception of the universe and John Locke's notion that all human knowledge is derived from sense experience. Where was free will in all of this? And where might God fit in? In the 1830s Emerson began to associate with other scholars who harbored similar doubts and questions, and together they initiated an intellectual movement that came to be known as *Transcendentalism*. Borrowing ideas from Samuel Taylor Coleridge, William Wordsworth, and other European Romantics, the Transcendentalists conceded the material world to rationalism and science but kept for themselves the mysterious, transcendent, inner world of intuition and personal experience. To find God, Emerson concluded, we must look within the self.

Like self-help writers today, Emerson was not as original as he perhaps claimed to be in holding this idea. Even the Puritans looked for God deep within. They examined their hearts for signs of divine election. (But they also examined the external world, for proof of God's blessing might be as tangible as a good crop or favorable weather.) In the Great Awakening of the 1740s, and in subsequent religious revivals in America, Protestant preachers pushed an emotionally anchored and deeply personal brand of faith, prioritizing, like the humanistic psychologists of the mid-20th century, the subjective experience of the "heart." Conversion was an inner event—a miracle of the heart rather than of history, an intuitive, irrational, personal experience, outside the purview of Newton or Locke. Emerson drew from different religious traditions and blended them with European Romanticism and an unbridled American optimism to produce a way of thinking about life— indeed a way of living—that exalted the inner self above all else. For Emerson, knowing God was the same thing as enlightened awareness of one's self. And from such enlightened self-awareness came freedom of action and

FIGURE 5.1 The great spokesman for American Transcendentalism, Ralph Waldo Emerson (1803–1882) wrote essays and poems, and gave countless lectures that celebrated a romantic and heroic image of the new American man. His most famous essay, "Self-Reliance," foreshadowed many of the key themes to be found in the popular psychology and self-help literature of the late 20th century. Among these were the affirmation of the inner self, the distrust of society and social institutions, and the belief that human growth and redemption come through an actualization of one's inner potential. Reprinted with the permission of Art Resource. The National Portrait Gallery, Smithsonian Institution/Art Resource, New York.

the ability to change one's world according to the dictates of one's ideals and conscience. The individual must have the courage to trust the inner force and live in accord with intuitively derived principles. Or, as the words of a popular sports drink ad recognize, "It's in you."

The mother of all American self-help essays is Emerson's "Self-Reliance." I remember reading this work in high school and hating it. What was the big deal? Like many of the classics, Emerson may be wasted on the young. High school students may not yet have the distance on their own culture to understand that the way they, as Americans, think about the world and about life is not the way everybody else thinks, or has always thought. Even today, Emerson is so quintessentially American that most American youth—perhaps most Americans—may, like fish who know nothing of water, not be able to hear him. Or if we do hear him, we hear the voice of a privileged White male, unfamiliar with the inner lives of many women, people of color, and the poor. There is no doubt that in some ways—his bombastic romanticism, for example, his lack of irony—Emerson sounds hopelessly old-fashioned and out of touch. But in other ways he seems very up to date. Despite the odd phrasings and dated metaphors, a number of the ideas expressed by this American voice from the middle of the 19th century seem especially familiar today:

> The magnetism which all original action exerts is explained when we inquire the reason of self-trust. Who is the trustee? What is the aboriginal Self, on which a universal reliance may be grounded? What is the nature and power of that science-baffling star, without parallax, without calculable elements, which shoots a ray of beauty even into trivial and impure actions, if the least mark of independence appear? The inquiry leads us to that source, at once the essence of genius, of virtue, and of life, which we call Spontaneity or Instinct. We denote this primary wisdom as Intuition, whilst all later techniques are tuitions. In that deep force, the last fact behind which analysis cannot go, all things find their common origin.[34]

Emerson is saying that all that is good in life—all that really matters to human beings—begins with a natural and intuitive sense of self more basic, more elemental, than thought, reason, and education. From this deep source of human individuality spring the joyful play of innocent children—"the nonchalance of boys who are sure of a dinner"—and the most noble achievements of the mature adult.[35] "A man should learn to detect and watch that gleam of light which flashes across his mind from within," he writes, "more than the luster of the firmament of bards and sages."[36] In other words, intuition is more valuable than Milton, Newton, or Locke—more important than a Harvard education. The gleam of light—be it an inspiration, a deep feeling, a new thought, a natural sense of what is or what might be—is a sign that "God is here within."[37] A man (or woman) who aspires to live naturally and well—even heroically—must summon forth the courage to trust the inner self:

> Trust thyself: every heart vibrates to that iron string. Accept the place the divine providence has found for you, the society of your contemporaries, the connection of events. Great men have always done so, and confided themselves childlike to the genius of their age, betraying their perception that the absolutely trustworthy was seated at their heart, working through their hands, predominating in all their being. And we are now men, and must accept in the highest mind the same transcendent destiny; and not minors and invalids in a protected corner, not cowards fleeing before a revolution, but guides, redeemers and benefactors, obeying the Almighty effort and advancing on Chaos and the Dark.[38]

Although Emerson writes of "great men" and "genius," Emerson directed his words to the everyday farmers, businessmen, and professionals who enjoyed the relative prosperity and the freedoms of living in America during the years leading up to the Civil War. By the standards of the day, his message was inclusive and egalitarian. As he rode the lecture circuit between 1840 and 1860, Emerson inspired thousands of Americans to think about their lives in the heroic terms that were once saved only for kings, conquerors, and the great men of history. Every freeborn man is potentially a great man—a "redeemer" or "benefactor" in the progressive drama of American life. You do not need to travel to London or Rome to find meaning in your life, "for traveling is a fool's paradise" and "the wise man stays at home."[39] You do not need to consult history and the great ideas from the past, "for history is an impertinence and an injury" and "the centuries are conspirators against the sanity and authority of the soul."[40] Do not worry about getting a well-rounded education so that you can formulate a coherent philosophy of life, for "a foolish consistency is the hobgoblin of little minds."[41] Stay at home. Do your work. Look deep within. Accept your "transcendent destiny." The God inside you—the inner self who is your God—is "absolutely trustworthy," "seated at [your] heart, working through [your] hands, predominating in all [your] being." With the inner self as your guide, you will advance in life, from "Chaos" to good order, from the "Dark" into light.

Like most of the self-help authors of the late 20th century, Emerson championed the individual over and against society. Indeed, his distrust of social institutions was nearly pathological—the extension of an American tendency that is as old as the republic: "Society everywhere is in conspiracy against the manhood of every one of its members," and "no law can be sacred to me but that of my nature." Therefore, "whoso would be a man must be a nonconformist."[42] The individualist keeps his distance and refuses to get ensnared in dysfunctional groups and relationships. Like a codependency counselor, Emerson cautions against irrational entanglements with those who are especially needy: "We come to them who weep foolishly, and sit down and cry for company, instead of imparting to them truth and health in rough electric shocks, putting them once more in communication with their own reason."[43] Even in relationships with friends, family, and lovers, a person must stay true to the inner self:

> Say to them, O father, O mother, O wife, O brother, O friend, I have
> lived with you after appearances hitherto. Henceforward I am the
> truth's. Be it known unto you that henceforward I obey no less law
> than the eternal laws. I will have no covenants but proximities. I shall

endeavor to nourish my parents, to support my family, to be the
chaste husband of one wife,—but these relations I must fill after
a new and unprecedented way. I appeal from your customs. I must
be myself. I cannot break myself any longer for you, or you. If you
can love me for what I am, we shall be the happier. If you cannot,
I will still seek to deserve that you should. I will not hide my tastes
or aversions. I will so trust that what is deep is holy, that I will do
strongly before the sun and moon whatever inly rejoices me, and the
heart appoints. If you are noble, I will love you; if you are not, I will
not hurt you and myself by hypocritical attentions. If you are true,
but not in the same truth with me, cleave to your companions; I will
seek my own. I do this not selfishly, but humbly and truly. It is alike
your interest, and mine, and all men's, however long we have dwelt
in lies, to live in truth.[44]

The Anti-Emerson: Freud

The Emersonian self was always too good to be true. Even as they admired
Emerson's idealism and optimism, American writers in the 19th and early
20th centuries tended to portray the inner self in darker shades and less transcendent forms. Like Hester Prynne in *The Scarlet Letter,* Nathaniel Haw-
thorne's characters look to their inner selves for inspiration and guidance,
but unlike Emerson they are never able to escape society's grasp. Pushed by
inner forces they cannot control, Melville's heroes drive themselves to destruction. Like Captain Ahab, they are conflicted at their very core and over-
matched in their battles with nature. The poetry of Emily Dickinson expresses the anguish and longing of the solitary American soul, focused
inward on itself. For Mark Twain, it is the self's pretensions and its raw
cussedness that assume center stage. Like Emerson, Twain believed in the
progressive development of the self, but his characters never transcend the
rough-and-tumble reality of frontier life. And Twain was funny and sar-
donic—which Emerson never was. Henry James invented characters who
ruminate over every nuance of consciousness, but their inner selves seem
ambivalent, diffident, or sometimes even missing. They lack Emersonian
vigor and clarity. They seem vaguely anxious, yet they do not know why.

The ambiguous and conflicted self portrayed in so much of the great literature (American and European) of the second half of the 19th century an-
ticipates Freud and the emergence of psychoanalysis as a cultural force in the
West. On September 5, 1909, Sigmund Freud arrived in Worcester, Massachusetts, to deliver a series of lectures at Clark University. His visit to Amer-

ica marked a giant leap forward for the psychoanalytic movement. Many Americans initially welcomed Freudian ideas, and before long educated men and women in the New World were speaking knowingly of such things as the Oedipus complex, psychosexual stages, fixations, and the id. Eventually, a number of psychoanalytically oriented theorists—Carl Jung, Alfred Adler, Harry Stack Sullivan, Karen Horney, and Donald Winnicott—attracted significant followings among American psychotherapists, their patients, and the educated lay public.

Although strongly influenced by the same Romantic thinkers that Emerson read, Freud developed a conception of the inner self that was decidedly non-Emersonian in most ways. Like Emerson, Freud believed that conflict between self and society was inevitable. But very much unlike Emerson, Freud ultimately sided with society. If the family and social institutions did not suppress the sexual and aggressive urges residing deep within all of us, chaos would ultimately reign, Freud believed.[45] More significantly, though, Freud believed that conflict would be inevitable even if we could set society aside. We simply want too much, and it is all contradictory. I want to love my father. I want to kill my father. I want my father to take me to a Cubs games. In our heart of hearts, we are fundamentally conflicted, ambivalent, chaotic. Even if society did not beat us down (but of course it does), we would still be anxious and miserable. For Freud (as opposed to Emerson), there was no clarity and single-minded purpose in the inner self. There was no purity, no innocence, no simple truth within. The deeper you went, the uglier it got.

Here is the real Freud: The person is a mystery, even to the self. All that we do, all that we think, all that we feel, all that we love and hate is determined by forces over which we have no control. And we rarely even know what these forces are. Our ignorance is so pervasive that, in most cases, we are completely in the dark about the meanings and the causes of some of our simplest acts and experiences—our silly mistakes, for instance, and our seemingly senseless dreams. Were we able to catch some glimpse into the unconscious arena of the self, we would shudder in disbelief, for even the most innocent comment or gesture may betray a shameful secret of the soul, a secret rooted in our primal desires, unconscious though they are, to kill, to love, to live, and even to die. In general, we are the anxious protagonists of a complex and tragic drama we call human life. Our misery is the inevitable by-product of relentless conflict. Though we may occasionally gain insight into the horrors of it all, there can be no redemption.

Sounds pretty bad, huh? It is—which is why American therapists, their patients, and the general public have *never* truly embraced Freud, even if poets and novelists have. Instead, we have cleaned him up and dressed him in the garb of can-do optimism and humanistic hope. From the beginning of the psychoanalytic movement, American therapists and scholars selected what they liked in Freud (early childhood is important, the unconscious is cool) and simply ignored or distorted many of his more disquieting ideas (when was the last time you heard anybody talk about his or her *death instinct?*). In the 1940s and 1950s, traditional psychoanalysis evolved into *ego psychology.* Ego psychologists, like Erik Erikson, deemphasized intrapsychic conflict and argued that the self (ego) is masterful and adaptive, and it de-

FIGURE 5.2 Sigmund Freud (lower left) came to America in 1909 to deliver lectures on psychoanalysis at Clark University. Seated next to Freud is G. Stanley Hall (a prominent psychology professor at Clark), and next to Hall is Carl Jung. Freud imagined a very non-Emersonian kind of inner self, ultimately unknowable and filled with conflict and anxiety. Despite Freud's popularity in America and his powerful influence on literature and the arts, his dark and ambivalent view of the self and self-development was never fully embraced (nor was it understood) by most Americans. More recent psychoanalytic formulations reaffirm the potential goodness and security of the inner self. Reprinted with the permission of Corbis. Photo by Bettmann/Corbis.

velops over time. In the 1960s and 1970s, psychoanalysts in America incorporated ideas from humanistic and existential psychologists (e.g., Victor Frankl, Rollo May) who celebrated the self's positive potential and urged clients to find redemptive meaning in their lives.

For Freud, the inner self was a very unsavory, very dangerous thing. For Americans, this has always been an unacceptable idea, for reasons both economic and cultural. First, how do you sell a therapy that claims you are really bad inside and not likely to get better? In a capitalist marketplace, this sounds like a loser. Some historians have argued that the psychotherapy industry sweetened Freud and dumbed him down to make him more appealing to the American consumer.[46] Second, Freud's ambivalent and ultimately tragic view of human life is difficult to square with the life experiences that most middle-class Americans know, or aspire to know. And it cannot be squared with America's cultural heritage. In his cultural history of psychotherapy, Philip Cushman argues that Americans' prevailing understanding of their inner self—the "human interior"—mirrors their sense of geography. Like the heartland of North America, the inner self is large and good, and our manifest destiny is to "liberate" it—to free it up and actualize its vast potential: "[For Americans] the human interior was conceived of as neither dangerous, secular, nor controlled by external events, as Europeans believed; instead it was inherently good, potentially saturated in spirituality, and capable of controlling the external world: it was an *enchanted* interior, a fitting partner for the enchanted geographical 'interior' that spread westward to the Pacific. It follows that whereas in Europe the path to wellness was through *control* of one's interior, in America wellness was to be found in the *liberation* of one's interior."[47]

Today, the American self-help industry, many psychotherapists, and the educated American public are more Emersonian than Freudian in their understanding of the self. They believe in the power and goodness of the inner self. They see the establishment of a secure inner self as the best early advantage a person can enjoy. They celebrate individual autonomy and distrust societal forces and institutions. They see the world as a dangerous place where many people suffer. They have faith in redemption. Lives can change for the better, people progress, upward and onward, guided by an inner light that is bright and true.

Self Psychology and Attachment Theory

As Americans tend to see it, the inner self is either good from the start, or it is made good through good early experiences in the family. In America today, the most influential theories of child development argue that good early experiences save the child from an alien, unredeemed world. Theirs is a message that Emerson (but not Freud) would have loved: Successful early development involves the transformation of an early interpersonal advantage into a good and gifted inner self that serves as an everlasting source of sustenance and strength in a dangerous social environment.

This idea is not only a staple of the self-help industry. It is also a cornerstone assumption in today's most respected clinical and scientific theories of socio-emotional development—so much a matter of faith that even behavioral scientists rarely seem able to summon skepticism about it. To flesh out my claim, let me focus briefly on two formal theories of development that are extraordinarily influential today. The first, Heinz Kohut's theory of *self psychology,* has had a strong impact on clinical practice, especially among psychoanalytically oriented therapists. The second, *attachment theory,* has had a profound effect on scientific research in developmental psychology over the past 25 years, the results of which have influenced even social policy. Although both theories are known and promoted by their advocates as objective, clinical-scientific theories, I believe that they can also be read as cultural texts, reflective of cultural and historical themes. It is no accident that both of these theories have proven wildly popular among clinicians and academics in *America.*

The most influential development in American psychoanalytic theorizing in the past 25 years has been the rise of Heinz Kohut's self psychology.[48] As a therapist, Kohut worked with patients whose central disturbance involved feelings of emptiness and depression. Many of these patients suffered from problems in narcissism. Through listening carefully and empathically to the stories his patients told, Kohut came to reject the standard Freudian categories for understanding mental health (such as sexual drives and the Oedipus complex) and came to adopt the view that narcissism stems fundamentally from problems in the construction of the inner self:

> In trying, again and again, in analysis after analysis, to determine the genetic [developmental] roots of the selves of my analysands [patients], I obtained the impression that during early psychic development a process takes place in which some archaic mental contents that had been experienced as belonging to the self become obliterated or are assigned to the area of the nonself while others are retained within the self or are added to it. As a result of this process a core self—the "nuclear self"—is established. This structure is the basis for our sense of being an independent center of initiative and perception, integrated with our most central ambitions and ideals and with our experience that our body and mind form a unit and a continuum in time.[49]

At the core of our being is what Kohut calls the *bipolar self*. Its two poles are (a) ambitions for power and success and (b) idealized goals and values. Linking the two poles are the person's special talents and skills. In Kohut's view, a person is driven by ambitions and guided by idealized goals and values in accord with talents and skills. The bipolar self is structured in the early years of life as the child interacts with important *self-objects* in the environment. Self-objects are people so central to our lives that we feel that they are, in some sense, parts of us. The bipolar self evolves through relationships with self-objects.

In most cases, the most important self-object in the first year or two of life is the mother. With respect to the development of the self, one of the mother's main roles is to *mirror* the child's grandiosity. This means that she must confirm and admire the child's strength, health, greatness, and specialness. She must reflect and celebrate the child's budding agency and power. The mirroring relationship establishes, consolidates, and affirms the ambition pole of the bipolar self, providing the child with an unconscious sense that he or she is good and special, and destined for greatness. Somewhat later in development, the mother or father may serve as the *idealizing* self-object. The child admires and identifies with idealizing self-objects as sources of strength, care, and calmness. The idealizing relationship establishes, consolidates, and affirms the second pole of the bipolar self, wherein are located idealized goals and values.

According to Kohut's theory, healthy mirroring and idealizing pave the way for the development of a secure, confident, and autonomous sense of self. Persons so blessed enjoy high self-esteem and self-confidence. They are not overly dependent on others but are able to engage in intimate and fulfilling relationships. When they are children, these people's parents generally support their grandiose strivings, while serving as models of responsibility, steadfastness, and calm security. By contrast, inadequate or faulty mirroring and idealizing can result in various kinds of self-injuries and deficiencies, including the many forms of narcissism. With their obnoxious egotism, narcissists may seem to have too much self for their own good. But the truth, according to Kohut, is that they have too little. Suffering from problems that stem ultimately from mirroring and idealizing deficiencies, narcissists lack a coherent and autonomous inner self.

Recalling chapter 4, we might say that the problem in narcissism is that early on in life the narcissist is never *chosen*. He is never the apple of his self-object's eye. He is never provided with the soothing and calming influence that comes from a proper idealizing relationship. From the standpoint of Kohut's self psychology, healthy mirroring and idealizing provide the early advantage that the growing child needs if he or she is ever to become an autonomous and effective adult. And it is very difficult to "make it" in America if you are not autonomous and effective—very, very difficult in this, the most individualistic of nations. It is the gift of a confident and empowered inner self, a self that I can depend on to hang in there through thick and thin, come hell or high water, a self that is true and good and beautiful and authentic and really, really *me,* me at my core—this is the psychological gift, the ultimate early advantage that Kohut says we all want, and need.

Coming more from the scientific lab than the therapist's couch, attachment theory contends that the first and most important psychological task we face as developing human beings is establishing a secure bond of love.[50] During the first year of life, infants form an attachment relationship with one or more important caregivers in their social environment. These caregivers are called *attachment objects.* In the second half of the first year, the infant comes to prefer the company of the attachment object, or objects, to other less familiar figures in the environment. Ideally, attachment objects are especially effective in assuaging the infant's anxiety during difficult moments and providing for the infant a secure base from which to explore the world.

Attachment theorists, such as John Bowlby and Mary Ainsworth, argue that attachment is a complex system that coordinates infant behaviors such as sucking, smiling, vocalizing, following, and eye contact in order to keep the infant and caregiver in close proximity to each other. The system serves the biological function of protecting the infant from a dangerous environment. Attachment has evolved as an innate but flexibly organized behavioral system in human beings and certain other primates. It is designed by natural selection to assure mother-infant proximity for the ultimate purpose of protecting the infant from predators and other dangers in the environment of evolutionary adaptedness.

American research psychologists have been especially interested in exploring individual differences in attachment relationships. Although it is true that virtually all babies in all cultures establish some form of attachment in the first year of life, the *quality* of these attachment bonds varies dramatically. Many babies are securely attached. They find great comfort in their attachment object's presence. When they are afraid, they seek out their attachment object as a safe haven. When they are in the mood to explore their world, they use their attachment object as a secure base. These fortunate infants are blessed in many ways. They become more independent and self-sufficient because of the security they feel in their attachment relationship. They internalize an inner image of a secure bond—what Bowlby calls a *working model*—that they take with them for the rest of their lives. In theory, this

FIGURE 5.3 Secure attachment. Attachment theory may be read as a cultural text reflecting American cultural and historical themes. From this standpoint, the securely attached infant may be imagined as one of "the chosen people"— gifted with both a secure working model of relationships and a coherent inner self. Tremendously influential in America today, attachment theory argues that secure attachment confers a special and long-lasting advantage upon the developing child, a psychological blessing that will redound in greater interpersonal efficacy and personal autonomy in the years ahead. Photograph courtesy of Dan McAdams.

inner image or prototype of what it is like to feel close to another person promotes successful interpersonal relationships in later years. Most important, securely attached infants consolidate a clear and strong sense of selfhood that will prove invaluable down the developmental road. They take with them for life an inner assurance that they can be effective and autonomous in the world. They know unconsciously that life will be okay, because it was so much more than okay at the very beginning. What Erik Erikson called the *basic trust* of early infancy leads logically, he and attachment theorists argue, to the healthy *autonomy* of the well-adjusted 2-year-old. Secure attachment, furthermore, should increase the chances for success and fulfillment with respect to many other challenges in later development—including, Erikson would argue, generativity in midlife.

But not everybody is chosen. For a variety of reasons, many infants are insecurely attached. Although they find some sustenance in their relationship with attachment objects, they nonetheless experience a range of problems in attachment. Some feel distant and cool in their attachment relationship, often avoiding even the best-intentioned overtures from the caregiver. Others feel ambivalence in the presence of their attachment objects—strong feelings of both love and hate. Still others seem disoriented and disorganized when they relate to their attachment object, and they are unable to use the attachment object as a secure base from which to explore the world. Insecure attachments are bad news in human development. Some research and much theory suggest that insecurely attached infants eventually fall behind their securely attached peers on many indices of social and emotional competence. They may feel less autonomy and independence in the world. They may suffer more problems in interpersonal relationships, for the working model they internalize leads them to expect that intimacy will come with the price of high anxiety. They may develop an inner self that is less resilient, less confident, less trustworthy. As M. Scott Peck warns in *The Road Less Traveled,* if I cannot fully trust my first attachment object, I may never be able to trust fully my inner self.

The Oprah Story

The life stories of highly generative American adults often affirm ideas about self-development that can be traced back to 19th-century American Transcendentalism and forward to widely endorsed popular and professional psychological theories in America today. Their self-narratives sound like Emerson, mid-20th-century humanistic theory, Kohut, attachment theory, and the gurus of American self-help. Narrative research shows that especially productive and caring American adults often identify an early advantage in their lives that (they believe) established for them a secure and coherent inner self. Some see the early advantage in ways that are consistent with Kohut and the attachment theorists—as a special relationship with a caring person (a self-object or an attachment object) in their childhood years. Others point to special skills and talents, fortunate events, and other sources that go beyond the nurturance and mirroring they may have experienced in the family. Whatever they identify, nonetheless, highly generative American adults tend to romanticize some feature of childhood so that a good and noble hero—the transcendent inner self—*emerges at the beginning of the story.* Like Emerson and many self-help experts, but unlike Freud, highly generative American adults tend to imagine their inner selves as good and innocent, deep and authentic. As everything else changes over the life course, their stories suggest, the good inner self remains true and stable—a source of continuity and sameness from one chapter to the next.

The self is good, but the world is dangerous. Highly generative American adults are more likely than less generative adults to recall early scenes in their lives in which they witnessed the suffering of others. Their stories suggest that, despite the optimism and confidence that may come from an early blessing, the protagonists know early on that the world cannot be trusted to make everybody happy. From Emerson to the codependency experts, American self-help advocates have glorified the self and cast suspicion upon society, social institutions, and the outside world most generally. Even attachment theorists, who maintain that the good self stems ultimately from a good and loving social environment, view the world to be hostile and threatening and assert the fundamental function of attachment to be the *protection* of the individual from danger. In our cultural folklore and our psychological theories, Americans celebrate all forms of individualism—rugged and otherwise. We love stories about how the good individual goes up against an unredeemed world.

Highly generative American adults, however, do *not* typically see themselves as going up against the world. As research reviewed in chapter 2 has shown, generativity is positively associated with extensive friendship networks and community involvements. Even though they may endorse the power of the individual, highly generative American adults tend to be well integrated into society. They are active in social institutions such as schools, churches, and community organizations. In their life stories, highly generative American adults describe many scenes in which they feel a sense of belonging and commitment to others. It is probably fair to say, therefore, that the protagonists of the stories told by highly generative American adults are not as distrustful of society as Emerson was. Nor do they show the disdain toward the social order that is expressed in many self-help books. Their attitude toward the social world is mainly one of *concern*. They know the world is a difficult place, and they want to make a positive difference in the world.

Highly generative American adults are optimistic about human development. Like the humanistic psychologists, but again unlike Freud, they believe in progress and redemption. Their stories also endorse the general humanistic idea that positive growth often involves a reactivation of or reconnection with the good and true inner self. As one of my research participants put it, "My life had been a mess, but then I found me." Development may be viewed as a journey inward: "My life's been about going deeper and deeper inside," concluded another highly generative adult. Although few people tell life stories that spell out the kind of step-by-step formulas espoused by self-help writers, highly generative American adults still tend to see life in very goal-directed and linear terms. Life moves forward, sometimes steadily, sometimes in fits and starts. If a setback occurs in the story, it is expected that the hero will eventually recover and move forward again. The hero should stay focused, eyes on the prize. Bad things will invariably occur, but redemption should follow.

Emerson aimed to inspire genius in every listener. Maslow and Rogers hoped to lead every person to full self-actualization. Self-help books promise the world. You can have it all—they all seem to say. Highly generative American adults are typically less naïve. They know you cannot have it all. Nonetheless, the life stories they tell often portray protagonists who struggle to achieve *many* different goals in life. Compared to less generative American adults, those high in generativity tend to tell life stories featuring stronger and more persistent efforts to achieve goals pertaining both to power and love. These stories often express frustration, disappointment, and conflict in the quest to achieve competing goals. Highly productive and caring as they often are, highly generative adults set high standards for fulfillment in their work and in their relationships. Their life stories suggest that, despite the claims of some self-help gurus, it is unlikely that you will ever feel all the strength and the love that you want (and perhaps deserve). Often the biggest struggle is *balancing* the competing goals you pursue: Work *and* family. Autonomy *and* attachment. Power *and* love. Getting ahead *and* getting along. How can I have the most of both? How can I balance my pursuits of these two very different prizes in life?

The topic of balance is a favorite on what today is arguably the most visible and influential single forum for self-help in America—the Oprah Winfrey television show. The tens of millions of American women and men who watch Oprah's show or read *O: The Oprah Magazine* regularly encounter discussions, presentations, features, images, and stories about how to find balance in life, how to deal with competing demands and goals, and how to cope with the stresses of work and love. But, of course, Oprah's show, her magazine, her former book club, her movies, her Internet and cable ventures, and her vast network of philanthropy are about much, much more. Through what has become a multimedia empire, Oprah gives image and voice to many of the most vexing problems in American domestic life today: sexual abuse, addiction, eating disorders, teen violence, divorce, AIDS, poor schools, poor health care, and race relations, to name but a few. At the broadest level, though, she offers a simple message to her predominantly female, middle-class constituency. "The message has always been the same," she said in a 2001 *Newsweek* interview: "that you are responsible for your life."[51]

Oprah Winfrey aims to revamp people's lives. Exemplifying the American self-help tradition, she urges people to take charge of their lives, to overcome their obstacles, to pursue their dreams, and to think about ways to give back to society.[52] One of the richest and most successful women in the world, Oprah seems to want to give back, as well. Her charity network has given away millions of dollars in scholarships and "Use Your Life" awards. Her philanthropy and her commitment to improving lives, especially the lives of young people, are consistent with a strong sense of generativity. Indeed, Oprah's public persona reinforces the generative image. She is widely viewed to be very empathic and nurturing. Media critics have marveled at her ability to establish an easy intimacy with her talk-show guests and audiences.[53] As a result, her shows are filled with intimate self-disclosures. She encourages guests to talk about their pain and trauma, and she freely talks about her own. The talk glides easily into the language of psychological dysfunction, psychotherapy, spiritual development, and the like. As some critics have noted, Oprah often makes use of psychological and self-help rhetoric even when she talks about social and cultural problems, as if "therapy" writ large were the solution to all the world's ills.[54]

Psychological theorists, psychotherapists, and self-help experts have long known that storytelling is one of the most effective tools for changing people's lives. Life-story telling is a major feature of the Oprah Winfrey show. In addition, Oprah tells and sells her own story. Born dirt-poor in Kosciusko, Mississippi, this African American heroine survived sexual abuse as a child to become first a radio reporter and then a news anchor, talk-show host, moviemaker, publishing czar, and finally international celebrity and philanthropist. The facts of her life seem to make for a classic American success story— but this time, the story of a Black woman rather than the predictable White man. While the story resembles the rags-to-riches narratives that Americans have known for centuries, the story also expresses themes and outlooks that are distinctively gendered and reflective of her African American heritage. Because of the rich mixture, there is something for almost every woman, and many men, to identify with in Oprah's story. As she has said, "I'm every woman. It's all in me."[55]

The Oprah Story, as portrayed and marketed in her public image, captures themes that are common to the American self-help tradition and my book's psycho-cultural-literary portrait of the redemptive self. Oprah has said that she believes her work obeys a higher calling. She has been chosen to make a difference in the world, to help people take charge of their lives and change for the better.[56] Oprah believes in the deep, good, true inner self: "What I teach is that if you are strong enough and bold enough to follow your dreams, then you will be led in the path that is best for you." Do not let other people dissuade you from following your own destiny. Resist society's norms and conventions if you feel they are keeping you from actualizing the self: "The voice of the world will drown out the voice of God and your intuition if you let it." Oprah's own redemptive life journey uses the languages of recovery and upward mobility: "I grew up a little Negro child who felt so unloved and so isolated—the emotion I felt most as a child was loneliness—and now the exact opposite has occurred for me in adulthood."[57] As evidenced in her own recovery from sexual abuse, people can survive traumatic experiences and come out even stronger: "Your holiest moments, most sacred moments, are often the ones that are the most painful."[58]

In sum, the Oprah Story is about redemption, generativity, and the power of the good inner self. In an article entitled "The Age of Oprah," a national journalist describes part of Oprah's early-morning routine. Before she gets on the treadmill and jumps into her day, Oprah pulls out a piece of personal stationery inscribed with one of her favorite quotations. It reads: "What lies behind us and what lies before us are tiny matters compared to what lies within us." The quotation is from Ralph Waldo Emerson.[59]

Six

GOD BLESS AMERICA

At a special mass held the night of September 11, 2001, Cardinal Francis George of Chicago asked God to grant again the gift of redemption. "The Lord is compassionate to all His creatures," he began. "We need our friends to remind us on a day filled with death and horror that there is compassion greater than ourselves, greater than the world and the universe itself . . . so let us pray that out of this evil, in God's own time, some good can come through His compassion."[1]

The world's religions provide the deepest sources for our understanding of redemption. Many Americans look to religion to support their redemptive hopes—to deliver them from suffering to joy, from bondage to freedom, from sickness to recovery, from frustration to the full actualization of the good inner self. Life-story research shows that highly generative American adults—productive and caring men and women in their middle-adult years—tend to construct narrative identities that underscore their moral steadfastness and deep belief that their lives are built on rock-solid values. For most of them, a religious or spiritual sensibility provides a prime source for moral depth and clarity. Religion is an ultimate resource for meaning and worth for many Americans. It should not be surprising to learn, therefore, that the redemptive self may often incorporate a spiritual dimension. Highly generative adults fashion narratives of lifelong commitment that often draw on the images and themes of a rich religious heritage. Their stories unconsciously tap into an evolving tradition of faith and spirituality that is quintessentially American.

America's Religious Fervor

Michael Newdow was standing in a checkout line in 1996 when he experienced a revelation. Looking down at the change he received after purchasing a bar of soap, he glanced at the words "In God We Trust." Newdow thought, "This is offensive. I don't trust in God." His chance to put his outrage into action had to wait a few years, until his daughter was old enough to enroll in the Elk Grove school district in Sacramento, California. Newdow filed suit, aiming to remove the words "under God" from the United States Pledge of Allegiance. An atheist's daughter should not have to say those words in the classroom, Newdow reasoned. Furthermore, Newdow believed that the words violated the American principle that government should not support religion—the separation of church and state. In the summer of 2002, a panel of the U.S. Ninth Circuit Court of Appeals agreed with Newdow, holding that the 1954 U.S. congressional decision to insert the phrase "under God" into the Pledge ran contrary to the Establishment Clause of the First Amendment. Although the panel's ruling was put on hold, pending a review by the entire court, the announcement of the ruling sparked an uproar. Politicians of all stripes denounced the panel. Radio talk shows went into overdrive. In the heat of the controversy, a *Newsweek* poll indicated that almost 9 out of 10 Americans supported the inclusion of "under God" in the Pledge. A message on Newdow's answering machine called him a "freakin' commie bastard."[2]

Every morning it is in session, the United States Senate begins business with a prayer from the Senate chaplain and the Pledge of Allegiance. President George W. Bush begins Cabinet meetings with a prayer.[3] When asked in the 2000 election debates who his favorite political philosopher was, Bush cited Jesus Christ. His opponent, Al Gore, also proclaimed his strong religious faith and claimed that he often asked himself, "What would Jesus do?"[4] Gore's running mate, Senator Joseph Lieberman, a devout Jew who refused to campaign on the Sabbath, repeatedly invoked the Almighty in his campaign speeches and asserted that religion was the only true basis for morality. The same *Newsweek* poll indicated that, by a 60 to 37 margin, Americans say it is "good for the country for leaders to publicly express faith in God."[5] Other polls indicate that solid majorities of Americans would be willing to vote for a Black, Jew, woman, or gay presidential candidate. But only 48% say they would vote for an atheist.[6]

The United States is one of the most religious industrialized democracies in the Western world. A total of 63% of Americans believe in God "without any doubts," and most of the rest profess some form of faith in God. Only

2.2% follow Michael Newdow to report they do *not* believe in God. One third say the Bible is the actual words of God, and 80% believe it is "divinely inspired." A total of 77% believe in heaven; 63%, in hell; 58%, in the devil. Almost two thirds of Americans claim a membership in a religious organization; one third claim to attend church or synagogue weekly or more often; 45% attend at least monthly.[7] By contrast, fewer than one French person in 10 goes to church *even once a year*. Great Britain has an established religion—the Church of England—with the queen as its supreme governor. But a mere 2% of the British regularly attend Her Majesty's church.[8] Organized Christianity attracts very few on Sunday mornings throughout Western Europe, from Ireland to Germany to Spain. It is almost inconceivable that a head of a European state would regularly begin important policy meetings by offering a personal prayer.

Religion is today at the heart of many of the most vexing social and political issues facing Americans. Abortion, euthanasia, stem cell research, school vouchers, the death penalty, state support of faith-based charities, relations with Israel and the Palestinians, the "war on terrorism"—all of these issues summon forth strong religious convictions and controversies. In the 19th and 20th centuries, religion's role was just as pronounced. Political

FIGURE 6.1 For Labor Day weekend in 2002, Glen Fritzler, a farmer near LaSalle, Colorado, created this gigantic (14-acre) corn maze, which spells out "God Bless America." Reprinted with the permission of Getty Images. Photo by Kevin Moloney/Getty Images.

scientist and historian Gary Wills writes that "religion has been at the center of our major political crises, which are always moral crises—the supporting or opposing of wars, of slavery, of corporate power, of civil rights, of sexual codes, of "the West," of American separatism and claims to empire."[9] Leading up to the Civil War, religiously-anchored arguments were employed with great force by abolitionists (as well as proponents of slavery). In later years, prohibition, women's voting rights, and civil rights all found their most passionate motivations in the discourse of faith.

The first nation to disestablish religion, the United States has spawned a tremendous amount of religious fervor and religious experimentation. Today Americans celebrate religious diversity. We speak with pride about the freedom we Americans enjoy to adopt whatever religious tradition we desire. Still, the dominant religious tradition is Christianity. About 80% of Americans identify themselves as Christians. Dividing up that large majority, approximately 29% identify with mainline, moderate Protestantism (e.g., Presbyterian, Methodist, Lutheran), 26% with Baptists and other conservative Protestant denominations, and 25% as Roman Catholic. Approximately 2.5% of Americans identify with Judaism, and another 2% with other non-Christian religions (e.g., Islam, Buddhism, Hinduism).[10]

The Second Great Awakening

Christianity's lock was even stronger in the 18th and 19th centuries, when Protestantism was what Wills describes as "the dominant force in American life," making up the "unofficial religious establishment of our politics."[11] Historians have often noted that America's deepest roots lie in two contrasting traditions of thought: Puritan Christianity on the one hand, and the European Enlightenment on the other.[12] One was spiritual and God-centered, whereas the other was rational, scientific, and humanistic. Nonetheless, Wills sees no contradiction between the two. American Protestantism and Enlightenment thought were both pragmatic and individualistic, and both expected tangible positive results:

> Newton's seeking the literal meaning of biblical prophecy was as appropriate as Jonathan Edwards's scrupulous study of the spider's habits. Literalism came as a liberation after centuries of priestly mystification. This was not only a genuine enlightenment; *it is something peculiarly American*. It helps explain the mystery of America's double heritage, from the Reformation Puritans and from Enlightenment philosophies. What looks like a contradictory coupling was still a

natural alliance in the seventeenth and eighteenth centuries. Insofar as the Enlightenment was religious, it was clearly Protestant—Voltaire admiring the individualistic Quakers, each with his or her own "inner light"; Benjamin Franklin developing his secularized Puritanism of self-scrutiny and improvement; the British deists testing God's claims by reason (confident he would meet the test). And Puritanism on its materialistic side was down-to-earth, antimystical, a *measuring* religion, good at keeping books, interested in *results*. This is the American tradition, in politics as well as religion.[13]

The traveling preachers who led revival meetings in the first half of the 19th century—during what church historians call America's "Second Great Awakening"—measured their success by the number of souls they saved. They were very good at keeping the books, interested in results. The most prominent of these was probably Charles Grandison Finney (1792–1875). A lawyer by training, Finney set up practice in Adams, New York, where he spent many hours pouring over legal texts. While perusing Blackstone's *Commentaries on Law,* Finney noted repeated references to Judaic principles and Christian scriptures. This moved Finney to buy a Bible, which he began to read assiduously. The reading stimulated an emotional upheaval, as Finney struggled to sort out just what his religious beliefs and feelings were. On October 10, 1821, while walking through the woods near his home, he underwent a religious conversion. He emerged from the woods convinced of his personal salvation and resolved to dedicate his life to spreading the gospel. The following day, when asked by a client to try his legal case, Finney reportedly replied, "I have a retainer from the Lord Jesus Christ to plead His cause; I cannot plead yours."[14]

Finney dropped his law practice to become an evangelist. Soon he was licensed by the Presbyterians. Drawing on the kind of homespun rhetoric he had used earlier in pleading with juries, Finney preached to enthusiastic crowds throughout upstate New York. He used what came to be known as the "new measures" of evangelism. These included encouraging men and women to pray publicly together, using colorful examples and colloquial language in sermons, praying for people by name, offering immediate church membership to converts, and holding services that lasted for days on end. Between 1824 and 1832, his revivals achieved spectacular success. Tens of thousands of people responded to his invitations to receive Christ as their "personal savior." In 1832 Finney began an almost continuous revival in New York City as minister of the Second Presbyterian Church. Although he repeatedly clashed with more conservative clergymen who objected to some of

FIGURE 6.2 Called the first professional evangelist, Charles Grandison Finney led religious revivals in Boston, Philadelphia, New York City, and hundreds of towns and villages in upstate New York during the 1820s and 1830s. Rejecting the Calvinist idea of divine election, Finney saw salvation as fundamentally an act of individual free will. As a major player in the Second Awakening in American church history, Finney also argued that the church should take an active role in righting society's wrongs. His ministry coincided with the upsurge of Jacksonian democracy and a populist celebration of the common man in America. Reprinted with the permission of Oberlin College Archives, Oberlin, Ohio.

his new measures, Finney continued to lead successful revivals in Philadelphia, Boston, and other large cities on the East Coast. In 1835 he moved to Oberlin College to become a professor of theology. Finney served as president of Oberlin from 1851 to 1866.

The religious doctrine that Finney championed has since become a staple of American Protestantism. Finney and other preachers of the Second Awakening rejected the Calvinist idea of divine election. Salvation was not something to be received passively by a few lucky beneficiaries of God's grace. Instead, individual men and women could actively bring Jesus Christ into their own hearts. Conversion became an act of free will, as each person made a personal decision to accept what God had to offer.

Finney's ministry corresponded with the rise of Jacksonian democracy in America. His message, like Jackson's populism, lifted up the common man (and woman) to be an active religious and political agent in the world, an empowered *individual*, free to choose, free to make something good and unique out of his or her life, as Emerson would also teach only a few years later. Finney preached self-reliance and personal responsibility for one's spiritual growth. But, unlike Emerson, he showed more concern for the problems of society. Finney challenged the church both to save souls and to take up the lead in cleaning up social sins. A great deal of the energy generated by the Second Awakening was channeled into voluntary societies and reform causes. Theodore D. Weld, one of Finney's most famous converts, thundered against the ills of slavery. Preacher Lyman Beecher, a rival of Finney's, singled out the intemperate use of alcohol as the greatest threat to American hopes for building a better society.[15]

If the Protestant preachers of the 19th century could actively critique American society, they could also reinforce its dominant values. During the heyday of Finney's ministry, the Frenchman Alexis de Tocqueville published his famous observations of life in America. Tocqueville marveled at Americans' fervent embrace of religion. "In America," he wrote, "religion is the road to knowledge, and the observance of the divine laws leads man to civil freedom."[16] Yet he was also puzzled by the easy juxtaposition in America of Protestant piety and the pursuit of material wealth: "One would think that men who had sacrificed their friends, their family, and their native land to a religious conviction would be wholly absorbed in the pursuit of the treasure which they had just purchased at so high a price. And yet we find them seeking with nearly equal zeal for material wealth and moral good—for well-being and freedom on earth, and salvation in heaven."[17]

The truth is that American religion, especially its dominant Protestant forms, has never had much trouble with the idea that you can be rich and still get to heaven. Jesus may have said that a rich man's entry into the kingdom of God is as difficult as a camel's passing through the eye of a needle, but Americans have never really believed this, or believed it applied to them. In the 19th century, Protestantism sanctified, as much as it critiqued, the growing free market system.[18] American religion accommodated itself to the demands of a growing commercial culture. Put differently, the preachers caved to—or were seduced by—capitalist lucre. The American dream of success found common ground with Protestant piety, because worldly accomplishment could be seen as a sign of God's blessing. It is probably fair to say that the same equation worked pretty well with the Puritans, too. But though material well-being might mean a bountiful harvest and a good roof on the barn in 17th-century New England, it could encompass lavish estates and multimillion-dollar fortunes in the 19th and early 20th centuries. The lords of capitalism and big business were role models for how good things could happen when God-fearing Americans worked hard and invested wisely. One of the greatest robber barons of them all—John D. Rockefeller—was a devout, Bible-thumping Baptist (and a great philanthropist). Americans

learned how to be crassly materialistic and deeply spiritual at the same time—
and we never forgot the lesson.[19]

In sum, Americans are as a group among the most religious people living
in the industrialized West today. Although American society enjoys tremendous religious diversity, this is still predominantly a Christian nation with a
strong Protestant heritage. American Protestants have always championed
an experience-based religion of the heart, through which salvation is conceived as an individual act of will. The Protestant heritage supports rugged
individualism, self-reliance, and upward social mobility. American Protestantism has been a driving force for social reform, from abolitionism in the
19th century to civil rights in the 20th. But it has also tended to reinforce the
American dream of material success, suggesting that spiritual growth and
material wealth can go hand in hand. When God blesses America, we have
traditionally believed, He provides riches for both heaven and earth.

Benefits of Religion

To the extent religion really does provide riches on earth for Americans
today, the benefits redound most notably in the realms of physical and mental health. For most of the 20th century, medical researchers ignored the role
of religion in health. With a few notable exceptions, clinical and empirical
psychologists expressed indifference, bemusement, or disdain toward religious belief, religious worship, spirituality, and the like. In the last 10–15
years, however, many researchers have finally turned their attention to religion. They have conducted medical, psychological, and sociological studies
and surveys that measure many different aspects of religious experience,
such as religious affiliation, church attendance and participation, religious
behaviors (e.g., prayer, meditation), and religious methods for coping with
adversity and stress. The bottom line finding is that, at least among Americans, religion tends to be positively associated with many features of physical and mental health. The statistical results are impressive and compelling.
At the same time, research also suggests that there are exceptions and complexities in the data. Some studies also show that religion can produce some
negative outcomes, too.[20]

Religious involvement is positively associated with many indices of physical health and wellness. Those who attend religious services on a regular
basis, for example, tend to live longer than those who are not involved in religious organizations, and they tend to lead healthier lifestyles. They are less
likely to use tobacco and illegal drugs, and they show lower levels of alcohol
abuse. Their blood pressure and cholesterol levels tend to be lower. Religious

involvement is associated with lower levels of heart disease, cirrhosis, emphysema, stroke, kidney failure, and cancer mortality. Following major surgery, highly religious adults tend to show fewer health complications and lower levels of stress compared to less religious adults. With respect to mental health, religious involvement is positively associated with self-esteem, life satisfaction, and overall psychological functioning. Religious involvement predicts lower levels of depression, delinquency, criminal behavior, and even divorce. A strong predictor of marital happiness is a couple's mutual involvement in religious activities. The positive effects of religion appear to be especially powerful among African Americans and among socially marginalized groups in American society.

The benefits of religion may stem from many sources. In the United States, churches, synagogues, and mosques provide members with close-knit communities where people share values and goals, and care for each other during difficult times. People develop close friendships in religious organizations; they join informal support groups of various kinds; they come to associate with a broad range of individuals who may be of help to them in many different ways. Ministers, priests, rabbis, and other religious leaders may provide counseling or offer advice as to how a troubled member may obtain help from social service agencies and other community-based resources. Religious involvement enhances social support and raises a person's *social capital*—the network of social relations upon which a person may draw to meet the many different challenges of life.[21] Higher levels of social support and social capital are themselves good predictors of health and well-being.

Religious values, furthermore, may encourage health-promoting behavior and discourage high-risk, antisocial activities that can compromise a person's health and well-being. For example, religious people are less likely to be smokers, resulting in the link between religious involvement and lower levels of emphysema. Religious ideologies provide people with answers to deep questions about life, providing a sense of security and hope in the face of adversity. Some researchers have speculated that the kind of security and optimism that some especially religious people enjoy may exert a calming physiological effect. Chronic activation of the body's sympathetic nervous system—associated with heightened levels of fear and anxiety—has been linked to illness and reduced longevity. Religious involvement may help to lower chronic stress and reduce the wear and tear on the body's vital organs that come from repeated overactivation of the sympathetic nervous system.

The positive effects of religion are especially evident when people express what psychologist Kenneth Pargament calls *intrinsic* religious values and *positive religious coping*.[22] Intrinsic religious values come from within; they

Box 6.1.   Some Benefits of Religion

Medical and psychological research shows that among Americans religious involvement predicts:

- Increased longevity
- Lower rates of heart disease
- Lower blood pressure
- Fewer strokes
- Lower levels of chronic pain
- Lower cancer mortality rates
- Lower cholesterol levels
- Higher levels of positive health habits
- Less stress following major surgery
- Fewer suicide attempts
- Lower levels of delinquency among youth
- Lower levels of criminal behavior
- Lower levels of alcohol and drug abuse
- Lower tobacco use
- Lower levels of depression
- Higher levels of life satisfaction, happiness, and self-esteem
- Better overall mental health
- Higher levels of marital satisfaction
- Lower divorce rates
- More satisfying friendship networks and social support

reflect religious choices that people have made freely and thoughtfully. By contrast, *extrinsic* religiosity may feel forced or coerced and is motivated by guilt, fear of rejection, or social conformity. Intrinsically religious people show higher levels of well-being, sociability, and intellectual flexibility, and lower levels of depression, anxiety, and social dysfunction than extrinsically religious people. When facing difficult periods in life, intrinsically motivated people often use such positive coping strategies as praying to God for assistance, seeking support from clergy and congregation members, and looking for positive blessings amid adversity. Studies have shown that these positive religious strategies are associated with higher quality of life and stress-related growth among hospital patients, more positive emotions among chronic pain patients, lower mortality rates among survivors of heart attacks, and less hostility among families of homicide victims. By contrast, *negative religious coping* strategies—such as questioning the powers of God, expressions of anger toward God or the church, and religious appraisals that emphasize God's wrath or the power of the devil—are associated with negative outcomes following periods of stress.

Pargament also suggests that fundamentalist forms of religion appear to show both positive and negative correlates. Research has consistently shown that adherents to strict, fundamentalist religious viewpoints tend to be more narrow-minded, authoritarian, and prejudiced. Among Christians, Jews, Muslims, and Hindus, strict fundamentalism is associated with distrust of people who hold other points of view and prejudice against such out-groups as homosexuals. Strongly conservative religious beliefs are associated with authoritarian traits, rigid and harsh codes of conduct, hostility toward others (especially those holding contrary beliefs), distrust and suspicion of education and the arts, and a general inability or unwillingness to comprehend complexity and nuance in the world. At the same time, Christian fundamentalism in the United States has been associated with a few positive features, such as optimism about one's own life and marital satisfaction: "Strict systems of religious belief and practice provide individuals with an unambiguous sense of right and wrong, clear rules for living, closeness with like-minded believers, a distinctive identity, and, most important, the faith that their lives are sanctioned and supported by God. These are strong advantages. They may help explain why, for many years, fundamentalist and evangelical churches in the United States have been growing in strength and membership more rapidly than their mainline counterparts."[23]

Religion and Generativity

The redemptive self is a narrative identity told and lived by many highly generative American adults. Generative adults are especially concerned about and committed to the well-being of future generations. As parents, teachers, mentors, leaders, activists, volunteers, and concerned citizens, generative adults tend to be actively involved in endeavors aimed at making their world a better place. Generativity is associated with positive family and community involvements of various kinds. For Americans, furthermore, it is often also linked to religion.

You do not have to be a religious person to be concerned about and committed to promoting the well-being of future generations. Many adults who have no religious affiliation, including agnostics and atheists, make positive and important contributions to children, their families, and their communities. But among Americans, research shows a positive statistical correlation between measures of generativity, on the one hand, and indices of religious and spiritual involvement, on the other.[24] Adults who report regular church attendance, frequent prayer or meditation, and concern about religious or spiritual issues tend to score higher on measures of generativity, on the average, than those adults who do not express high levels of religiousness and spirituality. Furthermore, adults high in generativity also tend to report that as children they were raised in religious households and involved in religious institutions, to a greater extent than adults low in generativity.[25]

In American society, it is not uncommon for adults to become more involved in religious organizations once they become parents. Young people who may have drifted away from the church in their teenage years often find that they want religion back in their lives once their own children are born. Religious organizations provide social and spiritual resources for families. Many offer religious instruction for children, support systems for young parents, youth groups for teens, opportunities for intergenerational activities, and a generally family-friendly environment. Research shows that religious mothers and grandmothers develop more positive relationships with their respective children and grandchildren. Religious fathers spend more time with their children.[26] Fundamentalist churches often reinforce rigid gender stereotypes, urging women to defer to their husbands and stay home with their families rather than work outside the home. They tend to celebrate the 1950s version of the all-American middle-class family—intact, father works, mom stays home with the kids. Although this idealized model of the American family may not be realistic in most contexts, fundamentalist churches nonetheless place a strong and salutary emphasis on parents' commitment to their children and to positive family life.[27]

Beyond the family, religious involvement is associated with such generative activities as staffing food pantries, running soup kitchens, mentoring disadvantaged youth, and raising funds for social ministries aimed at the disabled, the sick, and the dying.[28] Religious organizations often run schools and hospitals. They operate prison ministries. Religious organizations typically support community agencies and national or international bodies that provide social services for disadvantaged groups. African American churches have traditionally functioned as powerful, multipurpose institutions in Black neighborhoods, providing basic services for community members and mobilizing forces for community activism. It is through churches, synagogues, and other religious organizations that many Americans express their desires to become involved in the world beyond the self and to help and care for others who live beyond the orbit of their immediate family and friends.

My own narrative research suggests that highly generative American adults tend to center their lives on a value system that is clear and strong, and that

Box 6.2. Religion and Generativity

Recent empirical research has examined the relations between religious and spiritual involvement on the one hand and indices of generativity on the other. Although an adult does not have to be religious to be a generative person, the research shows that among Americans religious or spiritual involvement tends to be positively correlated with activities indicative of a concern for and commitment to the well-being of youth and future generations.

Social scientific research shows:

- Marriage and raising children boost involvement in religious organizations.
- Religious mothers and grandmothers develop more positive bonds with children.
- Religious fathers spend more time with their children.
- Religion increases positive intergenerational relationships in families.
- Religious individuals show more concern for others in their families and communities.
- Regular churchgoers give more time and money to charities and social service agencies.
- Religiosity is positively associated with volunteer work and civic involvement.
- Generative adults report more involvement with religious institutions as children.
- Measures of generativity are positively associated with participation in organizations and activities promoting religion and/or spirituality.

often, though not always, is derived from religion. In telling the stories of their lives, they are more likely than those scoring lower on generativity measures to claim that they internalized a coherent system of beliefs and values, usually linked to religious faith, in their childhood and adolescent years. They are more likely to say that, though they have changed and grown in many ways over time, those same values have remained strong and true. Highly generative adults are *less* likely to say that they have gone through tough periods in their lives in which they doubted or rejected their value systems or questioned deeply their belief in God. If the values and beliefs themselves have "changed," they have evolved gradually into more mature forms, building on a base of truth. They are *less* likely than individuals low in generativity to acknowledge that their values often conflict with each other. Highly generative adults rarely lie awake at night wondering whether or not God exists or if they have the world figured out right. They do not seem to struggle much about the correctness of their viewpoints, even though they tolerate others' points of view. They believe that their values are clear, consistent, and coherent, and have pretty much always been so. Their life stories suggest moral clarity and steadfastness.[29]

I must tell you that I was initially surprised to find these results. Having read too much Camus and Carl Jung in my intellectually formative years, I imagined highly generative adults as existentialist heroes, as always searching and questioning, pushing further and deeper than other people, continually scrutinizing themselves, continually becoming something new, never settling for the simple, conventional truths. Alas, highly generative adults are usually much more down-to-earth, much more in the world. Caring for and contributing to the next generation is more about changing diapers, teaching Sunday school, and getting people to sign your petition than it is about questioning the ultimate meaning of the universe.

Highly generative adults usually cherish simple values like the Golden Rule. Once these values are established, highly generative adults seem to say, one should not tamper with them too much. Cherished life values are too precious and too important to be overthrown or cast aside when challenges to their validity arise. Not that challenges should not be considered—but highly generative adults are typically able to deflect challenges or incorporate them into their own system as their values gradually evolve and mature. Highly generative adults may say today that they struggled when they were much *younger* to sort out their ultimate values and beliefs. But that was long ago. Today, in middle adulthood, there is too much to do, too many things to care for, too little time to waste on a searching reexamination of what is good and true, who is God, and what I believe in my heart to be right.

Case studies and autobiographies of adults who are strongly committed to social responsibility and moral action reveal the same pattern. In his book *The Call to Service: A Witness to Idealism*, Robert Coles writes that he found his initial inspiration for altruism in his father, who devoted a tremendous amount of time and energy to charitable work. "I frankly doubt I could continue," his father said, "if I looked too hard within."[30] Sociologist Molly Andrews has studied the lives of political activists who dedicated themselves to social change. Almost all of them developed strong political and ethical belief systems in their teenage and early adult years. They committed themselves to these value systems for life. They experienced relatively little inner conflict regarding the decisions they had made as activists. "Once having become politicized," Andrews writes, "they experienced virtually no moral conflicts which deterred them from the ongoing purpose of their lives' work."[31] Looking back on their work as elderly adults, they expressed no regrets.

Psychologists Anne Colby and William Damon have conducted one of the most illuminating studies of moral commitment in adult lives.[32] Colby and Damon asked an ethnically and politically diverse group of moral philosophers, theologians, ethicists, historians, and social scientists to nominate American adults who exemplified moral virtue and who dedicated their lives to making a positive difference in the world. The expert group nominated 84 such *moral exemplars,* each of whom demonstrated a sustained commitment to moral ideals and a willingness to risk self-interest in the service of a greater good. Each was a strong example—an exemplar—of moral virtue and principled action.

Colby and Damon traveled across the United States to conduct extensive interviews with a subsample of the 84. In all, they interviewed 23 moral exemplars (13 women and 10 men; 17 Whites, 4 African Americans, and 2 Latinas). The interviewees ranged in age from 35 to 86 years, with most at least in their 60s. Educationally, the final group ranged from completion of eighth grade to M.D.s, Ph.D.s, and law degrees. In terms of occupation, the group included religious leaders (a Catholic priest, a Buddhist monk, a Catholic bishop, a Protestant minister), businessmen (the founder of a large corporation, a wealthy entrepreneur), physicians, teachers, charity workers, an innkeeper, a journalist, heads of nonprofit institutions, and leaders of social movements. The social issues to which these men and women had committed their lives included poverty, world peace, the environment, civil rights, civil liberties, health care, medical ethics, and business ethics. Although Colby and Damon did not administer formal measures of generativity, it is probably safe to say that all of the moral exemplars they studied are highly generative American adults.

Colby and Damon were immediately struck by the importance of religion in the lives of the moral exemplars. All but one of the 23 identified an affiliation with a religious tradition, and the vast majority stated that religious and spiritual matters were at the center of their life's calling. Religious faith was a source of redemptive hope for most of the moral exemplars. It supported their "unremitting faith in humanity and its future."[33] Almost all of the moral exemplars, moreover, drew upon religious traditions and values to reinforce what Colby and Damon call an "impervious sense of certainty" about their life's work.[34] Like the highly generative adults at the center of this book, the moral exemplars identified by Colby and Damon expressed a deep confidence in the rightness and goodness of their viewpoints and commitments. Colby and Damon were initially surprised by this finding, just as I was. Their reading of past research on the psychology of moral development led them to expect that moral exemplars would be deeply reflective people who spent a great deal of time puzzling over and working out their philosophy of life. Although many of their respondents were very thoughtful and articulate, very few of them struggled with their faith, their commitments, or their life decisions. Based on the life stories they heard, Colby and Damon conclude,

> Character and commitment are played out in the realm of action, not reflection. Pondering moral problems is not the same as dedicating one's life to their solution. The capacity for single-minded dedication to a moral cause may have little to do with the capacity for reasoning about abstract moral principles. The will to take a stand may derive from a source entirely different from the ability to arrive at a sophisticated intellectual judgment. It may even be that some people who live out strong moral commitments tend at times to be impatient with extensive reflection, as if they instinctively fear that it may lead to hesitation and doubt.[35]

Colby and Damon observed a considerable amount of growth in the life stories of their moral exemplars. But it was growth *within a setting*. Life-narrative research in psychology suggests that fundamental beliefs and values—typically established by the end of adolescence or early adulthood—provide an *ideological setting* for a person's life story.[36] The setting is the backdrop upon which the story's action unfolds. In the case of the moral exemplars studied by Colby and Damon, growth and development occurred within the setting established by their early ideological commitments. Once they positioned themselves in the setting, moral exemplars sought out other like-minded people with whom to share their views. Through these social relationships, they learned more about the ideas and projects they had committed themselves to. They proved eager to take in information that might broaden, deepen, or enhance their original value commitments, actively receptive to what Colby and Damon call "progressive social influence."[37] As they learned more and gained in maturity, therefore, the moral exemplars gradually expanded and refined their beliefs and values. But they never abandoned those initial positions to which they had sworn allegiance. Ideologically speaking, they bloomed where they were planted.

The Development of Core Beliefs: Daniel Kessinger

To see how this kind of story unfolds, consider the moral career of Daniel Kessinger.[38] One of the first highly generative adults to participate in my life-narrative research, Kessinger was, at the time of his interview in 1991, a 48-year-old community organizer and director of a mental health agency. In

Kessinger's story, the protagonist establishes a strong ideological setting by the time he enters the sixth grade. Daniel tells his parents he will not attend the local junior high school (where all his friends are attending) because there are too many children there from rich families, and "this seemed immoral in some way." He convinces his parents to send him to a different school with a broader mix of social classes. His parents are not surprised by Daniel's demands. They have raised him to be keenly attentive to instances of inequality and injustice in the world. Their political socialization dovetails easily with Daniel's grade-school immersion in the Unitarian church. The church teaches tolerance, ecumenicalism, and social justice—values to which Daniel remains committed for the rest of his life. Putting his religious values into action, Daniel protests the exclusive use of New Testament readings in mandatory high school prayers. He tells his teachers and principals that the practice is an offense to the school's many Jewish students and to his own Unitarian sensibility.

Through progressive social influence, Daniel's beliefs and values broaden and become better articulated in his college years. Daniel's professors urge him to take a more critical stance toward his own beliefs in order to strengthen them, defend them against attack, and translate them into social action. As Daniel becomes more involved in the intellectual life at college, he also becomes increasingly active in campus politics and social issues. John F. Kennedy is the new American president, and Daniel's college is awash with the excitement of his youthful administration. These are halcyon days for the kind of young, White, liberal intellectuals with whom Daniel identifies. Inspired by the Kennedy Peace Corps and the brewing social ferment of the early 1960s, Daniel and his friends are motivated to push for greater social equality and justice. Expanding his concerns to encompass the issue of race, Daniel becomes involved with a group called Students for Racial Equality, and he works with college administrators to develop recruitment programs for Black youth. Later he organizes tutorial projects for minority children. Raising the ante further, he joins his fellow activists—now both White and Black—to march for civil rights in the American South. In a high-point scene in his life story, Daniel and his friends stare down a group of Klansmen during a rally in a small Southern town.

Throughout his early adult years, Daniel continues to expand upon and enact the values he learned as a child. Relationships with friends, professors, and fellow political activists contribute to the progressive enlargement of his moral agenda. He falls in love with a young woman who has made similar value commitments. Lynette is a psychology major whose main political concern is the Vietnam War. Daniel's views on the war are complex. He is not a pacifist, and he feels that many protestors have not thought through the implications of their views. It is wrong to refuse national service for purely selfish reasons, he believes. At the same time, he feels that this war is wrong, or at least wrongheaded. Lynette helps him sort through his thoughts and feelings about the war. They decide that they both want to serve their country in a way that promotes their work for social justice. They apply to join the Peace Corps—an appointment that will keep Daniel from having to go to war. In 1966 they are assigned to a small village in India to work with a group of Americans on a family-planning project. They talk to villagers about safe methods of birth control, distribute condoms, and contribute to the general health care initiatives sponsored by the American and Indian governments. They also get married. The 2 years in the Peace Corps prove to be a turning point for Daniel and Lynette. They come to realize that the most effective way to enact their values is to work within the system at the local level.

Daniel and Lynette return to the United States in 1968 to find a nation dramatically polarized by the Vietnam War. The alliance between liberal Whites and Blacks of the early 1960s has begun to dissolve with the emergence of a more militant Black consciousness. College campuses have been radicalized. Inner cities have erupted in violence. A new counterculture preaches the virtues of free love and free drugs. Still firm in the values he learned in the Unitarian church, Daniel feels increasingly uncomfortable with the radicalization of certain segments of American society, and he fears the growing backlash of the conservative White majority. Emotions run high on both the Left and the Right. Daniel's is a voice of reason and tolerance amid the growing chaos. As much as ever, he wants to work for a better world. He and Lynette believe in radical change, but he does not expect change to occur easily, nor without hard work:

> I had come back from India in some ways, eh, I'll call it *conservative*. I mean when you spend 2 years trying to change people's attitudes and stuff in a country like India, I mean one thing you come away with is a profound sense of how slow social change is. I mean the farthest thing from my mind was anything that was apocalyptic or immediate. I had a vision of social change taking place over a thousand years, with a lot of pain and false starts. Step by step.

Eventually Daniel and Lynette move to Chicago. He obtains an advanced degree and begins work as a community organizer. She becomes a social worker. At age 33, he is named executive director of a community mental health council. He starts with a small budget, but soon he is presiding over a multimillion-dollar operation that employs 55 full-time workers and 11 psychiatrists. As the United States moves politically to the right in the 1980s, Daniel pushes boldly in the other direction. He works hard for liberal and progressive political candidates in local elections, and he becomes active in protests over American military involvement in Central America. He designs and organizes a local food pantry and warming shelter and serves on a number of local boards and agencies to promote the health and welfare of community residents. "My life theme is creating a better world, " Daniel says. To do that, he adds, "I try to build things that institute the values I have." Those values were laid down in the Unitarian church and through his parents' passion for social justice. The fundamental values have not changed in quality, but they have broadened and become more refined through experiences with college professors, fellow activists, people he served in India, his colleagues in Chicago, and his wife Lynette. Daniel never abandoned the core beliefs he held as a child. But he built upon them and added to them to develop a personal ideology that supports a highly generative life:

> The Unitarians basically believe that each individual works out their own religious posture and their own path and their own way. And there's a side of me which obviously sees a lot of merit to that. On the other hand, I don't think that when everything in the whole religion brings it back to the individual you have a very good thing. This doesn't bring out the best in human beings. I could never be a Christian because I don't believe the myth. But there are some elements in Christianity that help people go beyond the individual. They bring out a collective commitment. The individual doesn't just stand alone. Part of me likes that a lot. You need that collective commitment if you are going to make positive change in the world.

Seekers Versus Dwellers

In the early and middle parts of the 20th century, many "experts" predicted that religion would nearly vanish from America by century's end. Advances in science would expose religion to be nothing more than primitive superstition. The spread of capitalism and wealth would replace traditional values with secular ones. Americans would look ultimately to science, technology, reason, government, economics, and other features of cultural modernity to find their life values and meanings. The experts, however, could not have been more wrong. What has happened instead is that Americans' religious and spiritual inclinations have gone in many different directions over the past 100 years. In the United States, religion has continued to flourish as it has evolved into a plethora of different forms. Unlike most Europeans and most citizens of modern industrial democracies, Americans continue to look to religion for happiness, meaning, and the support of their generative commitments.

It is estimated that there are over 2,100 religious groups in America today.[39] Of these, 17 claim over one million members. Included in the 17 are the estimated 1.5 million Muslims in America today. In the 1990s the major groups who gained the most members tended to be socially conservative Christian denominations. For example, the Church of Latter Day Saints (Mormons) increased membership by 19.3% between 1990 and 2000, to reach 4.2 million members. The conservative Churches of Christ gained 18.6% to reach 1.4 million. Assemblies of God, a Pentecostal denomination, went up 18.5%, for a total of 2.5 million members. The largest Protestant denomination, Southern Baptist, now claims about 20 million members, up 4.9% since 1990. By contrast, some mainline, socially liberal Protestant denominations have experienced significant declines in membership. For example, the relatively liberal United Church of Christ declined 14.8% during the 1990s.[40]

Many conservative Christian denominations today are described as "fundamentalist." Fundamentalism goes back about 100 years in the United States. In the early years of the 20th century, Darwinian science and secular commercialism seemed to put Christianity on the defensive. At the same time, new critical approaches to Christian theology began to suggest that biblical stories were more metaphorical than literal and that Christianity's truths were mainly, though importantly, symbolic. While these developments informed the faith of many educated, "liberal" Christians, they incited strong negative reactions in many others. As an example of the negative reactions, the Presbyterians drew up their five *fundamental* points to distinguish what they considered to be true believers from false professors of the faith. Outlined in 1910, the five points were (a) the inerrancy of scripture, (b) the virgin birth of Jesus, (c) the doctrine that Christ died for people's sins, (d) the bodily resurrection of Jesus, and (e) the authenticity of miracles. (Later, Christ's Second Coming was substituted for the authenticity of miracles.) The Presbyterians published a mass-circulation series of books called *The Fundamentals*. In 1918 a World's Christian Fundamentals Association was formed. By 1920 the term *fundamentalist* was in use to refer to those Christians and those churches committed to preserving the five fundamental truths of Christianity.[41]

Fundamentalist, evangelical, Pentecostal, charismatic, and other conservative Christian groups today set forth strict guidelines for belief and behavior and demand high levels of commitment from their church members. Critics of the "Christian Right" argue that these groups are intolerant and narrow-minded. Although the critics may have a point overall (recall that psychological research links fundamentalism to authoritarian values and rigidity), sociological studies still suggest a surprising degree of heterogeneity. For example, one study found that on most issues evangelical Christians claim toleration for other religious traditions, for a wide range of political viewpoints, and for feminism. Most neither hope to Christianize public schools, nor hope to secede into Christian enclaves. Although critics express concern about the growing political clout of conservative Christians in the United States, most evangelicals claim they prefer relational strategies to political activism. They mainly aim to persuade others to make voluntary decisions to "follow Christ," by setting good examples through personal relationships. Although their viewpoints on the family are more conservative than those of most other Americans, many evangelicals try to balance a belief in the male headship of the family with an affirmation of women's rights to work outside the home and make decisions for themselves.[42] Generativity among evangelical Christians is focused mainly on the family. They go to great lengths to assure that their children are raised in their faith.

Since the time of the Puritans, America has been a land of religious innovation. In December 2000, *Time* featured "new lights of the spirit," or religious innovators for the new century. Among those in the spotlight was Father Virgilio Elizondo of San Antonio, Texas. Father Elizondo has been instrumental in bringing Mexican traditions and customs into the Catholic service. He has also worked to develop a new theology to reflect the life experience of Mexican Americans in San Antonio. In that their lineage is both Spanish and Native American, most Mexican Americans are mestizos. So too, in a sense, was Jesus, Elizondo suggests—for Jesus was born in Galilee and raised in Nazareth, outside the mainstream of Jewish life. Like the modern-day mestizo, Jesus "became the rejected other, and only out of that position was he able to reject rejection," Elizondo says.[43]

While Elizondo aims for a Christian theology that speaks to Mexican Americans, Professor Jan Willis seeks to adapt Tibetan Buddhism to the life experience of African Americans. In the United States, Willis contends, Buddhism remains a religion for White elites. The few practicing African Americans belong to Soka Gakkai International, an approach that emphasizes simple chanting and appeals for prosperity. But Willis prefers a more rigorous meditational approach that, she insists, will help African Americans break loose from the psychological and spiritual shackles they have endured. "People tell you for centuries you are just cattle, just a beast of burden," she

Thank you for staying until after the closing prayer.

FIGURE 6.3 Lakewood Church in Houston, Texas, is one of a growing number of "mega-churches" in the United States—very large, "nondenominational" Christian churches that provide an enormous range of ministries, services, and activities. Lakewood blends conservative Christian theology with popular music, New Age language, and sophisticated marketing strategies to reach young adults and families who may be searching for spiritual fulfillment. For many conservative Christians in America, family life is the central arena for the expression of religious faith and generativity. Reprinted with the permission of Houston Press. Photo by Deron Neblett/Houston Press.

says of slavery's legacy. "The consequences of that remain with us and need potent, powerful medicine."[44] For Willis, African American Christianity, as strong as it has been, is not strong enough to heal the souls of Black folk. What is needed, she believes, is a more spiritual approach, emphasizing chants, devotional rituals, and the practice of visualizing oneself as the Buddha.

Beliefs and practices from Eastern religious traditions, deriving especially from Buddhism and Hinduism, have become important parts of many Americans' spiritual lives. In the 1960s and 1970s, college students began to experiment with Transcendental Meditation, yoga, and related practices from the East. It all seemed very daring at the time. (I thought I was quite hip in 1976 when I tried Transcendental Meditation.) But these practices have now become part of the American spiritual mainstream. Yoga is even taught in some public schools today. In recent years, notable segments of the American middle class have expressed strong interest in the Bahai faith, Native American religions, African religions, Falun Gong, Gnostic mysticism, and the Wiccans, to name but a few. Today, Americans shop for churches as if they were buying blue jeans (where do I find the best "fit"?), and they browse through a well-stocked spiritual marketplace that displays practices and beliefs from around the world. For a growing number, private spiritual practices have replaced institutionalized religion as the main source for confronting deeply personal issues and matters of ultimate concern.[45] Private spirituality, furthermore, is readily combined with the kind of self-help traditions I surveyed in chapter 5. In our therapeutic culture, religion is often described in terms of spiritual healing, emotional development, psychological fulfillment, and the like.

Taking stock of the current scene in America, sociologist Robert Wuthnow distinguishes between religious *dwellers* and spiritual *seekers*.[46] Dwellers typically align themselves with religious institutions. They are members of churches, synagogues, mosques, and other formal groups, and they work out their religious convictions through these institutions. They accept traditional forms of religious authority. They relate to the sacred through prayer and communal public worship. By contrast, seekers prioritize individual autonomy over religious authority. They tend to combine elements from different religious and spiritual traditions to craft the approach that is just right for them. Although some seekers are involved in formal religious institutions, many are not. In either case, though, they emphasize the ways in which their spirituality is separate from formal institutions. They believe that they have worked out their convictions on their own.

Is it better to be a dweller or a seeker? Critics of dwellers (they tend to be seekers) charge them with being overly conformist and stuck within authoritarian institutions. Critics of seekers (that is, dwellers) accuse them of being self-centered and oblivious to the communal function of organized religion. As an example of the second critique, the influential political scientist Robert Putnam worries that the seeker approach works to undermine Americans' sense of community. Seekers may be believers, he concedes, but they are not belongers. Their private spirituality may give them personal joy, but it does not contribute to the common good in any way. Furthermore, seekers themselves may be losing out by not linking up with traditional institutions. Churches and other religious bodies provide their members with substantial social capital, Putnam argues. By ignoring this opportunity, seekers may be isolating themselves from potentially beneficial relationships.[47]

With respect to the central concerns of this book, I have argued that religious practices and beliefs are linked to generativity for many Americans. Involvement in religion as a child is positively associated with measures of adult generativity. Involvement in religion is also linked to many manifestations of generativity—from developing better relationships with one's children, to volunteering to support worthy causes and charities. Especially generative American adults tend to draw upon religious traditions to support the moral steadfastness and continuity that they express in their life stories. These findings, however, all relate more clearly to dwellers than seekers. Because the seeker approach is a relatively new phenomenon, researchers have not had much time to examine its relationship to generativity.

The social sciences literature does yield some clues, however. Sociologist Michele Dillon and psychologist Paul Wink recently examined the relations between dwelling and seeking approaches to religion, on the one hand, and generativity, on the other. Dillon and Wink studied the lives of 183 men and women born in Berkeley, California, in the 1920s. The participants in this longitudinal study were followed up on regular intervals from early childhood into their later-adult years. Culling through a substantial amount of data for each individual, the researchers rated the extent to which each was involved as an adult in (a) traditional religious activities (dwellers: church attendance, belief in God, prayer) and (b) spiritual practices (seekers: meditation, other nontraditional practices, connection with a sacred Other). It turned out that patterns of dwelling and seeking were not cleanly either-or in any given life. Some of the participants combined both traditional religious affiliations and spiritual practices. The researchers also administered measures of generativity. The results showed that both patterns of religiosity or spirituality—dwelling *and* seeking—were positively associated with a concern for and commitment to promoting the next generation. Contrary to some critics' claims, the seeking pattern predicted an active involvement in improving the lives of the next generation.[48] The results are consistent with another study showing that spiritually involved middle aged baby boomers are more likely to value altruism and self-giving than are middle aged baby boomers who show no interest in spiritual growth.[49]

Americans draw upon religious and spiritual traditions in ways that both enhance the self and (ironically enough) enable them to get beyond it. Whether you are talking about Charles Grandison Finney's revivals in the 1820s, or the spiritual practices of New Age baby boomers, Americans have typically focused first on the good inner self, the heart, the soul: save it; redeem it; heal it; comfort it; make it feel really, really good, strong, effective, and peaceful. Then (and *only* then) can the person move toward a generative engagement with the outside world. Through prayer, music, worship, and community support, dwellers find sustenance for the soul. Through meditation and other nontraditional spiritual practices, seekers find *the same thing*. In America, the individual heart, the self, the soul—it always comes first. This does not necessarily make all Americans selfish (though it may contribute to selfishness for some). On the contrary, when the soul is sustained, Americans seem to believe, the person is freed up, empowered, and energized to look beyond it, to invest in productive and caring relationships with others, to commit to long-term projects aimed at improving the world for generations to come. For better and for worse, it seems to be the American way—to enhance the self (first) and to help others, to be happy (first) and to be good.

In characterizing generativity in midlife, Erik Erikson frequently invoked religion. He emphasized that the generative ethic of caring for others has a clear parallel to Christian teachings and referred, for example, to the "perfection of charity in the words of Christ."[50] Erikson cited the prayer of St. Francis as a classic example of choosing generativity in adult life: "Lord make me an instrument of thy peace; where there is hatred let me bring love . . . where there is darkness, let me bring light," for "in giving we receive."[51] The prayer is both generative and redemptive, like the ultimate drama in the Christian story, wherein Christ dies to bring his people life.

Many spiritual and religious traditions speak a language of generativity. Most religious institutions, furthermore, prompt adults to make long-term investments in the lives of youth, and many encourage a generative attitude to one's neighborhood, society, and world, as well. For Americans, religious institutions and personal spirituality continue to be wellsprings for both individual growth and commitment to others. The redemptive self emerges out of a backdrop of belief and value that is typically rooted in sacred traditions. For Americans, God, Jehovah, Allah, or some form of a sacred Other still soothes the inner self, redeems the single life, and opens up for the individual man or woman a world that asks for commitment.

Seven

BLACK (AND WHITE)

Like most Americans, I grew up a racist. It was not that the elementary school children of the second-generation immigrants living in Gary, Indiana, in the early 1960s hated Black people. We just did not quite consider them human. In our primitive minds, it was as if we and they were two different species. They all lived downtown, nearer the steel mills, in the older parts of the city, where our parents grew up before they were pushed south by the Black threat. We all lived south of the expressway—all the Serbs, Macedonians, Greeks, Poles, Irish, and other White kids, all with our ethnic and religious prejudices regarding each other, but all united in our belief that we were different from and better than our African American neighbors, though of course we did not call them that.

Interstate 94 cut a wide swath through the city, neatly bisecting it into Black and White. In the early 1960s Gary was almost exactly 50% Black and 50% White. Since the time of Franklin D. Roosevelt, Gary's working-class voters had always gone solidly Democrat. In some elections, the Republican party did not even field a candidate. In 1967 Richard Hatcher won the Democratic mayoral primary. Hatcher was a young, attractive nominee who promised to bring more federal dollars to a city that was beginning to suffer the loss of blue-collar jobs. But he was Black. Rallying to the crisis, the Whites organized seminars in church basements and went door-to-door to teach people how to "split their tickets." Rather than pull the Democratic lever to vote for all the Democrats as everybody had always done, people needed to learn how to vote for the Republican mayoral candidate (a guy named Radigan: he was White—we checked it out) and then to mark all the other Democrats. Many White ethnics had never split their tickets before, but they were eager to learn.

In the end, Hatcher won the election by a slim margin of votes. The interpretation of the results I heard at the time was this: All the Blacks voted for Hatcher, and *almost* all the Whites voted for Radigan. But a few dumbass Whites could not figure out how to split their tickets, or simply forgot, and that is how Hatcher won.[1] Indeed, it was simply inconceivable to me, as a sixth-grader, that a White person would (knowingly) vote for a Black man. So when I later heard the rumor that Teddy Puchowski's mother—a long-time Democratic activist—had *intentionally* voted for Richard Hatcher, I was agog. How could this be? I felt no hatred for Teddy—just shame and pity, as if his mother had been convicted of a crime and sent to prison.

As I moved into my teenage years, I started to realize that my racism was both wrong and stupid, and I tried to change my feelings, but it was very hard. In eighth grade, I attended an integrated school and was seated beside a Black girl in band class. Robin Teeter was funny, and we joked around a lot. But when a friend told me that people were starting to think that Robin and I "liked" each other (i.e., as girlfriend and boyfriend), I just stared at him, agog again. It was simply inconceivable. Ethnic Whites I knew would often concede that it was possible to be "friends" with a Black person on the job, but you would never bring one home, or marry one.

Even in my junior year of high school, now well-educated and professing strong opposition to all forms of discrimination and prejudice, I found myself surprised yet again. Matthew Banks (African American) and I were comparing notes on a really cute (White) girl sitting in the back row of math class. We were in total agreement that should she ever become available—she was dating some jerk at the time—we would definitely ask her out. We were comfortable with each other, so I teased him about making a play for a White girl. Matthew said, "Oh, don't worry. I'm not prejudiced." My puzzled look in response must have surely betrayed the truth: It had never occurred to me that a Black person would reject a White person out of "prejudice." How could Blacks be prejudiced against Whites? I mean, prejudice meant that you thought you were better, that you were on top. Might Blacks feel that sometimes? It seemed inconceivable. There I was—honor roll every semester, informed about current events, passionate about injustices in the world, idealistic and well-meaning, and almost an adult—and when it came to that most vexing of all American social issues—Black versus White—I still did not get it.[2]

"The problem of the Twentieth Century is the problem of the color-line," wrote W. E. B. Du Bois in 1903, in a prophetic and impassioned book about race in America.[3] Written for audiences both Black and White, *The Souls of Black Folk* aimed to penetrate what Du Bois characterized as the "veil" of African American experience. From the standpoint of White America, Black lives were hidden behind a veil—out of sight, beyond conception. Whites were clueless; they just did not "get it" when it came to imagining what it might be like to be Black. From the standpoint of African Americans themselves, Du Bois asserted, the veil hid the Black man or woman from the good, true inner self. In America in 1903, Du Bois asserted, Blacks could not see themselves for who they truly were, or might be. Instead, they viewed their lives through the eyes of the majority world. Du Bois wrote:

> The Negro is a sort of seventh son, born with a veil, and gifted with
> second-sight in this American world,— a world which yields him
> no true self-consciousness, but only lets him see himself through the
> revelation of the other world. It is a peculiar sensation, this double
> consciousness, this sense of always looking at one's self through the
> eyes of others, of measuring one's soul by the tape of a world that
> looks on in amused contempt and pity. One ever feels his twoness—
> an American, a Negro; two souls, two thoughts, two unreconciled
> strivings; two warring ideals in one dark body, whose dogged
> strength alone keeps it from being torn asunder.
>
> The history of the American Negro is the history of this strife—
> this longing to attain self-conscious manhood, to merge his double
> self into a better and truer self.[4]

One hundred years after Du Bois wrote these famous words, relations between American Blacks and American Whites have changed significantly. But the metaphor of the veil is still strangely and profoundly apt.

Du Bois's first meaning of the veil is interracial. Whites do not see Blacks, do not understand them, Du Bois said, as if Black life were, from the standpoint of the White majority, hidden behind a veil. The veil is partly a metaphor for segregation. Du Bois wrote *The Souls of Black Folk* just a few years after the U.S. Supreme Court concluded that enforced segregation did not violate the Constitution. In its 1896 decision in *Plessy v. Ferguson,* the Court upheld the state laws demanding separate but equal facilities for Blacks and Whites. In the second half of the 20th century, however, the Court reversed itself, and public sentiment moved away from sanctioned racism. In the 1954 *Brown v. Board of Education of Topeka* decision, the Court famously struck down the concept of "separate but equal" in the realm of public schooling. Federal legislation in the 1960s aimed to outlaw racial dis-

FIGURE 7.1 W. E. B. Du Bois (1868–1963) was an esteemed sociologist and the most important Black protest leader in the United States during the first half of the 20th century. In his celebrated first book, *The Souls of Black Folk*, Du Bois (1903) argued that American Blacks lived behind a "veil" that made them strangers to both White people and themselves. Du Bois repeatedly clashed with another giant in African American history—Booker T. Washington. Washington encouraged American Blacks to pull themselves up by their bootstraps within the White capitalist system, whereas Du Bois favored a more radical agenda that rejected full assimilation within the White mainstream and urged Blacks to construct a unique identity that was both African and American. Reprinted with the permission of Getty Images. Photo by MPI/Getty Images.

crimination in many realms of American life. Today, virtually all respected institutions and most major corporations in the United States claim to believe in the virtues of racial integration and diversity. And most Americans, Black and White, believe that substantial progress in race relations has occurred in the past few decades. In a 2000 nationwide poll, 58% of Blacks and 78% of Whites said that they perceived significant progress in eradicating racial discrimination since the 1960s. As one indication of a larger trend toward interracial acceptance, large majorities of Blacks (79%) and Whites (63%) reported that they approve of interracial marriage, up from 70% and 44%, respectively, just 10 years before.[5]

But progress is only half the story. The same nationwide poll exposed enduring differences between Blacks and Whites regarding their views of race in America, leading the authors of the article to conclude that "Blacks and Whites seem to be living on different planets."[6] For example, Blacks were nearly 4 times more likely than Whites to say they thought African Americans were treated less fairly in the workplace, in shops and malls, in restaurants, in bars, and in theaters. Two thirds of Blacks said African Americans were treated less equitably by the police, a view shared by only 25% of Whites. Blacks were 14 times more likely than Whites to say that they had been stopped by the police simply because of their race (42%, as opposed to only 3%). The poll also exposed the fact that despite all the nice talk about integration, Americans still live in a starkly segregated society. A total of 83% of Whites said they worked with only a few Blacks or none at all. A whopping 90% of Whites who attend religious services at least once a month reported that none or only a few of their fellow congregants were Black, while 73% of Blacks said that none or only a few of their fellow congregants were White. Both cultural and economic-structural forces are instrumental in keeping the veil up. It remains stubbornly true today that Blacks are substantially less educated, make dramatically less money, and enjoy far less family wealth, on the average, than Whites.

Blacks and Whites remain largely isolated from each other in their everyday lives. For the most part, they live in separate neighborhoods, work in separate settings, eat at separate restaurants, drink at separate bars, dance in separate clubs, learn at separate schools, and worship in separate churches. We live in a "country of strangers," writes David Shipler in a probing analysis of race relations in America. "When it comes to race, we do not know how to talk to one another."[7] The same theme is echoed in an in-depth series on "How Race Is Lived in America," run by the *New York Times* in 2000. A team of journalists spent 18 months interviewing Euro-Americans, African Americans, Asian Americans, and Hispanics regarding the influence of "race" on their lives. The stories they obtained conformed to no single pattern or bottom line. Yet nearly all the respondents described the feeling of being misunderstood. People from other ethnic and racial groups simply cannot conceive of what their experience is like, the respondents repeatedly claimed.[8] Misunderstood, disrespected, unseen—these are powerful impressions played out again and again in African American literature, responses to the veiled, shrouded experience of being Black in America, so powerfully depicted, for example, in Ralph Ellison's classic novel, *Invisible Man*:

> I am an invisible man. No, I am not a spook like those who haunted
> Edgar Allan Poe; nor am I one of your Hollywood-movie ectoplasms.
> I am a man of substance, of flesh and bone, fiber and liquids—and
> I might even be said to possess a mind. I am invisible, understand,
> simply because people refuse to see me. Like the bodiless heads you

see sometimes in circus sideshows, it is as though I have been surrounded by mirrors of hard, distorting glass. When they approach
me they see only my surroundings, themselves, or figments of their
imagination—indeed, everything and anything except me.[9]

Du Bois's second meaning of the veil is psychological. Because they must
continually view their behavior and their lives through the dominant lens of
the majority culture, Du Bois claimed, Blacks do not fully understand who
they themselves are, or might be. The good, true, and authentic souls of
Black folk are hidden from their very owners. A people owned for hundreds
of years by a foreign race were technically emancipated by the time Du Bois
wrote *Souls,* but they did not truly own their own lives, nor did they apprehend their own soulful authenticity, Du Bois believed.

Du Bois clashed sharply and repeatedly with the Black exponents of a
more conservative vision of African American uplift. In the early 20th century, many Black preachers and authorities like Booker T. Washington urged
African Americans to work their way up slowly and steadily in American society. By working hard as farmers and craftsmen, by pulling themselves up by
their bootstraps, Blacks would win the respect of White society and a piece
of the American Dream. In his autobiography, *Up From Slavery,* Washington
provided living proof that an African American could rise from nothing to be
a rich and influential man. In the mold of Benjamin Franklin and Horatio
Alger, Washington preached redemption through upward social mobility.

But Du Bois was more concerned with the emancipation of the Black
soul. More psychological, more skeptical of the capitalist status quo, and less
focused on material wealth than Washington, Du Bois wanted African Americans to free themselves from the social and cultural categories that stifled
their individuality and to construct new and authentic selves, in the spirit of
Emerson and the American romantics. There was no reason, in Du Bois's
mind, that Blacks could not and should not assume positions of prominence
in all areas of American life—from industry to arts to academia. African
Americans had already been instrumental in making America what it was.
"Would America have been America without her Negro people?" Du Bois
asked.[10] Even as they brought a unique African perspective to the New
World, Blacks personified some of the noblest virtues America had to offer:
"We the darker ones come even now not altogether empty-handed: there
are today no truer exponents of the pure human spirit of the Declaration of
Independence than the American Negroes; there is no truer American
music but the wild sweet melodies of the Negro slave; the American fairy
tales and folklore are Indian and African; and, all in all, we black men seem

the sole oasis of simple faith and reverence in a dusty desert of dollars and smartness."[11]

Many African American writers and scholars of the 20th century have struggled to lift the veil and to boldly articulate an authentic African American identity. From Richard Wright and Langston Hughes to Toni Morrison, Spike Lee, Cornell West, and the countless Black voices who speak with power and authenticity today, African Americans of the 20th and 21st centuries have repeatedly addressed the question of what it fundamentally means to be African American. Some of the parameters of this identity struggle were laid out 100 years ago in the tension between Du Bois and Washington. To what extent should Blacks subscribe to the traditional American Dream? To what extent should Blacks assimilate into the American mainstream? To what extent should they look to African roots for value and identity? How should a people who were once enslaved think about slavery today? What is the right model for social change? Martin Luther King, Jr.? Malcolm X? How might Blacks live in harmony with Whites? *Should* Blacks live in harmony with Whites? What is our history? Who are we today? Where are we going?

The question of African American identity leads naturally to the question of generativity, as well. What kind of future should our children enjoy? What kind of world do we want to create? Both Booker T. Washington and W. E. B. Du Bois envisioned a better world for future generations. Both believed strongly in the power of human redemption. For Washington, the language of redemption was mainly economic and religious. Blacks would rise up from slavery through hard work and perseverance, humility, moral steadfastness, and the disciplined pursuit of both material wealth and self-worth. For Du Bois, the language of redemption was mainly political and psychological-spiritual. Blacks should boldly emancipate themselves from the psychological shackles of slavery. They should defy the White majority. They should break through the veil, make themselves visible and noisy in all realms of American life. Washington and Du Bois imagined different stories for the future of their people and for the future of America. They struggled over different narratives of redemption and different understandings of how to translate strong drives for generativity into productive and caring human action.

Generativity in Black and White

How do Black Americans translate drives for generativity into human action? The sad truth in academic psychology is that few researchers have focused on the lives of African Americans. Most studies in social, personality, and cognitive psychology use undergraduates attending large research universities as research participants, the great majority of whom are White. Results from the few Black subjects who might participate are typically aggregated with those of all other groups. With some notable exceptions, studies of children and families in developmental psychology have usually used White participants, as well. When behavioral scientists do examine racial differences, their inquires are often premised on the assumption that minority groups in the United States are disadvantaged or deprived in some manner— showing lower levels of achievement, higher levels of delinquency, more social problems, and so on. Very few psychological studies have examined the lives of African American *adults*, and fewer still have examined positive aspects of those lives, such as leadership, altruism, generativity, and so on.

In 1994 I received a grant from the Spencer Foundation to launch the first major study of generativity among African American and among Euro-American adults. My students and I sampled 253 adults between the ages of 35 and 65 years, approximately half of them African American and approximately half White. About half of the participants were women and half were men. The sample was predominantly working class and professional, with Whites showing slightly higher family incomes than Blacks. The sample was also fairly well educated. Over 80% of the participants had obtained at least some education beyond high school. Again, Whites showed significantly higher education levels than Blacks. The participants in the study completed a series of questionnaires regarding generativity, mental health, personality patterns, parenting, friendships, religion, and social involvements.[12] Out of the large sample, we called back 74 participants for in-depth, life-story interviews. We aimed to interview those individuals, Black and White, who had scored either especially high or especially low on our measures of generativity.

One aim of the study was to examine the relations between generativity, on the one hand, and measures of mental health and social involvement, on the other. For both Blacks and Whites, individual differences in generativity proved to be significant predictors of mental health and constructive social involvements. For both Blacks and Whites, generativity was positively associated with self-report measures of life satisfaction, self-esteem, and life coherence, and negatively associated with depression. In other words, those midlife adults who scored high on our generativity measures also tended to report relatively high levels of subjective mental health, compared to midlife adults scoring lower on generativity measures. Compared to less generative adults, Black and White adults high in generativity felt better about their lives and expressed less depression and anxiety.

For both Blacks and Whites, furthermore, generativity was positively associated with constructive social involvements. In the realm of parenting, highly generative adults reported that they were more likely to serve as a role model and to pass wisdom down to their children than less generative adults. In the realm of friendships, highly generative adults reported more extensive and satisfying networks of social support than less generative adults. They provided more help and support for their friends, and they received more help and support in return. By contrast, less generative adults felt more isolated and dissatisfied in their social relationships. Highly generative adults reported greater religious observance than less generative adults. They attended religious services more frequently and engaged in religious behaviors, such as prayer or religious reading, more often than less generative adults. Highly generative adults also showed greater levels of political participation, as indexed by voting in national and local elections, working for political candidates, and writing letters to public officials. These patterns tended to play out in similar ways for both African Americans and Whites.

Blacks and Whites did show some differences, however. For the entire sample of 253 adults, African Americans showed on average slightly *higher* levels of generativity than White adults. They showed higher levels of overall concern for and commitment to the next generation and a greater number of generative acts expressed in the preceding two months.[13] In addition, African American adults showed higher levels on a number of social-involvement variables that were empirically associated with generativity for the overall sample. More particularly, African American parents were much more likely than their White counterparts to view parenting as an opportunity to pass on wisdom to and be a positive role model for their children. African American adults also reported substantially higher levels of family and community support and of religious involvement, compared to Whites. Whites, by contrast, showed higher levels of political participation.

The results I have described are based on a limited sample of African American and White adults between the ages of 35 and 65 years. The sample is not large enough or representative enough to produce conclusions that might be applied to all American adults. Given that our study is the only psychological study to date that has focused on generativity among African American adults, much more research needs to be done before clear conclusions can be drawn. Nonetheless, the findings suggest the plausibility of two ideas about generativity and race in America.

First, it appears that individual differences in generativity are associated with the same kinds of behaviors for both Blacks and Whites. Highly generative Black adults are similar to highly generative White adults in that they tend to show higher levels of well-being, less depression, greater social support, more generative patterns of parenting, and greater religious and civic involvement, compared to less generative Black (and White) adults. Whether you are African American or White, the data suggest, generativity brings the same personal and social benefits.

Second, African American adults tend on the average to show slightly higher levels of generativity overall, as well as higher levels of social support, religiosity, and the study's measure of generative parenting, compared to White adults. The mean differences between the Blacks and Whites in this study on the measures of generativity, though statistically significant, are very small. It is quite possible that the findings reflect something unique to this sample. Framing the results with a cautious interpretation, therefore, we might suggest that, on average, Blacks score roughly the same or slightly higher on generativity when they are compared to Whites. But even that cautious interpretation appears noteworthy. Academic psychology has a long history of assuming that African Americans suffer deficiencies when compared to Whites. Some researchers have underscored perceived disorganization and social pathology in Black families, pointing to the high incidence of out-of-wedlock births, unstable marriages, and social problems associated with poverty.[14] Others have pointed to higher crime rates and lower achievement among Blacks, compared to Whites. By contrast, a few researchers have recently emphasized the strengths and adaptive resources of African American adults and the resilience of Black families.[15] Our findings on generativity appear consistent with this more recent approach. While White Americans have enjoyed a plethora of advantages in American society since the beginning of the republic, the findings from our study suggest that when it comes to one very important psychological resource in adulthood—generativity—African Americans show no deficiencies whatsoever, and may even score slightly higher than their White counterparts.

Findings from our study are also consistent with some results that have repeatedly appeared in sociological studies on Black families in America. In our study, African Americans described more extensive and satisfying social support from friends and family than White individuals, and they reported substantially higher levels of religious involvement. Sociological research on African American families has consistently underscored the supportive influence of extended kin networks and of family friends and neighbors identified as *fictive kin*.[16] The sociological picture that is painted here is of more diffuse, flexible, and loosely organized support networks than would be the norm in middle-class White communities. Although our study did not directly examine the structure of support networks, the data indicate that so-cial support from family and friends is an especially important personal re-source among African American adults, and one that is positively associated with generative concern.

An even more characteristic personal resource for working-class Black families may be religion. As we saw in chapter 6, social sciences research has repeatedly documented the health benefits and psychosocial advantages as-sociated with church attendance and religious beliefs. For example, religious involvement tends to be positively associated with self-esteem and feelings of well-being, social support, healthy lifestyles, and even longevity, and it is negatively associated with substance abuse. Survey studies have shown that U.S. Blacks are more likely to be members of religious organizations than Whites and are more likely to attend services on a regular basis.[17] Blacks en-gage in more public and private religious behavior and rate religious values higher than do Whites.[18] They are more intrinsically religious than Whites— meaning that they are more likely than Whites to engage in religious behav-iors for personal and spiritual reasons rather than for such extrinsic reasons like conformity or fitting in with the group.[19] Historically, the Black church has proved to be an especially powerful force in the African American com-munity, serving not only as a house of worship but also as a social service center and an agent for political activism and neighborhood empowerment. Religious involvement may be an especially important personal resource for middle-aged Black adults and a strong support and catalyst for generativity.

While Black participants in our study reported higher levels of social sup-port and religious involvements, Black parents were also more likely than their White counterparts to view themselves as role models and sources of prosocial values and wisdom for their children. The parenting scales used in the study stressed the extent to which parents said they strive to teach their children values, provide them with clear-cut moral lessons and standards for ethical conduct, and view themselves to be role models whose particular val-ues and standards should be internalized by their own children. The higher scores among African American parents may reflect a more *vigilant* approach to parenting in a social environment that, compared to that enjoyed by middle-class Whites, may be perceived as potentially more dangerous. While White middle-class parents may bolster their children's self-esteem and en-courage their children's achievement strivings and interpersonal compe-tence in school and play, they may be somewhat less preoccupied with fend-ing off the dangers of street life—gangs and drug involvement, for example. Of course, parents of all stripes in America today worry about negative in-fluences that may be visited upon their children from the media and other threatening influences from the "outside." But given the legacy of racial discrimination in the United States and the gaping chasm between Blacks and Whites nationally on such social indices as education, wealth, crime, and teenage pregnancy, it should not be surprising that Black parents might be more vigilant. African American parents may be especially preoccupied with teaching life lessons and cautionary tales of adversity to their children, and they may expend considerable energy trying to pass on wisdom and advice.

Generativity can take many forms. In an environment perceived to be threatening, generative parents may need to focus their energies on protection and strong guidance to maximize the likelihood that their children will even make it to their adult years. Among many working-class Black families in America today, generative parenting may be as much about vigilance as it is about encouraging growth and the actualization of the self. In a less threatening social environment, by contrast, parents may have the luxury to channel their generativity into such things as promoting their children's autonomy and self-fulfillment. In a relative sense, many middle-class and upper-middle-class White parents may enjoy this kind of advantage. If they feel that their social environments are relatively safe, they may feel less urgency about guiding their children through a difficult world and may instead see their generative task as encouraging their children's individuality and uniqueness.

Jerome Johnson: A Life Story

A year or two before he was assassinated, the Reverend Martin Luther King, Jr., came to a small U.S. city to speak to civic and religious leaders and to rally citizens, Black and White, for civil rights. Jerome Johnson was assigned to be King's bodyguard.[20] Johnson was a Black policeman in his early 30s, an ambitious man who had been a football star in high school and who completed a tour of duty with the U.S. Air Force. Johnson dreamed of becoming a police chief, but he was frustrated. No Black man had ever even been promoted to sergeant in that city, let alone been seriously considered for chief. Johnson's fellow officers counseled against taking the promotional exam. His friends told him that he should be satisfied with what he had. Johnson was beginning to lose hope in his dream. He was seriously considering quitting the force. But when King came to town, Johnson's life turned around.

Jerome Johnson was one of the highly generative African American adults we interviewed in our study of generativity in Black and White. Indeed, Johnson's scores on our paper-and-pencil generativity measures were among the highest we have ever obtained. Now in his early 60s, Johnson tells what happened 30 years before:

[The turning point in my life] was back during the time I had mentioned earlier [in the interview], about my thoughts and feelings about not taking the promotional exam the department had. Even thinking about leaving the police force because I felt it was a hopeless thing that a Black could ever be a police chief. I mentioned before about quitting the basketball team [in college] and I have to say I had given strong thoughts to leaving the police force because of what I saw was happening to minorities there, you know, about [bad] assignments and all that stuff that happened. And then it was at the time I was assigned to be the bodyguard for Dr. Martin Luther King. And he was here, I think, maybe 2, 3 days. And so I spent some time with him. . . . [On the last day King] was getting ready to leave, and he was standing in front of the hotel and waiting for transportation to take him to the airport. And we started talking, and I told him how frustrated I was about the fact that no Black had ever been promoted. Maybe it's time to move on [I told him] because I didn't see there was anything that was gonna change at all. And he just said a couple of things, just very briefly he said, you know, he said, "Never give up." And that was basically the end of the conversation, and I thought about that before, but when he said it to me, and the way he said, "Keep the faith," you know, and "never give up," you know, and "never stop dreaming the dream," you know. And I held on to that, and I went on, and things changed. . . . He turned me around from walkin' out the door.

According to Johnson's life-story account, he did eventually take the exam, and he was eventually promoted to sergeant. In the years following, he continued to rise through the ranks in the police department. Johnson finally realized his dream and became the first African American police chief in that town. After serving for many years as chief, he took an early retirement. At the time of our interview with Johnson, he reported that he was now spending much more time with his wife and adult children than he was able to spend during his busy years on the force. Reflecting his strong generativity commitments, he also invests a great deal of time and energy these days in volunteer work with Black youth. He helped to set up a basketball league for young Black men in his community. Johnson's plans for the future include writing a book about his experiences on the police force. And he hopes soon to be a grandfather.

The turning-point scene in Jerome Johnson's narrative identity is a classic redemption sequence. The scene begins in hopelessness, but the situation is transformed by a fortuitous meeting with Martin Luther King, Jr. As he tells it from the vantage point of late middle-age, Johnson's life story is suffused with redemptive imagery. He begins the account of his life this way: "I was a Depression baby, so we went through some very difficult times, when there was, you know, no food and there was no money available. I do remember the struggles and things we had to overcome, and I really remember the hungry stomach and I remember the Christmases when there was nothing under the tree." But these difficult times eventually get better, and amid the suffering Johnson recalls scenes of kindness and care. People were poor, yes. But people helped each other out:

> I think about how growing up that things were like a real community. I mean, even though we were young and we were struggling and people all around you were struggling, we all, people contributed to each other, you know. If we didn't have enough food, someone would bring us something. Vice versa, my dad would bring something in, and we'd be able to share that with somebody else, and just kind of a community of responsibility that was there and I think has always made an impact upon me, that people reached out and helped each other then.

Jerome Johnson was an above-average student in school and a first-rate athlete. In a large and overwhelmingly White high school in the 1950s, he excelled in football and basketball. In his senior year, he was voted captain of the football team. Johnson made many friends among the White students. He remembers fondly the many good teachers he had, and the football coach who worked hard to bring more Black students onto the team. But like all his Black peers, Johnson was also victimized by racial prejudice. In one scene in his story, Jerome's mother runs home in tears after attending a basketball game in which the opposing team taunts her son by calling him a "nigger." In another scene, school administrators refuse to permit Johnson, as football captain, to walk out on stage with the homecoming queen and lead the traditional homecoming pep rally. The problem, of course, is that he is Black, and the homecoming queen is White. The image of a beautiful White woman and a strong Black man standing together on stage and jointly whipping the crowd into a frenzy was just too jarring for some White teachers, students, and parents to take in this small American city in the 1950s. Almost 40 years later, Johnson says that he still feels the pain when he recalls this humiliating event. In Johnson's story, the homecoming scene is simply not redeemable.

But many other scenes are. Repeatedly in the story, bad events turn into good outcomes. The high school "environment was very difficult to deal with," he concedes, but "I think the things I faced there helped me to be stronger in my lifetime." Through college and the Air Force, Johnson suffers his fair share of disappointments and setbacks, but he continues to grow in confidence and hope. Returning home after his military service, Johnson takes on a series of jobs but makes no progress until he joins the police force. By then in his mid 20s, he begins to make long-term plans for his life. He will marry and have a family. He will rise through the ranks, eventually to become police chief. He will do volunteer work in his community. He will build up a reputation as a good family man, solid citizen, and upstanding representative of the Black middle class. He will be a leader. When asked to describe the high point in his life story, Johnson gives a detailed account of how he planned carefully and worked so hard to become police chief, the strategic relationships he cultivated along the path, the vision he articulated for the future of the force. Throughout Johnson's story, he is the ever-hopeful protagonist who works hard to overcome obstacles and accomplish his goals. In his spare time, Johnson reads books about slave life and the history of Blacks—"what they went through and overcame." "I guess I'm kind of one-dimensional on this," Johnson admits. His favorite stories from childhood were his grandfather's tales of overcoming adversity.

Johnson's is a life story of steady progress. No sudden epiphanies. No thrilling climaxes. The scene with Martin Luther King, Jr., stands out as the only dramatic turning point. His story is focused mainly on doing good work for others, on the police force mainly, and secondarily as a community volunteer. Family life seems positive, but Johnson provides little detail about his relationships with his wife and children. There are surely other stories to tell there, but Johnson appears to see them as tangential to the main, progressive plot that defines who he was, is, and will continue to be. His fifth-grade teacher challenged the class one day when he said, "You're either on the destruction team or you're on the construction team in life; and you gotta make a choice now. Which of the teams are you gonna be on?" Johnson chose the construction team. Personal failures and frustrations get turned into good materials for the plot he continues to build. Potentially destructive events are given a constructive interpretation. Things keep building and growing. Redemptive sequences energize and direct the story's upward movement. Johnson entitles the current chapter of his life story "Give-Back Time." Even after a life of public service, he will now ratchet up his community involvements and redouble his constructive efforts to help the local Black youth.

Redemptive Scenes, Progressive Plots

Jerome Johnson is by no means the only highly generative African American adult we interviewed who told a life story filled with redemptive scenes. Despite the wide variation in the stories we heard, the theme of redemption was very common among highly generative Black adults, and relatively uncommon in the stories of less generative African Americans. For some highly generative Black adults, the theme of redemption was so pervasive that it served as something of a life credo. Florence Goodson is a 45-year-old divorced mother of one, employed as a marketing research manager. Summarizing the general trends in her life, she says, "The negativeness and the badness of the things I had to overcome emotionally—dealing with the lies [of men] and the different things he [her husband] said about me—it made me a better person, it made me a stronger person, it toughened me up." In Florence's story, redemption comes through hard-won struggles and considerable pain at the hands of abusive men. "That's not the way I would have chosen to get here, but it did force a lot of growth," she remarks. Her religious faith has promoted her forward movement: "Salvation is what helps me grow and to rise above."

For Francine Ross, "Any person with a little knowledge can turn their life around." For Robert Quicken, "I've gone through more shit than anybody I know, but I always come out of it, and I keep on going, keep on moving up." For Malcolm Smith, a 62-year-old accountant who is married and has one grown child, life began (literally) as a kind of redemption scene. His mother is raped in the opening episode of his story, which is ultimately how she becomes his mother. His birth is the positive outcome of a violent assault. What follows from childhood through midlife is one harrowing scene after another, culminating in Malcolm's recovery from a nearly fatal stab wound: "I was dead but the doctors brought me back alive"—the ultimate redemption sequence. "My philosophy in life," Malcolm says, "has always been to be positive instead of negative on any circumstances you deal with." "If you go with positive ideas, you'll progress; if you get involved in the negative, you'll drown."

A key finding in our narrative study of highly generative African American adults is the thematic link between redemption and life *progress*. The link is apparent in Jerome Johnson's life story, and in the brief examples from Florence Goodson, Francine Ross, Robert Quicken, and Malcolm Smith. Another highly generative African American woman, Jocelyn March, tells a story that begins with a chaotic childhood: "I had no direction and purpose when I was young," but eventually "I began to experience an awareness of the journey." After the birth of her daughter, Jocelyn began to see her life in terms of "stepping stones along the way." In her early adult years, Wronda Wagner did not feel that she had direction in her life, but then she went back to school to get her G.E.D. Only then did she feel she "was on the road to someplace." Today, age 51, married, and the mother of four, Wronda is proud, she says, of "how far I have come" and how much "my husband and I have grown." "We have been to hell and back, to be frank," she adds. Her big goal for the future is to "grow the bus company" that she and her husband began years ago. After successfully completing a 12-step program to recover from an eating disorder, Judy Savitch finally began to see her life as a progressive narrative. Even her children see it that way now, she remarks. Recently, her son said to her: "I wish you were like you are now when we were smaller." "I'm glad to have evolved," Judy says at the end of her life-narrative interview. Joellen Dorsett, a 39-year-old single woman who scores very high on generativity, concludes her interview with this paean to progress: "The things which do appear come from things which are not seen. What you see now is not what I am. I'm yet evolving. I'm yet progressing. I'm yet looking to be better. To have better for myself."

The essential movement in progressive life narratives like these is forward and upward.[21] Despite considerable pain and setbacks, the protagonists in these stories continue to grow, improve, make progress, move ahead, get better over time. Redemption sequences encode just such a movement, from bad to good, from negative emotion to positive emotion. But highly generative African American adults adopt a wide range of metaphors and discourses to convey the sense of a progressive life. Life may be a *journey* through which distance traveled symbolizes progress made. Life scenes may be viewed as "stepping stones" along the way. Life may be viewed as a sequence of *developmental stages.* Early stages may lay the groundwork for the successful engagement of later stages, an idea that is implicit both in many popular theories of human development and in many life stories of highly generative African American adults. History, too, may be viewed as a stage-like, progressive process. A number of highly generative Black adults in our study juxtaposed their life stories with the history of the African American people. Their basic metaphor was emancipation: from slavery to freedom — a progressive movement, for sure, though one not without setbacks and failures. A few highly generative Black adults remarked on how relatively "easy" their lives were compared to those of their parents, who faced considerably more discrimination and more overt prejudice when they were growing up. Things may not be so great now, but they used to be much worse.

Like developmental stages, *goals* can provide life with direction and purpose. A number of highly generative Black adults in our study underscored the importance of goals for directing life's journey. "I'm always preaching to my kids, you know, you can do it, you can make it, but you can't detour, you have to just keep a straight and narrow path toward the goal," remarked one highly generative Black woman. Unswerving focus on goals is the key to success, suggested another: "So most of what I can remember really growing up is the schooling, the discipline you got, you know, like marching really, strictly toward goals." In stories like these, losing sight of one's goals almost invariably leads to trouble. Even in the most progressive life narrative, life itself is precarious and contingent. Progress is never guaranteed.

Nor does progress make everything good. Redemption is rarely *total* in the life stories told by highly generative African American adults. Good things do emerge from bad experiences, but the good things that result often take the form of tough lessons about how to survive and move forward in a dangerous world. The highly generative Black adults in our study held strongly to a progressive story for their own lives, but they did not fail to see the dark clouds for the silver linings. Some victories resulted in as much ambivalence as progress. Even when success is achieved, the pain of early setbacks lingers on. Remember Elliot Washington, whose redemptive life story opened chapter 1 in this book. Washington tells how the racial discrimination he experienced in high school may have, ironically, promoted his successful vocation as a teacher and a scholar. Yet redemption is bittersweet:

> There was auto shop and machine shop. Those were closed shops. And the school counselor said, "You have to have the consent of the instructor to get into it." I said, "Well, what do I have to do to get the consent of the instructor?" She said, "Well, he puts in boys that he knows." And just walking by, I would see all of these White boys, these European descended boys in there. They'd be joking and laughing and carrying on. It was obvious that they had bonded with this man in a very, very close sort of way. There was no African descended student ever in those classes during the time I was there. I can tell you the reason why. If you went through machine shop course from the beginning to the end, when you got out of high school you would have had a trade. You could have walked out into any factory and gotten employment immediately because you were skilled. You had a trade. Same thing for the auto shop. In a way, it was fated. That doesn't bother me because if I had done that again, instead of going to college, I might have ended up in a factory! So, you know, some people say it and believe it. They say that God works in strange and mysterious ways. You know we all get our own

direction. It was fated that I wasn't going to get in there. But it was the level of hurt that you feel at being told you are different, that you are not allowed, you're not qualified to do this simply because of your ancestry.

The American Slave Narrative of Redemption

In Jewish and Christian traditions, the religious meanings of "redemption" presuppose sin. The suffering of God's people stems ultimately from their sinful nature, the book of Genesis tells us. Through burnt offerings, appeals to God, expiation, atonement, grace, or some other religious mechanism, sin is undone, even if only for a moment, and suffering, ideally, is relieved. In some conceptions of redemption, the deliverance from sin requires that the sinner first experience guilt or remorse. In the history of the United States, America's greatest "sin," to which is attached its greatest sense of collective guilt, may be the enslavement of the African American people. Indeed, Abraham Lincoln came to believe this to be the case, and he came to see the Civil War as America's great test of redemption.[22] In American cultural history, slavery provides what is arguably the most powerful symbol of an unredeemed world: A nation that celebrates freedom as its most cherished goal once kept many of its people in chains.

Southern slaves who escaped to the Northern states in the years before the American Civil War worked to abolish slavery in at least two ways. Like Harriet Tubman, some escaped slaves worked with abolitionists to organize safe houses and escape routes as part of the Underground Railroad. When Tubman was a young girl, a plantation overseer struck her on the head with a club, leaving her with permanent brain damage. As a result, she would lose consciousness several times a day. To compensate for her disability, Tubman increased her physical strength until she was strong enough to perform tasks that most men could not do. When her owner died in 1849, Tubman made her break for freedom, escaping from a plantation on the eastern shore of Maryland and finding her way eventually to Philadelphia. A year later she returned to Maryland to guide members of her family north to freedom. She soon became one of the Railroad's most active "conductors," making 19 trips back to the South to facilitate escapes. Her physical prowess and courage were legendary, as were some of her less than orthodox methods for promoting escape. It is said she sometimes urged the fainthearted and weary to continue their trek to freedom by threatening them with a loaded revolver. Despite huge rewards offered for her capture, Tubman helped more than 300 slaves to escape. Many slaves strongly identified with the Israelites—the

FIGURE 7.2 Known as "the Moses of her people," Harriet
Tubman (1820–1913) escaped to the North in 1849, only to
return to the Southern states 19 times to lead other slaves
to freedom. During the Civil War, she served as a nurse,
laundress, and spy with the Unionist forces along the coast
of South Carolina. She was present at the battle of Fort
Wagner, depicted in the 1989 movie *Glory,* in which 1,500
Black soldiers lost their lives. Of that horrific battle she
recalls, "Then we saw de lightening, and that was de guns;
and then we heard de thunder, and that was de big guns;
and then we heard de rain falling, and that was de drops of
blood falling; and when we came to get in de crops, it was
dead men that we reaped." [From Hine (1993), p. 1179. I am
indebted to Ruby Mendenhall, who, as a graduate student in
Northwestern University's Human Development and Social
Policy Ph.D. program, wrote an outstanding course outline
on Black Women and American Public Policy, from which I
learned of Harriet Tubman's words regarding this Civil War
battle.] Reprinted with the permission of Art Resource.
The National Portrait Gallery, Smithsonian Institution/
Art Resource, New York.

chosen people, enslaved to their Egyptian captors. To that end, Tubman received a most generative Old Testament sobriquet. She came to be known as "the Moses of her people."

A second way that escaped slaves worked to emancipate their brothers and sisters was to write accounts of their lives as slaves. The slave narratives are among the most powerfully redemptive texts in all of American cultural history. Under the sponsorship of Northern abolitionists, many escaped slaves wrote vivid, autobiographical accounts of their years in captivity. The narratives served a prime moral and political purpose: to educate Whites about the evils of America's "peculiar institution" and to rally the readership around the cause of abolitionism. If these works were to be effective, therefore, the authors had to exhibit unimpeachable credibility. Their mission was to tell the truth about slavery as it really was, not to fashion an imaginative, self-reflective story.[23] Each narrative, therefore, was a scripted argument against slavery, though told as a story. To that end, most of the slave narratives followed a common pattern that was established early in the history of this literary form.

The published narrative would typically open up with an engraved portrait, signed by the narrator.[24] The title page would include, as an integral part of the title itself, the claim that the narrative was "written by himself" (or some close variant: "Written from a statement of Facts Made by Himself;" or "Written by a Friend, as Related to Him by Brother Jones," etc.). Following the title page, a handful of testimonials, typically written by eminent abolitionists or White editors, would attest to the truthfulness of the tale and integrity of the author. The actual story would then begin: "I was born in . . ." The author would specify a place but not a date of birth, since slaves were rarely told their birth dates. Next, the narrator provided a sketchy account of parentage, often involving a White father. The next character introduced was typically a cruel master, mistress, or overseer, with vivid accounts of beatings and brutality, often inflicted on women slaves. Following this, the author might introduce a contrasting, noble African American character—one especially hard-working slave who refused to be beaten. Although this heroic character might meet a cruel fate, he served to foreshadow the author's inevitable rebellion and escape.

Slaveholders let the slaves practice a Christian faith, but they refused to allow for education. They rightly feared that, if a large number of slaves should learn to read, they would soon rebel. Therefore, the standard slave narrative described the many obstacles to literacy that the protagonist faced. For some narratives, learning to read marked a turning point in the life of the protagonist. Literacy also symbolized the African American's legitimate standing in the human community, as a literate, "speaking subject" rather than a commodity to be bought and sold.[25] The narrative also provided descriptions of especially pious "Christian" slave owners, who turned out typically to be the cruelest of them all. Devout Christian slave owners were the worst because they truly believed they were doing God's good work on their plantations. The narrator painted a stark contrast between the "false" religion of many slave owners and the "true" religion of the slaves. Another standard account was that of the slave auction, complete with horrific scenes of distraught mothers clinging to their children as they are torn away. The narrative chronicled how the prospect of freedom evolved gradually in the protagonist's mind, beginning as a fantasy and ending in a detailed plan that typically involved deceptive schemes and life-and-death risks. The narrative ended with the protagonist's arrival in the free states, his or her warm reception from Quakers or other religious and political figures, and the assumption of a new last name to signify a new social identity as a free woman or man.

The most famous and influential slave narrative was written by Frederick Douglass and published in 1845. "I was born in Tuckahoe, near Hillsborough, and about twelve miles from Easton, in Talbot County, Maryland," Douglass begins.[26] Douglass was lucky to live in Maryland, given its proximity to the free North. To escape from the deep Southern states of Georgia and Mississippi had to be much more difficult. His mother was Harriet Bailey, a dark Negro slave. His father was a White man:

> He was admitted to be such by all I ever heard speak of my parentage. The opinion was also whispered that my master was my father; but of the correctness of this opinion, I know nothing; the means of knowing was withheld from me. My mother and I were separated when I was but an infant—before I knew her as my mother. It is a common custom, in the part of Maryland from which I ran away, to part children from their mothers at a very early age. Frequently, before the child has reached its twelfth month, its mother is taken away from it, and hired out on some farm a considerable distance off, and the child is placed under the care of an old woman, too old for field labor. For what this separation is done, I do not know, unless it be to hinder the development of the child's affection toward its mother, and to blunt and destroy the natural affection of the mother for the child. This is the inevitable result.[27]

The story begins with a trauma. Even before the protagonist has reached his first birthday, he is taken away from his mother and given over to a

Box 7.1. The Slave Narrative: An Outline

A. An engraved portrait, signed by the narrator.
B. A title page: *Narrative of the Life of . . . , written by Himself.*
C. Testimonials from White abolitionists (e.g., William Lloyd Garrison, Wendell Phillips) and/or editors or literary figures, attesting to the truthfulness of the narrative and the integrity of the narrator.
D. The actual story:
  1. "I was born in . . ." (the opening specifies where the slave was born but does not give a birth date, as slaves were rarely told their birth dates)
  2. Sketchy account of parentage (often, the father is suspected to be a White man—typically the slave owner or a relative of the slave owner)
  3. Description of a cruel master, mistress, or overseer; accounts of whippings
  4. An account of a rebellious slave who refuses to be whipped—a foreshadowing of the narrator's evolution toward autonomy
  5. Record of the barriers to literacy; efforts to learn to read and write
  6. Description of Christian slave owners, with a suggestion that their religious faith made them even more brutal and heartless
  7. Descriptions of amount and kinds of food and clothing provided for the slaves, the work required, the typical day or week or year
  8. Account of a slave auction—families ripped apart
  9. Failed attempts to escape, pursuit by men and dogs
  10. The successful escape, typically involving deception, trickery, daring exploits
  11. Warm reception in the North by Quakers or other religious/political officials
  12. Taking a new name; assumption of a new social identity as a free woman or man
  13. Reflections on slavery.
E. An appendix with documentary material, such as bills of sale or newspaper items. The appendix might also include sermons, poems, antislavery speeches, and appeals for funds or moral support in the battle against slavery.

Adapted from Olney (1985).

stranger. Douglass suggests that the result of this common practice is to strip away the bond of love between caregivers and their infants—yet another strategy from the White man to undermine a sense of human community and care among his Black chattel. The strategy is only partly successful, for Douglass's mother sneaks back to see her son four or five times during his childhood, late-night journeys that hold tremendous risk. Douglass remembers her devotion, keeps a caring image of her in his mind as he moves through life. Slave children are given very little to do. They are barely fed and given inadequate clothing, so they spend a great deal of time feeling hungry, cold, and bereft. The tedium is punctuated by occasional scenes of horror. As a child, Douglass witnesses the murder of a slave who refused to be beaten. The murderer is an overseer named Mr. Gore:

> His savage barbarity was equaled only by the consummate coolness with which he committed the grossest and most savage deeds upon the slaves under his charge. Mr. Gore once undertook to whip one of Colonel Lloyd's slaves, by the name of Demby. He had given Demby but few stripes, when, to get rid of the scourging, he ran and plunged himself into a creek, and stood there at the depth of his shoulders, refusing to come out. Mr. Gore told him that he would give him three calls, and that, if he did not come out at the third call, he would shoot him. The first call was given. Demby made no response, but stood his ground. The second and third calls were given with the same result. Mr. Gore then, without consultation or deliberation with any one, not even giving Demby an additional call, raised his musket to his face, taking deadly aim at his standing victim, and in an instant poor Demby was no more. His mangled body sank out of sight, and blood and brains marked the water where he had stood.[28]

As we have seen throughout this book, highly generative men and women often identify something early on in their lives that they believe gave them a special advantage. Something occurs in the early chapters of the life story to convince the protagonist that he or she is *chosen*. For young Frederick, the positive turn in fortune happens when he is sent to Baltimore to work for a family named the Aulds. His new mistress, Sophia Auld, has never had a slave before. At first she is kind and considerate, and even consents to teach Frederick his ABCs. When her husband learns this, he commands his wife to desist immediately, for "learning would spoil the best nigger in the world."[29] As Frederick witnesses Mr. Auld's outburst, he suddenly becomes aware of how powerful the gift of literacy is. From this point on, he is determined to learn how to read and write. Because he is given plenty to eat in his new Baltimore home, Frederick is able to trade food and other favors to White boys in town, if they will help him learn to read. Frederick's move to Baltimore provides his narrative with the key early advantage that distinguishes the protagonist from all those suffering others. The move consolidates a steadfast conviction, and it convinces Frederick, furthermore, that God has *chosen* him for something good and special:

Going to live in Baltimore laid the foundation, and opened the gateway, to all my subsequent prosperity. I have ever regarded it as the first plain manifestation of that kind providence which has ever since attended me, and marked my life with so many favors. I regarded the selection of myself as being somewhat remarkable. There were a number of slave children that might have been sent from the plantation to Baltimore. There were those younger, those older, and those of the same age. I was chosen from among them all, and was the first, last, and only choice.

I may be deemed superstitious, and even egotistical, in regarding this event as a special interposition of divine Providence in my favor. But I should be false to the earliest sentiments of my soul, if I suppressed the opinion. I prefer to be true to myself, even at the hazard of incurring the ridicule of others, rather than to be false, and incur my own abhorrence. From my earliest recollection, I date the entertainment of a deep conviction that slavery would not always be able to hold me within its foul embrace; and in the darkest hours of my career in slavery, this living word of faith and spirit of hope departed not from me, but remained like ministering angels to cheer me through the gloom.[30]

Frederick spends 7 years with the Aulds. During his time in Baltimore, he learns to read and write. When he is sent back to the plantation, his original master finds Frederick to be much too independent and uppity for a slave's own good. He sends the teenaged boy to live for a year with a man named Covey, who is paid to "break young slaves in." Covey's brutal discipline almost works. After 6 months, Frederick is completely demoralized: "I was broken in body, soul, and spirit."[31] But in a key turning point scene, Frederick fights back one day after Covey beats him. For hours, they exchange blows. Striking a White man could bring the penalty of death in Maryland, but Covey is ashamed to admit that a slave hit him back. The admission would ruin his reputation as the best "nigger-breaker" in the region. "The battle with Covey was the turning-point in my career as a slave," Douglass writes. "It rekindled the few expiring embers of freedom, and revived within me a sense of my own manhood."[32] The redemptive sequence symbolized for him "a glorious resurrection from the tomb of slavery, to the heaven of freedom." "I now resolved that, however long I might remain a slave in form, the day had passed forever when I could be a slave in fact," he writes.[33]

It is still 4 more years before Frederick makes his escape. In the intervening time, he establishes close friendships with many slaves. He organizes

FIGURE 7.3 Frederick Douglass (1818–1895) escaped to
the free North in 1838 and
wrote a famous narrative of
his life as a slave. Along with
other narratives written by
escaped slaves and their abolitionist sponsors, Douglass's
account helped to mobilize
Northern sentiment against
the American institution of
slavery. As an autobiographical document, the account expresses psychological themes
often found in the life narratives of highly generative
American adults—such as an
early sense of being chosen,
an early awareness of the suffering of others, and redemptive turning points. Reprinted
with the permission of Art
Resource. The National Portrait Gallery, Smithsonian
Institution/Art Resource,
New York.

secret schools. On Sundays he teaches slaves how to read. "Their minds had
been starved by their cruel masters," he writes. "I taught them, because it was
the delight of my soul to be doing something that looked like bettering the
condition of my race."[34] He teams up with a small group of slaves to make an
escape plan, but on the night they are to make their break, they are betrayed
by an informant. His fellow conspirators are sold off to other plantations, but
by a lucky break Frederick ends up being sent back to Baltimore to learn a
trade. Under a new master, he negotiates a contract whereby he is free to provide for his own needs and find his own work so long as he gives over to his
master virtually his entire pay every week. Financially, the deal is a bad one for
Frederick, but it gives him the autonomy he needs to work out more clearly a
successful escape plan. Finally, "on the third day of September, 1838, I left my
chains, and succeeded in reaching New York, without the slightest interrup-

tion of any kind. How I did so,—what means I adopted,—what direction I traveled, and by what mode of conveyance—I must leave unexplained," Douglass writes, lest he compromise the efforts of those he has left behind.[35]

Literary scholars have argued that the slave narratives initiated a uniquely African American literary tradition.[36] As Henry Louis Gates, Jr., puts it, "The narratives of ex-slaves are, for the literary critic, the very generic foundation which most subsequent Afro-American fictional and nonfictional narrative forms extended, refigured, and troped."[37] Although the slave narratives were originally written to expose the horrors of slavery, they also expressed images and themes that have been incorporated and reworked ever since in Black autobiography, fiction, music, drama, and the cinema. Among the most important of these literary elements are a few that figure centrally in my conception of the redemptive self—in particular, the very theme of redemption itself, the sense of being chosen, and the early awareness of the suffering of others.

The slave narratives are powerful stories of the deliverance from bondage to freedom—what I described in chapter 1 as the redemptive move of emancipation. This same move is a dominant motif in the most celebrated Black autobiographies of the 20th century, such as Richard Wright's *Black Boy,* Maya Angelou's *I Know Why the Caged Bird Sings,* and *The Autobiography of Malcolm X.* Although the protagonists of these stories are not literally enslaved, their growth and development over time involve many of the social and psychological dynamics that Frederick Douglass himself knew and worked through. The redemptive move in these life narratives is often visualized as *vertical,* as Booker T. Washington suggested in his autobiography, *Up From Slavery*—up from the plantation to the town, up from the South to the North, out from under oppression's thumb and struggling to move up in a society that still wants to hold you down. Herbert Leibowitz writes that African American autobiographies often present "remarkable portraits of men and women under siege who create dynamic identities despite social handicaps that would have stopped less resolute persons in their tracks." "The dominant pattern in these autobiographies, following the Augustinian model," he goes on to explain, "is the triumphant reversal—from slavery to freedom, ignorance to understanding, follower to leader, and, sometimes, criminality to spirituality."[38]

The authors of the slave narratives often drew upon Christianity as a source for their redemptive tales. The reasons for this are threefold. First, White abolitionists, who often assisted in the production and publication of the slave narratives, typically grounded their convictions in their Christian faith. Second, Christian images and themes resonated with the White readership for these stories. Third, Christianity had taken strong hold among the slaves themselves. The slaves embraced Christianity as a balm for their grievous wounds, a source of comfort amid relentless distress. In Christianity, furthermore, they found inspiration for quiet resistance and for hope that somehow, someway, they would eventually be delivered from their oppression.[39] The Black church has offered sustenance and inspiration for African Americans ever since. And Christianity has provided the African American community with some of its most powerful messages of spiritual, political, economic, and social redemption. Indeed, redemptive imagery is at the heart of one of the most stirring passages of African American public rhetoric ever crafted:

> I have a dream that one day on the red hills of Georgia the sons of former slaves and the sons of former slave owners will be able to sit down together at the table of brotherhood. . . . I have a dream that one day the state of Alabama, whose governor's lips are presently dripping with the words of interposition and nullification, will be transformed into a situation where little Black boys and Black girls will be able to join hands with little White boys and White girls and walk together as sisters and brothers. . . . I have a dream that one day every valley shall be exalted, every hill and mountain shall be made low, the rough places will be made plains, and the crooked places will be made straight, and the glory of the Lord shall be revealed, and all flesh shall see it together.[40]

Like the life stories of highly generative adults, the early chapters of the slave narratives typically juxtapose accounts of the suffering of others (as well as the self's suffering) with a sense that the protagonist of the story enjoys an inherent advantage—is chosen or called for a special destiny. Douglass's accounts of the beatings he observed as a child are set next to his telling of how he came to believe in "a special interposition of divine Providence in my favor."[41] It makes sense that those slaves, like Douglass, who had escaped to the North would indeed come to see their own lives, in retrospect, as having been blessed. Compared to those they left behind, they were surely the fortunate ones. Indeed, one of the earliest and most influential slave narratives, published in 1789, was written by one Olaudah Equiano—a name that means "one favored."[42]

But in a more communal sense, African American slaves identified themselves as a chosen people, like the enslaved Israelites in the book of Exodus. Like the Israelites crossing the Red Sea, and like the Puritans crossing the Atlantic, they were on a *pilgrimage*. Writes one scholar, "The central metaphor of the Black spiritual autobiographer of the late 18th and early 19th centuries might be summarized as: 'I am as Mr. Christian [of *Pilgrim's Progress*] was, a spiritual pilgrim in an unredeemed world.'[43] They also identified with Jesus, whose suffering was necessary if the world was to be redeemed. Although some slaves might be more favored than others, the Black slaves *as a people* were chosen for a special destiny, many believed, as one scholar puts it: "African American Christians believed they were the chosen people, not because they were Black, nor because they suffered, but because their history fit the pattern of salvation revealed to them in the Bible. They saw themselves in Christ, the suffering servant. Their lives modeled the paradoxes of the gospel: in weakness lies strength, in loss, gain, in death, life."[44]

Early Danger and the Opponent

Beyond those themes that are central to the redemptive self, the slave narratives express many other images and motifs that have assumed prominence in African American literary traditions. Two of them are especially noteworthy for their psychological importance in adult life stories. I call them (a) *early danger* and (b) *the opponent.*

The eminent psychologist Jerome Bruner wrote that the prospect of danger often gives stories their narrative thrust and direction.[45] European folktales like "Cinderella" and "Snow White and the Seven Dwarfs" often begin in innocence and goodness, but the plot thickens with the introduction of some kind of threat to the goals or well-being of the protagonist. The narrative movement is from initial safety to subsequent danger. By contrast, a comprehensive study of African American folktales concluded that danger emerges as a force at the very beginning of these stories.[46] Traditional folktales told by American Blacks tend to begin with the narrative assumption that life is tough and unfair. Protagonists are born into a world that is immediately perceived to be untrustworthy. The narrative movement is from immediate danger to some kind of response on the part of the protagonist to this threatening or challenging environment.

Similarly, it is not uncommon for middle-class White Americans to romanticize their early years and describe the early chapters of their life stories in glowing and innocent terms. There is a "once upon a time, in a faraway place" quality to many of these stories—like the opening of European fairy tales. By contrast, the slave narratives introduce the opposite form. In the beginning, there is trouble. Before he reached his first birthday, Frederick Douglass was ripped away from his mother. The protagonist knows early on that the world is a very threatening place. In a famous essay called "The

White Negro," Norman Mailer writes, "Any Negro who wishes to live must live with danger from his first day, and no experience can ever be casual to him."[47]

Early danger is a staple in African American autobiography. Richard Wright's *Black Boy* begins with a cataclysmic event: The 4-year-old boy sets his house afire and is viciously whipped by his mother. In *The Autobiography of Malcolm X*, the hero is surrounded by danger. He is born into a family of eight children in Omaha, Nebraska. He knows poverty, hunger, and deprivation from an early age. Klansmen and other bigots harass his family, burn down his house, and eventually murder his father, a Baptist preacher. Malcolm and his brothers are separated and farmed out to relatives and friends. His mother suffers a mental breakdown.[48]

In life stories like these, the legacy of early danger lives on, even if the protagonist rises to success and fame. More generally, African American autobiographies speak eloquently of the need to be vigilant in a world that can never fully be trusted. Very few Whites fully understand this sense of wariness. In a *New York Times* interview, Houston A. Baker, Jr.—a distinguished professor of African American studies—reflected on the sense in which even the most accomplished Black women and men in American society never lose the edge: "It's not that White academics don't work extraordinarily hard," Baker said. "But what they have that I lack is a sense of leisure, an *absence of endangerment,* a look of being unconcerned that at any moment they could die."[49]

In reading through the interviews of African American men and women in our study of generativity in Black and White, I was struck by how often the theme of early danger arose—both for highly generative and less generative Black adults. One indication of this tendency was displayed in each participant's description of the single earliest scene in his or her life story. Approximately 60% of the earliest memories from African American participants involved death, physical injury, violent behavior, or some other threatening event that evoked the protagonist's fear.[50] Included among these episodes are accounts of being bitten by a dog, getting spanked, receiving an electrical shock, experiencing a nightmare, learning that an aunt has died, and seeing father pull a gun on the mother. With a few exceptions (e.g., the gun incident), the events tend not to be traumatic in and of themselves; nor are they really surprising as early memories. What is perhaps surprising, though, is that so *many*—well over half—of the earliest memories signal some form of danger.

Early danger is also apparent in the participants' overall description of the "first chapter" in their life story, in response to the opening section of our life-story interview. Again, a strong majority of African American adults in the sample introduced danger into their accounts at the very beginning of the interview. Recall Elliot Washington's opening from chapter 1: "In early childhood my father was dead; he died before I was born." Philip Jordan, a 47-year-old computer technician, began with an account of finding his father dead on the floor. Jerome Johnson, the former police chief, began by saying, "I was a Depression baby, so we went through some very difficult times, when there was, you know, no food and there was no money available." A highly generative Black woman who has enjoyed considerable success in both work and family life, Judy Savitch began this way: "Let's start with early childhood, and first I'm gonna say there was a lot of confusion in my life." Jocelyn March is a highly generative single mother who has virtually nothing to say about her childhood years. She began instead with adolescence: "When I was a teenager, my life was chaos, confused all the time, no sense of direction, no one had a purpose, no one in the family had any goals." Yet another participant emphasized how she was "bullied" as a child. And another stated he was "always nervous as a child" and worried that his father would beat him. And yet another listed a long litany of mishaps and danger. Sonny Clay—a 35-year-old, unmarried man, scoring very high in generativity—is an ebullient conversationalist who seemed to revel in the dangers he had known:

> When I was a child, I was more or less accident-prone. The first injury I recall was I got chewed up by a dog at age 13, and it was traumatic. Okay, I made it through that. The following summer, I got hit by a car. I survived that. About 6 months after being hit by a car, I hit a tree and broke my collarbone. After that, I must have been 15, one of my best friends got killed. That was June of 1976. In November of 76—1976 was a year when a lot of crisis situations happened to me—my father, uh well, August of 1976 I got shot in the eye and [temporarily] lost my eyesight. November of 1976 my father passed away. In 1976 I had a little brother being born in December. This was a crucial year in my life that I won't forget. Okay. I survive all of that, that trauma. So I started working and all the stuff, you know, living good, but still it put a lot on my mind.

Sonny's account suggests that an early awareness that the world is a very dangerous place can be perceived to leave a psychological legacy with the protagonist: "It put a lot on my mind." Very few participants in our study described as many dangerous situations in early life as did Sonny. Yet many accounts were noteworthy for how *quickly* the theme of danger was introduced into the story. Nonetheless, the stories are not completely given over to negative events, as is clear in the cases of Elliot Washington and Jerome Johnson. The life stories are not *all* about danger, or even primarily about danger or threat. The respondents described a wide range of experiences through the narratives. The point instead is that the stories tend to *begin* with danger. A narrative context is established early on: The world is not completely trustworthy. As I emphasized in chapter 3, life-narrative accounts reflect both what has really happened in people's lives and the interpretive frames that people commonly use to make sense of experience. In that most of the African American participants in our study grew up in working-class or impoverished families, it should not be surprising that early scenes of deprivation and threat might be recalled. But a story's beginning also indicates how the person today reconstructs and approaches life overall. Even after they have enjoyed considerable success as adults, many African Americans may continue to underscore the precariousness of human life.

Going back to Aristotle's *Poetics*, various theories of narrative suggest that story plots are often propelled by the protagonist's confrontation with an *opponent*—an enemy or force that stands in the way of the hero's goal striving.[51] The opposition between the good protagonist and an evil other is especially stark in African American literature, going back to the slave narratives. The reasons are clear. The slave owners, the overseers, the entire system of American slavery—these constituted the evil and overpowering antagonist. One expert on slave narratives puts it this way: "One reason why early Black autobiography deals as often as it does in melodramatic extremes and diametrical opposites is due to this perception of America as bereft of a sense of the natural order of things and of the differences between things, so blinded had Whites become because of their bigotry, greed, and fear."[52] The stark contrast between protagonist and opponent is also a central idea in African American folktales. The author of a comprehensive study of these stories observes, "The characters find themselves almost in perpetual opposition; we watch how antagonists throw themselves, enthusiastically and playfully, into the eternal dramas pitting humans against animals, men against women, master against slave, God against the devil."[53]

In our study of generativity in Black and White, the life-story interviews of African American adults were noteworthy for their clear identification of an opponent with whom the protagonist does battle. Many of the participants were quick to point to a force, factor, organization, or person who represents in their life the bad, sinful, evil, destructive, or dangerous things in the world—or in the self—against which the (good) protagonist fights. In some cases, the opponent was on the outside, as in the many cases in which authors identified the prime antagonist to be "the street." In other cases, the opponent was imagined as inside the self—an internalized enemy represented as a personal failing, a bad aspect of the self, a force within. While some opponents grew out of the early danger in life identified by many participants, other opponents appeared much later in the story or had nothing to do with the original childhood dangers. The clear identification of a struggle between a protagonist and an opponent gave many of these life stories—for both highly generative and less generative Black adults—a strong narrative thrust and clear story line.

The most common opponent identified in these life stories was "the street." This rich term connoted a wide range of temptations and dangers associated with urban street life—alcohol abuse, drugs, prostitution, crime, and violence. At the same time, "the street" carried many positive meanings, such as spontaneous socializing, music, dance, and intense relationships with others. As such, the street served as an especially alluring and dangerous enemy in the minds of many of our respondents—a source of strong ambivalence. Another general, though less complex, opponent was racial prejudice. Many respondents explicitly identified racial prejudice as a major obstacle in their life striving. While some viewed the enemy to be a large societal system, others were more concrete, taking aim at "White people in general," "certain White women," or "racist people." When asked to identify the central theme in her life story, one less generative participant identified "prejudice and people controlling other people," and she provided many accounts of discrimination suffered at the hands of Whites. Another respondent identified his opponent in life as "Jewish people as a group," this despite the fact that his lifelong best friend was a Jew.

While a number of African American adults in our study identified an opponent in the outside environment, a few viewed the antagonist as within. A 41-year-old benefits counselor and mother of one, Lillian Downes claimed she struggled regularly with "the demons that come up and haunt me," as she called them. She described the "demons" as those aspects of her self that stem from failures she experienced in romantic relationships. In adolescence, Lillian needed to move away from home to escape these demons, so that she could, she said, "come into my own." The implicit struggle is between the good, true, inner self—like that described by Emerson and the self-help gurus in chapter 5—and internal self-objects or representations that work against her true nature. In a similar manner, Jocelyn March set up a clear battle between the true self and the false self. She described the false self as the cool conformist who won social prestige but never related intimately to others. In her earliest memory, Jocelyn provided an early model of the false self—a popular (and White) girl in her elementary school class who proved to be an unreliable friend. She castigated herself afterward for ever trying to imitate and be accepted by the popular girl. The false self reached its zenith in the narrative during adolescence, when Jocelyn cultivated a "cool" persona on the street. She gained social acceptance from gang members and other peers because she was so cool and mysterious. Although this social strategy carried with it the incalculable advantage of assuring her survival in a dangerous social world, Jocelyn looked back on adolescence as a time in which her perennial opponent—the false self—dominated her life: "I think myself, that wasn't even me. I was never there any of those years. It was not me. It was like I had given another person the opportunity to occupy my body and carry me through life, and it worked."

In their personal battles against a wide range of opponents, the African American adults in our sample mobilized resources and marshaled forces of many different kinds. Although they had opponents, they also had many allies. The traditional Euro-American emphasis on rugged individualism seems tempered in these stories. The protagonists often enjoy considerable support from a community of family, friends, and institutions that are allied with them against the opponents of life. Mothers and grandmothers were held in highest regard as allies in the struggles of life. Religion, too, played a major role. For both highly generative and less generative African American adults in our study, religious faith was described as an invaluable resource. For some participants, religion provided a social network that brought with it friends and social support. For others, it provided a forum for expressing their talents, as in singing in the church choir, or opportunities for being of service to others. For still other participants, religion translated into daily rituals such as prayer and meditation. For virtually all of the participants, though, religious faith was invoked as a strong ally in the battle against opponents and a safe haven in the face of danger. Indeed, four of the participants remarked that God or spiritual forces *literally* saved their lives. To the extent that the participants viewed life as a morality tale, religious faith was always cast on the side of the protagonist and against the opponent, providing comfort, inspiration, guidance, and strength.

In sum, the slave narratives introduced an African American literary tradition that has given voice to a set of psychological themes that also figure prominently in the life stories of the Black adults who participated in our study of generativity (and narrative identity) in Black and White. The most powerful of all the themes is redemption. The slave narratives, like the life stories of highly generative Black adults, are extraordinarily redemptive, reg-

---

Box 7.2. *Psychological Themes in Slave Narratives
and in African American Autobiographies*

Themes of the redemptive self that figure prominently in slave narratives, in classic
African American autobiographies, and in the life stories of highly generative
African American adults at midlife:

- Early advantage: sense of being chosen for a special destiny
- Suffering of others: sensitivity to pain and oppression of other people
- Redemption: emancipation, enlightenment, upward social mobility

Other psychological themes from slave narratives and classic African American
autobiographies that are frequently expressed in the life stories of midlife African
American adults, both highly generative and less generative:

- Early danger: opening scenes of threat; the world cannot be trusted
- The opponent: identification of a clear antagonist; good versus evil

---

ularly employing the discourses of emancipation, enlightenment, and upward social mobility. Relatedly, these stories affirm the protagonist's early
concern for the suffering of others and the sense that he or she had been chosen early on for a special destiny. These three themes—redemption, suffering of others, and chosenness (early advantage)—have been identified again
and again in this book as parts of the thematic core of the redemptive self, a
life-story form that is especially characteristic of highly generative American
adults, both Black and White.

In addition, the literary tradition that was spawned by the slave narratives
features two life-narrative themes that appear to be especially central in African American narrative identity, and less common among Whites. In our
research, the life stories of African American adults at midlife, those both
high and low on generativity, often portray early scenes and chapters that are
fraught with danger. And they often feature a stark contrast between the
good protagonist and a strong opponent. These stories suggest that no
matter how accomplished and beloved the protagonist feels, he or she still
harbors a lingering sense that this world is not completely secure and that
there are many tough battles still to be fought. The war is between the good
inner self and the enemy forces that seek to keep the self *down* or lead it
astray. Or, as Jerome Johnson's fifth-grade teacher put it, the world presents
you with an epic contest between "the construction team and the destruction team" in life. And you have to pick a side.

Race in America: The Future

At the beginning of the 21st century, newspaper articles were reporting that African Americans were no longer the largest racial, or ethnic, "minority group" in the United States. The 2000 census showed that Hispanics now outnumber Blacks, for the first time in our history. Asian Americans are also increasing in number, and many people now identify themselves as "mixed race." America is no longer simply Black and White; it is increasingly multiracial, multicultural.

Americans seem to express two very different responses to this increasing diversity. The first is to deny it, or to argue that it no longer matters. People are people. Racial and ethnic categories are passé. The second response is to celebrate the diversity. Each group is different and special. No single culture encompasses us all. Each of these two general responses contains a great deal of complexity and contradiction within it. Each can be expressed in both positive and very negative ways. And each has a special resonance for thinking about narrative identity among Black and among White Americans today.

The concept of racelessness—the idea that race no longer matters—has adherents across the political spectrum. Many liberals have traditionally argued that racial categories are but excuses for discrimination. If we could just get beyond the color of people's skin, they seem to suggest, we would enjoy a more egalitarian and just society. In arguing against affirmative action and other programs that are perceived to benefit minority groups, conservatives have often sounded a similar tune. College admissions officers, for example, should ignore race and focus exclusively on a candidate's "merit," many argue. Both sides can find scientific "support" for their views from the biologists, who usually argue that race is not a biologically meaningful category, anyway. As Werner Sollors, a distinguished professor of African American studies, recently put it, "There's no biological concept of race that any [reputable] scientist believes in. There's only racism."[54]

That American society may one day transcend race is an implication that could be drawn from a number of observations being made today. For example, a recent study of interracial love and intimacy shows a sixfold increase in Black-White marriages between 1960 and 2000.[55] Increasing numbers of young people, furthermore, appear to cross racial lines in their friendships and dating. Interviewed about his close friendship with an African American boy, one White teenager said, "We think just alike, act just alike and dress just alike. Robert and the other [Black] people I hang with don't care that I'm White."[56] Popular culture—from music to sports to television commercials—is breaking down many racial barriers. Many White teenagers enjoy rap and other music commonly performed by Black artists. White sports fans wear the jerseys of their favorite Black basketball stars and running backs. Advertisers showcase multiracial images and messages to sell products to people united in their common patterns of consumption—a big tent under which we can all enjoy Kentucky Fried Chicken and drive the sexiest SUVs. According to one recent analysis, popular culture may be moving America toward a raceless future, creating a new transracial American Dream.[57]

At the same time, many people of color recoil at the prospect of a transracial future. If the United States is to be a truly diverse society, they suggest, it should celebrate differences rather than subordinate them to a homogenized megaculture. In an effort to explore and affirm cultural differences, American universities have developed interdisciplinary programs in African American, Asian American, and Latino/Latina studies. Rather than look to a transracial future, these programs aim to give full expression to the unique historical, literary, religious, scientific, and cultural experience of a particular people. Racelessness goes completely against this grain. To this end, when a White person tells a Black person that he never even thinks of the latter as Black ("I just see you as a person"), the comment may be heard as deeply disrespectful. It suggests that Black is not even worth seeing, or that to see a person as Black is automatically demeaning. The implicit assumption behind the comment is that since Black could not possibly be beautiful, it is best to eliminate race as a characteristic. But many African Americans see race as a deep vessel of history and culture. To ignore race, then, may be tantamount to disregarding a heritage that is at the very heart of African American identity.

While much of Western society looks mainly to Europe for its values and orientation to life, Black Americans may look to Africa to find a different point of view. A number of Black scholars argue for the validity of *Afrocentric* philosophies, psychologies, and modes of inquiry.[58] Afrocentric approaches celebrate synthesis over analysis, harmony over discord, the community over the individual, and subjective emotional experience over cool Eurocentric rationality. In his study of race in America, David Shipler describes a similar set of distinctions, but in more down-to-earth terms: "Many African Americans describe 'black culture' with definitions of contrast: black is better than white in one or another dimension, such as the inventiveness of humor, the closeness of family, the honesty of friendship, the spontaneity of feeling, the dignity of struggle, the sexuality of love, the rootedness of reality, and the suffering of the streets."[59] Whether or not one buys into these generalizations, it is clear that to scoff at or disregard people's cultural categories is very much like my refusing to believe, at age 17, that a Black person could be prejudiced.

As multicolored as America may be today, the distinction between Black and White still summons forth our most troubling history and our most vexing cultural dilemmas. America is still divided between Black and White; all other distinctions are, in my opinion, secondary. For this reason, I have focused my attention in this chapter on patterns of generativity and narrative identity among Black (and White) American adults in their midlife years. In our survey research, African American adults appeared to be as generative as, or slightly more generative than, their Euro-American counterparts. For both Whites and Blacks, high levels of generativity bring the same psychological and social benefits—better mental health, more generative patterns of parenting, more supportive relationships with family members and friends, and higher levels of religious and political involvement.

In making narrative sense of their own lives, African American adults at midlife draw upon their own personal experiences and a wide range of cultural resources and influences. In form and content, furthermore, their stories seem to draw implicitly on a rich African American literary tradition, some of whose origins lie in the autobiographies of emancipation and uplift written by escaped slaves in the 18th and 19th centuries. Among the psychological themes that distinguish these narratives from common Eurocentric forms are the emphasis on early danger in life and the clear identification of the life opponent. African American life stories often suggest that the world cannot be fully trusted and that the protagonist must be ever ready to do battle with a rival force that aims to hold down the good inner self, or to lead it astray. Like the slave narratives, furthermore, the narrative identities of highly generative Black adults at midlife are striking exemplifications of the redemptive self. W. E. B. Du Bois was surely right when he said that America would not be America without its Black citizens. In their robust portrayal of the redemptive self, the narrative identities of highly generative African American adults are as profoundly *American* as any life stories you will ever see.

Eight

CONTAMINATED PLOTS,
VICIOUS CIRCLES

For Tanya Williams, it seems that good things almost always turn bad.[1] Even the best thing that ever happened worked out that way. "Tell me about the best thing that ever happened in your life," the interviewer asks Tanya. Tanya's life-story high point is the birth of her first child. Tanya is 21 years old when the child is born. She is ready to be a mother. The delivery is perfect. The baby is beautiful. This is a happy story, the interviewer assumes, like the many "first births" we have heard. Among midlife American adults, the birth of one's first child is probably the single most commonly told life-story high point. And so it is for Tanya. But Tanya does not end the telling with the baby's birth. Instead, she immediately flashes forward 3 years: "The baby's father was killed, you know." Stabbed in the back five times, found dead in a motel room. Tanya did not *have* to tell the story this way. She did not have to end her account of the happiest moment in her life with the death of the baby's father. But that is how she thinks of the sequence. That is *the story* as she conceives it and feels it, a story that reinforces her belief that "in general good things do not happen to me." In truth, good things *do* happen in Tanya's life story, but often they are later ruined by bad things.

We were interviewing Tanya because she scored so *low* on our self-report measures of generativity. She is one of the many midlife American adults we have interviewed who scores in the low-generativity range, indicating that they do not feel that they are exerting a positive impact on future generations. To this point in my book, these individuals have lurked in the background. Theirs are the life stories to which we may contrast the redemptive narratives provided by Elliot Washington (chapter 1), Deborah Feldman (chapter 2), Jerome Johnson (chapter 7), and other highly generative American adults at midlife.[2] Many low-generativity individuals are simply not very involved in the kinds of activities that we associate with adult generativity: raising children, assuming leadership roles, mentoring and helping young people, getting involved in civic or religious organizations, and so on. They say that they have little desire to have a positive impact on the next generation. Others, like Tanya, are somewhat involved but feel that their efforts are failures.

Tanya's generative efforts are focused mainly on her children; she is a mother of four. She has also occasionally filled in as a substitute Sunday school teacher at her church. But her very low scores on generativity scales suggest that she does not feel that her generative efforts are effective or satisfying. Like many adults who score in the extremely low range of generativity, furthermore, Tanya shows relatively high scores on measures of anxiety and depression. She has good reason to feel anxious and depressed. Money is very tight; she and her family have been on and off public assistance for a number of years. Although she is technically married, she receives no financial support from her husband, for he is in prison. Tanya has battled alcohol and abusive men for much of her life. She has struggled with so many problems and faced so many obstacles to happiness that she feels she can make *no progress* in her life. She cannot sustain a forward life movement. "I'm 41 years old, but I still feel kind of lost," Tanya says. "I know what to do when I get up every day, but do I really know where I am going?"

It was not always this way. Tanya's life story begins in a promising manner. She recalls a happy childhood in a working-class, racially integrated neighborhood. Her mother loves her. Her sister and she stay up late at night telling ghost stories. She learns to ride a bike. Things begin to take a negative turn around the time of puberty. In junior high school, she discovers she has a "mischievous streak," like her father. "They tended to tell me that I was like my father, which caused me a lot of problems." As she tells it, she inherits her father's "love of the street." Like him, she embarks on a very rough and dangerous life in her early teenage years. It is as if she has no choice in the matter. She must live out his destiny. By age 13, she is drinking. By age 15, she is experimenting with drugs.

The pattern established on a large scale for the opening chapters of Tanya's life story is repeated again and again in individual story scenes. Things typically begin well in many scenes, as indeed her life begins well with a happy childhood. But they eventually turn bad, as when puberty ushers in her love of the street. The characteristic narrative movement that Tanya repeatedly describes is what I call a *contamination sequence*.[3] In a contamination sequence, a very good or emotionally positive life-narrative scene (or a series of scenes) is followed immediately by a very bad or emotionally negative outcome. The bad ruins, spoils, sullies, or contaminates the good that precedes it. A contamination sequence is the opposite of a redemption sequence. In our research, contamination sequences are not as commonly told in life-narrative accounts as redemption sequences. But most life stories contain at least one strong contamination sequence. Unfortunately, Tanya's story contains many.

In one contamination sequence, Tanya tells of the happiness she felt in her late 20s when she marries a man who, she is convinced, loves her dearly. But once her husband proves sexually unfaithful, life deteriorates rapidly. Tanya becomes depressed and angry. She drinks more and becomes more heavily involved in drugs. Soon she is selling drugs to support her habit. Her anxieties mount as she now fears she will be busted by the police. Thieves break into her apartment and steal her money. With the pressure building, she becomes distraught one evening and calls a "stress line." She tells the person on the phone, "Please, someone come and help me with my daughter before I kill her." As Tanya tells the story years later, the authorities arrive shortly after her call and take her daughter away. Astonishingly, she is surprised even today that the authorities believed her daughter was in danger. (What else were they to believe?) Her threat to kill her daughter was "simply a manner of speaking," she maintains. She did not mean to be taken literally. (Eventually, her daughter is returned to her care.)

The contamination form is equally apparent, if less dramatic, in Tanya's account of an important scene from adolescence. Here she describes her triumphant graduation from eighth grade. "That was something I achieved on my own, and I felt very proud." Still, what follows immediately in her account is failure: "That was the last time I walked across the stage," she remarks. After graduating, Tanya becomes, in her words, "the black sheep in the family."

In another contamination sequence, Tanya returns to problems with men. Now she is in her early 30s, still married to the man who cheated on her. Trapped in what she sees as an abusive marriage, Tanya takes up with a much younger man. With Marvin, she finds comfort and excitement. Marvin provides Tanya with the love and the respect that she feels she has always deserved, and never received, from men. But Marvin sells drugs for a living, and Tanya knows that this line of work will lead to ruin. She and Marvin's mother convince him to quit selling and look for a respectable job. Marvin agrees to turn his life around. He is to start a new job on Monday. Marvin promises to call Tanya late Saturday night, after he returns from a party. The call comes instead from one of Tanya's friends. Marvin got into a fight at the party and has been seriously injured. He is in the hospital, fighting for his life.

Marvin dies in the hospital, now the second dead lover in Tanya's life story. The point of greatest contamination in the story, however, occurs just before Marvin dies. The account is hard to believe, but Tanya insists it is true. Marvin is in and out of consciousness for two days. Tanya refuses to visit him in the hospital. After all, she is still a married woman, and she does not want her husband to learn of her affair with Marvin. However, a few of Tanya's girlfriends know of the affair, and they urge her to visit Marvin. Maybe her presence can help him to recover. Tanya agrees to go to him. When she enters the hospital room, the first things she sees are two enlarged photos, "blown up about as big as his window." The photos show Tanya, lying on satin sheets in her own bed. Apparently, Marvin had taken these photos of Tanya during a secret rendezvous. Marvin gave the photos to his mother, who has known about the affair all along. Marvin's mother had them enlarged, and she has now tacked these two photos up on the wall of Marvin's hospital room! Tanya thinks the photos are there to taunt her, but Marvin's mother, who seems nearly delirious, claims she hung them up to rally her son, to cheer him up and out of his dying state. The photos have been hanging on the wall for two days. Everybody has seen them. Tanya feels "stripped." She is humiliated and exposed as an unfaithful wife. Word of the photos reaches her husband, and he is enraged. And then Marvin dies. "He was the best one I ever had, and I'll never have him back," says Tanya. "I loved him. I find that when I care a lot about someone that they leave me, or they die, or someone else takes them away."

The contamination pattern plays itself out in an early memory, too. In a bizarre scene from childhood, Tanya and her sister are playing with frogs under an apple tree. They are happy and carefree. But a storm is brewing, so they run into the house. Lightning hits the tree and splits it in half. They return after the storm to find the frogs "turned into slime" by the lightning. After relating this event in her interview, Tanya moves directly into an account of how the White kids in her neighborhood "used to tease us and call us crispy critters," presumably for the dark color of her and her siblings' skin. Like the frogs, Tanya has been burned to a crisp. She is Black, but, more important, she will turn out to be the black sheep in her family. Puberty was like the lightning that burned her soul and made her bad. She cannot undo what fiery nature has wrought. Instead, she is doomed to repeat the contamination sequence again and again. As a result of the repetition of violence, humiliation, and betrayal, Tanya today feels empty and heartless at her core. In a chilling self-commentary, she admits, "I know of some of the events to make me come to this point. But I really think there's something else deep inside, that maybe I don't even know myself, that really makes me feel that I don't care. When I say I don't care, I'm talking about I don't care. I really don't care about things. I'm only doing what I have to do. I'm alive, so I have to live."

Contamination and Stagnation

In everyday talk, an English expression that captures well the meaning of a contamination sequence is "a fall from grace." The allusion is to two well-known ancient stories. The first is Lucifer's fall from paradise. Originally an ally of God, Lucifer is cast out of heaven for insubordination. His movement is depicted as literally a "fall"—from heaven above to the underworld below. The second tale is from the book of Genesis. In the beginning of their life stories, Adam and Eve enjoy the perfect world that God has provided for them. Once they disobey the Creator, however, they are thrown out of their paradise, as well, and left to fend for themselves in a hostile environment. For the first humans in Genesis, the story begins in happiness, goodness, and innocence, but sin becomes the ultimate contamination. Once sin enters the story, furthermore, there seems no getting back to the original goodness. Innocence lost is lost forever. Human actors seem doomed throughout the Old Testament to repeat their contaminations again and again. One step forward, two steps back. Around and around. Forty years wandering were the Israelites, and getting nowhere—lost like Tanya in the wilderness.

Contamination sequences are not simply bad happenings in a person's life. There are plenty of bad occurrences—some worse than others. But contamination sequences are a special category of negative life experiences. In contamination, there first exists something that is very, very good. The protagonist of the story tastes the sweetness of life; enjoys the goodness; experiences the beauty, the truth, the excitement, the wonder. And then—and often quite suddenly—it is all lost. Spoiled. Ruined. The turn toward contamination is especially devastating because that which preceded the onset of the bad was itself so good. The contrast can be almost unbearable.

It is virtually impossible to be 30 years old or more and not own at least one contamination sequence in your life story. No period of the life course, furthermore, seems immune from the possibilities of contamination. Say you build a model airplane, take it to class for "show and tell," and the class bully breaks it in half. Say you are deeply in love with the perfect man or woman, and then your lover dumps you. Say you win a high honor in your

FIGURE 8.1 Contamination: a fall from grace. William Blake depicts one of the most famous stories of contamination in Western literature: the temptation of Eve. Once Eve succumbs and convinces her husband to do the same, their perfect state of affairs is ruined. In the Old Testament creation story, sin functions as the original contamination, compelling God to cast his children out of the Garden of Eden. William Blake, English 1757–1827, *The Temptation and Fall of Eve* (illustration to Milton's *Paradise Lost*), 1808, pen and watercolor on paper, 49.7 × 38.7 cm (19⁹/₁₆ × 15 ¼ in.), Museum of Fine Arts, Boston. Gift by subscription, 90.99. Reprinted with the permission of Museum of Fine Arts. Photograph copyright 2005, Museum of Fine Arts, Boston.

profession, and then your mother dies before she can see you receive your award. In box 8.1, I have listed a few condensed examples of contamination sequences we have observed in life-story interviews with midlife adults. If you cannot find one that fits roughly to a sequence in your life story, feel free to pencil in your own.

Although almost everybody can summon forth a contamination sequence from the past, people differ with respect to how many such sequences they recall and how important the general idea of contamination is in their life stories. Tanya Williams recalls a large number of contamination sequences, and she tends to construct the broad narrative of her life in contamination terms. Even when a positive event in her story is not immediately followed by a negative outcome, she tends to provide a negative interpretation, or

---

Box 8.1. *Condensed Examples of Contamination Sequences From Life-Story Interviews*

In a contamination sequence, a very good or emotionally positive life-story scene is immediately followed by a very bad or emotionally negative scene, outcome, or narrative interpretation. Note: "P" stands for the "protagonist" in the story.

Marriage is wonderful → Partner states he wants a divorce.
P feels pride at high school graduation → Father says P looks fat crossing the stage.
New house is a long-awaited joy → Repair bills become a nightmare.
Sex is great before marriage → Now married, spouse is no longer interested.
P finally stands up to a bully and is winning the fight → Bully's friend beats P up.
P worships new professor → Professor criticizes P's work publicly, humiliates P.
P is pregnant, happy → Husband is killed in auto accident, P miscarries.
P receives a valuable gift → Gift is stolen.
P loses weight, looks great → New attention from men makes P nervous, neurotic.
Birth of beautiful baby → Baby develops serious illness.
P enjoys senior class party → Friends go their separate ways, P is depressed.
P is winning the race, steps from the finish line → Body gives out, P finishes dead last.
P enjoys kissing boyfriend on porch → Father shines light on them, humiliation.
P is playing happily in the park → It gets dark and parents seem to have abandoned her.
P is accepted to prestigious law school → Later, P's fiancé is rejected from same school.
Wedding ceremony, wonderful party after → Best man gets drunk and shoots himself.

"spin," for the event. For example, her eighth-grade graduation is a positive event, but she ends the account of the event by remarking that she never "walked across the stage" again. The general movement in her story, furthermore, is from a relatively happy childhood, as she mainly recalls it, to a much more complicated and distressing adult life. The key transition period—her fall from grace—is puberty, when she first experiences her "love of the street."

Contamination sequences in narrative identity are associated with depression, anxiety, and low self-esteem in adults. Research that my students and I have done shows a strong positive correlation between contamination themes and measures of psychological distress. Those individuals, like Tanya, whose stories tend to emphasize contamination are the same people, by and large, who report relatively high levels of depression and anxiety in life and low levels of life satisfaction, happiness, self-esteem, and sense of life coherence. Contamination themes are also *negatively* associated with generativity. Midlife adults who, like Tanya, are low in generativity tend to construct narrative identities that emphasize contamination. Low-generativity adults tend to tell life stories containing significantly more contamination sequences than the life stories told by highly generative adults.[4]

Contamination is one of a set of features that tend to appear in the life stories of American adults who fall at the very low end of the generativity continuum. What do we know about the narrative identities in this group? For one, we know that these individuals construct life stories that tend *not* to feature the main narrative themes that are featured in this book—for example, early advantage in life, sensitivity to the suffering of others, moral depth and steadfastness, redemption sequences, and future growth. Compared to high-generativity individuals, those low in generativity tell life stories that show the central themes of the redemptive self less often. But what *do* their life stories show?

In her doctoral dissertation in the field of counseling psychology, Martha Lewis conducted a very close reading of 34 life-story interviews from adults extremely low in generativity.[5] The small sample in Lewis's intensive study comprised only those adults whose generativity scores on paper-and-pencil measures put them in the bottom 20% of the distribution. In other words, the adults whose life stories Lewis examined scored in the bottom fifth of the distribution of generativity scores for all individuals who have participated in our research studies. Included in Lewis's group was Tanya Williams.

Lewis found that most of the life stories she read began with an *early psychological injury* or setback from which the protagonist never seems to recover. According to these stories, the psychological injury may be the result of inadequate care or support from parents, emotional conflict between parents, or the loss of a parent or sibling to death, illness, or separation. In some, but not all, instances, these early injuries are structured as contamination sequences. For example, one participant told how family life was very enjoyable until the birth of a disabled sibling. Another described a similarly happy early childhood that ended at age 6, when her mother died. "It felt like the end of the world," she says. It is not uncommon to find negative, even traumatic, experiences in the early chapters of life stories. What Lewis found so distinctive in the stories of low-generativity individuals, however, was how powerful these early scenes were in *setting the tone for the entire story.* The injury never seems to heal. A small setback triggers a negative cascade of bad events. An early trauma plays itself out again, later in the story. In the life stories of adults very low in generativity, early injuries seem to symbolize the deep belief that there is something fundamentally wrong or broken in life. If only this problem could be repaired, the author imagines, things might turn out right and good.

Lewis also observed that the main characters in the life stories of low-generativity adults tended themselves to be especially nongenerative. Characters who might serve as positive role models in the story—parents, aunts and uncles, pastors, supervisors, and authority figures of many kinds—tend instead to exert a negative influence. Fathers fare worse than mothers on this score. Mothers may seem overwhelmed or distant, whereas many fathers are described as irresponsible, uncaring, or abusive. When the protagonists look outside their family for guidance, moreover, they find precious little. "I really needed outside, adult guidance," laments one respondent. But "there was no modeling; nobody knew how." Another says, "I've never really had what I call mentors in my work, or in my life. . . . I had to try to figure it out on my own." Because they find so few generative sources in their environment, the protagonist in these stories often ends up feeling that the only person to be truly trusted for help and guidance is himself or herself. The result may be a rugged, but bitter, self-reliance: "I don't depend on nobody to do nothing for me. . . . I live with a friend, and my friend is always saying, 'You need some money, you need this, you need that.' And I always say, 'No,' because I don't want him to feel like I depend on him to give me this money, or I'm dependent on him to give me a ride someplace, when I'm working. I work full time. I know where the bus stops are. . . . That was the hardest thing with my ex-husband, too. He always wanted me to depend on him, and I couldn't."

The life stories of adults low in generativity tend to lack a forward, upward thrust. Many of the respondents in Lewis's study remarked that they found it very difficult to ascribe overall direction and purpose to their lives. Some suggested that they had drifted through life, avoiding tough decisions and life-shaping commitments. Others suggested that the course of their lives was determined by outside forces—family, friendships, institutions, the economy, history, or luck. In the face of these powerful external forces, the protagonists, in their stories, have been able to exert very little control in determining the direction of their lives. To the extent they have made important decisions, some suggested, the decisions have been focused mainly on *avoiding* problems rather than *approaching* positive goals. As in the case of Tanya Williams, life presents some people with so many overwhelming problems and tough obstacles, that merely surviving the dangers of the day may be considered something of an achievement. It is tough to make long-term, positive goals under conditions of extreme deprivation.

The motto in some life stories told by adults low in generativity is that "living for the moment" or "going with the flow" is preferable to higher aspirations and long-term aims. Whether because goals have not been achieved in the past or because of a life philosophy that questions the value of focusing attention on the future, a number of the respondents in Lewis's study expressed strong ambivalence about the idea that a life should move in a particular, self-chosen direction. Although most low-generativity adults will still articulate some goals for the future, their goals tend to be focused mainly on the self rather than on promoting the well-being of others, and they tend to be short-term, concrete goals, such as losing weight, refurbishing the kitchen, or taking a class on yoga. One 60-year-old man who scored at the bottom of the generativity distribution describes his life direction this way: "I want to keep doing exactly what I want to do. I want to follow my own interests, or lack of interests. I like to drink coffee. I'd like to spend more time in the coffeehouse. I like to run and work out, and maybe take some interesting classes. Maybe travel. But I don't really want much responsibility, and I have no [large] aspirations for me. I don't want to aspire to anything."

If the plot of a life story does not move forward, how does it move? Some life plots are regressive, in that the main character steadily loses ground over time. Stories involving fatal illnesses, advanced aging, and the course of Alzheimer's disease typically follow a backward, regressive pattern.[6] Most of the life stories told by midlife adults low in generativity, however, show random, sporadic movement, sometimes forward, sometimes backward. Sometimes, the story seems to move in a vicious circle. Traumas, disappointments, failures, and losses from the early chapters of the story reappear and play themselves out again and again in later chapters. A young man's first romantic relationship ends after he tells his teenage lover that he cannot commit himself to her for the long run. Over the next 20 years, he experiences three more relationships that follow the same pattern; in each case, the relationship ends when the man expresses his uncertainty regarding a long-term commitment. A woman is fired from a succession of jobs. In each case, she gets along famously with her coworkers but ends up having serious disagreements with the boss. A man goes into a tailspin whenever he feels he is not getting the respect he deserves from his subordinates. It has been like that ever since his younger brother ridiculed him for being such a bad baseball player, way back in junior high school.

The past leaves a heavy burden for many adults low in generativity. Negative patterns experienced in childhood and the adolescent years make repeat performances through middle adulthood. Old injuries and insults never seem to go away. Contamination sequences suggest that even when life moves forward, there is bound to be reversal up ahead. The protagonists in these stories seem unable to build anything positive upon the past. Nor are they able to leave the past behind. Having lost both parents by the time he was 16 years of age, one 38-year-old man scoring very low in generativity concludes, "You never get over it; you just get used to it. And that holds true, at least for me personally, for any loss. I was 10 when I lost my dad. That was 28 years ago. Any big event that you go to afterwards, you think, 'I wish my mother and father were here to see this. . . .' Not a day goes by where I don't think of it." Another 36-year-old man recalls the divorce of his parents, when he was 5, as the turning point in his story. Life held so much promise for him at the beginning. But because his parents divorced when he was 5, he believes, he has been unable to achieve any important goals in his life. "What might have been?" he wonders: "What would have happened if certain things had not happened? If I would have had an actual family unit that would have stayed together, what would I be now? A senator? A doctor? Would I have gotten a college degree? An M.A.? A Ph.D.? I've got the brains. I probably would have been a fantastic literature teacher, or sportscaster. . . . What if I had gone ahead and taken a chance with [a woman I loved] and got married? Maybe I would have had some beautiful kids by now. . . . What if?"

In sum, adults who score at the very low end of the generativity spectrum tend to tell life stories that emphasize contamination over redemption and that feature a set of narrative themes suggesting problems in life *movement*. The plots in these stories tend to stagnate around early injuries and repeated conflicts. The story's main characters seem unable to make progress in life. They get very little help from the characters around them. The entire setting for the story seems threatening or neglectful. Authority figures who should provide generative support for the main characters during their times of need repeatedly fail them. They, in turn, feel that they are failures in their efforts to be generative toward others, or else they find little need in their lives

---

Box 8.2. Life Stories of Adults Low in Generativity

An intensive study of narrative identities constructed by midlife American adults scoring very low in generativity shows a general pattern of contaminated plots and vicious circles. These life stories tend to begin with an early psychological injury that is repeated again and again as the plot unfolds. The stories tend to lack the progressive, forward plot movement that is so common in the life stories of adults high in generativity. Preoccupied with self concerns and focused mainly on the present moment, adults low in generativity imagine goals for the future that focus mainly on the short-term needs of the self.

How does the story begin?
  Early psychological injury
  Neglecting or abusive characters; no generative role models
How does the plot develop?
  No upward or forward thrust; stagnation and regression
  Vicious circles, repetition of problem scenes
  Contamination sequences: good scenes are spoiled by bad outcomes
How does the story end?
  Reluctance to project into the future; living in the moment
  Short-term, concrete goals focused on the self

---

to be generative toward other people. The future chapters of the story promise to bring more of the same. The main characters in these stories seem to have lost faith that good things can come out of suffering and sacrifice. They dare not trust in redemption. To the extent that they set goals for the future, their goals are short term, concrete, and focused mainly on the self.

Contamination and Repetition

When asked to describe the "opposite" of generativity, Erik Erikson typically gave two different answers. The first answer was *stagnation*. People who are not generative feel stagnant, stuck, immobilized. They cannot move forward. They are unable to *generate* outcomes that extend their care and commitment to future generations. They feel that they cannot produce anything of lasting value. It is as if adults low in generativity are writers afflicted with a serious case of "writer's block." They sit in front of the word processor for days on end, they struggle to create something original, but nothing seems to come out right.

Erikson's second choice for generativity's opposite was *self-preoccupation*. Rather than invest in future generations, some adults invest principally in themselves. They are so preoccupied with their own problems and pursuits that they cannot free up enough energy and will to care for others and to commit themselves to enterprises beyond the self. While highly generative adults focus attention on children and the future, adults low in generativity think mainly of their own problems and concerns. In a sense, *they are their own children.* Given the way their lives have gone, they may conclude that the people who need their care the most are none other than themselves.

Life stories told by adults low in generativity express both of Erikson's characterizations. The protagonists in these stories often seem overwhelmed by external forces and by the power of their own internal needs. Although they are likely to be involved in important and even nurturing relationships with other people, they still expend an inordinate amount of energy and time caring for themselves and working on their own satisfaction. Efforts to move forward in life, furthermore, are frequently stymied by contamination sequences and the repetition of traumatic, frustrating, or conflicted scenes. The very plots of the stories seem to stagnate. Unproductive, self-absorbed, and loath to expect too much from the future, protagonists go around and around in circles.

Writing at the end of World War I, Freud was struck by how often his patients described scenes and behaviors in their lives that involved going around and around in circles.[7] Soldiers came home from the front only to find that they could not leave the trenches and the gasmasks behind. Many experienced flashbacks about the war, reliving traumatic scenes in their dreams and in waking life. Expressing symptoms of what we now call *posttraumatic stress disorder,* many of these men seemed compelled to repeat or relive the past again and again, even though they did not want to do so. Freud's observations prompted him to explore the same phenomenon in patients whose experiences had nothing to do with war, or even with trauma. He began to see that many people felt an irrational need to repeat unsatisfying past experiences. This *repetition compulsion* puzzled Freud, for it seemed to serve no pleasurable or productive purpose. Why should anybody ever want to relive negative events? Freud speculated that many cases of repetition compulsion may represent efforts to undo or master the past. By replaying the frustrating or traumatic scene again and again, the person may be unconsciously trying to loosen the grip of the event upon his or her entire personality. It is as if the repetition of the bad event serves to "get it out of my system" or enables me "to get used to it" and "learn to live with it."

The life stories of adults who are especially low in generativity resemble at times the pattern of repetition compulsion that Freud identified. For some, a particular early loss or injury is repeatedly invoked as the reason for failures in life. For others, a particular negative scene provides a model for future negative scenes. The original scene itself is not repeated in the story, but later scenes seem to resemble the original one. It is possible that, as Freud suggested, people who construct their lives as fated stories in which the protagonist is destined to repeat an early negative experience over and over may be learning how to work through that experience so that, eventually, the experience will loosen its grip. But the impression I get when I read these stories is that many of the narrators are simply stuck, like Tanya. Repetition leads to more repetition, rather than to mastery. Something dramatic needs to happen to shake them out of the loop.

Another psychologist who wrote extensively about repetition and contamination in life narratives was the late Silvan Tomkins. In the 1960s and 1970s, Tomkins fashioned a bold and provocative theory of personality that is only now beginning to be appreciated by psychological researchers and clinicians. Tomkins called his conception *script theory*.[8] According to Tomkins, human beings are fundamentally like playwrights who create scripts in which they play the leading roles. From the earliest weeks of life onward, Tomkins contended, people unconsciously fashion *scripts* to organize and make sense of their lives and to set the stage for future action. Scripts comprise individual *scenes* in life, and at the center of every important scene are one or two basic *emotions*. Basic emotions are either positive or negative. The basic positive emotions are joy and excitement. The basic negative emotions include fear, sadness, anger, guilt, shame, and disgust. Emotions are the great motivators in life, Tomkins argued. We act in order to experience positive emotions or to avoid experiencing negative ones. But emotions are also the great *organizers*, for it is around basic emotional experiences that life scenes and scripts are ultimately constructed.

The life stories told by midlife adults low in generativity are very similar to what Tomkins called a *nuclear script*. Nuclear scripts are marked by confusion and ambivalence. The past is seen as a series of frustrating and conflicted scenes. Many of these scenes may promise positive emotion, but they usually fail to deliver. Yet these scenes from the past continue to exert a strange hold upon the "playwright," making it very difficult for him or her to write a script for the future that sets forth clear goals aimed at experiencing positive emotions. Instead, the person living a nuclear script is irresistibly drawn toward and repelled by negative-emotion scenes from the past. He or she cannot quit wondering "what might have been" and how things could have turned out so much better had one or two good breaks happened along the way. At an unconscious and completely irrational level, furthermore, the person may feel that it is still possible to go back to the past and undo it.

There is no chance to move forward with confidence and the full expectation of positive emotion until the past has been redone in some sense. But of course it is too late to redo it, literally speaking. There is no getting back into the Garden of Eden once the hero and heroine have been thrown out.

Nuclear scripts usually begin with a *nuclear scene*. A nuclear scene is essentially a contamination sequence from early childhood. The scene begins with the child's feeling great joy or excitement in the presence of parents or other potentially generative characters. But these older characters betray or disappoint the child, or else they prove powerless to prevent the turn from good to bad. What begins, therefore, as joyful or exciting turns frightening, enraging, disgusting, shameful, or sad. Most people are able to separate spoiled events from the general plot of their life narrative, or they are able to accept them as the way things had to be even if they were very painful. Some people even manage to conceive of contaminated events as necessary obstacles or stages on the way to redemption.

Still other people, however, come to construe contaminated childhood scenes in their lives as a foreshadowing of what is to come. The contaminated childhood scene becomes the origin of a nuclear script. A nuclear script begins to form when the person seeks to reverse or undo the original scene, to turn what became a bad scene into a good one again. Tomkins suggested that the person living the nuclear script may be motivated to reexperience the same emotional sequence that appeared in the original nuclear scene. Moving through life, he or she may unconsciously seek out new scenes that replay the positive opening of the nuclear scene. Yet the same kinds of negative outcomes end up occurring again, and again. The person comes to expect that this sequence will continue to recur. Yet he or she is unable to give up on the counter expectation—or wish—that the kind of contamination sequence experienced in the first place may someday be undone, that he or she will someday have an experience that is just like the original one that turned bad. *Except this time, it will stay good.* The joy and excitement I felt in that childhood scene will come back to me just as they were at that time, and they will stay with me, forever.

Tomkins's idea of a *script* is similar in many ways to what I call a *narrative identity*.[9] Like the life stories that people construct to make sense of their past, present, and anticipated future, scripts are products of the imagination as much as they are grounded in reality. To a certain extent, we choose our stories and our scripts. We decide what kinds of emotional sequences to highlight, how to connect one scene to another, what to remember and how to remember it, and what to expect for the future. These narrative decisions, like those made by any dramatist or novelist, are influenced by the reality of our lives. Nuclear scripts, therefore, reflect contamination and repetition as they have indeed been experienced in a given life. But Tomkins believed that nuclear scripts also reflect the idiosyncratic ways through which the person has decided to tell and "emplot" his or her own life. People who tend to understand their own lives in terms of nuclear scripts are not able to incorporate their contaminated scenes into a progressive narrative of the self. Instead, they feel compelled to repeat contaminated scenes, perhaps in an effort to undo them. They hold on to the hope that if the pain of the past could only be erased, *then* their lives might move forward in a satisfying and generative way. *Then* they might be able to switch their focus from themselves to future generations or to the society in which they live. For some people, redemption means nothing less than the complete decontamination of the past. But this is a tall order for even the most ingenious playwright.

Confession

How do we try to decontaminate the past? How do we seek to undo the bad that has already been done? When we feel that we may be partly or largely *responsible* for the bad outcome that occurred, when we feel that it may be, in some sense, "our fault," we may seek to *confess.* By publicly acknowledging wrongdoing, the confessor aims to wipe the slate clean—to reinstate the good situation that preceded the bad. Confession may assuage the guilt and shame a person feels for having committed an immoral or unfortunate act. It may repair relationships damaged by the original transgression. It may make amends with victims, family, friends, and the community at large. It may open the door to punishment or some form of repayment or recompense through which a kind of equilibrium may be restored. From a religious perspective, confession may put a person back into good stead with God and the cosmos. From a legal perspective, confession may signal an acceptance of responsibility and a willingness to be rehabilitated.

Confession is a cornerstone concept in Christian religious traditions and in Western morality and jurisprudence.[10] Convoked in 1215, the Catholic Fourth Lateran Council made annual confession obligatory. In so doing, the church established a social ritual that has had profound effects on how Westerners have come to think about their lives ever since. In his book *Troubling Confessions,* Peter Brooks writes, "The image of the penitent and the priest, in the intimate yet impersonal, private and protected space of the confessional, represents a potent social ritual that both its friends and its enemies over the centuries have recognized as a shaping cultural experience."[11]

As Brooks sees it, the practice of confession signaled the emergence of a narrative self in Western culture. The telling of transgression to an accepting audience became a standard form of self-expression, a sanctioned way of telling "the real story" about the self. The form is modeled today in autobiographies, tell-all books, television talk shows, reality TV, and the occasional mea culpa offered by a public official or celebrity caught in an intrigue.[12] Indeed, the very existence of a confession ritual suggests that people have stories that they often "keep to themselves," secret, inner selves that are hidden from even their closest confidantes. We often believe, therefore, that personal truth and authenticity can be expressed and experienced through the telling of the secret story. Such a telling may mark the full expression of the inner self to an audience—be that audience the priest, the good friend, the therapist, the police, the jury, the reader, the television viewers, the voting public, or God. In Western culture, we are "confessing animals," writes the French philosopher Michel Foucault.[13] We feel the urge to confess, even at the expense of condemnation and punishment.

A good Catholic girl and a straight-A student, Katherine Ann Power confessed her sins to her parish priest on a regular basis.[14] Twelve years of parochial schooling and the strong influence of her devout and principled parents instilled in Power a sense that life should be lived according to a higher calling. "I grew up on stories of the saints—the ones who got their heads chopped off for the greater good," Power remarks. "I always imagined how glorious that kind of sacrifice would be."[15] At Brandeis University in the late 1960s, Power and many of her friends became increasingly radicalized regarding the war in Vietnam. They saw the war as a great evil, and they looked for opportunities to express their moral outrage. When President Nixon expanded the war into Cambodia, Power resolved to carry out public actions that might undermine the military effort.

In her senior year, Power dropped out of college and joined a group of four other young people who were deeply opposed to the war. The group planned to rob the State Street Bank and Trust Company of Boston in order to "liberate funds from a collaborationist establishment to support the movement against the Vietnam War."[16] On September 23, 1970, they carried out the plan. Power was assigned to drive the getaway car. During the robbery attempt, however, one of the group's members shot and killed Walter Schroeder, a Boston policeman. Officer Schroeder left behind a wife and nine children. Under the felony murder law of Massachusetts, because all five members of the group engaged in a felony when the murder occurred, all five were chargeable with murder.

For the next 23 years, Power lived as a fugitive from the law. She remained on the FBI's Ten Most Wanted list longer than any other woman in American history. Power changed her name, moved around the country, and cut off all contact with her family. Horrified by the death of Schroeder and deeply ashamed of her part in the crime, Power experienced bouts of severe depression, accompanied by guilt and the fear of being caught. Running from the law, however, kept her busy and constantly vigilant—activity that, she believes, staved off suicide. Eventually Power married a man named Ron Duncan and settled in Oregon, where they raised her son. She became co-owner of a restaurant in Eugene. She made friends in the community. Still hiding from the law, Power tried to atone for the damage she had done. For example, she gave a great deal of her income away to charity, in keeping with her Catholic beliefs: "In Catholicism, the catechism of forgiveness is that if you have done something very, very wrong, you can be forgiven by naming your act, knowing how it came to happen, and removing yourself from the environment that contributed to it. I did that and then I vowed that I would make my life an act of contrition for my wrong to the Schroeder family."[17]

All of the kindness and the generativity she expressed in her family life and among her friends and neighbors was not enough. Power still felt tremendous guilt about the murder, and she felt that over the past 23 years she had been living a lie. All of the good things she had done since September 23, 1970, all of the loving relationships she had formed—they were all based on a lie. She was not the person other people thought she was. In order to atone fully for her crime and to reestablish her authenticity as a human being, Power concluded, she needed to confess. She needed to give herself up to the authorities. In September 1993 she turned herself in, waived her right to a trial, pleaded guilty to manslaughter, and began serving an 8- to 12-year sentence in the Massachusetts Correctional Institution in Framingham. She did not wish to contest her role in the crime, even though some legal experts believed that the government might not be able to prove its case against her. After all, she had not even known about the shooting until well after it occurred. Her role was the naïve and unsuspecting driver of the getaway car used in a botched bank robbery. In 1995 psychologist Janet Landman asked Power why she agreed to plead guilty:

> It was an act of redemption . . . it was an act of redemption for my dishonesty with the people I had to lie to in my fugitive life, the declaration in action that I understood the importance of authenticity, honesty, owning up, speaking, in order . . . in order to be, in order to be somebody that anybody could trust ever. I thought . . . that people would be very angry and very hurt that I was not what I seemed, but I think part of that, part of why they know that is

because I insisted on pleading guilty. How could they trust me? How could they not assume some sleazy level of inability to be honest and to act with integrity if I had said, "Oh, maybe I did it and maybe I didn't do it. What can you prove?" It would feel like disowning everything I had ever done.[18]

Confession can serve to restore the integrity and wholeness of narrative identity. For some people who feel that their lives are contaminated by bad events for which they themselves may be responsible, confession may help to

FIGURE 8.2 Katherine Ann Power (right) leaves prison in 1999, after serving 6 years for her role as the getaway driver in a botched burglary that resulted in the murder of a policeman on September 23, 1970. Power lived as a fugitive from the law for 23 years before her guilt and her need to experience honesty in her relationships with others motivated her to turn herself in and confess to the crime. For some people, confession can serve a redemptive purpose in narrative identity by decontaminating the past and freeing the story's protagonist to move forward in life. Reprinted with the permission of AP/World Wide Photos.

undo the wrong and open up new opportunities for growth and development. In some life stories, confession may help to decontaminate the past and free the protagonist from vicious circles and stagnant plots. Katherine Ann Power came to believe that redemption in her life story could be achieved only through public confession. She had to give herself up before she could hold out hope of redeeming a contaminated past. After serving 6 years in prison, she was released for good behavior in 1999.

Redemption Through Recovery: Alcoholics Anonymous

Jefferson Singer is a research psychologist and a clinician who has worked extensively with alcoholics and drug addicts.[19] In therapy sessions with Singer, men and women suffering from substance abuse describe how alcohol and drugs have contaminated their lives. Too often, their repeated efforts to beat the addictions end up looking like vicious circles. After a destructive binge or a really bad trip, they resolve to kick the habit. They get a job. They try to make new friends. They try to stay clean. But the frustrations of their new life and the temptations of the old prove too powerful, and they relapse. The cycle repeats. Singer believes that for many addicts the only way to break the cycle is to create a new life story. The "problem of achieving sobriety for some chronically addicted men [and women] is a problem of their ability to create good stories, stories that achieve a coherence and authenticity," Singer writes.[20] The new story is more than just a few new words. It must instead integrate the addict into a caring and productive social environment, Singer maintains. The new story must enable the addict to commit the self to long-term relationships and productive roles. The new story must be coherent and authentic, and it must eventually provide opportunities for generativity.

The construction of a new life story and the integration of the addict into a potentially productive and caring community are central aims of Alcoholics Anonymous (AA) and other well-known 12-step programs, such as Narcotics Anonymous, Overeaters Anonymous, Gamblers Anonymous, and Al-Anon. Interestingly, these programs begin with a kind of confession. The first step toward sobriety in AA is to confess the very addiction that brings you there in the first place.[21] You must admit that you are powerless to control the addiction. Life has become unmanageable, and there is nothing that you can do about it on your own. The only constructive thing left to do, then, is to surrender your will to a higher authority. According to AA, only a power that is greater than the self can free you from the contamination and the vicious circles of your life. You must decide to turn your will and your life over to the care of God. AA leaves it up to you to decide who or what God is. The key thing to know is that God is outside you. *You are not God.* Once you realize that you cannot control your life and that you, therefore, are not like God, then you are able to join a new community of fellow alcoholics who are themselves equally powerless over their own lives but eager to help you with yours:

> The fundamental and first message of AA to its members is that they are not infinite, not absolute, *not God.* Every alcoholic's problem had first been, according to this insight, claiming God-like powers, especially that of control. . . . To be an alcoholic within AA is not only to accept oneself as not God; it implies also affirmation of one's connectedness with other alcoholics. It is this connection that historically has provided for hundreds of thousands of people a way out of active alcoholism and the path into a life of health, happiness, and wholeness.[22]

A washed-up Wall Street trader and a hopeless drunk, Bill Wilson sat down at the bar in November 1934 to have a drink with a fellow alcoholic named Ebby.[23] But when Ebby showed up, he told Bill he did not want to drink anymore. He had "got religion," Ebby claimed. Ebby said he had joined an evangelical Christian group that was dedicated to temperance. An offshoot of the Young Men's Christian Association (YMCA), the Oxford Group used the kind of conversion experiences popularized by Charles Grandison Finney (chapter 6) and other Protestant evangelists to transform drunks into upstanding citizens (and good men of God). Men could be saved from the bottle by committing themselves to Christ. Ebby's conversion did not stick, however. Weeks later, he was back on the bottle. But Wilson was intrigued by the whole idea and began thinking about how he might decontaminate his own life. Still, Wilson continued to drink. After a 3-day bender in December, he checked himself into a hospital. Wilson had finally hit rock bottom:

> My depression deepened unbearably and finally it seemed to me as though I were at the bottom of the pit. I still gagged badly on the notion of a Power greater than myself, but finally, just for the moment, the last vestige of my proud obstinacy was crushed. All at once I found myself crying out, "If there is a God, let Him show Himself! I am ready to do anything, anything!"
>
> Suddenly the room lit up with a great white light. I was caught up into an ecstasy which there are no words to describe. It seemed to me, in the mind's eye, that I was on a mountain and that a wind not of air but of spirit was blowing. And then it burst upon me that I was

a free man. Slowly the ecstasy subsided. I lay on the bed, but now for a time I was in another world, a new world of consciousness. All about me and through me there was a wonderful feeling of Presence, and I thought to myself, "So there is the God of the preachers!" A great peace stole over me and I thought, "No matter how wrong things seem to be, they are all right. Things are all right with God and His world."[24]

On Wilson's road to recovery, this was the first step. He gave up the belief that he could control his own life. He acknowledged a power greater than the self. But this was not enough. He needed to tell somebody about it. He needed to establish a new community through talk, though telling a story and listening to the story of another. The opportunity to do so arose in the early summer of 1935 when Wilson met Dr. Robert Holbrook Smith, a proctologist from Akron, Ohio. Smith was also an alcoholic. In a fateful conversation that is now seen as the "founding moment" in the history of AA, "Bill W." convinced "Dr. Bob" to quit drinking. One anonymous drunk helped another. Both men were now committed to a life of sobriety. More important, though, their little talk became the model for AA and all of the 12-step programs that have followed its lead. Bill W. and Dr. Bob went on to establish AA. By century's end, AA groups could be found in 140 countries. In a 1990 survey, 13.3% of American adults reported that they had attended a 12-step program of some kind. In the same year, *Life* magazine named Bill Wilson one of the 100 most important Americans of the 20th century.[25] Aldous Huxley regarded him as that century's "greatest social architect."[26]

The 12 steps that Bill W. and Dr. Bob developed take the alcoholic from confession to self-examination to generativity. Once the alcoholic has admitted powerlessness and surrendered the will to a higher Other, he or she takes a moral inventory of life and tries to sort out the many different ways that his or her own actions have hurt others. The person humbly asks God to remove shortcomings and to help him or her make amends. The constant focus on improving the self with the assistance of God and the AA community helps to pull the person out of the life patterns that lead to vicious circles. There is a sense that life is moving forward. But optimism must always be tempered, for one is always in a recovery mode. Alcoholism is forever, according to AA. Even one drink can recontaminate the entire recovery, undo years of good work, and return the alcoholic to the contaminated and repetitive script of long ago. Furthermore, a return to contamination would let down the entire group. AA aims to build strong community through personal storytelling. Members talk incessantly about their hitting bottom, their ongoing recovery process, and the daily struggles to maintain sobriety and move forward. The storytelling itself also serves the function of generativity. Experienced AA members pass their stories down to those who are newer to the group. An "older" generation of alcoholics cares for a younger one by passing on the wisdom they have accumulated. The wisdom is conveyed through life-story telling. Indeed, the wisdom *is* the stories. In AA generativity becomes the performing of one's own narrative identity.

What is the story? How is it performed? Although every alcoholic's story is unique, observers of AA have long noted that the stories told in AA sessions tend to conform to a general pattern or script.[27] The pattern conforms in a general way to Bill W.'s own narrative: Excessive drinking leads to isolation; eventually the hero hits rock bottom; the hero begins to experiment with different solutions to the problem, but none work; eventually the hero joins AA; in AA the hero acknowledges powerlessness and begins to rebuild a life through the help of some larger force and the AA group; recovery happens gradually, an ongoing process; the hero eventually feels gratitude and seeks to help others. In the AA story, alcoholism itself is seen as a disease. The cure is to embrace humility, identify with other alcoholics, and find one's place in a new community.

In telling their stories to others, members of AA provide the vivid details that make their stories unique. They often use humor and other performance methods to capture their audience's attention and to differentiate their stories from those told by others. At the same time, their stories follow roughly the general redemptive pattern that prevails in AA. Speakers articulate the long and harrowing disintegration that marked the progress of their "disease." In the most extreme cases, alcohol eventually had come to control all their significant actions and decisions. They lost jobs, friends, and family. At rock bottom, they lost control of even the mundane events of daily life. Yet the downward spiral is viewed as having been necessary. The suffering had to occur. It was all part of some master plan. Recovery, too, follows a kind of preordained plan. The hero works through the 12 steps. He or she eventually moves past fear and shame to acceptance and serenity. Struggles continue, but life steadily improves. Redemption is never complete, nor total. But for the time being, the alcoholic's life story has become decontaminated. Vicious circles have been overcome. The future looks good. The story suggests that life should continue to progress.

When people feel that significant chunks of their lives have been wasted, they need to create stories that give some kind of redemptive meaning to those lost years. In the stories that many men and women tell in AA, the drunken years are often reconstrued as comprising a painful but necessary course of development. "I had to hit rock bottom," some of them say, "before I could begin the process of recovery." Contaminated episodes and vicious circles from the past come to be seen as the necessary early chapters in a long story of recovery. By "re-storying" their lives as redemptive tales, recovering alcoholics are able to wrench meaning and hope out of a most difficult course of events. In the words of the great psychotherapist Victor Frankl, they may be able to derive a sense of *tragic optimism* from a contaminated past.[28]

When Criminals Reform

For Charlie McGregor, the problem was not so much alcohol. It was drugs, gangs, and a life of crime. In his autobiography, *Up From the Waking Dead*, McGregor details the contaminated plots and vicious circles of his early life, and how he was eventually able to leave that all behind.[29] The story goes like this:

> McGregor was born in Harlem, to a single mother who beat him terribly because she thought he was less intelligent and less attractive than his lighter-skinned older brother. He became involved in gangs and drugs as a means of achieving a sense of power and self-respect amid a powerless ghetto existence. His young adulthood, however, was largely spent behind bars. Although he found a "family" of sorts in prison, he longed for female intimacy and material success. Each time he was released, however, he found that these goals were unattainable through legal means, so he returned to criminal behavior.
>
> Finally, in prison for the last time, he was exposed to a social service organization called Reality House, run by former Harlem gang members like himself, but who had achieved respectability in mainstream society. After seeing the respectful way prison officials treated the counselors from the organization, McGregor agreed to go along to the group's meetings. He soon found that this "new family" was a far more peaceful and understanding group than his incarcerated peers. Upon his release from prison, he approached the agency to find a job, so he could be like one of the counselors he so admired. Although the process was anything but easy, several years later, Charlie McGregor became a licensed drug therapist, public speaker, and minor celebrity, who used his new position to help young people avoid making the mistakes he made.[30]

McGregor's story is one of many studied by criminologist Shadd Maruna in an ongoing effort to trace and to understand the lives of criminals who have "gone straight." Maruna has examined published autobiographies of men and women like McGregor, and he has conducted extensive question-naire- and interview-based research with prison inmates and ex-convicts.[31] Criminologists have long sought to figure out why some career criminals like Charlie McGregor eventually turn their lives around and give up their crim-inal ways while many others continue to commit crimes. The term crimi-nologists use for giving up crime is *desistance*. Years of research suggest that the single biggest predictor of desistance is age. Criminal activity peaks out in the teens and early 20s. After that, as people get older, they commit fewer crimes. But what is it about getting older that makes a difference? Do older people simply have less energy for crime? Do they get smarter with age? Do their life prospects improve? Furthermore, many career criminals, even as they grow older, continue to commit serious crimes, suggesting that age it-self is not a foolproof predictor of desistance.

Maruna believes that desistance often depends on formulating a poten-tially *generative narrative of the self*. This kind of narrative identity must do two things: First, it must *salvage a good self from the past,* so as to suggest that one's life has not been completely wasted. Second it must integrate the per-son into a *productive and caring social niche for the future.* As people grow older, they may find it somewhat easier to create this kind of a life story for themselves than they did when they were younger. Still, accomplishing such an identity task amid the daunting obstacles facing many men and women who have committed serious crimes is very difficult. It is difficult to find a positive message from a past life of crime. And it is difficult to secure a niche in society that meets the ex-convict's needs for constructive self-expression and caring relationships with others.

People who eventually desist from crime create many different kinds of narrative identities to make sense of their lives. The case of Charlie McGregor, however, illustrates what Maruna considers to be an especially compelling and fairly common form. McGregor's story fits well with what Maruna calls a classic *reform narrative*. As illustrated in figure 8.3, the reform narrative can be broken down into five basic chapters. Each chapter contains its own plot outline and its own *imago*. An *imago* is the main role or persona that the cen-tral character plays in the chapter. Put another way, an imago is that chap-ter's hero. Imagoes suggest some of the traits and goals associated with a given role, and some of the conflicts and challenges faced during a particu-lar segment of a person's life story.[32]

The reform story begins with contamination, as Maruna shows. In child-hood the hero is victimized by a negative turn of events. As one ex-convict puts it, "I was born with a silver spoon in my mouth—or at least one of

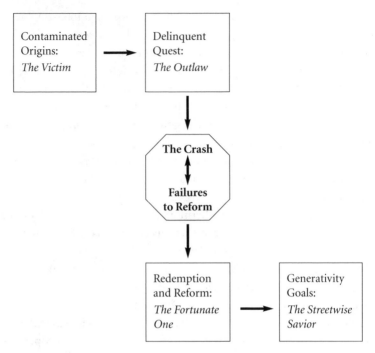

FIGURE 8.3 Desistance from crime: the reform story (adapted from Maruna, 1997).

sturdy nickel plate—but at age five . . . it was abruptly snatched and probably my mouth was torn."[33] The implication in this passage is that life *might have* turned out very well. The beginning held promise. But the early advantage was soon lost. In the case of Charlie McGregor, matters turned bad when his mother began to believe that he was not as smart or as beautiful as his older brother. Once she made this judgment, she began to beat him.

Maruna insists that, by creating an opening life chapter centered on victimization, ex-convicts are doing more than simply making excuses for the fact they eventually turned into criminals. They are also providing a narrative through which they can salvage what they believe to be their essential goodness and innocence. Their contaminated first chapters say something like this: "Once upon a time I was good, but then bad things made me bad; life might have turned out much better had I not been victimized." The basic structure of a contamination sequence is the move from positive to negative. The good news in the sequence is that *goodness was once there,* if only for a fleeting moment. Maruna believes that ex-convicts need to believe that they were once good. The opening chapters of their narratives express a longing for the precontaminated state. Like Ralph Waldo Emerson and the self-help gurus I discussed in chapter 5, they want to believe in the good and true inner self.

In adolescence, the reform story moves from contamination to crime. The victim becomes the delinquent. The delinquent is a much more assertive imago than the victim. The delinquent actively seeks out opportunities for success and for close human relationships. But the venue for this seeking is the streets, the gangs, the criminal subculture that draws in those young men and women who feel they have no place in the conventional world. In adolescence the hero finds success in crime and may forge bonds of friendship and loyalty within gangs and other delinquent groups. One ex-convict brags that his gang "literally ruled the neighborhood" and that "every time I served another sentence [in prison], I came out more of a hero in my neighborhood." Another writes, "To the rest of my family, I was 'the successful one,' as if I were a lawyer, doctor, or accountant—only I was a burglar."[34]

The reform story may portray the delinquent imago in highly romanticized terms. The hero is the "romantic outlaw" or the "heroic vigilante."[35] Charlie McGregor describes himself as the prince of the Harlem underworld: "Regardless of all the dudes around me, I am the finest. I am so clean, junkies stop shooting up and whores stop flatbacking to remark, 'That is the sharpest nigger we ever seen.'"[36] As his reputation grows, the hero faces up to the toughest challenges of the streets and the prison. He passes the big tests of strength or loyalty or bravery. For one ex-convict, a big test was learning (in the penitentiary) how to fight back:

> From that point on, nobody fucked with me again. It was the animal
> sense of wariness and respect for one who would fight back savagely.
> They all said I was a good kid. This recognition was my downfall in
> a way. If I hadn't fought back, if I'd submitted to the threats and be-
> come somebody's punk, I'd never have gone back [to prison]. Instead
> I had gained respect and self-assurance. I had lost my fear of them—
> the guards and the other prisoners. I had learned new tricks and
> become one of them.[37]

The romance of the delinquent quest, however, soon wears off. The self-respect the hero gains from "success" is accompanied by fear, shame, and humiliation. The "family" he gained in the gang or in prison proves unfaithful and fleeting. Drugs, alcohol, prison—they all take their increasing tolls as the hero moves through young adulthood. The hero now enters a downward spiral. His crimes and his punishments become more severe. He begins to look for a way out. In chapter 3 of the reform story, the hero may hit bottom.

Maruna describes "the crash" as an especially low point in the narrative. The hero may feel that he has now committed a crime so despicable, or experienced a humiliation so dreadful, that he must try to do something to turn his life around. Many ex-convicts describe epiphanies and moments of clarity that followed such devastating experiences as the death of a son, the murder of a lover, or a confrontation with a victim.

But these potential turning points in the story often lead instead to vicious circles and repetitive loops. The hero tries to go straight and make it in the conventional world. But he is repeatedly blocked in his efforts by lack of skills, poor social networks, and other obstacles to reform. Eventually, he returns to crime and repeats the patterns of previous years. Again, he spirals downward, hitting new low points, bottoming out at levels even beneath where he has been in the past. New resolutions may lead to new attempts to go straight. But they are frustrated again, and the cycle repeats. "You're caught in a vicious cycle," one ex-convict reports. "It's money, drugs, money, drugs—and it just goes round and round. It's like a roundabout."[38] Charlie McGregor writes that he "recited a whole list of resolutions. . . . I promise to get married and raise a family. I promise to get a square job and stay out of trouble. Promises I had made a million times before." But then "the street dude in me . . . perked up and laid some heavy shit on me, 'Nigger, if you squaring up, you better find yourself some rich broad to lay up with, 'cause you ain't gonna make it by your lonesome. That job the parole officer has lined up for you only pays chump change. How you gonna get sharp with no money to spend? . . . Without money, you're nobody.'"[39]

The story enters chapter 4 when a bottoming-out experience and the subsequent resolutions that the hero makes finally seem to stick. The hero is able to break the vicious circle when he perceives that there are opportunities for fulfillment in the conventional world of work and love. Maruna writes that the critical difference between earlier crash-and-resolution events on the one hand and the true turning point event on the other is not to be found in the event itself: "Rather it seems to be more connected to the perceived possibilities for identity change in the life circumstances and situations narrators face following the turning point episode. In other words, even though narrators 'see the light' during an alleyway shootout some Friday night, they might ignore the sign if they do not perceive any structural opportunities to achieve the sort of agency [power, self-respect] and communion [love, connection] they could obtain through criminal behavior."[40] Once they see opportunities for gainful work and for interpersonal intimacy outside the criminal environment, main characters begin to adopt the imago of "the fortunate one." They come to realize that they have finally gotten a lucky break in life.

Once victimized, they are now sensing that the good inner self has its chance to make the big comeback. And they are very grateful—to new friends, lovers, employers, counselors, and other people outside the criminal world who are willing to take a chance on them, who believe that they are redeemable.

Religious belief may be part of the process of redemption for some ex-convicts. Like Bill W. in AA, they may come to believe that their move forward in life is due to the power of a higher being. Many come to believe that their life is now orchestrated by a higher power for a certain purpose. One ex-convict writes, "All of the times I have lived when I should have died were not accidental; they were part of a design that God has set aside for me as one of his children." Another writes, "One of my first lessons was to be grateful, to know I wasn't in control."[41] Maruna observes that a story suggesting "God has turned me into a new person" may be more convincing in the social circles wherein ex-convicts reside than one that simply asserts, "I decided I wanted to change myself." The religious invocation may give the story a sacred stamp. For many Americans, indeed, a religious meaning may be the only kind of meaning that is powerful enough to exert the kind of redemptive force that the reform narrative seems to demand. After a life of contamination, victimization, delinquency, vicious circles, and failed attempts at reform, the hero is now chosen for a blessing. This point is conveyed powerfully by an ex-convict, who is also a recovering drug addict:

> I believe that all recovering addicts are the Chosen Ones. That's my point of view. I feel we are all chosen by God, because we're loved. . . . Like, I feel addicts are lucky when they learn recovery. Because the people who are not addicts, they're not—they still have their problems. People who are in recovery and go through programs, they learn how to live life on life's terms. . . . So I feel we're special because we're learning how to deal with the world. And, the people that aren't addicts, they don't know how to deal with the world because they're never taught. So, I just feel like we're the special ones.[42]

Note the imagery in this evocative passage. No longer are we talking about contaminated sequences and vicious circles. No longer is the protagonist a hapless victim or an aggressive delinquent. Instead, the hero of the story is one of the *chosen people*—special, gifted, advantaged, redeemable. As in the redemptive life narratives I have featured throughout this book, the imagery of chosenness in this passage seems to open the way toward a mature and generative approach to life. Because the hero has been singled out for a blessing, he or she feels gratitude and a need to give back to others. In most of the redemptive stories I have described in this book, the narrators say that they were advantaged early on in life. For Maruna's ex-convicts, however, early life was all about contamination and victimization. The sense of being special had to come much later in the story, after years of pain and suffering. But the blessing eventually arrives.

In Maruna's fifth and final chapter in the prototypical reform narrative, the imago of "the fortunate one" gives way to "the streetwise savior." The blessing leads to generativity. The protagonist dedicates the self to generative goals. Those goals may include raising children and doing productive work that benefits others. In many cases, the goals involve working constructively with young men and women who are already involved in crime or helping other young people avoid a life of crime. The ex-convict has a special expertise here. The street-smarts gained over the years can now be put to good generative use. Ex-convicts describe this critical turn toward generativity in many different ways. I leave you with three brief examples:

> Because of my past life and conversion, I have a special burden in my heart for prison inmates.
> I was confident my own life was ruined beyond repair, but I found I could derive a certain vicarious satisfaction by becoming concerned with the future of the younger inmates—kids who had gotten into trouble once or twice, but who still had a useful life ahead of them if they could be straightened out in time.
> Daily I look into the upturned, eager faces of youth filled with potential . . . . I also know that one bald-headed old ex-con is not going to convert the world, but I humbly thank God that it is the kind of world where one man can make a big contribution— that I can be a part of molding plastic, young life.[43]

Breaking the Cycle

We began this chapter with stagnation and self-preoccupation, but we have come back now to generativity. We began with contaminated plots and vicious circles, but we have ended up with redemption and the belief in a progressive narrative of self. Contamination sequences capture the move in narrative from highly positive to highly negative emotional states. Adults low in generativity tend to construct narrative identities that contain a greater number of contamination sequences than do the stories constructed by adults high in generativity. These same life stories, furthermore, often portray heroes who fail to make substantial progress in life. The life stories of adults low in generativity tend to have a circular and repetitive quality. Problematic patterns of living are repeated again and again, suggesting vicious circles and plot loops from which the protagonist seems unable to escape. These same kinds of patterns can be found in narratives of addiction and the kinds of stories that criminals tell in accounting for their movement from childhood victimization and the delinquent quest to the downward and repetitive spiral of crime and punishment.

The stories of reformed addicts and criminals, however, also suggest ways of breaking the cycle and moving forward to redemption. In cases where people feel responsible for the misfortune they have known, confession can serve to decontaminate the past and set the person on a more positive life trajectory. In the kinds of stories often told by recovering addicts in 12-step programs, the first step in decontamination involves giving up one's will to a higher power. The hero then systematically takes stock of the many ways addiction has harmed family, friends, and coworkers, and then he or she tries to make amends. Addiction is viewed as an illness from which the hero can never fully recover. But progress in life can still be made through extensive self-monitoring and the support of the 12-step community.

In the reform narratives examined by criminologist Shadd Maruna, protagonists break through the vicious circle when they are able to find mature roles in society that provide them with self-respect and interpersonal intimacy. When this happens, many ex-convicts come to believe that they have finally experienced a blessing in life. In gratitude, they then seek to give something back. They work to help those younger men and women who may be headed toward a life of crime. By sharing with others their personal stories of victimization, delinquency, and reform, ex-convicts express their newfound generativity. They come to see their own personal redemption as intimately tied to their strong desire to do something good for the next generation.

Unfortunately, Tanya Williams does *not* feel that she has done something good for the next generation—this, despite the fact that she is a mother of four and a part-time Sunday school teacher. Tanya loves her children, of course. But she does not believe she is contributing in positive ways to their development and welfare. Tanya is too preoccupied with her own problems to focus her attention fully on the problems that other people face. Reflecting the realities of a very tough life and her own negative way of telling stories about herself, Tanya's narrative identity is filled with contamination sequences and vicious circles. In her story, the protagonist has never been able to recapture the good and true inner self that she lost once she became an adolescent. "These days, I am desperately seeking myself," Tanya remarks. At the end of the life-story interview, Tanya says she is looking for a "stepping stone" in life.

"Can you give me a stepping stone?" Tanya asks the interviewer.[44] She is hoping that the interviewer might be able to offer her some piece of advice, some pearl of wisdom that could move her life forward. Tanya is hoping for a stroke of good fortune or a positive turn of events that might break the vicious circle of her life. She wants to take that first forward step along the path to a better place. In desperately seeking herself, Tanya aims to decontaminate her past and return to the good and true inner self she knew long ago. In looking for that stepping stone, Tanya holds out the hope for redemption.

Nine

WHEN REDEMPTION FAILS

In their midlife years, the most caring and productive American adults tend to tell a certain kind of story about their lives. I call this story *the redemptive self.* As they reconstruct the past and imagine the future, highly generative American adults shape their lives into a narrative about how a gifted hero encounters the suffering of others as a child, develops strong moral convictions as an adolescent, and moves steadily upward and onward in the adult years, confident that negative experiences will ultimately be redeemed. Redemption may take the form of atonement for past wrongs, upward social mobility, political or emotional emancipation, recovery and healing, personal enlightenment, or the progressive development and fulfillment of the good inner self. Like any narrative identity, this story provides life with some degree of meaning and coherence. But more than other kinds of life stories, the redemptive self underscores the narrator's belief that bad things can be overcome and affirms the narrator's commitment to building a better world. It is a story that supports a generative life—a narrative identity artfully designed to encourage and sustain a caring and productive outlook on adult life.

This is a good story told by some very good people. Generative adults are committed to the growth and well-being of future generations. In their roles as parents, teachers, mentors, leaders, activists, worshipers, and productive citizens, especially generative men and women contribute in positive ways to their families, neighborhoods, schools, churches, and society. They build and sustain the institutions that make a good society good. They work to make a good society better. They want to give something back to the world. They want to leave a positive mark on posterity. They want to make a positive difference. A life story that features the power of human redemption is a good life story to make if you are in the business of making the world a better place. And should not we all be in that business? Would not the world be a better place if more people were dedicated to making it so? I am not so cynical as to believe that it would not. Throughout this book, I have tended to feature the positive qualities of the redemptive self, for I do sincerely believe that aspects of the story are worth affirming. You may wish to draw creatively upon this story's images, plots, and themes in creating a narrative identity for your own life.

So, what could ever be *wrong* with a story this good?

In this chapter, I turn my attention to the limitations and the dangers of the redemptive self. Just as no single person can truly claim to lead a perfect life, the life stories of highly generative American adults are not without their failings. Even the most productive and caring midlife adults will admit to a litany of shortcomings, conflicts, and frustrations. We all struggle with our shortcomings, our character flaws, our petty jealousies, and our deep disappointments and defeats. Unless we are completely out of touch with the reality of our own lives, we will admit that we are—each and every one of us— *flawed,* and the lives we lead are flawed. What we are less likely to realize and admit, however, is that the very stories upon which our lives are based may themselves be flawed. No story is perfect—not even a story of redemption.

It seems almost un-American to find fault in narratives of atonement, upward social mobility, political and emotional emancipation, recovery and healing, personal enlightenment, and the development of a good inner self. These kinds of stories are the "mom and apple pie" of narrative identity. *But this is precisely my point.* In a profound sense, it *is* un-American to take issue with the redemptive self. Understood more deeply, to look critically upon the redemptive self is to look critically upon certain aspects of American culture, for the redemptive self is a story that celebrates some of the most cherished values in our American heritage.

The redemptive self is a characteristically American story that supports a characteristically American brand of generativity. But there are surely other brands—life stories that work just as well to affirm generative lives under very different cultural conditions and with respect to different cultural (and subcultural) traditions. Put differently, *generativity is a human universal, but the redemptive self is not.* In every human society, productive and caring adults in their midlife years shoulder the burdens of promoting the growth and well-being of future generations. These adults make sense of their own lives through some kind of story that makes good sense within their own culture. The redemptive self is a life story that highly generative *American* adults tell. It is a story that makes good sense in the context of American culture and history. But Americans are wrong to think, as we sometimes do, that our story is superior to all the others. And we are especially wrong to think, as I fear we often do, that ours is the only story out there.

I come now not to bury the redemptive self, but I do not wish to idolize it either. We need to step further back from the life story that highly generative American adults tend to tell. We need to see it from a greater cultural distance in order to afford a more objective evaluation. Let us, therefore, cast a cool, analytical eye upon a way of telling a good American life that seems so, well, good. It is not *all* good.

Problem 1: Individualism and Its Discontents

In all societies, generativity links people together across generations and within social groups and institutions. It should come as no surprise, therefore, that highly generative American adults tend to feel they are well integrated into society. To a greater extent than most other Americans, highly generative American adults are actively involved in civic, religious, and political organizations. They are joiners and doers. Furthermore, they often enjoy strong bonds of love and friendship in their families and communities. They receive and provide high levels of social support. They know many people. And many people like and respect them.

Despite their many friendships and affiliations, however, highly generative American adults—both men and women—can be strong individualists. The American brand of generativity gives prime importance to the "I." Here are those common expressions of generativity that we so value in America: "*I* want to make a positive difference in the world." "*I* want to give something back." "*I* want to leave a legacy for *my* children." In telling their redemptive life stories, highly generative American adults will often credit other people for helping them along in life, but they will credit larger groups or societal institutions much less often. Although highly generative American adults often work through social institutions to make the world a better place, they typically express some ambivalence or even suspicion toward such traditional institutions as governments, churches, schools, the military, and the like. Like most Americans, they tend to believe that the world becomes a better place mainly through the efforts of hardworking *individuals*— each man and woman doing his or her part, following his or her inner calling and direction. This individualistic conception of good work was captured perfectly by the first President Bush when he initiated his "Thousand Points of Light" program. Each day, the Bush administration would identify an individual American—a point of light—who had brightened up the world with his or her own generous or heroic behavior.

It is perhaps ironic but especially revealing that the life stories of the most caring and socially integrated American adults at midlife express so vividly the efficacy and the discontents of American individualism. Many life stories of highly generative American adults are tributes to the noble achievements of the individual self. Highly generative adults *do* make a positive difference in the world—each of them, individually. But generative achievements may come with a cost. To a greater extent than is the case with less generative adults, highly generative American adults experience a conflict between what psychologists call *agency* and *communion*.[1] *Agency* refers to the tendency to expand, defend, or express the self; *communion* refers to joining the self with others in bonds of love, friendship, and community.

A common refrain in the life stories of highly generative American adults is the difficulty narrators express in simultaneously fulfilling their strong needs for both personal agency (power) and communion (love).[2] The conflict may be expressed in many ways. In one woman's story, social activism consumes so much time in her early adult years that she is never able to squeeze in a husband and a family, much to her regret. For another highly generative woman, balancing her work as a teacher with her family responsibilities pits a more public form of generativity against a more private one, and neither seems to get its full due, she believes. For chapter 6's Daniel Kessinger, the more successful and powerful he becomes as a community organizer, the more difficulty he has relating to his close friends and his family. The relationship with his 11-year-old daughter is especially complex. He wants to provide guidance and discipline, but he also wants to love her unconditionally. When he exerts too much control, she rebels and withdraws her love. When he lets up and allows her to do what she wants to do, he feels guilty—a "slacker" father who does not have the guts to say *no*.

It is as if highly generative adults want too much from the world. They want to feel powerful, effective, and free; at the same time, they want to feel loved, accepted, and bonded to others in enduring communities of care. Of course, at some level, we all have strong needs for agency and communion. But highly generative American adults seem to want it all *more*—or better, they tend to play out the inherent conflicts between power and love, between freedom and belonging, in more dramatic terms in their self-defining life stories. In so doing, highly generative American adults are expressing a dynamic that cultural historians have long associated with life in America. As Michael Kammen describes it in a classic study of American culture, "the push-pull of both wanting to belong and seeking to be free has been the ambivalent condition of life in America, the nurture of a contrapuntal civilization."[3]

Among the first observers of American life to document this contrapuntal dilemma was the French social philosopher Alexis de Tocqueville. In the 1830s de Tocqueville admired Americans' can-do initiative, and he singled out American family life, church attendance, and participation in local politics as strong forces for bonding Americans together into harmonious and dynamic social communities. At the same time, however, he warned against the centrifugal forces of unbridled American individualism: "The citizen of the United States is taught from infancy to rely upon his own exertions, in order to resist the evils and the difficulties of life; he looks upon social authority with an eye of mistrust and anxiety, and he claims its assistance only when he is unable to do without it."[4] Self-sufficiency may often be a good thing, de Tocqueville suggested, but it tends to devalue those other goods that can come only from group support and collective action. Furthermore, individualism may push people away from larger collectives and into the private retreats of family and close friendships, ultimately undermining a democratic polity. In this regard, Tocqueville wrote that individualism often "disposes each member of the community to sever himself from the mass of his fellows and to draw apart with his family and his friends, so that after he has thus formed a little circle of his own, he willingly leaves society at large to itself."[5]

Many social critics have followed de Tocqueville's lead in decrying the excesses of American individualism. Invoking images of the cowboy, the robber-baron, the traveling salesman, and the couch potato, social observers have repeatedly depicted Americans as solitary individualists, sometimes rugged, sometimes ugly, sometimes just "hanging out." In a searing indictment of modern life, Christopher Lasch described American society in the 1970s as a "culture of narcissism."[6] A few years later, sociologist Robert Bellah and his colleagues drew directly upon de Tocqueville's writings to expose the deep difficulties Americans' experience in finding ways of expressing their longings for community.[7] "Clearly, the meaning of one's own life for most Americans is to become one's own person, almost to give birth to oneself," Bellah wrote in *Habits of the Heart*.[8] The language of the individual self is so powerful and pervasive in America that we do not even know how to talk about community life, except to describe how relationships with others are either good or bad *for the self*. Striking a similar note at the turn of the 21st century, Robert Putnam lamented Americans' loss of "social capital."[9] In *Bowling Alone*, Putnam argued that many indices of healthy community life in the United States have declined since the 1950s. With notable exceptions, we do not join clubs anymore; we do not get involved in political and civic activities the way we used to; we spend most of our free time watching television, playing video games, and driving to the mall.

While sociological critics warn of the breakdown of community in American life, psychological critics sound another warning: they suggest that unmitigated individualism ultimately compromises the very self it extols. In psychological circles it has almost become a cliché to underscore the importance of social relationships for the development of the healthy self and to lament, in the next breath, the obstacles to intimacy and community in modern Western life. The more incisive analyses go beyond the immediate contexts of family and friends to articulate the complex historical and economic forces at work, in the spirit of Marx and critical theory. For example, Philip Cushman views American cultural history as "a story of an increasingly lonely people trying to live decently in a world of . . . isolation, uncertainty, and doubt."[10] To fill the void, Cushman argues, capitalist industry and the psychotherapy business have worked hand-in-hand to create a consumerist culture wherein psychological health is reduced to feeding an "empty self." Selves, relationships, and communities become commodities that are bought, sold, and consumed in an effort to satisfy a hunger that never seems to wane. The basic hunger is loneliness, argues James Lynch, in a recent book that documents the medical consequences of social isolation (e.g., heart disease).[11] Rugged individualists that we are, we Americans tend to be in denial about our loneliness, Lynch insists. Yet some of us are fully aware of just how isolated we are. The great American novelist Henry James maintained that loneliness was the starting point for all of his literature, and Emily Dickinson's poetry depicted the pain and illusion of the solitary life.[12] Of course, people (and eminent writers) are lonely the world over, but de Tocqueville thought that Americans might be at especially high risk for social isolation: "Americans acquire the habit of always considering themselves as standing alone, and they are apt to imagine that their destiny is in their hands. Thus, not only does [American] democracy make every man forget his ancestors, but it hides his descendants and separates his contemporaries from him; it throws him back forever upon himself alone, and threatens in the end to confine him entirely within the solitude of his own heart."[13]

We can even be lonely in a crowd. David Riesman's *The Lonely Crowd*, originally published in 1949, was one of the most influential sociological analyses of American character ever written.[14] Like a number of other social science books appearing in the early postwar years, *The Lonely Crowd* expressed more concern about mindless conformity than it did about the dangers of American individualism.[15] Riesman sought to understand the different social and psychological mechanisms through which Americans learn to conform to the norms and rules of society. In premodern societies, people are *tradition-directed,* Riesman argued. They conform to clear-cut religious and cultural traditions, and violations of tradition produce the experience of *shame.* The Renaissance and Reformation gave birth to forms of society that demanded the *inner-directed* character type. For inner-directed people, society's values and norms are learned early in life, leaving behind a "psychological gyroscope" that provides guidance for the rest of life. Inner-directed people conform to society's basic values because those values are consistent with the character structure they learned as children. Violations of these standards result in the experience of *guilt.*

Riesman believed that inner-direction was beginning to give way in the middle years of 20th-century America to an *other-directed* character structure. The other-directed person looks to people in his or her immediate environment for guidance and standards. The other-directed person conforms not so much to authoritarian traditions or internalized values and goals but to the social contingencies that prevail in a given situation. For the other-directed person, being liked and fitting in to the immediate environment are prime motivators for social life. Not fitting in results in *anxiety.* Epitomized in the anxious company man of post–World War II America, the other-directed person gets through life by playing roles and performing in accord with the exigencies of the social moment. Compared to the inner-directed person, he or she seems more agreeable, friendlier, shallower, more flexible, and more anxious: "The other-directed person tends to become merely his succession of roles and encounters and hence to doubt who he is and where he is going," Riesman wrote.[16] "The other-directed person has no clear core of self to escape from; no clear line between production and consumption; between adjusting to the group and serving private interests; between work and play."[17] Without the crowd, he is nothing.

A common interpretation of Riesman's work is to identify the inner-directed man as an individualist and the other-directed man as a conformist. But this is not quite right. In Riesman's view, both types conform their behaviors to norms and standards that ultimately derive from the outside. The key differences pertain instead to development and stability. For the inner-directed person, external norms and values are internalized early on in life and remain relatively stable thereafter. Consequently, the inner-directed person feels that he or she behaves in accord with a relatively stable ideological core. The other-directed person, by contrast, either ignores these internalized values or never internalizes them in the first place. Instead, the other-directed person adjusts his or her behavior to the dictates of ever-changing social conditions. In a sense, the other-directed person is more of a "work in progress," but the "work" (or psychological development) does not appear to be aimed in any particular direction. Consequently, he or she may feel un-rooted and even alienated, especially when conformity to the group proves too difficult to achieve.

At the end of his book, Riesman invents a new character type, which he calls the *autonomous person*. The autonomous person is both principled and flexible, Riesman seems to suggest, and capable of living in "freedom." Tipping his hand as a champion of American individualism in its best sense, Riesman ultimately finds fault with both the inner- and the other-directed types, because neither appears to live up to the full potential inherent in being a free man or woman living in a mature and dynamic democracy. For Riesman, as for Erich Fromm (1941) in his famous book *Escape From Freedom*, too many individuals shrink from the obligations of freedom.[18] In the last sentence of his book, Riesman expresses his deepest commitment to American individualism: "The idea that men are created free and equal is both true and misleading: men are created different; they lost their social freedom and their autonomy in seeking to become like each other."[19]

Unlike de Tocqueville, Bellah, Putnam, and many others who claim Americans are too individualistic, Riesman ended up suggesting that, if anything, we are not individualistic enough. Yet for all these authors, and for so many others who have observed and critiqued American social life over the past 200 years, the problem of individualism appears to be *the* central problem in American culture. How do free individuals live together in community? What is the appropriate relationship between the self and society? How can I express the self's agency and still be connected to others in meaningful and loving communion? Both inner-directed and other-directed and seeking autonomy and community, freedom and belongingness, power and love, highly generative American adults live out the drama of American individualism and its discontents. Their life stories reflect the satisfactions, as well as the frustrations, that de Tocqueville observed and imagined for a people so deeply committed to the free expression of the individual self.

Problem 2: American Exceptionalism

The narrative identities of highly generative American adults celebrate the uniqueness and the giftedness of the good inner self. The protagonists in these stories believe that they are the chosen people—chosen by God, good fortune, positive circumstances, a special talent or relationship, or some other advantage that they experienced as a child to live out an inner truth that will redound to the benefit of others. Theirs is a manifest destiny to make the world a better place, to give back for the blessings they have received. As children, they sensed they were called to do something good with their lives. In their adolescent years, they committed themselves to a set of values and beliefs, often anchored in some religious tradition, that have sustained their efforts ever since. Their principles are simple, self-evident truths that guide their behavior and keep them focused and steady in an unredeemed world. They stay the course. They fight the good fight. No matter how bad things get, no matter how many mistakes they make, they own an inner confidence that tells them that in some fundamental sense they are justified, they are right, they are good, they are special, they are the *exception* to the rule.

To the ambivalent among us, to the hand-wringers and nay-sayers, to the academic skeptics and political realists, to the folks who wake up in the middle of the night and wonder if they are indeed doing the right thing, the simple sincerity and quiet confidence of some highly generative American adults can be damn annoying. True belief can look like arrogance (or ignorance). Sustained commitment can seem rigid, narrow, or even blind. And how do we feel when our truths are different from theirs? When the commitments we make conflict with the commitments they make? Please know that there is no empirical evidence to suggest that highly generative adults are any more narrow-minded, dogmatic, or arrogant than individuals low in generativity. Personality traits like these can be found among highly generative adults, those low in generativity, and everybody in between. But the *life stories* that highly generative adults live by portray a main character who is chosen for goodness, who believes steadfastly in a deep inner truth, and who moves forward in life with the confidence that comes from being distinguished and exceptional. The *story* may have a kind of arrogance about it, even if the *person* living it seems humble and nice.

It is often said that almost everybody in America thinks he or she is above average. The idea is evoked with charm and humor in Garrison Keillor's stories of Lake Wobegon, Minnesota, where "all the women are strong, all the men are good-looking, and all the children are above average." Of course, only half of the population can technically be "above average" on any given dimension. But researchers have continually found evidence for the Lake Wobegon effect on a wide range of dimensions, from self-ratings of intelligence to estimates of one's own driving ability.[20] Some psychologists argue that believing in one's own superiority, even when such a belief is an illusion, protects self-esteem and psychological morale.[21] Indeed, cross-cultural research shows that Americans in general do have higher levels of self-esteem than people of most other nations.[22] Boosting children's self-esteem has become something of an unquestioned obsession among middle-class parents and teachers in the United States over the past 30 years. Yet empirical research shows clearly that high self-esteem does *not* necessarily translate into better performance in school or work; nor does it predict success in the interpersonal domain. Instead, high levels of self-esteem can often feed narcissism, grandiosity, and the sense that one is entitled to special treatment in the world.[23]

We are taught in America that every individual is unique and special. Everybody has a special talent or gift to offer. About 20 years ago, developmental psychologist Howard Gardner proposed a new theory of intelligence that emphasized the many different kinds of cognitive abilities that people express.[24] Gardner argued against the commonly held notion that intelligence is that single quality measured on IQ tests, for which some people show high scores (indicating they have a large amount of intelligence) and others show lower scores (indicating they have less). Instead, there are multiple, independent intelligences, Gardner argued—linguistic, spatial, mathematical, kinesthetic, musical, and personal intelligences—and more. Many American educators and parents totally love this idea. If my student or child does poorly in one kind of intelligence, there is always the possibility that we can find another one upon which he or she can be declared above av-

---

Box 9.1. How High Is Your Self-Esteem?

On typical self-esteem questionnaires, people rate the extent to which they agree or disagree with items like those listed below (from Slater, 2002). On the average, Americans tend to score higher on self-esteem measures than people in many other countries, and among Americans highly generative adults tend to score especially high. More importantly, highly generative American adults tend to tell life stories affirming a message that follows easily from high self-esteem—the message that "early on in life I realized that I was especially fortunate or blessed and that I was destined to live an *exceptional* life." The narrative identities of highly generative American adults, therefore, reflect a cultural preoccupation with self-esteem, giftedness, and related ideas—all *psychological* forms of what historians have termed *American exceptionalism.*

On the whole I am satisfied with myself.

I feel that I have a number of good qualities.

I am able to do things as well as most other people.

I feel that I am a person of worth, at least the equal of others.

I take a positive attitude toward myself.

I feel I do not have much to be proud of.

erage, or even gifted. In a related vein, educators and parents speak knowingly today of different learning styles, "right brain" versus "left brain" learners, and various learning disabilities and deficits that can be clearly delineated to show that, though everybody cannot do everything well, anybody can surely find *some* particular domain of functioning somewhere wherein he or she shows exceptional ability.

The quest for distinctiveness knows no bounds in America today. We even look for our specialness in the terrible things that happen in life. An especially compelling narrative in contemporary American life is the story of recovery from victimization. Memoirs like Mary Karr's *The Liar's Club* and Kathryn Harrison's *The Kiss* depict protagonists as victims of emotional and sexual abuse in childhood who manage to find enough redemption in life to write about their victimization in artful and moving ways.[25] Part of what makes these stories so powerful is the protagonist's innocence. The heroine is always good and pure in the beginning. In the fashion of most American stories about childhood, and along the lines of most theories about children articulated by American developmental psychologists and other experts, there must be a good, true, inner self on stage for the first act. Enter an abusive antagonist, however, and the age of innocence abruptly ends. In stories of abuse, the antagonist may be a parent or other family member, magnifying the horror of innocence lost, trust betrayed. In a perverse sense, the innocent protagonist has been *chosen* for special suffering. Redemption lies in the resilience and determination the protagonist displays in overcoming his or her singular nemesis. The good and true inner self wins out in the end, or at least survives to tell the story.

Some critics have suggested that Americans revel in their victimhood. In her book *I'm Dysfunctional, You're Dysfunctional,* Wendy Kaminer writes that, in contemporary American life, "everybody wants to be a survivor." Even if they were not fortunate enough to experience real abuse as a child, Kaminer sardonically suggests, many Americans reconstruct the past in especially negative ways in order to set up a recovery narrative for themselves. They exaggerate childhood disappointments and search long and hard to find childhood scenes of betrayal in order to create a story about innocence lost. The story's main goal, then, becomes "healing your 'inner child'—the wounded child who took refuge from deprivation and abuse in some recess of your soul."[26] Comfortably sipping wine in their spacious suburban homes, upper-middle-class Americans need something to overcome. Horatio Alger cannot be the path to redemption for them. Instead, they may look to self-help and the modern recovery movement for lessons of spiritual uplift. They may find in their special suffering as childhood victims a redemptive story that will win them self-esteem and social approval. Writes Kaminer, "Like Contestants on 'Queen for a Day,' Americans of various persuasions assert competing claims of victimhood, vying for attention and support."[27]

The possibility that some recovering victims may indeed have made it all up has not been lost on the skeptics. In *A Child Called "It"* and two other autobiographical books, Dave Pelzer tells the story of growing up in a family that is so dysfunctional as to defy belief. Pelzer describes how his mother, Catherine, starved him for 10 days, smeared feces on his face, made him eat dog feces (with worms in it), made him eat his own vomit, burned his arm over a stove, and kept him hidden away from his four siblings throughout his childhood. He goes on for 13 grotesque pages narrating an episode in which his mother stabbed him. (In one book she stabbed him in the stomach; in another, it was in the heart.)

Pelzer gives no explanation for why his mother hated him so much, and how it was that she proved to be kind and caring to almost everybody else. Pelzer refuses to provide the identities of family members, in order, he claims, to protect their privacy. But one reporter tracked down a brother. Now 40 years old, the younger brother denies that his mother ever abused Dave. Dave was never ostracized from the family, his brother claims: "He was very close to me and Robert" (another brother). "We were 'The Three Musketeers.' But David had to be the center of attention. He was a hyper, spoiled brat." Pelzer's grandmother, Ruth Cole, remembers him as a "disruptive kid, only interested in himself, with big ideas of grandeur." His grandmother claims that as a young man Dave bragged that celebrities, like Chuck Yeager, would attend his wedding. "But it was just a few family members in the garage," she says. "His books should be in the fiction section."[28] Fiction or not, Pelzer's books have sold millions, topping out best-seller lists for months on end. His fans believe him. They identify with him. They marvel at his resilience and his ability to transform his life into a narrative of redemption.

Even in our sufferings (those real and imagined), we Americans strive for distinctiveness. As good as it is to be above average, it is so much better to be one of the chosen people. To be blessed with that unique advantage. To be the exception to all the mundane rules. Historians use the term *American exceptionalism* to suggest that from the beginning the United States was, or considered itself to be, the exception to the rules. This special nation, "under God," dedicated to those simple propositions of freedom and equality under the law, blessed with an abundance of natural resources like no other nation on earth, whose manifest destiny was to expand across the North American continent and subjugate its native peoples, to spread the good news of democracy to the four corners of the globe, to welcome the huddled masses and stand up against all evil empires, and perhaps to become its own empire in the 21st century—this special, chosen nation is too special to be subject to any systems or orders larger than its good sovereign self. Whether the United States is viewed as the leader of the world or a global bully, liberator or oppressor, it remains a singular force, apart from all the other states and principalities, separated by geography or politics or wealth from all the others, exceptional in reality to be sure, but also and especially exceptional in its own "mind" and through its own self-defining myths.

The United States—today the world's only superpower—may be exceptional even in its own (self-proclaimed) *innocence*. A major theme in *America*'s narrative identity is the innocence of the good inner self.[29] Again and again, historians and cultural observers have remarked on the extraordinary ways in which the self-images of Americans, and of America itself, are rooted in a basic sense of goodness and innocence. The chosen people are decent people at their very core—and not just decent in the ways that people all over the world may be decent, but exceptionally decent, exceptionally pure and even simple, good and innocent, bordering on naïve. The comparison is made most frequently to Europe. In de Tocqueville, Herman Melville, Walt Whitman, Henry Adams, Henry James, and many writers of the 20th century, American innocence is played off against European experience; idealism, against cynicism; exuberance, against a somewhat weary but realistic appraisal of the world. A German colleague of mine admires Americans for their can-do enthusiasm about changing the world: "Students in America often say, 'I want to change the world. I want to make a difference.' We do not say that in Europe. It sounds too presumptuous, almost silly. It is not that we don't want to make a difference in the world. But one person? Making a difference all by himself? Get real!"

Innocence is most noticed when it is "lost." In my lifetime, Americans seem to have lost their innocence at least half a dozen times! For the baby boomer generation, the dramatic assassination of John F. Kennedy has always been depicted as a loss of innocence. But then we lost our innocence again in Vietnam. And Watergate. A couple of decades later, innocence was lost big time with the September 11 attacks on the Pentagon and World Trade Center. In a moving account written the week after September 11, 2001, Andrew Sullivan described how the bombings blew up more than buildings and bodies. They also exploded the narrative that we Americans are separate and special and destined to be protected in an unredeemed world:

To arrive from elsewhere onto American soil was always and every-where a relief. It presaged the joy of security again, of family and friends and faith and work. We knew what days were for; and knew also that even when disaster struck or news shocked, the days them-selves would encompass what we had to deal with. They would bracket us, shield us, support us.

I look at the calendar now and see the last time I felt this way. I check my voice mail and hear voices recorded before it changed. I haven't erased them. Something stops me. I want to remember their unwitting innocence—of dates fixed and dinners planned, of trips scheduled and work to be done, of assumptions of regularity that seemed banal before they ended, when they suddenly seemed more precious than the gorgeous sun that beat down on that Tuesday morning. I miss that blithe assurance that things will be what they have been—if not in degree but in kind. I miss the America that knew deeply it was different, apart, protected, somehow open to the world and yet immune from its worst evils.[30]

Like the most cherished national narratives of the American heritage, the life stories of highly generative American adults speak a language of excep-tionalism. Because of our special blessings or sufferings, because of our good and innocent inner nature, because of the simple truths we steadfastly be-lieve in, we are the exceptions, destined to make a positive difference in the world. In their best expressions, these stories may inspire people to take on attitudes and projects aimed at benefiting others, advancing society, and en-hancing the world we will bequeath to our children's children. As national narratives, these stories promote patriotism and idealism and can succor a nation even during its darkest days, at Gettysburg, for example, or after September 11.

But the same stories can sometimes seem naïve, arrogant, and dismissive of the real gifts and legitimate concerns of others—be those others the people outside the orbit of our own generative efforts or, on a national level, those living in very different kinds of societies with different values, beliefs, and goals. These kinds of stories can unwittingly (and sometimes quite con-sciously) suggest that I am good and you are evil, that I was chosen and you were overlooked. Throughout history, those who have considered them-selves the chosen people have often made more enemies than friends. At a fundamental, philosophical level, furthermore, a belief that we are the chosen people—be that belief psychological or political—seems to contradict a be-lief in equality. How can *everybody* be chosen? How can everybody be gifted?

How realistic is it to think that everybody can be *called* to fulfill his or her own manifest destiny? What happens when my destiny undermines yours? How can every individual be the *exception* to all the rules? And why should any nation or individual be entitled to lord it over all the others?

Problem 3: Redemptive Violence

Generativity is about giving birth to things. It is about creating life and nurturing that life along. It is about bettering the lives of the next generation. On first blush, therefore, nothing would seem to be more antithetical to generativity than violence and destruction. The impulse to kill or destroy would seem to run in direct contrast to the impulse to create and to nurture. Yet we can doubtlessly think of many examples in which it seems necessary to destroy or even kill in order to promote life and growth. We tear down abandoned buildings to clear the way for houses or office suites. We pull out the weeds from our gardens in order to promote the growth of our flowers and vegetables. We slaughter cows and pigs in order to feed human beings. We fight and kill other human beings when our lives or the lives of our loved ones are threatened. Indeed, human beings often attempt to justify their aggressive acts in the name of generativity: "I did it for my family." "I did it for my country." Sometimes these justifications seem compelling to us, sometimes not.

There is no evidence to suggest that highly generative American adults are any more aggressive than adults lower in generativity. Indeed, if we define aggression in terms of criminal activity, antisocial behaviors, and the like, then they are probably *less* aggressive, in that highly generative adults, overall, tend to be fairly well integrated into society. Nor is there any clear evidence to support the idea that American citizens are any more or less aggressive than citizens of other nations. Aggression is defined differently in different societies, and its expression is strongly shaped by cultural, economic, and religious norms, and by unpredictable events such as war and political unrest. In all societies there are some people who act in especially destructive and violent ways, and many others who strive to live relatively peaceful lives. Furthermore, in all societies certain individuals are socialized to be more aggressive than others. We expect and promote certain forms of aggression in soldiers, police officers, and athletes. We expect a less aggressive attitude and gentler behavior among nurses and social workers. To a large extent, moreover, the very concept of aggression is gendered, associated more commonly with the behavior of men than with the behavior of women.

But I am not mainly concerned here about individual behavior. I am concerned instead about the *story*. The redemptive self is not a violent story, *but it is a story that can be read as one that might conceivably condone aggression in the name of redemption.* The ways in which this could be accomplished in narrative are many. For example, the protagonist's belief that he or she is chosen to be the good exception in the world might conceivably be used to justify aggression in the service of promoting selfish needs and wants. If I am the exception, I can break the rules to promote my own agenda, at the expense of yours. The protagonist's strong commitment to a clear set of values, his moral steadfastness and ideological certitude might function to transform a life story into a morality play, featuring the good hero against the bad world. In accounting for the dogged efforts of the famous Supreme Court jurist Oliver Wendell Holmes to find pragmatic solutions to legal dilemmas, historian Louis Menand argues that the American Civil War taught the young Holmes a basic lesson: "It is that certitude leads to violence."[31] Moral fervor is a potent force in many life stories told by highly generative American adults. Be they Christian conservatives or card-carrying members of the American Civil Liberties Union, the protagonists in these stories may tend to see life itself as something of a mission. I am here to do God's work, or at least *good* work. If I encounter resistance, I will need to fight for what is right. I know what is right. My fight, therefore, will always be the good fight.

From the early 19th century to the present day, Americans have used redemptive rhetoric to justify national expansionism, imperialism, opportunism, and a range of other violent acts and programs. They have used it to justify wars that historians have characterized as well intentioned, and wars that history has judged in much less charitable terms. "The belief that one is carrying out divine purpose can serve legitimate needs and sustain opposition to injustice," wrote Jackson Lears on the eve of the U.S. invasion of Iraq in 2003. "But it can also promote dangerous simplifications—especially if the believer has virtually unlimited power." "The slide into self-righteousness is a constant threat."[32] As just one glaring example of self-righteousness, notice how President William McKinley, in 1898, justified the seizure of the Philippines after winning the Spanish-American War: "I am not ashamed to tell you, gentlemen, that I went down on my knees and prayed to Almighty God for light and guidance that one night. And one night late it came to me this way. . . . There was nothing left for us to do but to take them all and to educate the Filipinos and uplift and civilize and Christianize them, and by God's grace do the very best we could by them, as our fellow men for whom Christ also died."[33]

In his book, *Hellfire Nation*, James Morone suggests that ever since the Puritan days, Americans have been subject to a moral fervor that reinforces the twin urges of reforming others as we redeem ourselves.[34] Moralizing divides the world into the righteous *us* and the malevolent *them*. From this perspective, war may be conceived as a crusade: "Onward Christian soldiers, marching as to war, with the cross of Jesus going on before." The crusader theme is central to Ernest Lee Tuveson's classic study of American national destiny, *Redeemer Nation*. Tuveson describes the American mission: "Providence, or history, has put a special responsibility on the American people to spread the blessings of liberty, democracy, and equality to others throughout the earth, and to defeat, if necessary by force, the sinister powers of darkness."[35]

In order to redeem the world, the chosen people must fight the holy war. They must defeat the forces of evil and chaos. Throughout American history, those "evil" forces have often been projected onto non-Christians, people of color, governments with competing ideologies ("Godless communism"), and many other outsiders who were not deemed to be among the gifted. About 100 years ago, the statesman-historian Albert J. Beveridge delivered a famous address to the U.S. Senate, stating the purpose and calling of the American nation. His audience loved these words:

> God has not been preparing the English-speaking and Teutonic people for a thousand years for nothing but vain and idle self-contemplation and self-admiration. No. He made us master organizers of the world to establish system where chaos reigned. He has given us the spirit of progress to overwhelm the forces of reaction throughout the earth. He has made us adept in government that we may administer government among savage and senile peoples. Were it not for such a force as this the world would relapse into barbarism and night. And of all our race, He has marked the American people as His chosen nation to finally lead in the redemption of the world.[36]

With its racist overtones and bombastic claims of moral superiority, this kind of rhetoric has, thankfully, gone out of fashion. But American politicians still brand as "evil" certain foreign regimes, and they still call upon redemptive imagery to rally citizens for war. Many critics of the American (and British) war on Iraq in 2003 saw the Bush administration as arrogant and self-righteous in its refusal to bow to world opinion and seek a peaceful resolution to the conflict. Many in the Islamic world saw the war as a revival of the Crusades. Most Europeans strongly opposed the war, depicting the Americans as cowboys, bullies, or worse.

But defenders of the American policy insisted that force was the only viable means for achieving the desired ends—be those ends deposing Saddam Hussein, destroying weapons of mass destruction, or liberating the Iraqi people. In a very influential paper, analyst Robert Kagan argued that the United States is perfectly positioned today to impose its will on the world. The strong European sentiment against the use of such force reflects a historical divergence of Europe and the United States, Kagan contends. After two bloody world wars, the weakened European nations have come to value cooperation and conciliation in world affairs. As participants in the European Union, they tend to see themselves as thoroughly integrated within an international community wherein disputes are resolved through mediation and common interests. By contrast, Americans are more comfortable going it alone, both because of their unsurpassed military might and because of a history of independent action. If any single nation can make the world a better place, it is the United States, Americans tend to believe. In Kagan's view, they should seize the moment.[37]

Even vigorous apologists for the constructive use of American power will concede that (White) Americans used the language of redemption to justify the displacement of millions of indigenous people from their native North American lands. Historian Richard Slotkin analyzes how White Americans, between 1600 and 1860, came to understand their own relentless and ultimately successful campaigns to tame the wilderness, defeat the Indians, and expand their domain to encompass the vast land that is today the United States. He argues that White Americans justified these acts of violence in terms of *regeneration*. In order to generate something new and good, we needed to destroy the old. We purged the land of its original inhabitants. We stole the land from others who claimed it was theirs. We glorified the violent heroes who were so instrumental in helping us win this ongoing war—the hunters, pioneers, and Indian fighters.

Slotkin asserts that violence in the name of regeneration and redemption is the most striking theme of the American story: "The first colonists saw in America an opportunity to regenerate their fortunes, their spirits, and the power of their church and nation; but the means to that generation ultimately became the means of violence, and the myth of regeneration through violence became the structuring metaphor of the American experience."[38] "The land was ours before we were the land's," wrote Robert Frost.[39] "The process by which we came to feel an emotional title to the land," claims Slotkin, "was many deeds of war."[40] War in the name of regeneration and redemption— war aimed at wiping out the *old* so that we can start fresh anew, or war aimed to rescue *them* from their own badness, to make them *good*, like us.

The most primal meanings of redemption are religious. In the Christian religion, the prototypical redemptive sequence is Christ's death and resurrection. The sequence is designed, Christians believe, to save humankind from its sin. Because Christ died on the cross but then came back from the dead, believers are redeemed from their own sinful natures. They will enjoy everlasting life because Christ died for them. But why does Christ need to be killed in the first place? Feminist theologians Rita Brock and Rebecca Parker point out that brutal violence is at the heart of the Christian redemption story. God sends his son to earth *to be murdered.* This violent act becomes the touchstone for the redemptive process. Only through violence can Christians ultimately be saved. In their deepest understandings of faith, Brock and Parker suggest, Christians are conditioned to associate violence with regeneration and redemption. And in emphasizing so strongly the death and resurrection of Christ, traditional Christian theology implicitly condones the use of violence in the service of noble purposes. As Brock and Parker see it, the Christian version of redemption ends up normalizing, if not encouraging, aggression in the service of "a higher calling," "the pursuit of the good," "the improvement of mankind," and other potentially dangerous ventures, even when they may be well-meaning.[41]

Problem 4: Can Everything Be Redeemed?

Although she retired from teaching a few years back, Melinda Taylor still substitutes in the local schools and tutors children who are having problems learning to read. At age 61, Melinda expresses her strong desires for generativity in the classroom, with her many female friends who routinely look to her for support, and through involvement in local politics ("I am a bleeding-heart liberal") and many charitable organizations. Melinda's life story contains many of the key features of the redemptive self. Her early advantage is that she is a star in school: "I was the one who got all the A's." Strong role models in her school and in the community teach her the value of living an honest and caring life. "For as long as I can remember, I have always tried to live by the Golden Rule," she says. Her parents, however, often disappoint her. Her mother fails to show up for the big performance of the third-grade play. Her father criticizes her first boyfriend. Still, Melinda describes these negative scenes as opportunities for growth. Redemption typically takes the form of learning and self-development. Painful experiences teach her key lessons or catalyze the process of maturation. "Most of the bad things that have happened to me have turned out to be growing experiences," Melinda says.

The worst of the bad things happen in her late 30s and 40s. On her 37th birthday, Melinda is diagnosed with breast cancer. She struggles through the tough period of radiation and chemotherapy. But her good friends support her all the way, and she proves to be a survivor. Looking back on her "cancer years," Melinda describes them as one of the *high points* of her life. Some of her best experiences in teaching occur during those years. And the illness brings out the best in her friends and family. She never felt more loved and appreciated than when she was stricken with cancer.

The low point in her life occurs in 1980. On the night that Ronald Reagan defeats Jimmy Carter in the U.S. presidential election, Melinda receives a phone call from a man who claims his wife is having an affair with Melinda's husband. "I was pretty upset by the election, as you can imagine. But the news on the phone completely wrecked me." She is shocked: "I thought our marriage was really great. I loved him, and I thought he loved me." She confronts her husband, and he admits to the affair. Still, she is willing to forgive him if he promises to break off the relationship with his lover. He cannot decide. Figuring that this event will work itself out in a positive way, she says she will wait for his decision:

> My friends said I should have told him to get out. But I didn't want
> to do that. I was trying to understand it through his eyes. I figured
> he was in a midlife crisis, and I was just going to see it through. So
> I waited longer than they say is necessary, I guess. A 2-year wait is
> pretty much enough, but I waited 4. *But it was a wonderful time for
> me.* It was very painful, but it was such a *growing time* that by the
> time I decided in 1984 that I wasn't going to wait any longer—
> because I kept getting this, "I'll know by tomorrow, I'll know by
> next month, I love you both, I don't want to get a divorce," well . . .
> I ended up okay with it. Around this time there was an article in the
> local paper about divorce, how people recover from it and so on.
> Well, I knew I could handle that. I didn't want to have a big lawsuit
> or, well, that just wasn't me. So I told him we should get a divorce,
> and he did not argue with me at all. Eleven days after the divorce was
> final, he married the other woman. So, I guess he worked through all
> his wavering and so on and decided that's what he wanted to do. And
> I look back at the end of it, and I see it as a real period of *hope.* It's
> been almost 15 years now, but you know I *learned so much* from that.

Precisely what Melinda did indeed learn from her husband's affair, her 4 years of patience, the final breakup, and the humiliating fact that he married her rival just days after the divorce was finalized is never made clear. But like virtually all the negative experiences in Melinda's life story—from her mother's negligence to her fight with cancer—this one ends up redeemed: "I did come out on the other side a better person, and probably a happier person. I was unaware that I was unhappy in our marriage, but now I think I was." If things are to get better, they have to be bad first. The marriage must have been bad, she has now decided; narrating it that way (I must have been unhappy, even though I wasn't aware I was) helps her to narrate her divorce as something that brings an improvement. No matter how large the setback in Melinda's life, growth always seems to follow. Melinda always puts the bad stuff behind her and moves forward. Life continues to progress. No regrets. No ambivalence.

There is much to admire in Melinda's story. The main character is extraordinarily resilient and upbeat. The plot is well crafted to illustrate meaningful growth and development. It is clear that Melinda's redemptive identity supports a very generative life. But, in my reading of the text, the redemptive sequences feel forced. When her mother fails to show for the big performance, little Melinda never sheds a tear. Instead, she says, "I learned to be more independent." When her husband's affair is exposed, she rejects the expected role of enraged wife and assumes instead the patient role of therapist—hoping to see him through his midlife crisis. (One need not consult the research on infidelity to know that this response is pretty odd.) He tells her he cannot decide whom he loves more—his wife or the other woman. Melinda waits for her unfaithful husband to sort it all out—she waits for 4 long years! Finally, she files for the divorce. Now, like magic, he is able to decide. He marries her rival virtually before the ink is dry on the divorce papers. And still Melinda never expresses a word of bitterness or regret. It was a "growing" experience for her. A period of "hope."

Melinda's story illustrates the lengths that some people will go to make redemptive narratives out of difficult life events. But does Melinda go too far? Does she seem more defensive than resilient? Does her redemptive story do full justice to the emotional dynamics of traumatic events like cancer and divorce? Do we believe her when she says that virtually every negative experience in her life has led to growth? One interpretation of her narrative is that she is deceiving the interviewer by presenting an identity story that is too upbeat to be true. Another, more interesting, interpretation is that she may be deceiving herself. So committed is she to the redemptive form of life-story telling that she is unable to experience and understand life difficulties in any other way. Many psychotherapists who work with narrative suggest that the best, most life-enhancing, and most authentic life stories are "true to lived experience."[42] Authentic life narratives encompass the full panoply of emotional life. The best narrative identities draw upon many different images, themes, and plots to provide a rich and differentiated sense of self. But when every negative event leads to redemption, a story may seem constricted, simplistic, and psychologically unsatisfying.

Some especially bad things that happen in life may not be redeemable. What about a child's death? What about a profound disability? What about murder? In the wake of the most devastating events, people struggle to find meaning and purpose. They will often look for silver linings and life lessons. But should we be surprised when they sometimes do not find them? Is it realistic to expect that all suffering will lead to redemption? Indeed, is it even morally *right* to expect it? To take the most extreme examples from the 20th century, what redemptive meaning might we find in the extermination of 6 million Jews or in the atrocities of Stalin and Pol Pot? In an article entitled "Against Redemption," James Young observes that many post-Holocaust writers in Europe are careful not to represent the last century's most horrific events in redemptive terms.[43] Even to suggest that something good might have come out of the systematic murder of so many people is to insult the dead, their families, and perhaps even the cosmos. In making sense of that which is grotesquely senseless, we must find forms of expression that go beyond redemption, Young suggests. We have to use different kinds of stories— more complex stories that do justice to the lived human experience and to suffering so intense and so pervasive that to hope for redemption in its wake is to trivialize the suffering itself.

For over 15 years, Professor Henry Greenspan has taught a college class on the stories of Holocaust survivors.[44] The students read testimonials written by survivors of the Nazi concentration camps. At the end of the semester, they meet one or two of the authors themselves and listen to them reflect on the stories they have written. One of Greenspan's interests in the class is to examine how a survivor may tell the "same" story again and again. He finds that the story of the same event may change subtly with repeated tellings. In one of Greenspan's examples, a survivor named Leon gives repeated accounts of an event he witnessed in which one of his friends in the camp was executed by a Nazi guard. When he tells the story the first time, Leon begins his account by underscoring the selective quality of narration: "The memory is selective, no question. And the selection is probably toward suppressing traumatic events and concentrating on others that have some human or *redeeming* quality."[45]

It is difficult to see much that is redemptive in his first telling. A 19-year-old prisoner named Lieberman steals a loaf of bread to give to his sister, who

FIGURE 9.1 Is every event redeemable? Some events in people's lives, and in world history, may be so horrific that constructing a redemptive narrative in their wake may be nearly impossible, or an affront to those who suffered the event. Redemptive narratives typically sustain hope and commitment, but they can sometimes also be heard as justifications or rationalizations for magnitudes of human pain that should never be justified or rationalized. Stories of redemption sometimes oversimplify complex emotional realities by suggesting that negative feelings will inevitably give way to positive. Redemptive narratives may also raise expectations for future growth, improvement, recovery, or even *retribution* in instances when such hopes might be baseless or even destructive. Reprinted with the permission of Getty Images. Photo by Ezra Shaw/Getty Images.

is starving in another camp. The Nazi guards find out. They march Lieberman and a number of other inmates out to a Jewish cemetery, where they are all instructed to chop up gravestones and haul them in wheelbarrows so that the gravestones can be used to build roads. Then SS corporal Schwetke shoots Lieberman in the head, and they bury him in the cemetery. Nonetheless, the story may be understood in terms of categories that are familiar to the students in Greenspan's class and that make sense within the framework of the redemptive self. The students can see Lieberman as a noble victim who gives his life to save his sister. Schwetke is readily cast as the evil antagonist. Leon plays the role of the witness who grieves the death of his friend. There is something very understandable and heroic about it all. Even though Lieberman died, Leon survived, and we can feel sympathy and inspiration in his story. Indeed, Leon's very telling of the story may itself be redemptive in that it helps us to understand his experience and it may help Leon cope with a traumatic event from his past.

But Leon's subsequent tellings call into question this redemptive interpretation. Over the course of 2 months, Leon tells Greenspan the same story two more times. He changes some of the details and fills in others. We learn the following: (a) Corporal Schwetke was not known as an especially brutal guard; indeed, he was one of the nicer ones; (b) Lieberman was one of the favorites of the Nazi guards; (c) the guards were proud of the hardworking Jews who were their prisoners; and (d) after Lieberman was shot, the inmates buried him themselves, and *they felt absolutely nothing*. Leon completely rejects Greenspan's suggestion that the story has some kind of redemptive meaning. He does not agree with the students who suggest that the telling itself helps lesson the trauma of the memory. It is all instead a nightmare that can never be fully conveyed, understood, or redeemed:

> Yeah. Yeah. Yeah. You [Greenspan] see a cause and effect relationship—a crime and a punishment. But, see, this is a good example of how hard it is to convey. You pose the question. I owe you an explanation. There are a few elements you couldn't have known.
>
> You see, in a perverted sort of way, the SS were proud of this camp. We had become their expert workers. They used to show us off! They used to say, in German, they never saw *Juden* work in such a fashion. Despite the killing all around us, we imagined this was a little island of security. And the Lieberman incident destroyed the whole thing.
>
> You see, this was the moment of truth. Lieberman was a favorite. Even to them, to the Germans, he was a favorite. He had smiling black eyes, with so much life in them. All of a sudden we see no one's life is worth a damn. The very Germans you thought took this almost paternal interest—they would kill you with as much thought as it takes to step on a cockroach. And so our pipe-dream was shattered right there. It was suddenly and dramatically shattered, along with Lieberman's skull.[46]

And regarding the burial of Lieberman, Leon says,

It was a feverish thing. A feverish feeling. A terrible intensity. When Lieberman was shot—the moment before there was sun—, even in a cemetery you were conscious of the world around you—, but with this execution, the whole thing came to a standstill. It is like—, the only reality left over here is death. Death—and we performing— like a mystic ritual. I wasn't aware of *anything* around me.

There would have been six of us. Six left. Six automatons digging the hole. . . . And even the SS man Schwetke, he ceased to be real. All of a sudden, he has left this known-to-you universe. And become something else. . . .

This is probably what makes it so unbelievable. The pure land- scape of death. . . . Even sound, even sound would be out of place. There is no sound actually. There is no sound.[47]

There is no redemption, either. Leon is telling Greenspan that every cate- gory he and the students want to use to extract a positive message from the story cannot justifiably be used. Yes, Lieberman steals the loaf of bread to help his sister, but she is going to die anyway. His act is probably more stu- pid than heroic. Why should the Germans shoot Lieberman? He is one of their favorites. The killer himself is probably the one guard least likely to pull the trigger. The Jewish prisoners are harboring the misplaced hope that they will be protected somehow, that their captors have some modicum of respect for them as hard workers and as human beings. But when Lieberman is shot, the hope is quashed forever, and the entire scene becomes unreal. Leon does not grieve for Lieberman. He and his fellow prisoners feel nothing now. They have become automatons, insensate machines digging a hole. There is no sound because there is nothing meaningful now to hear, or ever again. A pure landscape of death. And telling the story of it later does nothing to re- move the silence, the void, the impossibility of ever making sense of some- thing so horrifically senseless.

Few Americans have known the nightmares that Leon has known, but all of us suffer in our own ways. Some people suffer more than others. And some sufferings resist an upbeat, redemptive narration. Yet we live in a soci- ety that expects, even demands, happy endings to tough stories. *I believe there is a kind of tyranny in the never-ending expectation in American life that bad things will and should be redeemed.* When people tell us their problems, we anticipate that they will also tell us how they have solved them. And when they do not tell us that, we may want to help them find the happy endings we all want. We value and we expect improvement, growth, recovery, upward mobility, and the like. We listen intently for the redemptive message in a life narration. When we do not hear it, we are troubled or confused. How can that be? Surely, *something* good *must* have come out of that!

No! Nothing good came out of it. Don't be a fool. Don't be so naïve.

Many psychotherapists help their patients develop more redemptive understandings of their lives, in order to promote psychological well-being and meaningful participation in society. For the most part, this is good. But a few mental health experts have recently argued that the emphasis on redemption may be too strong, especially among American counselors and therapists. Israeli psychologists Nahi Alon and Haim Omer, for example, write that many people's lives would be enriched if they were more aware of the narrative power of *tragedy*.[48] In classic Greek or Shakespearean tragedy, the hero suffers a fate that he or she cannot avoid and for which he or she is not fully responsible. Oedipus cannot avoid the fate of killing his father and sleeping with his mother, no matter how hard he tries. The tragic hero learns that suffering is an essential part of life, even when the suffering has no ultimate meaning, benefit, or human cause. Suffering is to be endured, but not necessarily redeemed. Human beings are moral agents to be sure, but not every action or event makes sense in a moral framework. Sometimes we are just lucky, or unlucky. Fate, happenstance, blind chance, serendipity—tragedy teaches us that lives sometimes turn on these capricious factors.

Tragedy also teaches us other lessons that serve as a psychologically useful counterpoint to the redemptive self. For example, tragedy calls into question the belief that any particular individual is blessed with an innocent and good inner self that is destined to achieve good things. Buried in the rich soil of Oedipus's inner self are the seeds of both goodness and destruction. Indeed, the very qualities that so distinguish him as a great leader—his kingly goodness and responsibility, his love of truth, his uncanny ability to solve riddles—contribute to his downfall, as he pushes himself with all his might to find the secret that ultimately destroys him.

Tragedy gives fuller expression to the ambivalence and the complexity of human lives than do many other narrative forms. It looks with skepticism upon the kind of ideological certitude celebrated in the redemptive self. Surely, it is good for people to have strong moral principles, but many would say that the principles need to be flexible, and they need to be open to change as the world changes. The tragic hero anguishes over the moral complexities in the world. He does not settle for simple truths and pat answers. For him, there can be no "evil empire," and no "chosen people." At the same time, the tragic hero knows that decisions made and actions taken may sometimes not matter in the long run. Individuals can be overtaken by larger forces and by events beyond their control. Furthermore, one's best intentions can lead to the worst results. The most generative parents cannot assure that their children will not grow up to be sociopaths. The most committed public servant cannot know that her actions will not turn out to be blunders. Paradoxically, knowing that one's best actions may not always make the big difference, or even that they may backfire, can be liberating, Alon and Omer suggest. It may be okay if I fail in my goal to change the world for the better. But, of course, it is good to try.[49]

Finally, and perhaps most important, tragedy opens people up to each other and sometimes brings them closer together. In my own life, some of the moments in which I have felt closest to other people have been moments of deep sadness and pain. New friends whom I did not yet know very well showed up at my father's funeral. From then on, they were friends for life. My wife struggled with a health scare. Never had I loved her more. One of the most powerful feelings of community I ever experienced happened at a hastily arranged religious service, held the evening of September 11, 2001. From soldiers to sorority sisters, people often report that shared suffering bonds them to others in a powerful and enduring way.

People also report that others are easier to like and to know when they admit to their own vulnerabilities and flaws. Tragedy suggests that we are all flawed. We always have been, and we always will be. Tragedy rejects as folly the notion that selves can ever be perfected. The redemptive self can sometimes seem impenetrable and aloof in its deep and solitary commitment to improving the self and the world. The person whose story celebrates his or her unique giftedness, moral certitude, and redemptive quest to make over the world may evoke our admiration, but he or she may also scare us off a little bit, or put us off, or make us feel inferior. Which reminds me of my secretary's remark many years ago after I gave her 4 or 5 new interviews to type, taken from adults *low* in generativity. Before the new ones, she had typed up a batch of 50 life-story interviews of highly generative adults. "I like these new ones better," she said. "They don't take themselves so seriously."

Reprise

In box 9.2, I have summarized this chapter's critique of the redemptive self. I have suggested that for all its efficacy and worth, the narrative form that highly generative American adults tend to follow in making sense of their own lives has some potential limitations and shortcomings. The story tends to affirm (a) an individualist approach to life, (b) the belief that one is exceptional and distinctive, (c) a strong moral agenda that may sometimes excuse aggression in the service of noble purposes, and (d) a naïve or insensitive belief that all suffering can be redeemed. The potential problems with the redemptive self encompass both psychological and social issues. On the psychological level, for example, the expectation that all bad things should be redeemed may keep a person from experiencing life in its full emotional richness. On the social level, the same expectation may trivialize the suffering of others by insisting that all things will turn out good in the end. In a similar vein, the strong commitment to distinctive individual accomplishment, so characteristic of the redemptive self, may have the unintended effect of separating the story's protagonist from those he or she loves and shortchanging the social institutions to which he or she is committed.

The shortcomings and the limitations of the redemptive self reflect cultural concerns that have been at the heart of American national identity for the past two centuries. Alexis de Tocqueville warned of the potential dangers of unbridled American individualism. Since the 19th century, cultural observers have taken Americans to task for their arrogant exceptionalism and their deeply held belief that they are the chosen people. Violence in the name of redemption and regeneration is as old as the republic itself, as witnessed

---

Box 9.2. *Potential Problems and Limitations*
of the Redemptive Self

1. Individualism and its discontents
    - Conflict between power (freedom) and love (belonging)
    - Dangers of social isolation
2. American exceptionalism
    - Arrogance, sense of superiority and entitlement
    - Failure to take seriously others' points of view
    - Drive for distinctiveness, celebrity
3. Redemptive violence
    - Aggression in the service of noble purposes
    - Excessive moral fervor
    - The good "us" versus the bad "them"
4. Can everything be redeemed?
    - Naïve optimism, defensiveness
    - Emotional constriction
    - Trivialization of suffering
    - Denial of tragedy

in expansionism and imperialism in the name of manifest destiny and other purportedly lofty principles. Americans are known for their pragmatic, can-do, optimistic spirit. But this attitude about life finds it difficult to allow for the possibility that life's deepest meanings may be found in tragedy, as well as redemption.

All this is to say that the redemptive self is a problematic story. It is a story that reflects cultural and psychological tensions with which Americans have struggled for a very long time. And we continue to struggle with them. But we should not forget that there is no good story that is free of struggle and tension. There is no perfect life narrative, just as there is no perfect society. Every narrative identity is like a double-edged sword. It cuts both ways. The redemptive self affirms a generative commitment to society, but it opens itself up to the dangers of individualism. The redemptive self celebrates the power of human resilience, but it may also fall into arrogance and self-righteousness. The redemptive self sustains hope, but blind hope is naïve.

I hope I have convinced you that the life stories highly generative American adults tell are not without their flaws. I hope I have convinced you that we should not extol these life stories too much, that these narrative identities are not universal tales of goodness and health. But I hope I have not been *too* convincing. I did not spend eight chapters exploring the redemptive self only to "shoot it down" in chapter 9. In American society today, the redemptive self still expresses many of the noblest aspirations and mature commitments of men and women in their midlife years. This is still a compelling story told by adults who are indeed trying to make the world a better place in which to live. Our effort to gain some cultural distance on this narrative in order to see its limitations, as well as its strengths, should not be misread as a campaign to tear the story down. A healthy skepticism can enrich our personal lives and enhance our participation in a democratic society. We should, therefore, be able to appreciate both the good and the potentially bad when it comes to American identity. Knowing the limitations and the shortcomings of the stories we live by may help us cope with our failings in constructive ways, and even help us to transcend them.

Ten

CULTURE, NARRATIVE,

AND THE SELF

If you are looking for the redemptive self, you should know that it is not hard to find. You need go no further than the Oprah Winfrey show, the self-help aisle at your local bookstore, or Hollywood's latest drama about the humble hero who overcame all the odds to find vivid expressions of the power of redemption in human lives. You can hear the voice of the good and gifted inner self in contemporary theories of child development that showcase the mother-infant attachment bond, in the essays of Ralph Waldo Emerson and the poetry of Walt Whitman, and in the testimonials that Americans love to give whenever they are convinced that they have finally found something or someone in their lives that feels so true and so right.

You can follow the good inner self as it perseveres and moves steadily forward to embrace steadfast life principles, even in the face of contamination, when you hear it expressed in the 12-step programs promising recovery from abuse, in the spiritual autobiographies written by New England Puritans, and in Lincoln's Gettysburg Address. You can hear many of the same kinds of messages in Christian Sunday sermons, in the slave narratives from the antebellum South, in political rhetoric calling Americans to noble purpose, and in the high literature of Melville, Whitman, Steinbeck, Ellison, and Angelou. And you can hear the redemptive self in many of the life stories told today by highly generative American adults in their midlife years.

The redemptive self is an American identity. The life stories that highly generative American adults tell are as much about American society as they are about the lives of the middle aged adults who tell them. These stories of manifest psychological destiny speak to us on many levels. They provide narrative explanations for how caring and productive adults in their midlife years believe they have come to be caring and productive adults over time, and how they believe they will continue to be caring and productive in the future. As such, these stories reflect the psychological efforts of individual men and women to find coherence and meaning in their lives. But as cultural expressions, the life stories of highly generative American adults also project values and grapple with issues that have been at the center of American cultural life for over 200 years.

Highly generative American adults are the *chosen people* in two very different senses. As I suggested in chapter 4, American adults who score high on measures of generativity tend to tell life stories in which the protagonist enjoys a favored status in the childhood years, even as he or she witnesses the suffering and disadvantaged status of others. In these storied reconstructions of the past, the protagonist feels chosen for a good and special destiny. But in a second sense, highly generative American adults—those men and women who most exemplify a caring and productive engagement of the world—are especially well positioned in midlife to be *the chosen spokespersons for their culture.* They narrate lives that capture many of those issues, values, and themes that are at the heart of their culture. Of course, every person's life is set in culture, and therefore every person's life story says something about the society in which the narrator lives, but I contend that highly generative American adults are more *representative* of culture than most other people. I believe that their life stories resonate most clearly and contend most dramatically with many dominant cultural narratives in American society.

It has often been said that a society is best reflected in its most troubled and marginalized members. We can learn something important about a given society by examining the lives of those individuals who are labeled by the society as deviant in some way. According to many psychoanalytic writers, for example, individual psychopathology may be viewed as a window into culture. The repressed neurotics of Freud's day most likely expressed conflicts inherent in the strict norms of middle-class Victorian society.[1] The alienated youth of the 1960s may have given voice to an identity crisis that was as much cultural as individual.[2] The narcissistic personalities described by Heinz Kohut and Christopher Lasch in the 1970s and 1980s may have reflected the grasping materialism of American culture during that time of diminishing expectations.[3]

Although I believe that there is some truth in the notion that cultural problems are expressed in individual pathology and deviance, I have taken the opposite tack in this book. I have focused on the generative people. It is to the best-adjusted, most fully functioning, and most productive and caring adults—men and women in the prime of their lives—that I have turned to discern some of what is most characteristic and problematic in American culture. I have chosen a sample of people who are not distinguished by pathology or by celebrity, or by anything particularly glamorous or sexy about their lives. I have chosen them, instead, because they are committed to making the world a better place for the next generation. It is through listening to the life stories of these especially generative adults, I believe, that we may hear cultural themes and variations that we have never fully appreciated before.

But why choose the highly generative adults? I propose that generativity is the most powerful psychological force linking adults to cultural norms, values, and traditions. The most generative adults in a given society are those members most attuned to that society's most cherished (and contested) ideas and practices, because they are the members most responsible for passing those ideas and practices on to the next generation. By saying that highly generative adults are attuned to society's central ideas and practices, I do not mean to suggest that they always embrace or even agree with the dominant cultural ideals. Indeed, many highly generative adults work hard to defy conventions in order to promote agendas and viewpoints that they believe to be in the best interest of themselves, their families, and future generations. Generativity comes in conservative, liberal, and even radical forms. There are generative Republicans and generative Democrats; generativity runs deep on both sides of America's increasingly sharp political divide. Some highly generative adults are knee-jerk conformists, whereas others love the role of cultural rabble-rouser. What I am suggesting is that highly generative adults are more likely than most other members of a given society to be *meaningfully engaged* in the prevailing traditions, norms, values, ideas, controversies, and practices of their culture. Highly generative adults are the norm bearers and destiny shapers in society. They fully embrace the generative roles of creating, maintaining, and passing culture on to the next generation.

In chapter 2, I described research that links generativity to social support, civic engagement, religious participation, and other indices of social integration. Compared to less generative adults, highly generative men and women enjoy larger and more satisfying friendship networks, participate to a greater extent in the political process, and show higher levels of community and religious involvement. They are deeply invested in society's most important institutions, but they are also the individuals—by virtue of age, status, resources, and commitment—best positioned to change those institutions. Culturally speaking, highly generative adults are the movers and shakers. They are among society's most notable cultural stakeholders.

Because of their deep investment in cultural institutions and their active engagement with culture's most significant ideas and practices, highly generative adults are among the best candidates, in my view, to express a society's valued and representative narrative identities. Their life stories are fertile ground for generating themes and meanings that go well beyond the individual life to inform our understanding of culture. Their stories, therefore, are not just about themselves as individuals, but they are also the stories of the culture to which they have given so much and within which their lives are so deeply enmeshed. In saying that highly generative adults express representative narrative identities, however, I do not mean to suggest that their individual life stories perfectly match the dominant cultural narratives of the society in which they live. In the case of the highly generative adult, the relation between narrative identity and culture is likely to be more complex than straightforward. It is my goal in this last chapter to spell out some of that complexity.

The Relationship Between Self and Culture

What is the relationship between the individual self and culture? In the minds of many Americans, there is little relationship at all. Many Americans see life in highly individualistic terms. We strive to live out fully our own individuality, or we strive to make our selves into the kinds of persons we individually want to be. We may concede that parents, lovers, friends, teachers, and a few other important individuals have had some impact on us as we have developed over time. But we tend to be rather obtuse in sorting through how societal institutions, for example, may have shaped our identities. Beyond making vague references to things like "my religious heritage" or "the American Dream," we tend to have remarkably little insight into the ways our lives are framed by cultural categories, values, and norms. Of course, even to claim that one's life is mainly a matter of individual self-making is itself a strong cultural statement, reflecting the dominant cultural norm of American individualism. It is that cultural norm, you might say, that has convinced many Americans that self and culture have rather little to do with each other.

Anthropologists and sociologists have always seen it as something of a solemn duty to educate Americans about the complex relation between self and culture. As any student who hopes to pass an introductory anthropology course has to know, human beings are highly social animals whose lives have their fundamental meanings in culture. But these beginning students, eager to receive good grades, often adopt an oversimplification that runs directly opposite to the suppositions they may have had going into the course. Rather than assuming that the self and culture have little to do with each other, they now conclude that the self is completely determined by culture or, in the extreme, that self and culture are virtually the same thing. This naïve expectation has it that every member of a given society is like a little replica of that society. All Peruvians share a basic similarity by virtue of growing up and living in Peru. All Japanese are basically alike, and different from the French. Although this kind of thinking may have the virtue of focusing some attention on interesting cultural differences, it leads to stereotyping and tends to ignore the often ingenious ways that people in all societies develop lives that sometimes go against the dominant norms and values of their own culture.

Still, you cannot really blame the students for coming to these kinds of conclusions when you realize that a few social scientists once came close to suggesting the very same thing themselves. In the 1930s and 1940s, a number of psychologically oriented anthropologists and cultural observers argued that culture and personality together comprised a tightly linked and coherent system. According to the *culture and personality* view, consistent expressions of culture could be observed in a wide range of cultural practices, from methods of child rearing, to modes of economic production, to art and folklore. All of these expressions worked neatly together to produce what Abraham Kardiner called a society's *basic personality type.*[4] In her 1934 book *Patterns of Culture,* the anthropologist Ruth Benedict made famous the distinction between Apollonian and Dionysian cultures.[5] Apollonian cultures expressed themes of order and reason in their art and religion, and employed child-rearing practices ideally suited to inculcate the values of order and reason in the next generation. People growing up in Apollonian cultures learned to be rational and orderly in their lives. By contrast, Dionysian cultures emphasized the emotional expression of the self. In their child-rearing methods, art, folklore, religion, and other cultural practices, Benedict suggested, people living in Dionysian cultures placed strong value on deep feelings and intuitions, the full expression of passion, and ecstatic experiences.

Benedict viewed her distinction between types of cultures in a relatively nuanced way. Some cultures were more tightly integrated or pure in their embrace of the Apollonian or Dionysian ideal, whereas other cultures might be less consistent and more mixed.[6] Nonetheless, the initial distinction she made between cultural types encouraged other writers to make grand and

FIGURE 10.1 Ruth Benedict (1887–1948) was an acclaimed anthropologist who, along with Margaret Mead and others in the 1930s and 1940s, argued for the "culture and personality" point of view in the social sciences. Benedict's observations of common tendencies in art, ritual, folklore, religion, child-rearing methods, and other social practices *within* particular cultures led her to argue that a culture is an integrated and well-organized whole. From Benedict's perspective, any given culture is likely to engender a certain kind of corresponding personality or self. Therefore, the person is a microcosm of the culture in which he or she lives, and the culture itself is "personality writ large." Reprinted with the permission of Vassar College Library, Special Collection. Photo by Arthur Muray, New York.

oversimplified claims about the relation between culture and self. The most extreme example may be the analysis provided by Geoffrey Gorer and John Rickman in their 1949 book, *The People of Great Russia*.[7] Gorer and Rickman argued that the Russian people displayed a passive and dependent personality type that was reflected in their cultural practices and institutions. For example, the practice of swaddling infants in Russia might encourage passivity and dependence at a very early age. Because their culture traditionally encouraged passivity, the Russians *preferred* the kinds of authoritarian governments they endured under the czars and even the brutal communist dictatorship of Stalin, Gorer and Rickman reasoned. Their preference for this authoritarian leadership could be linked to their experience of having been swaddled as infants.[8]

Efforts like that of Gorer and Rickman to make sweeping claims about national character met with resounding criticism in the 1950s and afterward. Many social scientists (and educated lay readers) argued that it was ludicrous to reduce the cultural complexity of an entire nation-state to parental practices involving swaddling or toilet training. Furthermore, they objected to any neat correspondence between personality types and cultural norms, and they took issue with the general idea, associated especially with Benedict, that cultures are well-organized wholes. According to many critics, the culture and personality advocates overestimated both the match between self and culture, and the overall coherence of culture itself.[9] Cultures are not random collections of people, to be sure; they certainly show *some* coherence and organization. But any given culture also shows many inconsistencies and complexities. As the anthropologist Clifford Geertz put it, "The elements of a culture are not like a pile of sand and not like a spider's web," but are rather "more like an octopus, a rather badly integrated creature—what passes for a brain keeps it together, more or less, in one ungainly whole."[10] In that any given culture is loosely integrated and only modestly coherent at most, no single personality type or "self" pattern will map onto it in a neat and easy way.

Most psychologically oriented anthropologists today emphasize the dynamic and multifaceted relation between self and culture. Robert LeVine writes that culture is "an organized body of rules concerning the ways in which individuals in a population should communicate with one another, think about themselves and their environments, and behave toward one another and toward objects in their environments." Importantly, he adds that the "rules are not universally or constantly obeyed, but they are recognized by all and they ordinarily operate to limit the range of variation in patterns of communication, belief, value, and social behavior in the population."[11]

A culture provides a common framework or set of categories for a given set of individuals. Included in the framework are many different kinds of stories about how to live a good or worthwhile life. Although not all individuals in the set will abide by or even endorse the entire framework, almost everybody recognizes the framework, if only dimly, and finds that he or she has to come to terms with the framework in order to function adequately in the set. Indeed, the framework may itself contain inconsistencies; cultural norms may encourage contradictory forms of thought and behavior, as when a culture glorifies stories of sex and youth but places strong restrictions on the expression of individual desire. People do not, moreover, always match up neatly to the cultures in which they reside. Instead, each person makes use of the cultural resources that are available to him or her. In the words of one authority, each culture provides "a tool kit of habits, skills, styles, perspectives, norms, roles, and values out of which each individual can construct a potentially unique strategy of action."[12] People act and think selectively and strategically within a culture. They can embrace certain aspects of their culture, ignore certain other aspects, and actively resist yet others.[13]

A dominant cultural frame in American society is *individualism*. Like Canada, Australia, and the democracies of northern and western Europe, the United States is consistently described as an individualist culture. Individualist cultures prioritize personal autonomy, the freedom of the self, competition, individual achievement, and the relative importance of personal over common goals. This pervasive meaning framework suggests that we as Westerners tend to see people as potentially self-sufficient agents endowed with fundamental rights—such as the rights to "life, liberty, and the pursuit of happiness," the right of free speech, and the right of assembly. We view society as comprising autonomous agents who freely choose to behave as they do.

By contrast, cultural *collectivism* gives priority to the group or collective over and against the individual, underscoring the values of group harmony, cooperation, solidarity, and interdependency. The emphasis on collectivism is especially strong in many traditional societies and in Asia, the Pacific Islands, and Africa. Collectivist values are at the heart of Eastern Asian religious and cultural traditions, as evidenced in Buddhism and Confucianism. The Buddha taught self-renunciation as a goal of human life, through which the person transcends the limits of the individual self and finds connection to others and the cosmos. Confucius codified a social doctrine of familial and community obligations. In the Confucian tradition, social order takes precedence over individual expression. A person needs to know his or her proper place in the hierarchical order of things. In many collectivist cultures, special emphasis is placed on the vertical (across generations) relationships between parents and children. Sons and daughters are obligated to serve their parents and show them considerable deference (filial piety); ideally the same obligations are to be expressed toward the authority of the state.[14]

Social psychologists Hazel Markus and Shinobu Kitayama argue that individualist and collectivist cultures give rise to different conceptions of the self.[15] As spelled out in table 10.1, Markus and Kitayama propose that in Western, especially North American middle-class, cultures, there is a strong belief in the independence of self from others. The self is mainly defined in terms of internal attributes such as motives, abilities, talents, or "personalities," and a major cultural task is to discover, actualize, or confirm these personal attributes of self. The "real me" is experienced as an inner sense of distinctiveness. Relations with other people may help to support the actualization or fulfillment of the "real me," while also serving as a basis for comparison (how am I doing compared to you?).

By contrast, many non-Western, especially Asian, cultures (and to an important extent some non-European groups in the United States) do not value such a strict separation or independence of the self. These cultures, in-

TABLE 10.1. *Key Differences Between Independent and Interdependent Conceptions of Self*

Feature	Independent	Interdependent
Definition	Separate from social context	Connected with social context
Structure	Bounded, unitary, stable	Flexible, variable
Characteristics	Internal, private (abilities, thoughts, feelings)	External, public (statuses, roles, relationships)
Tasks	Be unique Express self Realize internal attributes Promote own goals	Belong, fit in Occupy one's proper place Engage in appropriate action Promote others' goals
Role of others	Self-evaluation: others are important for social comparison, reflected appraisals	Self-definition: relationships with others in specific contexts define the self
Basis of self-esteem	Ability to express self, validate internal attributes	Ability to adjust, restrain self, maintain social harmony

Adapted from Markus and Kitayama (1991), p. 230.

stead, believe in the fundamental connectedness or interdependence among those within an in-group. The self is made in reference to the relationships of which it is a part. From an interdependent standpoint, the "real me" is not experienced as an internal distinctiveness so much as a sense of self expressed in the intricate roles and shifting situational demands of daily social life. The major cultural task is to fit in, adjust to the relationships, while constraining, taming, or otherwise conditioning internal desires or wishes to facilitate the paramount goal of interpersonal harmony.[16]

The redemptive self is a narrative identity framed within an individualist culture that tends to construe people as more or less autonomous, independent agents. Many of the story's themes emphasize this individualist/independence idea. For example, the protagonist of the redemptive self experiences an early advantage that distinguishes him or her from all others. *I* am blessed; *others* suffer. Because of my special status as a person chosen for a good destiny, I have an obligation and opportunity to be of good use to other people. The protagonist of the story develops warm and caring relationships, to be sure. But the protagonist is still depicted as an independent agent who does good work *for* others in the world. What motivates this good work, furthermore, is often a personalized set of values and beliefs that further distinguishes the story's protagonist from others. The generative hero stays true to the deep principles internalized in childhood and the teenage years. Throughout the story, the moral steadfastness of the generative hero trumps the shifting demands of social situations. Americans admire the man or woman of principle who does what is "right" no matter what. Accordingly, the protagonist of the redemptive self often draws inspiration for generativity in the simple and elegant truths that may be found in religion or in the sacred Emersonian *me*.

At the same time, the redemptive self implicitly rejects, or calls into question, many of the excesses and the negative features we often associate with cultural individualism. The protagonist in this story is rarely depicted as greedy, selfish, exploitative, materialistic, or even self-serving. He or she may be chosen for distinction early in life, but it is the distinction that presages caring for others and working to make a better world for future generations. There are many stories in our society about reaching the pinnacles of fame or celebrity, triumphing at the expense of others, amassing gargantuan riches, or retiring happiest in the end with the greatest number of "toys," the biggest house, and the most luxurious SUV. These are *not* the kinds of life stories, however, that highly generative American adults tend to tell. Their stories tend to emphasize, instead, their commitment to prosocial goals and their efforts to make their own lives better so that they can make better the lives of others. We may occasionally make fun of the "do-gooder" qualities in these stories. But an individualist society like ours depends dearly on do-gooders and on a general respect for life narratives in which independent protagonists do good things to help other individuals.

What Do You Know When You Know a Person?

I contend that the redemptive self is a narrative identity that captures important and valued life themes that are especially salient in an individualist culture like ours. The redemptive self is a story that links the individual person with culture. But the story itself, the culture, and the person are different from each other, as well. Just as the culture and personality theorists of the 1930s and 1940s were mistaken to insist that culture and personality are nearly one and the same, so it would be a mistake today to assume that the story I have described in this book, the generative persons who tell this story, and the culture in which they tell it are all tightly linked and virtually interchangeable. Instead, the linkages are subtle and variable. A person is not a culture; a culture is not a story; a story is not a person. Rather, a person lives in a culture and tells a story about his or her unique life within that culture. Let me expand on this idea a bit further now by considering a question that I find especially fascinating, even if it may seem, on first blush, quite elementary. It is a question about the nature of persons: What do you know when you know an individual person?

The branch of psychology that is concerned mainly with the study of persons is *personality psychology.* Since the time of Freud, personality psychologists have struggled to devise a system for capturing the most important dimensions and facets of human individuality. They have proposed many competing frameworks for classifying and categorizing people in ways that specify how individuals are different from each other. In recent years, the field of personality psychology has moved toward some consensus on this issue. Although not all personality psychologists see it the same way, a number of scientifically oriented personality researchers and theorists today agree that human individuality can be captured well with respect to three different levels of personality variables. I call these levels (1) *dispositional traits,* (2) *characteristic adaptations,* and (3) *integrative life narratives.* Each of the three addresses different aspects of a person, and each relates to culture in a different way.[17]

Level 1: Dispositional Traits

When we meet a person for the first time, we immediately and unconsciously begin the process of assigning basic personality traits. We may note how friendly, compassionate, persevering, dominant, anxious, emotionally stable, fun-loving, excitable, or open-minded the person seems to be. We know that people differ from each other in very broad and basic ways, and we assign hundreds of adjectives to people we know in order to label such differences. We also know that any given label is but a crude generalization. Even the most generous person can sometimes be stingy. Even the friendliest individual will occasionally have a bad day. Despite the many exceptions to all the rules, we still believe that over time and across varied situations different people *tend* to show consistent differences in their behavior. If we did not believe this, we would not have over 4,000 words in the English language that refer to relatively stable personality traits.[18]

Personality psychologists have developed and validated many different instruments to assess individual differences in basic personality traits. Most of these measures are self-report questionnaires—simple tests that ask people to rate themselves on various dimensions or answer a series of yes/no

282 THE REDEMPTIVE SELF

or true/false questions. It turns out that people are pretty good at rating them-selves, that these ratings tend to be similar to the ratings that their friends and acquaintances make of them on the same dimensions, and that people's scores on many well-validated personality trait measures are reasonably good pre-dictors of general trends in their actual daily behavior as observed over time and across different situations.[19] It also turns out that scores on traits are rel-atively stable over time, especially across the adult years. If you score toward the extraverted end of the introversion-extraversion continuum, for example, the chances are reasonably good that 10 years from now when you take the same scale again you will again score toward the extraverted end. Of course, some people show dramatic change over time, but the general tendency is to-ward relative stability and consistency in dispositional traits.[20]

After many decades of scientific research on dispositional traits, person-ality psychologists are coming around to the idea that most of the hundreds of traits that can be invoked in describing human behavior in the English language can be found in a five-factor statistical space, now routinely called the *Big Five.*[21] In box 10.1, I have listed these five super traits or trait cate-gories as they are most commonly labeled. As you can see, each dimension in the Big Five is bipolar. In other words, it is viewed as a line segment with two end points. Most people would be expected to score somewhere toward the middle of any given dimension, but some people find themselves at one extreme (e.g., flaming extraverts) or another (e.g., withdrawn introverts). Almost any personality trait that is commonly measured on a well-validated questionnaire can be fit into one of the Big Five categories, or else it can be seen as something of a blend of two or more Big Five dimensions.

Extraversion/introversion (E) is the first broad dimension of the Big Five. At one end of the continuum, you have outgoing, energetic, and socially dominant tendencies; at the other end, you have people who are more with-drawn, private, and socially inhibited. The second dimension is neuroticism (N), and it encompasses a wide range of negative tendencies in personality. People at the high end of the neuroticism continuum may show chronically high levels of anxiety, depressiveness, emotional vulnerability, and generally negative mood. Individuals low in N-related traits are emotionally stable, calm, and rarely plagued by strong negative feelings. Of course, people's feel-ing states can shift dramatically from one day to the next, even moment by moment. You do not have to be high in N to feel depressed when your lover leaves you. N, however, refers to an overall general tendency. Although we all experience bad feelings at one time or another, individuals high in N suffer from negative feeling states more often and with greater intensity. They seem to be dispositionally inclined toward negative emotional experience.[22]

Box 10.1. Level 1 of Personality: The Big Five Traits

Extraversion (E)
    Sociable—Retiring
    Fun loving—Sober
    Affectionate—Reserved
    Friendly—Aloof
    Spontaneous—Inhibited
    Talkative—Quiet

Neuroticism (N)
    Worrying—Calm
    Nervous—At ease
    High-strung—Relaxed
    Insecure—Secure
    Self-pitying—Self-satisfied
    Vulnerable—Hardy

Conscientiousness (C)
    Conscientious—Negligent
    Careful—Careless
    Reliable—Undependable
    Well-organized—Disorganized
    Self-disciplined—Weak-willed
    Persevering—Quitting

Agreeableness (A)
    Good-natured—Irritable
    Soft-hearted—Ruthless
    Courteous—Rude
    Forgiving—Vengeful
    Sympathetic—Callous
    Agreeable—Disagreeable

Openness to Experience (O)
    Original—Conventional
    Imaginative—Down-to-earth
    Creative—Uncreative
    Broad interests—Narrow interests
    Complex—Simple
    Curious—Incurious

Adapted from McCrae and Costa (1987).

Conscientiousness (C) and agreeableness (A) map roughly onto the domains of work and love, respectively. Individuals high in C are hardworking, dutiful, persevering, well organized, and focused. Those on the other end of the C continuum may be unreliable, lazy, disorganized, and lacking in drive and focus. It should not be surprising to learn that of all the Big Five trait domains, C is the one that consistently predicts high levels of job performance, especially in occupations that call for autonomy and individual initiative.[23] Agreeableness encompasses a vast array of prosocial tendencies, such as altruism, nurturance, and sympathy. People high in A are warmhearted, caring, kind, and generous; those low in A are obnoxious, callous, and mean-spirited. Although individual differences in personality traits are fairly stable over time, there is some evidence that people in general increase on both C and A as they move from their adolescent years into and through adulthood. Part of growing up and becoming socialized in culture involves learning how to be a conscientious and loving person.

Finally, openness to experience (O) brings together traits that assess open-mindedness, flexibility, tolerance for change, cognitive complexity, and other tendencies that spill over into the realm of thought and intelligence. Although people high in O are not necessarily more intelligent than those low in O, they may be more *intellectual,* showing more interest in ideas and issues, and a preference for conceptual complexity.[24] At the low end of the O continuum lie tendencies toward concrete and practical issues over intellectual ones, narrow and rigid categories of thinking, and a reluctance to embrace change and complexity. People high in O tend to see those low in O as simplistic and narrow-minded; but those low in O may see people high in O as impractical and lacking in conviction.

A growing body of research suggests that people in many different cultures and language traditions may use terms like those encompassed in the English Big Five to describe basic differences in personality traits. Researchers have found that when they statistically analyze self-report scales administered to people in different societies, respondents implicitly divide up trait descriptors in ways that are roughly similar to the way people do it in English-speaking societies. Comparable five-factors structures have been found in German, Dutch, Portuguese, Chinese, Japanese, Korean, Hebrew, Hungarian, Estonian, and Filipino language traditions, among others.[25] Some enthusiasts have proclaimed that the Big Five is a universal structure for personality traits, whereas other researchers point to the rough but less than perfect similarities found cross-culturally as evidence of considerable variability. In either case, it is clear that people in many different cultures routinely employ basic trait descriptors like those found in the Big Five when they think and talk about basic differences between persons. In this sense, different cultures may see personality in somewhat similar ways.

What, then, is the relationship between broad personality traits and culture? Although the Big Five provides a trait taxonomy that may be used in many different cultures, the taxonomy itself is not especially useful for thinking about differences *between* cultures. There are extraverted and introverted people, to be sure; but it makes much less sense to talk about extraverted and introverted cultures. There are at least two reasons for this. First, trait terms carry meanings that mainly pertain to how one person is different from another in overall behavioral style. But a culture requires and allows for many different kinds of styles to be expressed by many different kinds of people. When trait terms are used to label cultures, they usually end up sounding like simplistic stereotypes (which is what they are when applied to culture).

Second, trait terms (and the scales that measure them) are explicitly comparative within a local reference. When residents of Kyoto, for example, rate themselves on trait items (e.g., "How conscientious are you?"), they are implicitly comparing themselves to people they know, such as their family, friends, and neighbors in Kyoto, Japan. Residents of Los Angeles do the same thing—comparing themselves most likely to other people who are part of their own cultural world. There are no universal norms or standards for trait ratings. Consequently, it makes little sense, in my view, to say that Japanese are more "reserved" than Americans, that the French are more "arrogant" than the Russians, or that people living in a small Indian village are less "conscientious" than those living in Palo Alto, California.[26]

Cultures may, however, have an influence on how individual differences in traits are *expressed* in behavior. Being an extravert in Japan may involve different ways of showing outgoingness and social dominance than those that prevail in New York City. Cultural norms and mores are likely to shape how traits are played out in social behavior. But this is very different from saying that cultures match up with or reflect particular *amounts* of a given trait. Few if any societies specialize in producing neurotics, nonconscientious adults, or people with extraordinarily high levels of openness to experience. Similarly, extraverts are extraverts all over the globe; they are more outgoing, fun-loving, and sociable than introverts in general, no matter where you are. The "where they are" shapes *how* they express their E, much more than it shapes *how much* E they have. Given the tremendous variability in human individuality (including broad temperamental differences apparent at birth), cultures have to allow for and give some expression to a wide trait range. You will find extraverts and introverts, mildly neurotic and relatively stable people, and individuals falling at, say, the 75th percentile on C and the 5th percentile on A *the world over*. With respect to Level 1 dispositional traits, therefore, different cultures are likely to present you with pretty much the same sort of thing.

Level 2: Characteristic Adaptations

As you get to know a person, you move beyond initial trait attributions to consider a person's needs, wants, goals, fears, conflicts, interests, and the like. I may describe a college student I know as high in conscientiousness and openness to experience, but unless you know about her passion for the piano, her liberal political views, her skepticism about organized religion, her ambivalence about authority, her tendency to approach new situations with extreme caution, her current desire to be a professor of mathematics, her preference for high-energy friends who challenge her, and the way she often defends against anxiety through the mechanisms of intellectualization and humor, you really do not know her well at all. Characteristic adaptations are those *specific* features of human individuality that speak to what people *want* or *value* in life and how they pursue what they want and avoid what they do not want in particular *situations,* during particular *time periods,* and with respect to particular *social roles.* While dispositional traits sketch an outline of human individuality, characteristic adaptations fill in many of the details.

Among the most important characteristic adaptations in a person's life are a person's particular goals, strivings, projects, values, and fears, and the characteristic methods a person employs to pursue valued goals and deal with important conflicts and fears.[27] Compared to dispositional traits, characteristic adaptations are more specific, more contextualized, and more changeable. Extraversion is a very general and stable tendency in personality that accounts for consistencies in behavior across many different situations and over time. Indeed, the very power of the trait concept is its ability to account for broad and stable tendencies. By contrast, characteristic adaptations speak to the particularities of everyday life, to specific situations and roles, and to those important aspects of human individuality that may be very much here today but gone (or different) next year. My college student's goals in life, her passions and interests, her attitudes about religion, her political beliefs, and her characteristic ways of dealing with authority and coping with stress are likely to change with time and development. She may become a political conservative. She may loose interest in math and aim for law school. She may formulate new dreams and develop new fears and conflicts. She may eventually move from a life stage of identity struggle to one more focused on generativity. Although dispositional traits are hard to change, Level 2 of personality offers ample opportunity for self-improvement and personal development while reminding us that sometimes we must change in response to unexpected life challenges and new situations.

There is no Big Five–like taxonomy for Level 2. Personality psychologists have enumerated so many different kinds of characteristic adaptations that no single, comprehensive system seems able to hold them all. Different ideas about characteristic adaptations, furthermore, come from different theoretical traditions with different and often conflicting assumptions about human nature and the nature of individual differences between people. Nonetheless, characteristic adaptations that are most directly associated with motivation—such as motives, goals, and strivings—have often been organized in terms of two basic dimensions. The first is an approach/avoidance dimension. Some goals are aimed mainly toward achieving something (e.g., power, love, money, health) and others are aimed mainly toward avoiding something (e.g., pain, loneliness, embarrassment).[28] The second dimension relates roughly to self/other. Some goals are more self-oriented (power, achievement, agency), and others are more concerned with interpersonal relationships (love, intimacy, communion).

Characteristic adaptations appear to be much more sensitive to cultural differences than dispositional traits. Important differences, for example, between individualist and collectivist cultures can be demonstrated in the areas of motives, goals, and values. Individualist cultures tend to prioritize the person's goals over the goals of the group. Individualist cultures tend to value the person's efforts to explore and expand the self and to achieve personal fulfillment and self-actualization. By contrast, collectivist cultures tend to prioritize the aims of the social order over and against individual goals. Individual projects should be aimed at promoting social harmony within the collective. Certain forms of agentic, self-oriented goals tend to be especially valued in individualist cultures, whereas certain forms of communal, other-oriented goals tend to hold higher station in collectivist cultures. Cultural differences may also prevail on the approach/avoidance dimension. One team of researchers has shown that people in individualist cultures enumerate relatively more goals that are aimed at achieving desired ends (approach), whereas people in collectivist cultures show more goals aimed at avoiding undesirable ends (avoidance).[29]

Nonetheless, cultural differences in preferred characteristic adaptations are almost always a matter of degree rather than kind. As we saw in chapter 2, human beings have evolved to be especially sensitive to social cues signaling getting along (communion, other-oriented goals) and getting ahead (agency, self-oriented goals). Accordingly, all human societies must leave some room for the pursuit of both general sets of goals—those aimed at promoting the collective, and those aimed at promoting the individual. Living well, to say nothing of simply surviving, requires sensitivity, furthermore, to both approach and avoidance goals in daily life. People need to be able to take advantage of positive opportunities when they arise, and they need to know when they should draw back to avoid or escape the many potentially negative situations that will surely come their way.

Level 3: Integrative Life Narratives

If dispositional traits sketch the outline and characteristic adaptations fill in the details, then what else do we need in order to account for human individuality? We need to consider *meaning*. What does a life mean as it evolves over time and in culture? What kind of meaning does a person make out of his or her life overall? As I argued in chapter 3, we ultimately make meaning out of our lives through stories. Beginning in late adolescence and young adulthood, we construct integrative narratives of the self that selectively recall the past and wishfully anticipate the future to provide our lives with some semblance of unity, purpose, and identity. Personal identity is the internalized and evolving life story that each of us is working on as we move through our adult lives. Therefore, even if I have a good sense of my own dispositional traits and the many characteristic adaptations that fill in the details of my daily life, I still do not really know who I am until I have a good understanding of my narrative identity.

Integrative life stories are layered on top of dispositional traits and characteristic adaptations in the structure of human personality. In some cases our stories fit well with our dispositional tendencies and our specific adaptations. In other cases, our stories diverge dramatically from other aspects of our personality.[30] With respect to their overall function and developmental course, life narratives contrast most sharply with dispositional traits. As basic stylistic tendencies in behavior, dispositional traits may be readily traced back to temperament differences in infancy. You can see the precursors of introversion, for example, in what developmental psychologists have identified as high levels of behavioral inhibition in some one-year olds.[31] By contrast, life narratives are only loosely tied to behavior per se. A woman with a redemptive life narrative, for example, may behave in many different ways in many different situations. Knowing something about her life story may give you no more than a weak clue as to what her actions will be. If you want to predict her behavior, you would do better to know her traits. But if you want to know how she makes sense of her life, you had better know her story. Life stories, furthermore, do not even become a force in personality until well after traits (and characteristic adaptations) have come on the scene. People begin to put their lives into full narratives in their late teens and early 20s, as I argued in chapter 3. And they continue to work on their stories, encountering substantial change and development in identity, long after traits seem to have settled down to a more or less stable form. Traits get organized early (though some change is always possible); stories follow much later and continue to develop for the rest of life.

Like characteristic adaptations, integrative life narratives are sensitive to and reflective of cultural differences. Indeed, I would submit that life stories are more reflective of and shaped by culture than any other aspect of personality. Stories are at the center of culture. More than favored goals and values, I believe, stories differentiate one culture from the next. I have argued throughout this book that the stories people live by say as much about culture as they do about the people who live them and tell them. Our own life stories draw on the stories we learn as active participants in culture—stories about childhood, adolescence, adulthood, and aging. Stories capture and elaborate metaphors and images that are especially resonant in a given culture. Stories distinguish between what culture glorifies as good characters and vilifies as bad characters, and they present the many varieties that fall in between. Stories depict full and fragmented lives that are exciting, frightening, infuriating, enlightening, admirable, heroic, dignified, ignoble, disgusting, wise, foolish, and boring. Stories teach us how to live and what our lives mean.

Culture, then, provides each person with an extensive menu of stories about how to live, and each of us chooses from the menu. Because different people within a given culture have different experiences and opportunities, no two people get exactly the same menu. We cannot eat everything off the menu we do get, so our narrative choices spell out, more than anything else, our precise relationship with our culture. When the food comes from the kitchen, we doctor it to our own tastes. We add pepper or salt; we mix things up and throw some things away; we nibble from somebody else's plate; we may even send the order back and ask to see the menu again. This is to say that we choose and we appropriate in the making of a narrative identity. We select from competing stories, and we modify those stories we choose to fit our own unique life, guided by the unique circumstances of our social, political, and economic world; by our family backgrounds and educational experiences; and by the dispositional traits and characteristic adaptations that also comprise our individuality. A person constructs a narrative identity by appropriating stories from culture. *Self and culture come to terms with each other through narrative.*

Table 10.2 summarizes the main ideas I have presented in this chapter regarding the three different levels of personality and their relation to culture. As I suspect you now see, persons and cultures could never match up as neatly as some social scientists thought in the first half of the 20th century. Not only is a culture too large and complex to be embodied in a single person, but also a single person is too complex and multifaceted to reflect any single cultural stereotype. Instead, persons and cultures relate to each other in intricate and uneven ways. A person's dispositional traits are not especially representative of any particular cultural form, though culture may influence how traits are expressed in behavior. The content, structure, and priorities of a person's characteristic adaptations—personal goals, strivings, values, fears, conflicts, and interests, for example—are all shaped by culture. Individualist and collectivist cultures emphasize somewhat different characteristic adaptations, although they still leave room for substantial variability. Integrative life narratives are the most culturally nuanced aspects of personality. Each culture provides a panoply of stories about how to live, and people pick and appropriate those stories that seem to work best for them, ignoring

TABLE 10.2. *Three Levels of Personality and Their Relation to Culture*

Level	Definition	Function	Significance for Culture
I. Dispositional traits	Broad and basic dimensions of behavioral style that account for consistencies across situations and over time (e.g., extraversion/introversion, depressiveness, the Big Five). Individual differences in traits are relatively stable over time.	Dispositional traits sketch a behavioral outline (what I do)	Similar trait labels and systems found across many different cultures and languages. Different cultures encode dispositional differences in relatively similar ways.
II. Characteristic adaptations	More specific motivational and strategic variables that are contextualized in time, situations, and social roles (e.g., motives, goals, coping strategies, relational patterns, domain-specific styles, interests, beliefs, and values). Some characteristic adaptations show substantial stability over time; others are more changeable.	Characteristic adaptations fill in the details of human individuality (what I want; what I believe)	Cultures differ substantially on their most valued goals, beliefs, and strategies for social life. *Individualism* and *collectivism* encourage different patterns of characteristic adaptations.
III. Integrative life narratives	Internalized and evolving life stories that reconstruct the past and imagine the future to provide a person's life with identity (unity, purpose, meaning). Life stories change substantially over time. The *redemptive self* is one kind of integrative life narrative—noteworthy for its association with generativity at midlife and its reflection of many cherished American themes.	Integrative life narratives tell what a person's life means in time and culture (who I am)	Cultures provide a menu of stories for the life course and specify how stories should be told and lived. In modern societies, many different stories compete with each other. Persons must choose some stories and resist others.

and actively resisting many others. Given the central role of individual choice in the making of narrative identity, therefore, life stories provide especially powerful examples of the strength of culture to shape lives and the strength of individuals to make lives out of culture.

In focusing throughout this book on the redemptive self, I have chosen a particular narrative identity that reflects some of the most valued and contested stories in American cultural history. The redemptive self is an especially *American* narrative identity, because it draws so heavily and creatively from an American anthology of narrative expression. This is not to say that the redemptive self is the primary or the most prevalent narrative identity in America today. The menu of cultural narratives in American society runs for many pages. Individual American adults appropriate many different kinds of stories to make sense of their own lives. The redemptive stories I have featured in this book are noteworthy for their association with high levels of generativity among men and women at midlife. They are stories associated with the mature adult's efforts to leave a positive legacy for future generations. These are not stories that necessarily resonate with teenagers, twenty-somethings, or many senior citizens. Different life stages have their own favorite stories.

In that I believe generativity to be the cardinal psychological challenge and virtue of the middle adult years, and in that any good society depends dearly on the generative efforts of its citizens, I have privileged the life stories told by highly generative American adults in midlife. There may be many problems with these stories, as I suggested in chapter 9. But they are still among the most inspiring stories that I know for leading a worthy life in our middle adult years. Generative adults in America show a wide range of dispositional traits and characteristic adaptations. There are neurotic and emotionally stable parents committed to the development and well-being of their children. There are introverted and extraverted community activists; conscientious and lazy Sunday school teachers; agreeable and obnoxious Little League coaches; and blood donors, altruists, and inspiring leaders who run the gamut from high to low openness to experience. Generativity, furthermore, is associated with many different goal priorities, value systems, religious ideologies, political affiliations, defense mechanisms, coping strategies, and interest patterns. Surveying generative adults' traits and adaptations may be a good start, but you will know them most deeply and distinctively through their stories.

In saying that the redemptive self is a characteristically American life story, I do not mean to claim that it is solely or exclusively American. The American cultural menu features stories that can be found on other cultural menus, as well. The very idea of redemption, for example, appears in all of the world's major religions, as I indicated in chapter 1. Nonetheless, Americans have developed their own characteristic variations on this common theme, as also indicated in chapter 1. Almost all of the themes comprising the redemptive self—from the sense of childhood advantage to the adult conflict between power and love—can be found somewhere in stories from other cultures. But again there are characteristic American formulations of these ideas, as in the notions of manifest destiny and American exceptionalism. Most important, Americans have tended to *pull all of these themes together* into coherent narrative packages that have been featured again and again in the texts of American autobiographies, political rhetoric, self-help psychology, fine literature, and the popular media.

Different cultures have probably always displayed as many commonalities as distinctions. As economic interdependence, the Internet, and other global forces work to shrink our world further and mix different people and cultures together in the 21st century, the idea of a pure and distinct culture becomes even more untenable. Increasingly, cultures may be viewed as evolving and unsettled hybrids. Traditional values compete with the demands of cultural modernity. Different ethnicities and interest groups promote their own cultural agendas. In American society, for example, "secular humanists" battle with "religious fundamentalists" in what has been described as an ongoing series of "culture wars." In a complex society like ours, therefore, different stories compete for dominance; some stories win, and others lose. In American culture today, the redemptive self aspires to be a winning story. It is by no means a perfect story, but it still deserves a close look if you are searching for a life narrative that makes good meaning for an American life well lived.

Epilogue

AN AMERICAN'S CONFESSIONS

AND FINAL THOUGHTS

We research psychologists are trained to be objective observers of human behavior. We learn disciplined methods of data collection, reliable techniques for psychological assessment, rigorous statistical procedures for testing hypotheses, and tight logical schemes for keeping our biases out of the analyses we do. In most of the studies my students and I have performed over the years, we have taken all the appropriate steps to minimize bias. When measuring individual differences in generativity, for example, we employ the best-validated psychological instruments. When coding unwieldy life-narrative accounts for redemption and contamination themes, we rely on objective and quantitative scoring systems that have been painstakingly designed and cross-validated. We go through extensive training procedures to assure that our coding is reliable and unbiased. We subject our predictions to stringent statistical tests.

But we are not completely objective, and we should not be. Our personal inclinations get played out in the questions we decide to study, the hypotheses we decide to test, and, most important, the interpretations we decide to offer. There is a great deal of subjectivity in social sciences research. This is especially true when it comes to studying life narratives. In this book's prologue, I introduced my inquiry as a venture in the narrative study of lives. As a narrative psychologist, I systematically analyze the texts of people's life stories to obtain a better understanding of both the people who tell the stories and the culture within which those stories are told. Although I have drawn extensively on my own and others' research to make this book's arguments,

I have also provided my own subjective reading of many psychological and cultural texts. As a result, I have arrived at an interpretation of the redemptive self that is, I freely confess, highly subjective.

But confession is de rigueur for the narrative study of lives. The greatest power that the narrative psychologist has is the creativity that comes from a subjective stance in the world. As an interpreter of life narratives, I am subjectively positioned in a particular time and place, and gifted with a set of personal and intellectual experiences that deeply inform what I have to offer you. It is my responsibility to draw deeply from my subjectivity. But it is also my responsibility to confess my stance so that you can evaluate my perspective in your own subjective reading of my work.[1]

What should I confess? You already know that I admire an especially generative teacher from my undergraduate years. You know that I loved the Chicago Bulls in high school. You know that I grew up in a racist community. My fascination with the American problem of race can be traced back to those early experiences in Gary, Indiana. Religion, too, has fascinated me for most of my life, setting the emotional table for chapter 6 in this book. When I was 5, the neighborhood church lady scooped my brother and me up from our front yard one Sunday morning and hauled us off to Bible hour. (My mother assented to the abduction.) I imbibed many fiery sermons growing up in the Baptist church, the phrasings and cadences from which have been known to leak into my lectures at Northwestern University. I left the Baptists in high school because I believed they were not "intellectual" enough for me. A few years later, I married the daughter of a Lutheran minister.

The central concerns in my book are generativity and redemption in America. I fancy myself to be a highly generative American adult. I would score quite high on the Loyola Generativity Scale, but then again I designed it. I have known my share of redemptive experiences. I grew up in a very humble family in which nobody before me had ever received a college education. With a Ph.D. and a high academic position today, I certainly have in my life followed the redemptive path of upward social mobility. In addition, I have known powerful experiences of redemption via atonement and enlightenment. But other classic American forms of redemption are pretty much outside my personal orbit. I have never come close to feeling "enslaved" in any manner, so I have never experienced redemption via emancipation. I have never had an experience of recovery. When I look back on my life, some of the most vivid scenes are antiredemptive: strong contamination sequences are very clear from my childhood years.

My perspective on the redemptive self is both admiring (chapter 2) and critical (chapter 9). Like many highly generative American adults, I have formulated a life story in which the childhood protagonist does indeed experience an early advantage. Mine took the form of a lucky break, at least as my father told it, regarding my premature birth: "Danny, you had a 50–50 chance to live!" I think he made it up, but I believed him when I was little, and always felt special because of this. God had *chosen* me. Therefore, I would make something special out of my life, something good and something very different from the hardscrabble existence that was Gary, Indiana. But, in other ways, my story departs substantially from the redemptive self. I do not feel that my inner "me" is completely good and innocent. I do not have strong memories of empathizing with the suffering of others when I was young. I have rarely felt that power and love are in conflict in my life. Finally, the belief system that I began to formulate in adolescence is still something of a work in progress, and I have absolutely never known complete moral certitude. My academic training has taught me to be suspicious of simple truths in life. It bothers me to no end, therefore, when highly generative American adults say that they know deep in their hearts what is right and good. How can anybody know?

While I admire the redemptive life stories that many highly generative American adults tell, I also find a good number of these stores to be too neat and upbeat for my tastes. My sentiments run toward tragedy and irony when it comes to life narrative. I do not expect suffering to be redeemed, though I hold out hope that it will be. I am intrigued by the fatal flaws in human character, the mixed motives, the garbled messages, the half-truths, the partial epiphanies, the discontinuities and digressions, and the randomness of it all, even as I sift through in search of coherent patterns. Life is not a simple story, though we try to make it into one. Some variations on the redemptive self are rich and complex, like Elliot Washington's narrative in chapter 1. But others are no more complex than Horatio Alger's stories. From my subjective standpoint, I would like a little more complexity.

My taste for tragedy and complexity in human lives doubtlessly reflects the fact that I came to psychology by way of Freud. Reading *Civilization and Its Discontents* as a college freshman was a turning point in my life story. Freud's influence in psychology has waned considerably over the past three decades, but certain features of his perspective have survived. One of these is the idea that people do not fully understand themselves because their lives are complexly determined by a messy multitude of forces and factors. The messiness of life, the way life defies a simple and totalizing interpretation, is a favorite theme today in the writings of *postmodern* psychologists, like Kenneth Gergen.[2] Freud found the complexity and the messiness in an unconscious inner realm, whereas postmodern thinkers look to the mixed-up, constantly shifting, media-saturated world of contemporary social life in postindustrial societies. We are bombarded today by a befuddling multitude of different messages and images. We are forced to play a dizzying array of different social roles. We can pretend to be anybody on the Internet. We feel that our lives are forever in flux. We move from one confusing social performance to another. Amid such chaos and complexity, what might a single life ever mean? How might we ever be able to narrate it all into a convincing life story?

The concept of narrative is key in the psychological writings of postmodern thinkers.[3] Lives are like texts, they suggest, narratives that continue to be written and rewritten over time. But what are texts? They are nothing but patterns of words, pictures, signs, and other sorts of representations. There is nothing substantially "real" about them. Literary texts have no inherent and stable meanings. Language is indeterminate. Every word is ambiguous in and of itself, and its particular meaning in a particular moment is dependent on its relation to other equally ambiguous words with which it is spoken or written.

If lives are like texts, then lives, too, have no inherent meanings, according to the postmodern view. People may think they understand who they are, that their lives "stand for something" or "express something true." But they are mistaken, just as readers are mistaken when they think they have found a single meaning in the words that make up a particular novel or short story. If lives are like texts, people construct selves in and through the sharing of texts in conversation, or *discourse*. Narrative identities are made through talk. But the talk is strongly determined by the changing social demands of postmodern life. Every new experience changes the story of your life, a story that *you* are *not* really writing anyway. The story is being written for you by a messy social world. The story is but a relentlessly shifting pattern of words that has no central message, no unity, and no stability, because the social world (that is, its author) has no meaning, unity, or stability either. A lot of sound and fury, perhaps. A randomly changing tale told moment by moment, signifying nothing.

If I thought life narratives signified nothing beyond the swirl and confusion of contemporary life, however, I would not study them. If I thought that American adults themselves were not the real authors of their own stories, appropriating discourses and narratives that prevail in their own culture (as I argued in chapter 10), I would not assert that narrative identities provide lives with some degree of unity and purpose while offering insights, as well, into culture. No matter how messy it gets out there, people want to make sense of it all. Life-story telling continues apace.

In his 1994 novel, *After Gregory,* Austin Wright portrays a troubled post-modern hero living in a contingent world. Peter Gregory is a high school English teacher whose affair with one of his students is about to be exposed.[4] Other things have gone badly, as well. Recently, his wife and children left him. Two years ago, he drove his car the wrong way on a highway exit ramp, causing a chain-reaction collision. A woman and her two daughters were killed. On a raw November night, he tries to kill himself by throwing his body into a freezing river. But when Peter hits the river, he changes his mind. He finds himself swimming against the current with greater power and effectiveness that he imagined he could summon. He sees the lights on the distant shore, and these tell him to fight, to live on. But to live on as a different person, for the old self—that is, "Peter Gregory"—seems to have died in the water. He scrambles ashore, shivering and exhausted, but now a new self. Later, he explains: "Peter Gregory wrote a suicide note and drowned himself in the river. I swam out on the other side."[5]

Wright's novel is a parable of the ever shifting postmodern self. Peter Gregory is the first in a parade of selves to serve as protagonists in the novel, each appearing in succession in the body originally inhabited by Peter. The former Peter Gregory hitchhikes to New York, changes his name a number of times, tries on a series of new roles, and makes new friends. Eventually, he meets the billionaire playboy and philanthropist Jack Rome, who offers him $30 million to finance a completely new life under the name of "Stephen Trace." Rome awards Stephen one of his patented "*Me*-grants"—a grant to make a new self from scratch. The only condition of the Me-grant is that Stephen cannot revisit the world of Peter Gregory in any way. He must sustain for the long run the clean break he believes he has already made. If he can do that, he can construct virtually any kind of self or selves that $30 million can buy. With some misgivings, the former-Peter-now-Stephen takes up the challenge. He purchases a beautiful new house on Long Island Sound. He cultivates new interests, tastes, friendships, and religion. Jack Rome even provides him with a new wife.

A self-made man himself, Jack Rome is fascinated with the prospect of the making and the killing off of multiple "me's." He wonders about the malleability of the postmodern self. Is there any stability to selfhood at all? Can we continue to shift and fluctuate with each new social performance, each new opportunity for discourse? Rome thinks not. Rome bets a colleague that Stephen will not be able to comply with the conditions of the Me-grant. Within 2 years he will go back to being Peter Gregory, Rome wagers. His colleague bets that Stephen will make it. The self is infinitely flexible, he asserts, able to transform itself into virtually any form that shifting social life comes to demand.

Stephen finds it difficult to keep aspects of his former self out of his new life. He finds that many of his thoughts and feelings feel still very much like Peter Gregory. He is plagued by dreams and fantasies replaying and reworking his earlier days. And he longs to sneak back to the old town of Peter Gregory. Despite the postmodern role playing, he never seems able to make a clean psychological break. Still, Stephen likes his new life and his new wife well enough. When Rome dies in a plane crash, however, Stephen's grant support is withdrawn. His new wife leaves him to marry the colleague who bet Rome that Stephen would never go back to being Peter Gregory. Stephen moves west, takes the name of Mitchel Grape, and starts up a relationship with Bonnie Brown, who is a social activist. He tells her about his previous selves. She does not believe him at first. But after a while she begins to encourage him to reconnect to his past: "Time to think about your life, she said. You had a wife, you had children. They meant something to you. People can't live divided from themselves. You need to heal yourself. Close your wounds. Bring your divided selves together. A re-union."[6]

Bonnie sounds like an American self-help book. Our hero follows her advice. He goes back to the town of Peter Gregory. There he finds but few traces of his former self. Now what should he do?

What do you think?

He takes out paper and begins *to write his story*—the one story of his many selves. He endeavors to reconstruct his past and reimagine his future to create a narrative identity aimed at providing his life with some semblance of unity and purpose. But who might be the readers of the story? Peter Gregory's former wife, for one, and his children. He will run a personal advertisement in a number of newspapers across the country. It will read, "Peter Gregory your once husband and father is alive and well and has *a story* for you. Please write or call."[7]

I bet it will be a story of redemption.

Notes

1. Langewiesche (2002), p. 47.

2. I borrow the term "the good society" from a book of the same name written by Bellah, Madsen, Sullivan, Swidler, and Tipton (1991). The authors of this thoughtful volume consider the problems Americans have in sustaining commitment to and finding meaning in societal institutions. They also introduce to the arena of political science the psychological concept of *generativity*. Generativity is a central idea in *The Redemptive Self*.

3. As *psychological* documents, the Declaration of Independence and the Preamble to the Constitution emphasize very different human aspirations. The Declaration sets people free from oppressive authority to pursue their own happiness and individuality. By contrast, the Constitution challenges free people to bond *together* into a good society in which the welfare of future generations is assured (generativity).

4. Erikson introduced the term *generativity* in his classic 1950 book, *Childhood and Society*. Other key sources for the concept include Kotre (1984); McAdams and de St. Aubin (1998); and de St. Aubin, McAdams, and Kim (2004).

5. For Erikson, generativity was the centerpiece of the seventh of eight stages in his life span theory of psychosocial development. Each stage is defined by a polarity between a positive and a negative outcome. For Stage 1, for example, the polarity is *trust* versus *mistrust*. For Stage 7, it is *generativity* versus *stagnation*. Each stage, furthermore, is associated with a specific virtue. For Stage 7, the virtue is "care." By adding virtues to each stage, Erikson argued that psychosocial developmental concerns often have a strong moral or ethical meaning, as well. See, especially, Erikson (1964). Browning (2004) provides a very thorough examination of generativity as an ethical concept. Wakefield (1998) traces philosophical thinking regarding generativity back to Plato's *Symposium*.

6. I take these virtues from Bennett (1993).

7. See, for example, McAdams (1985, 1993).

8. The main studies documenting differences in life stories between highly generative and less generative adults are described in chapters 2, 3, and 8 of this book.
Published first in scientific journal articles and in chapters of professional books, the
studies were reported originally in the following sources: Himsel, Hart, Diamond,
and McAdams (1997); Mansfield and McAdams (1996); McAdams and Bowman
(2001); McAdams, Diamond, de St. Aubin, and Mansfield (1997); and McAdams,
Reynolds, Lewis, Patten, and Bowman (2001). Related findings, also described in later
chapters of this book, have been obtained in life-narrative research by Colby and
Damon (1992) and M. Andrews (1991).

9. Many classic theories of personality pit a striving for self-expression and a
striving for loving community against each other as *the* two fundamental motivations in life. The most general expression of this is probably Bakan's (1966) distinction between *agency* and *communion* as the two basic modalities of all living forms.
For Bakan, *agency* refers to self-expansion, self-defense, and all strivings that put the
self first and foremost; communion refers to merging the self with others in various
ways, as in erotic love, friendship, family life, and community. Similar distinctions include Freud's (1920/1955) aggressive instincts (*Thanatos*) versus sexual instincts
(*Eros*), Adler's (1927) strivings for *superiority* and *social interest,* Angyal's (1941) basic
needs for *autonomy* and *surrender,* Rank's (1936/1978) *fear of life* (which motivates us
to separate from others) and *fear of death* (which motivates us to seek union), and
Hogan's (1982) evolutionary tasks of *getting ahead* and *getting along.* In my own life
story model of identity, I have argued that the two basic thematic lines in life narratives concern agency/power and communion/intimacy (McAdams, 1985).

10. In Kammen (1991).

11. In "Song of Myself," Walt Whitman celebrated an exuberant and sprawling
American identity. Among my favorite lines are these: "Do I contradict myself? / Very
well then I contradict myself, / (I am large, I contain multitudes.)." In Murphy (1977),
p. 737.

12. Bellah, Madsen, Sullivan, Swidler, and Tipton (1985).

13. For almost 100 years, empirically minded personality psychologists have tried
to delineate clear types of human personality, but with only modest success. Loevinger
(1976) sets forth a developmental typology, suggesting that people can be characterized broadly in terms of their overall stage of ego development. But even Loevinger
admits that there is much more to personality than a person's ego stage. Block (1971)
and York and John (1992) have developed useful typologies that bring together groups
of variables into more or less coherent patterns. But these typologies are much more
complex and their boundaries are much looser than traditional notions of character
types typically suggest. Most current scientific thinking has it that personality is a
complex mixture of different personality traits and other variables, set in a complex
social context. We will consider personality traits and their relations to life stories, as
well as the relationship between personality and culture, in chapter 10.

14. The idea that identity is an internalized and evolving narrative of the self is
the central idea of my life story model of identity (McAdams, 1985, 1993, 1996b, 2001c)

and appears in a number of other theoretical approaches (e.g., Gregg, 1991; Hermans, Kempen, and van Loon, 1992; Singer, 1995).

15. In the late 1990s, empirical psychology witnessed the emergence of a movement toward *positive psychology*. An important leader in this movement is Martin Seligman, former president of the American Psychological Association. Positive psychology seeks to establish a scientific understanding of positive and prosocial aspects of human functioning, including human happiness and well-being, psychological resilience, human virtues such as honesty and gratitude, prosocial aspects of religious faith, and moral development (see Seligman & Csikszentmihalyi, 2000). For the most part, the concept of generativity seems to fit well the positive psychology emphasis.

16. Most empirical psychologists have traditionally been more comfortable linking up with the biological sciences than with their sister disciplines in the social sciences, and most have proven positively phobic about the humanities. The past decade and a half has witnessed many fruitful efforts to integrate psychology—especially cognitive psychology—with the brain sciences and with biology. Among the best trade books written in this vein in recent years are Antonio Damasio's (1994) *Descartes' Error,* Joseph LeDoux's (1996) *The Emotional Brain,* Steven Pinker's (1997) *How the Mind Works,* and Daniel Schacter's (1996) *Searching for Memory.* By contrast, empirically minded psychologists lately have had relatively little to offer the educated public regarding the relation between psychology, on the one hand, and society and culture, on the other—beyond, that is, a few reductionistic attempts to derive culture from genes and traits. If you go back a few decades, however, you can find smart and provocative books written by psychologists for educated lay audiences, as well as professionals, aiming to explore the relation between self and culture. Written by a rigorous empiricist, David McClelland's (1961) *The Achieving Society* is one good example. Other examples come more out of the psychoanalytic tradition, such as Norman Brown's (1959) *Life Against Death,* Erik Erikson's (1963) *Childhood and Society,* Philip Rieff's (1966) *The Triumph of the Therapeutic,* and Ernest Becker's (1973) *The Denial of Death.* Psychologically informed sociologists have also written important and widely read trade books in this vein, including most notably David Riesman's (1949/1961) *The Lonely Crowd,* Christopher Lasch's (1979) *Culture of Narcissism,* and Robert Bellah et al.'s (1985) *Habits of the Heart.*

17. The narrative study of lives is an interdisciplinary movement in the social sciences, one aimed at exploring and interpreting the narrative or story-like dimensions of people's lives and social-cultural contexts. Ruthellen Josselson and Amia Lieblich edited a groundbreaking book series in the mid-1990s aimed at showcasing the best scholarly work being done on narrative studies of lives, bringing together psychologists, sociologists, anthropologists, literary scholars, education researchers, and researchers in other disciplines. See, especially, Josselson and Lieblich (1993). More recently, the American Psychological Association launched a book series entitled *The Narrative Study of Lives* (e.g., Josselson, Lieblich, & McAdams, 2003; Lieblich, McAdams, & Josselson, 2004; McAdams, Josselson, & Lieblich, 2001). Other noteworthy research contributions to the narrative study of lives include Crossley (2000),

Franz and Stewart (1994), Josselson (1996), Maruna (2001), Nasby and Read (1997), and Rosenwald and Ochberg (1992). The conceptual and philosophical frameworks that underlie narrative studies of lives are discussed in many sources in psychology and sociology. Among the most influential or comprehensive are Barresi and Juckes (1997), Bruner (1986), Cohler (1982), Denzin (1989), Freeman (1993), McAdams (1999), Polkinghorne (1988), Sarbin (1986), and Shotter and Gergen (1989). A related movement in the helping professions is *narrative therapy,* an important source for which is White and Epston (1990).

18. From Didion (1979), p. 11.

Chapter 1

1. Elliot Washington is a pseudonym for a participant in one of the life-story research projects conducted at Northwestern University in the mid-1990s. To protect confidentiality and assure anonymity of all research participants whose life stories are described and analyzed in this book, minor facts and details for each case are modified, and pseudonyms are always used. The procedure is in accord with the principles of the Institutional Review Board at Northwestern University. Funded by a grant to Dan P. McAdams from the Spencer Foundation, the study in which Elliot Washington participated examined the life stories of highly generative and less generative African American and Euro-American adults between the ages of 35 and 65 years. The study is further described in later chapters. Methodological details and full results of the study can be found in McAdams and Bowman (2001); McAdams, Reynolds, Lewis, Patten, and Bowman (2001); and Hart, McAdams, Hirsch, and Bauer (2001).

2. James (1902/1958), p. 383 (italics in original).

3. The entry for *redemption* in the 15th edition of the *New Encyclopaedia Britannica* (1997) is cross-referenced with that of *salvation.* The term is defined this way: "In religion, the deliverance of mankind from fundamentally negative or disabling conditions, such as suffering, evil, finitude, and death; also, in some religions, the restoration or raising up of the natural world to a higher realm, or state." The entry continues:

> While salvation or redemption is a universal religious notion, the doctrine is
> perhaps most characteristic of Christianity, in which context it signifies the
> action of God within history whereby mankind is delivered from sin and
> death through the life, death, and Resurrection of Jesus Christ. In Christian
> theology, emphasis has been placed on the voluntary and loving character
> of Christ's sacrificial act and substitutionary activity of Christ in doing for
> men what they could not do for themselves, and on the needed response of
> men in faith, worship, and newness of life to this initiative of God in Christ.
> In the Bible, redemption has a more limited context. According to the

New Testament, "In him, we have redemption through his blood, the forgiveness of our trespasses according to the riches of his grace" (Eph. 1:7). The biblical metaphor is that of buying back a parcel of land or of purchasing someone from slavery. In popular Christianity, it is the individual soul that is thus redeemed—according to some, by virtue of voluntary faith, and according to others, on the basis of divine election.

4. A very thoughtful analysis of narratives of secular redemption in social gerontology and the study of adult psychological development can be found in Manheimer (1989).

5. Kakutani (2001), p. 4-1. A similar but more general point is made by Crossley (2000), who sees "restitution" themes as endemic to many modernist narratives. She writes,

> Restitution narratives are characteristic of modernity and constitute the culturally preferred narrative in contemporary culture. To recap, these narratives incorporate the modernist expectation that for every suffering there is a remedy. This "remedy" could be in the form of some sort of medical intervention which "cures" the disease or some form of political activism which "solves" the problem by implementing a particular policy or vision. The important feature of such restitution narratives is that they incorporate the assumption that by acting on the world in some way, a "solution" is forthcoming. (p. 169)

6. I owe thanks to Peter Zeldow for coming up with the idea of coding *People* magazine stories for redemption themes.

7. "Stories of Hope," *People* (2002, September 16), p. 49.

8. *People.*

9. Written in 1630, Winthrop's precise words were as follows: "For wee must Consider that wee shall be as a Citty upon a Hill, the eies of all people are uppon us." From Winthrop's lay sermon delivered on board the *Arbella*, "A Modell of Christian Charity," in Bellah, Madsen, Sullivan, Swidler, and Tipton (1985), p. 26.

10. The fact that New England Puritans modeled themselves after the biblical Israelites has been noted and analyzed in detail by many scholars. Among the best sources on this idea are Bercovitch (1974, 1975), Bush (1999), Delbancho (1999), K. Erikson (1966), Glaude (2000), and Wills (1990).

11. Winthrop's precise words: "The end is to improve our lives, to doe more service to the Lord, the comforte and encrease of the body of Christ whereof wee are members, that our selves and our posterity may be the better preserved from the Common corrupcions of this evill world, to serve the Lord and worke out our Salvacion under the power and purity of his holy Ordinances." From Bellah et al. (1985), p. 25.

12. See T. R. Cole (1992).

13. See Shea (1968).

14. Delbancho (1999), p. 28.

15. Ibid., p. 29.

16. See Shea (1968).

17. For example, the eminent historian Sacvan Bercovitch writes,

Early New England rhetoric provided a ready framework for inverting later secular values—human perfectibility, technological progress, democracy, Christian socialism, or simply (and comprehensively) the American Way— into the mold of sacred teleology. And the concept [Cotton] Mather advanced of the American who stands for the New World, in spite of, or beyond, the forces of secular time, justified the claims of a long progression of solitary keepers of the dream. The greatest of them are also the leading figures of our cultural tradition, from the Great Awakening through the American Renaissance, Edwards through Emerson. Each of them, in his own way, responded to the problems of his times by recourse to what I have described as the genre of auto-American-biography: the celebration of the representative self as America, and of the American self as the embodiment of a prophetic universal design. (1975, p. 136)

18. Quoted in Glaude (2000), pp. 79–80.

19. In the introduction to his edited volume on the classic slave narratives, Gates (1987) writes,

One scholar, Marion Wilson Starling, estimates the total [of escaped slaves] at sixty thousand. Of this number, over one hundred wrote book-length "slave narratives," as we call them, before the end of the Civil War. Between 1703 and 1944, when George Washington Carver published his autobiography, Starling concludes that *six thousand and six* ex-slaves had narrated the stories of their captivity, through interviews, essays, and books. No group of slaves anywhere, at any other period in history, has left such a large repository of testimony about the horror of becoming the legal property of another human being. (p. ix)

20. See, for example, W. L. Andrews (1986), Davis and Gates (1985), Gates (1987), and Glaude (2000).

21. See Pennebaker (1989, 1997); Pennebaker, Mehl, and Niederhoffer (2003). Also see Francis and Pennebaker (1992), Greenberg and Stone (1992), and King and Miner (2000).

22. Pennebaker (1989, p. 218).

23. See Wegner, Schneider, Carter, and White (1987).

24. See, for example, Affleck and Tennen (1996); Aldwin, Sutton, and Lachman (1996); Park, Cohen, and Murch (1996); S. Taylor (1983); and Tedeschi and Calhoun (1995).

25. Wollman and Felton (1983).

26. Taylor, Lichtman, and Wood (1984).

27. Affleck, Tennen, and Gershman (1985).

28. Affleck, Tennen, Croog, and Levine (1987).

29. Tedeschi and Calhoun (1995).

30. Taylor et al. (1984).

31. Tedeschi and Calhoun (1995), p. 38.

32. See Franklin (1961), p. 39; and Leibowitz (1989).

33. Franklin (1961), p. 16.

34. Bellah, Madsen, Sullivan, Swidler, and Tipton (1991).

35. Quoted in Bush (1999), p. 52.

36. de Tocqueville (1835/1956), p. 156.

37. Quoted in Wills (1990), p. 213.

38. On Horatio Alger, see Decker (1997), Scharnhorst (1980), and Tebbel (1963).

39. In Scharnhorst (1980), p. 31.

40. The historian was Kenneth S. Lynn, in Scharnhorst (1980), p. 9.

41. In *Made in America: Self-Styled Success From Horatio Alger to Oprah Winfrey,* Jeffrey L. Decker (1997) traces American narratives of self-made success over the past 150 years. He argues that over this time the emphasis in success stories shifted progressively from *character* (e.g., virtue and will) in the 19th century, to *personality* (effective traits, social skills) in the early 20th century, and finally to appearance and *image* in the media-saturated world of today. Over this time period, furthermore, success stories became more inclusive, incorporating immigrants first, and then women and minorities. Decker argues that success stories have lost a good deal of the moral authority they once had. We no longer expect successful people to be "good" people, even though we still wish to be successful ourselves. Decker is especially astute at exposing the contradictions and ambivalences in American success stories, as in that most celebrated of all American novels about success, F. Scott Fitzgerald's *The Great Gatsby.*

42. See Carnegie (1936/1981) and Covey (1989).

43. For example, Klinkenborg (2002).

44. See, for example, Bellah et al. (1985), Decker (1997), Hochschild (1995), and Shulevitz (2001). The dangers and limitations of American success stories, and other redemptive myths, are central topics in chapter 9 of this book.

45. To read an empirical psychological study based on a critical view of the American Dream, see Kasser and Ryan (1993).

46. The full study is described in McAdams et al. (2001) and in McAdams and Bowman (2001). I will return to aspects of this study in chapter 2.

47. The 8 scenes described by the midlife adults via the interview and the 10 scenes described by the students in written form were content analyzed for redemption imagery according to a 4-point scheme. The scene received a quantitative score of +1 if the author explicitly described a turn from a clearly negative situation to a positive one. Following the research of Tedeschi and Calhoun (1995), furthermore, all

scenes that initially received the score of +1 were further analyzed for three additional themes: (a) enhanced agency (feelings of self-confidence, power autonomy, and so on), (b) enhanced communion (feelings of heightened interpersonal closeness, love, intimacy, and so on), and (c) enhanced religious or spiritual insight. Consequently, a maximum score of +4 was possible—for a scene with an explicit redemptive turn from negative to positive which, in turn, led to enhanced personal agency, enhanced friendship or love, and enhanced religious or spiritual insight. For each participant, individual scene scores were summed to arrive at a total redemption score.

48. For example, Grossbaum and Bates (2002).

49. Each scene was rated on a 5-point scale to determine how much positive emotion it contained, from a score of 5, meaning extremely positive story with very happy ending, and a score of 1, meaning extremely negative story with a very sad ending. These positivity scores were modestly significantly correlated with scores for redemption sequences in the life narratives. Through a multiple regression statistical procedure, I pitted positivity against redemption to see which predicted more strongly the self-report outcomes of depression, self-esteem, life satisfaction, and life coherence. In the multiple regression, redemption consistently proved to be a statistically significant predictor of these outcomes, whereas the narrative positivity variable dropped out as a good predictor and failed to account for a significant amount of the variance in psychological well-being.

Chapter 2

1. Gen. 1:11 RSV.

2. Gen. 1:24 RSV.

3. The concept of inclusive fitness was first articulated by the eminent evolutionary biologist William Hamilton (1964).

4. The term *environment of evolutionary adaptedness* (EEA) is used by many evolutionary biologists and psychologists. I first encountered it in Bowlby's (1969) book on attachment. Bowlby argued that the bond of love between human mother and infant served the biological function of protecting the infant from predators in the EEA. Among the best and most engaging resources on social life and evolutionary challenges in the EEA are books by Pinker (1997), E. O. Wilson (1978), and R. Wright (1994); and the scholarly monograph by Tooby and Cosmides (1992).

5. Robert Hogan (1982, 1987; Hogan, Jones, and Cheek, 1985) developed an entire personality theory around the ideas of getting along and getting ahead. He calls it *socioanalytic theory,* for its roots in Freudian psychoanalysis and George Herbert Mead's sociological role theory. Socioanalytic theory asserts that human beings are biologically predisposed to live in social groups that are variously organized into status hierarchies. Group living provided our evolutionary ancestors with advantages in cooperative ventures, such as defense against predators. At the same time, high status within one's group included decided advantages, providing first choice of food,

romantic partners, living space, and whatever other desirable commodities and privileges the group afforded, ultimately promoting reproductive success. Therefore, human beings are genetically mandated to seek acceptance and status, to seek to be liked and to be powerful. As Hogan puts it, "Getting along and getting ahead are the two great problems in life that each person must solve" (Hogan et al., 1985, p. 178). These two great problems, argues Hogan, are always addressed and resolved in the context of ritualized social interaction. Social behavior is an elaborate game, governed by rules and conventions, scripted into roles and routines, and mastered by the most skillful game players among us. This was just as true in the EEA as it is today, Hogan asserts. This is not to trivialize social behavior as inauthentic or lacking in sincerity. Rather, role-playing and impression management are unconscious, central, biologically programmed tendencies for all human beings. He writes as follows: "Self-presentation and impression management are not trivial party games. They are fundamental processes, rooted in our history as group-living animals. They are archaic, powerful, compulsive tendencies that are closely tied to our chances for survival and reproductive success" (Hogan et al., 1985, p. 181).

6. See de Waal (1996).

7. The concept of reciprocal altruism was first spelled out in scientific detail by Trivers (1971).

8. E. O. Wilson (1975).

9. Kotre (1984), p. 10.

10. Speaking of books on identity, I cannot help but plug my own modest effort in this regard: McAdams (1985). Among the best books on Erikson's concept of identity are Breger (1974), Erikson (1958, 1959, 1968), Josselson (1996), Langbaum (1982), and Lapsley and Power (1988). In chapter 3, I will return to the concept of identity to argue that a person's internalized life story *is* his or her identity, or at least is a central component of that identity.

11. Many theorists and researchers have discussed the complex ways in which social class, gender, and cultural conditions influence generativity. Among the best sources are Cohler, Hostetler, and Boxer (1998); E. R. Cole and Stewart (1996); Keyes and Ryff (1998); MacDermid, Franz, and de Reus (1998); and Rossi (2001). The larger and related question regarding the overall relationship between generativity and society is the subject of this edited volume: de St. Aubin, McAdams, and Kim (2004).

12. Problems and frustrations in generativity are central concerns in the following sources: K. Erikson (2004), Kotre (1984), and Kotre and Kotre (1998).

13. A considerable amount of research has examined Erikson's contention that generativity marks a discrete midlife *stage* of development. Predictably, these studies have examined the relation between age and various measures of generativity, including measures of generative behaviors, attitudes, and self-attributions. The results of these studies vary, from a few showing no relation between generativity and age (e.g., Whitbourne, Zuschlag, Elliot, & Waterman, 1992), to others that have documented a smooth stage sequence (e.g., Snarey, 1993; Vaillant & Milofsky, 1980). A number of studies, including a nationwide survey of over 3,000 U.S. adults, suggest

that generativity concerns and behaviors may peak in the midlife years (e.g., Keyes & Ryff, 1998; McAdams, de St. Aubin, & Logan, 1993; Peterson & Stewart, 1990; Rossi, 2001). Nonetheless, the developmental course of generativity is still strongly and sometimes unpredictably shaped by social and cultural forces. To suggest that generativity is neatly situated within a discrete stage of midlife, therefore, is probably to suggest too much. The course of adult development is not nearly so neat and predictable (Dannefer, 1984; Elder, 1995). Furthermore, Stewart and Vandewater (1998) have shown that the *motivation* to be generative may be very high in young adulthood, but that many people may not be typically able to actualize fully their generative desires until they reach the midlife years (e.g., their 40s). The conclusion to be drawn here is that generativity may be an especially salient psychosocial issue in midlife, but that generative concerns and issues can arise at virtually any point in the adult life course (McAdams, 2001a).

14. Over the past 15 years, researchers have developed a number of different measures of individual differences in various aspects of generativity. Some researchers have used clinical ratings (Bradley, 1997; Snarey, 1993; Vaillant & Milofsky, 1980) to assess the extent to which different adults have achieved developmental tasks associated with generativity. Others have used the Q-sort ranking procedure to evaluate the extent to which an individual's overall profile of personality traits exhibits features indicative of generativity (Himsel, Hart, Diamond, & McAdams, 1997; Peterson & Klohnen, 1995). Still others have employed content analysis procedures designed to detect generativity themes in imaginative autobiographical narratives (McAdams & de St. Aubin, 1992; Peterson, 1998; Peterson & Stewart, 1990). My own research program has focused on three interrelated aspects of generativity: generative concern, generative goals, and generative actions (McAdams & de St. Aubin, 1992; McAdams, Hart, & Maruna, 1998). On the Loyola Generativity Scale (LGS), adults rate the extent to which they agree or disagree with 20 statements designed to assess the strength of a person's overall conscious concern for the next generation. To measure generative goals, we employ a procedure developed by Emmons (1986) for identifying the person's most important daily strivings—the things that a person is typically trying to accomplish in daily life. To measure acts, we present people with a checklist of behaviors indicative of generativity (e.g., "read a story to a child," "performed a community service") and ask them to determine how many times they have indeed performed each act in the past two months. Measures of generative concern, generative goals, and generative acts tend to be positively correlated with each other. Of the three measures, the LGS has the most psychometric reliability and validity, and it is typically the measure we depend upon the most.

15. Research support for a connection between generativity among parents and parental involvement in children's education comes mainly from Nakagawa (1991).

16. Research support for a connection between generativity and authoritative parenting styles comes from Peterson, Smirles, and Wentworth (1997) and Pratt, Danso, Arnold, Norris, and Filyer (2001).

17. Research support for a connection between generativity, on the one hand, and

parental value socialization and emphasizing the passing on of wisdom in family lessons and stories, on the other, comes from Hart, McAdams, Hirsch, and Bauer (2001); McAdams (2004); and Pratt, Norris, Arnold, and Filyer (1999).

18. Research support for a link between generativity and social support comes from Hart et al. (2001).

19. Research support for associations between generativity, on the one hand, and religious, political, civic, and volunteer activities, on the other, comes from many sources: E. R. Cole and Stewart (1996), Hart et al. (2001), Peterson (2002), Peterson and Klohnen (1995), Peterson et al. (1997), and Rossi (2001). The most impressive data in this regard come from Rossi's (2001) nationwide sample of over 3,000 American adults, in which generativity measures proved to be especially strong predictors of caring for others in the family and contributing time and money to volunteer and charitable activities.

20. Research support for a connection between generativity and moral development comes from Pratt et al. (1999).

21. Research support for a connection between generativity and mental health (including self-reported quality of life) comes from many sources: Ackerman, Zuroff, and Moscowitz (2000); de St. Aubin and McAdams (1995); Grossbaum and Bates (2002); Keyes and Ryff (1998); McAdams et al. (1998); Peterson et al. (1997); Snarey (1993); Stewart and Ostrove (1998); Vaillant (1977); and Vandewater, Ostrove, and Stewart (1997).

22. Generativity has been linked to high needs for power (agency) and intimacy (communion) in Ackerman et al. (2000); de St. Aubin and McAdams (1995); McAdams, Ruetzel, and Foley (1986); Peterson and Stewart (1993); and Rossi (2001).

23. Rossi (2001).

24. Some studies show that women score slightly higher than men on generativity; other studies show no gender difference. Generativity is sometimes positively associated with education, though this relationship tends to be modest (e.g., Kim & Youn, 2002). Results connecting generativity to the many outcomes described in chapter 2 remain statistically significant when differences in education are partialed out. Therefore, the positive associations between generativity, on the one hand, and indices of psychological well-being, social support, parenting effectiveness, societal involvement, moral development, and other positive outcomes, on the other, are not due to differences in education or social class.

25. These studies are described in McAdams et al. (1997); McAdams and Bowman (2001); and McAdams, Reynolds, Lewis, Patten, and Bowman (2001).

26. The logic of these studies involves developing a hypothesis or prediction about group differences from a small subsample of the data and then testing that hypothesis objectively through careful content analysis of the remaining data. In the second phase of hypothesis testing, it is imperative that all scoring or coding of interview transcripts be done in a "blind" manner. This means that trained coders applied objective rating and scoring procedures to the interview data without access to any other information about the respondents and without knowledge of the study's hy-

potheses. The painstaking procedure for data analysis begins with literally thousands of pages of interview transcripts that are subjected to rigorous content analytic procedures performed by many different coders, resulting in quantitative scores for each story. The scores are then subjected to statistical tests to test various hypotheses about how the life stories told by highly generative adults differ from life stories told by less generative adults. At the end of the day (actually, after many years of work), these rich, qualitative interview transcripts are translated into reliable quantitative scores that are then subjected to conventional statistical procedures. The studies are noteworthy—probably unique—for their blending of qualitative and quantitative methods in psychological research. The best description of the overall methodology can be found in McAdams et al. (1997).

27. I heard this little tune at Children's Memorial Hospital in Chicago on August 2, 2001. My daughter thought I was crazy to write down the lyrics.

28. For example, Bercovitch (1975), Cushman (1995), Kammen (1972), and Kazin (1984).

29. The theme of American exceptionalism is also found in American literature, as shown in Kazin (1984).

30. In a classic research report, Brown and Kulik (1977) maintained that the vivid recollections most Americans of a certain age have of the Kennedy assassination constitute *flashbulb memories.* Like a photograph, the memory captures forever the concrete experience of the happening, where the person was, what he or she was doing, thinking, and feeling at the dramatic moment the flash went off. Other researchers have suggested that memories of dramatic, public events like the Pearl Harbor invasion, Kennedy assassination, the Challenger explosion (January 28, 1986), and the September 11, 2001, attacks in the United States tend to be reworked in our minds over time, revised and edited in accord with our changing understandings of the past, present, and future. The cognitive psychologist Ulric Neisser (1982) preferred the term *benchmark memories* for these recollections. Over time, these events become established in our memory as "the places where we line up our own lives with the course of history and say, 'I was there'" (p. 48).

31. Eisenberg and Miller (1987); Hoffman (1981).

32. See, for example, de St. Aubin (1996).

33. M. Andrews (1991); Colby and Damon (1992); Dillon and Wink (2004); Rossi (2001).

34. Gettleman (2002), p. A8.

35. See Wills (1992).

Chapter 3

1. Sources on Bob Love: Berkow (2002); Love and Watkins (1999). Quotes come from Berkow (2002, p. C-18; emphasis added). Love lost the aldermanic election.

2. "Second Acts," *People* (2002, September 30), p. 124.

3. The idea that identity is an internalized and evolving life story is probably the main idea behind virtually everything I study as a psychologist. My life-story model of identity is described in detail in McAdams (1985, 1990, 1993, 1996a, 1996b, 1999, 2001c). Among the best scholarly sources on the overall role of storytelling in human lives are Bruner (1986), Charme (1984), Cohler (1982), Freeman (1993), Josselson (1995), MacIntyre (1984), Polkinghorne (1988), Ricouer (1984), and Sarbin (1986).

4. Bruner (1986, 1990).

5. Bruner (1986), p. 17.

6. Bruner (1990), pp. 49–50.

7. The term *episodic memory* was coined by the cognitive scientist Endel Tulving. An excellent and up-to-date source on research into episodic memory is Tulving (2002).

8. This case comes from Tulving (2002), pp. 12–16.

9. The relative independence of semantic and episodic memory leads to some fascinating possibilities. For example, some case studies of amnesia suggest that, although an individual may lose most or all recollection of events from his or her past, he or she may still retain valid semantic information about the self. For example, a woman with the kind of amnesia shown by K. C. may give responses on a self-report personality scale suggesting that she thinks of herself as a relatively "extraverted" person, and these responses may be consistent with the way other people see her. But how did she come to the conclusion that she was extraverted if she can recall no personal memories from her past? The commonsense understanding of personal trait ratings is that people base judgments of themselves on past experiences, but, if you can remember no past experiences, then how do you judge? As counterintuitive as it may seem, it may be the case that we do not or need not rely on past experiences to make these judgments. In other words, I may just "know" that I am an extravert (or a depressive, or a very nice person) without needing to provide episodic evidence for my conclusion. An example suggesting this possibility is the case of D. B., described in Klein, Cosmides, Costabile, and Mei (2002).

10. Freud (1905/1953).

11. Damasio (1999).

12. Ibid., p. 30.

13. A similar idea was expressed by Julian Jaynes in a classic book from the 1970s, *The Origins of Consciousness in the Breakdown of the Bicameral Mind.* Jaynes argued that consciousness is an operation of the human mind involving the construction of an analog space with an analog "I" that observes the space, moves metaphorically within the space, and *narrates* that movement over time:

> In consciousness, we are always seeing our vicarial selves as the main figures
> in the stories of our lives. . . . Seated where I am, I am writing a book and
> this fact is imbedded more or less in the center of the story of my life, time
> being spatialized into a journey of my days and years. New situations are
> selectively perceived as part of this ongoing story, perceptions that do not

fit into it being unnoticed or at least unremembered. More important, situations are chosen which are congruent to his ongoing story, until the picture
I have of myself in my life story determines how I am to act and choose in
novel situations as they arise. . . . Consciousness is ever ready to explain anything we happen to find ourselves doing. The thief narratizes his act as due
to poverty, the poet his as due to beauty, and the scientist his as due to truth,
purpose and cause inextricably woven into the spatialization of behavior in
consciousness. But it is not just our own analog "I" that we are narratizing;
it is everything else in consciousness. A stray fact is narratized to fit with
some other stray fact. A child cries in the street and we narratize the event
into a mental picture of a lost child and a parent searching for it. A cat is up
in a tree and we narratize the event into a picture of a dog chasing it
there. . . ." (Jaynes, 1976, pp. 63–64)

14. As William James noted more than 100 years ago, human selfhood is reflexive. There is always an "I" and a "me." The "I" is that basic sense of self as an agent,
the sense of subjectivity that we all take for granted most of the time. The "me" is
what the "I" sees (the object) when it looks upon itself—it is the self-concept, all
those things that a person attributes to himself or herself. In the second year of life,
children begin to attribute various distinguishing characteristics to themselves, including their names, their favorite toys, their likes and dislikes, and so on. With the
development of language, the self-concept grows rapidly to encompass a wide range
of things "about me" that can be verbally described. To be included in the mix eventually are memories of events in which the self was involved. According to Howe and
Courage (1997), *autobiographical memory* emerges toward the end of the second year
of life when children have consolidated a basic sense of "I" and reflexively begun to
build up a primitive understanding of "me." Although infants may be able to remember some events (primitive episodic memory) before this time, it is not until the
end of the second year, Howe and Courage contend, that episodic memory becomes
personalized and children begin to organize events that they experience as "things
that happened to me." From this point onward, the "me" expands to include autobiographical recollections, recalled as little stories about what has transpired in "my life."

15. In the second year of life, children begin to express the kinds of social emotions that suggest they are at least dimly aware of themselves as the objects of other
people's observations. Pride, shame, and guilt (which probably develops somewhat
later) are examples of social emotions. The development of social emotions accom-
panies the emergence of a clear sense of self (as both "I" and "me") in the second year
and the understanding that the self is separate from, but in relation to, others.

16. Baron-Cohen (1995); Wellman (1993).

17. Autobiographical memory and storytelling emerge and develop in a social
context (K. Nelson, 1988; Welch-Ross, 1995). Parents typically encourage children to
talk about their personal experiences as soon as children are verbally able to do so
(Fivush & Kuebli, 1997). Early on, parents may take the lead in stimulating the child's

recollection and telling of the past by reminding the child of recent events, such as this morning's breakfast or yesterday's visit to the doctor. Taking advantage of this initial conversational scaffolding provided by adults, the young child soon begins to take more initiative in sharing personal events. By the age of 3 years, children are actively co-constructing their past experiences in conversations with adults. By the end of the preschool years, they are able to give a relatively coherent narrative account of their past experiences, independent of adult guidance (Fivush, 1994). In conversations with adults about personal memories, young children become acquainted with the narrative structures through which events are typically discussed by people in their world. The sharing of personal experiences functions as a major mechanism of socialization and helps to build an organized personal history from a growing base of autobiographical memories.

18. Arnett (2000).

19. The sociologist Anthony Giddens writes that "a person's identity is not to be found in behavior, nor—important though this is—in the reactions of others, but in the capacity to keep a particular narrative going" (1991, p. 54). In accord with Giddens (1991) and the philosopher Charles Taylor (1989), I have argued in many places that the unique problems cultural modernity poses for human selfhood require modern men and women to become especially adept at assimilating their lives to culturally intelligible stories (McAdams, 1996b, 1997, 2001c). In the modern world, the self is a reflexive project that a person is expected to "work on"—to develop, improve, expand, and strive to perfect. Modern people see the self as complex and multifaceted, as containing many layers and depth, and as changing relentlessly over time. At the same time, they feel a strong urge to find some coherence in the self, to fashion a self that is more or less unified and purposeful within the discordant cultural parameters that situate their lives. From the media to everyday discourse, modern life is filled with models and examples of how to live a meaningful life, and how not to. Yet virtually every positive model has its drawbacks, nothing close to consensus exists, and, even if some modest level of cultural consensus could be reached, modern people are socialized anyway to find their own way, to craft a self that is true to who one "really" is. (This point will be expanded in chapter 5.) As a consequence, people pick and choose and plagiarize selectively from the many stories and images they find in culture, in order to formulate a narrative identity. Identity is not a problem that is unique to cultural modernity, but it is especially characteristic of it. In modern life, constructing your own meaningful life story is a veritable cultural imperative.

20. The fourth and last stage of cognitive development in Piaget's (1970) famous theory, *formal operations* refers to the adolescent's and adult's purported ability to engage in hypothetico-deductive thinking and to reflect rationally on the process of subjective thought. Breger (1974) argued that the onset of formal operations in adolescence helps to usher in the concern for identity. Identity becomes an especially engaging abstraction for the formal thinker: "The idea of a unitary or whole self in which past memories of who one was, present experiences of who one is, and future

expectations of who one will be is the sort of abstraction that the child simply does not think about." But "with the emergence of formal operations in adolescence, wholeness, unity, and integration become introspectively real problems" (Breger, 1974, p. 330). The idea that one's life, as complex and dynamic as it increasingly appears in the emerging adult years, might be integrated into a meaningful and purposeful whole may represent, therefore, an especially appealing possibility to the self-reflective adolescent or young adult.

21. Habermas and Bluck (2000).

22. The developmental psychologist David Elkind (1981) coined the term *personal fable* and articulated a Piagetian cognitive theory for its emergence. According to Elkind, personal fable is one form of adolescent egocentrism, resulting from the adolescent's naïve efforts to use the newfound power of formal operations to develop a logically organized hypothetical scenario for his or her own life.

23. A central conclusion from the research literature in cognitive psychology is that autobiographical memory helps locate and define the self within an ongoing life story that, simultaneously, is strongly oriented toward future goals (Conway & Pleydell-Pearce, 2000; Pillemer, 1998; Stein, Wade, & Liwag, 1997). Most authorities in this area believe that memory for past events is sometimes quite accurate, but sometimes not, and that people often reconstruct the past to fit their current views of themselves and their future goals. For example, Brewer (1986) has argued that "recent personal memories retain a relatively large amount of specific information from the original phenomenal experience (e.g., location, point of view) but that with time, or under strong schema-based [attitude- and personality-driven] processes, the original experience can be reconstructed to produce a new nonveridical personal memory that retains most of the phenomenal characteristics of other memories" (p. 44). Similarly, Thompson, Skowronski, Larsen, and Betz (1996) have contended that memory for recent events is largely reproductive but that memory for distant events tends to be reconstructive. Schacter (1996) concluded that memory systems in general, and autobiographical memory in particular, "do a remarkably good job of preserving the contours of our pasts and recording correctly many of the important things that have happened to us." And yet, "Our [autobiographical] stories are built from many different ingredients: snippets of what actually happened, thoughts about what might have happened, and beliefs that guide us as we attempt to remember" (p. 308). Taking a more reconstructive position, Barclay (1996) has construed autobiographical memory as a form of *improvisation* whereby the person puts together a more or less plausible account of the past, which functions primarily to maintain personal coherence rather than provide an objective report of what has transpired in a person's life.

24. Like many cognitive psychologists, I adopt a moderately reconstructive view of autobiographical recollections. Personal goals and other concerns shape the encoding and recollection of what Singer and Salovey (1993) call *self-defining memories* and other important features of the life story. Reconstruction exerts a distorting effect, especially with regard to memories from long ago. But for life stories the great-

est degree of reconstruction may involve *selection* and *interpretation,* rather than outright distortion of the truth (Bluck & Levine, 1998). People select and interpret certain memories as self-defining, granting those memories privileged status in their narrative identity. Other potential candidates for such status are downgraded, relegated to the category of "oh yes, I remember that, but I don't think it is very important," or to the category of the altogether forgotten. To a certain degree, then, narrative identity is a product of choice. We choose the events that we consider most important for defining who we are and providing our lives with some semblance of unity and purpose. We endow them with symbolic importance, lessons learned, integrative themes, and other personal meanings that make sense to us in the present as we survey the past and anticipate the future.

25. Morris (1999), p. xii.

26. Ibid., p. 181.

27. The sociologist Erving Goffman (1959) built a highly influential theory of social behavior around the metaphor of playacting. From Goffman's perspective, Ronald Reagan would have been the norm, not the interesting extreme case, in this thoroughly dramaturgical framework for comprehending social life and identity.

28. Pasupathi (2001).

29. Thorne (2000); Thorne and McLean (2003).

30. Freud (1923/1961).

31. Mead (1934).

32. See McAdams (1998). Many different psychologists have proposed that human behavior is guided by internalized agents of various sorts. Freud's (1923/1961) *superego* is perhaps the best-known example. As an internalization of the Oedipal parents, the superego performs the function of observing the self and monitoring psychic activity with respect to internalized standards for good and bad behavior. Following Freud, object relations theorists (e.g., Fairbairn, 1952; Guntrip, 1971) and psychoanalytic self-psychologists (e.g., Kohut, 1977) proposed a variety of models for psychological functioning in which significant persons (*self-objects*) in one's environment are internalized in one way or another and their personified mental representations influence and monitor psychic activity in various ways. For example, Kohut spoke of internalized parental imagoes that help structure the self, and Watkins (1986) has spoken of internalized dialogues that take place between various personified agents of the psyche. A related idea comes from attachment theory (Bowlby, 1969; Main, Kaplan, & Cassidy, 1985), which assumes that infants develop internalized mental images of their mothers or caregivers, images that remain in their minds as working models for subsequent interpersonal relationships.

33. For research reviews, see McAdams (1999, 2001c); Pasupathi (2001); C. E. Smith (2000); Thorne (2000).

34. Lachman (2001).

35. The life-story interview is a research tool, but it can also be used in a less formal way for self-discovery and other purposes, as described in chapter 10 of McAdams (1993).

Chapter 4

1. Melville (1850/1892), p. 144.

2. The historian Michael Kammen (1972) wrote that the idea of America as a utopian place was implanted in European minds long before the Pilgrims and the Puritans set sail for the New World:

> The *idea* of Europe, for example, emerged historically well after Medieval Europe had become a recognized reality in the political, religious, and economic realms. Whereas the idea of America, as El Dorado and Paradise, surfaced before the fact of America, prior to colonization, and thereby conditioned the form the "facts" would take, and even what people would make of them. Sir Thomas Moore's *Utopia,* for example, preceded by more than a century the utopian schemes of Puritan Boston or Pilgrim Plymouth. There is a sense in which Americans, from the outset, could not fully control their own destiny because they had a mythology before they even had a country. (p. 9)

3. In *God's New Israel: Religious Interpretations of American Destiny,* Conrad Cherry (1998) writes,

> The rudiments of the theme of American destiny under God emerged in the English colonization of the New World. The new nation that was to appear would inherit from the thirteen colonies an English language, legal system, and set of social customs, all appropriately adapted to the American environment. It would fall heir also to a religious view of history that had developed in the mother country. By the time they launched their colonial enterprises in the seventeenth century, the English had been taught from childhood that the course of human history is directed by God's overruling providence and that God's redemptive efforts centered on England and English Christianity. These assumptions about history were frequently joined with the millennialist belief that God and his chosen English saints were actively defeating the powers of Satan, the first major victory being the Protestant Reformation. The establishment of the colonies, therefore, was hardly considered an ordinary undertaking. Many in England saw it as an opportunity to extend the influence of their civilization through which God was working for the redemption of humankind. For others colonization was a chance to bring England to its senses by achieving on new soil what they had not been able to do at home. The Quaker William Penn was moved to announce that his "holy experiment" in religious toleration was meant to be God's own "example to the nations." The letters of the Jesuit father Andrew White claimed that the settlement of Maryland was continuously presided over by the providence of God and that the "first and most important design" of the colony was "sowing the seeds of religion and piety." (p. 25)

4. Bercovitch (1974, 1975) spelled out the seventeenth-century Puritan Myth in great detail, arguing that it has continued to exert a strong influence on American identity ever since:

> The emigrants thought of themselves as a "new Israel" on an "errand" to found "a city on a hill." To the modern reader (and all too often, to the modern scholar) the terms mean anything—i.e., nothing in particular. To the Puritan their meanings are both precise and complex. "Errand" implied the believer's journey to God and the communal calling to the New World; "new Israel" signified the elect, the theocracy as it was prefigured in the Old Testament, and the blessed remnant which, according to prophecy, would usher in the millennium; "city" meant a social order and the bonds of true visible church; the concept of "hill" opened into a series of scriptural landmarks demarcating the march of redemptive history: Ararat, Sinai, Golgotha, and the Holy Mount of New Jerusalem. Each of the terms, then, presents the same constellation of meanings. Each of them tells us that the Puritan impulse was profoundly eschatological; that the eschatology was at once private and public, applicable as it were in the same breath to saint and society; and that the forms of that society expressed the saint's relationship to his church, his fellow-man, the spiritual life to come, and God's grand design for mankind. (1974, p. 7)

5. Cherry (1998), p. 64.

6. Ibid., p. 65.

7. I borrow the term (and conception of) *redeemer nation* from a book of the same name, by Tuveson (1968).

8. Quoted in Tuveson (1968), dedication page.

9. Clymer (2002) reports on a conference of historians and political scientists to discuss Reagan's place in history. The consensus of the gathering was that, despite his reputation in some circles as a man with few intellectual gifts, Ronald Reagan did indeed hold a coherent and well-articulated political philosophy. The political scientist Hugh Heclo argued at the conference that the core Reagan idea was "a sacramental vision" of America. According to Heclo, "God's unique relation to America was the central chord [in Reagan's philosophy] from which all else followed" (p. A-17).

10. Ibid.

11. Quoted in Reeves (2001).

12. Marx (2003).

13. See, for example, Tajfel and Turner (1979).

14. From Williams (1972), p. 3.

15. Emerson (1841/1993), p. 38.

16. Weber (1904/1976).

17. Evidence in support of the idea that highly generative adults reconstruct their past in ways suggesting they felt an early advantage in life comes mainly from case

studies provided by Colby and Damon (1992) and from two rigorous, content-analysis studies conducted by my students and me. In the first (McAdams, Diamond, de St. Aubin, & Mansfield, 1997), extensive life-story interviews of 40 highly generative adults and 30 less generative adults were transcribed and coded by a team of researchers, using objective content-analysis procedures designed to assess the extent to which the protagonist in the story (a) enjoyed a special blessing or advantage in his or her family, (b) experienced a secure and trusting relationship with parents, or (c) received substantial care and assistance from a nonfamily source at a young age. The results showed that as a group the highly generative adults were significantly more likely to describe a childhood event in which they experienced a blessing or advantage, compared to less generative adults. They were no more likely, however, to enjoy a trusting bond with their parents or to receive special care from nonfamily sources. In a second study, we examined the life stories of 41 highly generative adults and 33 less generative adults, all ranging in age from 35 to 65 years. Approximately half of the sample was African American and half was Euro-American. Each interview transcript was coded for the extent to which the subject described an early advantage that he or she enjoyed in life before the age of 12 (as described in the Life Chapters portion of the interview and in the reconstruction of an earliest memory and an important childhood memory). Among the highly generative adults, 63% of the life stories showed an explicit early advantage, compared to 19% among the less generative adults.

18. In McAdams et al. (1997), highly generative adults were 5 times more likely than less generative adults to recall a childhood incident in which they felt empathy for the suffering of another or witnessed an injustice experienced by another person. In a second study, among 74 midlife adults, those high in generativity were 3 times more likely than those scoring low in generativity to spontaneously describe such an event from childhood.

19. See chapter 10 for a discussion of human nature, culture, and the development of self.

20. I prefer to see a person's life story as a *psychosocial construction* rather than a mere *social construction*. The latter term suggests that culture completely determines the nature of the story. My view is that the individual is as much an author of his or her own story as culture is; in some cases, the individual's story reflects master narratives and common themes in society, but in other cases a person resists culture's dominant viewpoints and develops a story that, in some sense, is at odds with culture. Of course, this is all very complex, because we all live in many different cultures, and a story that is in dispute with one of those cultures (e.g., a person's religious culture) may be consistent with another culture (e.g., a person's professional culture). For now, I assert that the term *psychosocial construction* simply works better in this context, because the *psycho* part reminds us that individuals take part in their own self-making. For more on the term *psychosocial constructionism,* see McAdams et al. (1997).

Chapter 5

1. American self-help books come in many different forms and address many different problems. A few of these volumes are written by academic and research-oriented clinical psychologists who aim to explicate principles of self-help derived from formal theory and scientific research (e.g., Prochaska, Norcross, & DiClemente, 1994). Many others are written by therapists, counselors, ministers, and others in the helping professions, who focus mainly on their own clinical experiences (e.g., Anthony, 1991; Miller, 2002; M. S. Peck, 1978). The last 15 years have witnessed an explosion of books on recovery from addiction, abuse, and other traumatic experiences (e.g., Beattie, 1992; Forward, 1989). Recovery books are sometimes based on or linked to 12-step programs such as Alcoholics Anonymous. Some self-help authors draw on Christian traditions (e.g., Bradshaw, 1988; Moore, 1992), while others incorporate Eastern spirituality, mysticism, and New Age philosophies (e.g., Vanzant, 1998). Going back to Dale Carnegie's (1936) *How to Win Friends and Influence People,* self-help authors have also addressed problems and opportunities in people's occupational lives, with a strong emphasis on business success and entrepreneurship (e.g., Covey, 1989; Ringer, 1977). Rarely, however, are the claims made by self-help authors subjected to the rigors of scientific evaluation. Many books are filled with wildly unsubstantiated claims and some ideas that are downright wacky. For example, Louise Hay's (1984) *You Can Heal Your Life* (over 3 million copies sold) says that acne comes from not accepting yourself and appendicitis results from a "blocking of the flow of the good" (p. 150). Many authors offer little real expertise beyond their own intuitions and the quality of their personal experiences. It should come as no surprise, then, that scientifically oriented psychologists and clinicians, as well as many other serious observers of American social life, are highly critical and even dismissive of the entire self-help industry, even as that industry generates billions of dollars every year. For example, Kaminer (1992) offers a scathing critique of the recovery movement, support groups, and many other features of the self-help genre in her *I'm Dysfunctional, You're Dysfunctional.* While I share many of Kaminer's concerns, I do find a small number of self-help books to be thoughtful and helpful. More important, I regard some of the most popular self-help books to be illuminating *cultural* texts that help us understand how Americans think about their lives and their world.

2. Peale (1952/1982).

3. Ibid., back cover.

4. Ibid., p. vii.

5. Ibid., p. 13.

6. Ibid., p. 2.

7. Ibid., p. 30.

8. The material on W. Clement Stone comes from his *New York Times* obituary, written by Martin (2002, September 15).

9. Rogers (1951).

10. Maslow (1968).

11. Dyer (1976/1995), pp. 71–72.

12. M. S. Peck (1978), pp. 15–16.

13. Ibid., p. 56.

14. Ibid., p. 82.

15. Ibid., p. 24.

16. The source for these claims is the front and back cover of Covey (1989).

17. Covey writes, "Principles are guidelines for human conduct that are proven to have enduring, permanent value. They're fundamental. They're essentially unarguable because they are self-evident" (1989, p. 35).

18. Covey (1989), p. 33.

19. Ibid., pp. 42–43.

20. Ibid., p. 107.

21. Ibid., p. 316.

22. Beattie (1992), dedication page.

23. Ibid., chapter titles, table of contents.

24. Anthony (1991), p. 20.

25. Forward (1989), p. 12.

26. Kaminer (1992), p. 18.

27. Covey (1989), p. 108.

28. Quotation at Forward (1989), title page.

29. Dyer (1976), p. 34.

30. Vanzant (1998), back cover.

31. Anthony (1991), pp. vii–viii.

32. Quotation at Peale (1952/1982), p. vii.

33. Kaminer (1992) is especially critical of the anti-intellectual streak in American self-help. For all the talk of introspection and self-exploration, she points out, self-help authors are quite reluctant to encourage honest and searching examinations of life—the kinds of practices that might produce ambivalence and increase inner turmoil.

34. Emerson (1841/1993), p. 27.

35. Ibid., p. 21.

36. Ibid., p. 19.

37. Ibid., p. 30.

38. Ibid., p. 20.

39. Ibid., p. 34.

40. Ibid., p. 28.

41. Ibid., p. 24.

42. Ibid., pp. 21–22.

43. Ibid., p. 33.

44. Ibid., p. 31.

45. See, especially, Freud's (1930/1961) *Civilization and Its Discontents.*

46. Cushman (1995).

47. Ibid., p. 118.

48. See Kohut (1971, 1977) and Wolf (1982). My discussion of Kohut is adapted from McAdams (2001b), pp. 142–143.

49. Kohut (1977, p. 177).

50. On attachment theory, key sources include Ainsworth (1989); Ainsworth, Blehar, Waters, and Wall (1978); Bowlby (1969); Cassidy and Shaver (1999); and Sroufe and Waters (1977). Also, see McAdams (2001b), pp. 89–110.

51. Clemetson (2001), p. 44.

52. Some observers criticize Oprah Winfrey for promoting an individual-centered, self-help approach to problem solving rather than addressing the more structural, economic, and political sources of social problems. Oprah scholarship, of which there is a considerable amount, seems divided on the issue. While numerous articles praise Oprah for exemplifying important virtues and bringing an empowering message to a broad range of people in contemporary American society (e.g., K. Dixon, 2001; Haag, 1993), others are much more critical. For example, Abt and Seesholtz (1994) argue that Oprah in particular and TV talk shows in general create superficial "pseudo-intimacy" that turns people and their emotions into a spectacle. J. R. Hill and Zillman (1999) worry about the "Oprahization" of the criminal justice system, suggesting that Oprah's empathic approach to criminals—who are sometimes framed as victims—may make Americans too soft on crime. Cloud (1996) suggests that Oprah's rags-to-riches life narrative is an example of "tokenism" in the American media. According to this argument, the White middle class embraces Oprah and her story because the story proves to them that American society is fair and free from racial prejudice. The fact that a poor Black woman can rise to the top may be used to defuse the critics who bemoan racial inequality, the unequal distribution of resources in American society, crumbling schools in the Black inner cities, and other vexing social issues. Ironically, Oprah's message of self-help may end up blaming the victims, from this point of view, by suggesting that if African American people are unable to pull themselves up by their own bootstraps, the way she did, then they have only themselves to blame.

53. For example, see Haag (1993).

54. J. Peck (1995).

55. Clemetson (2001), p. 44.

56. Decker (1997).

57. Clemetson (2001), p. 45.

58. Ibid., p. 44.

59. Ibid., p. 48.

Chapter 6

1. I thank Dick Anderson at Trinity Lutheran Church for providing me with this passage from Cardinal George's homily on September 11, 2001.

2. On the Pledge of Allegiance controversy, see Fineman (2002).

3. "Bush Pushes Plan for Faith-Based Aid," Associated Press story in the *Chicago Tribune* (2002, April 12).

4. Wheatcroft (2000).

5. Fineman (2002), p. 24.

6. Lee (2002).

7. In their authoritative review of the sociology of religion, Sherkat and Ellison (1999) report that 29% of Americans claim to attend church at least once per week. Goodstein (2001) reports that Gallup polls for the past three decades consistently show that between 39% and 43% of Americans say they attended church or synagogue during the past week. In the 10 days following the September 11, 2001, attacks, that number shot up to 47%, but by the end of November in that same year, it had dropped back to a typical figure—around 42%.

8. Wheatcroft (2000).

9. Wills (1990) adds, "If we neglect the religious element in all of those struggles, we cannot understand our own corporate past; we cannot even talk meaningfully to each other about the things that will affect us all" (p. 25). Nonetheless, until quite recently social scientists have mainly dismissed religion as a fading factor in modern life. John Dewey, for example, believed that a progressive democratic society must ultimately cast aside the authoritarian strictures of religious belief. Marx famously dubbed religion "the opiate of the masses," and Freud saw it as nothing more than an illusion derived from infantile wishes and identifications. Following World War II, psychologists either ignored religion altogether or associated it with prejudice, ethnocentrism, and politically reactionary viewpoints (e.g., Adorno, Frenkel-Brunswik, Levinson, & Sanford, 1950). With a few notable exceptions (e.g., Allport, 1950; James, 1902/1958), American psychologists have traditionally shown very little interest in the empirical study of religious experience and belief. In the past decade or two, however, things have begun to change. James Fowler's (1981) *Stages of Faith* presents an influential stage model of faith experience to developmental psychologists. Empirical psychologists such as Emmons (1999) and Pargament (2002) have conducted important scientific research on the role of religion in personality functioning and social relationships. For an authoritative review of psychological research on religion and spirituality, see Emmons and Paloutzian (2003). A spate of books has appeared on the intersection of religion, psychotherapy, and mental health (e.g., Levine, 2000; Nielson, Johnson, & Ellis, 2001). Most recently, the John Templeton Foundation has funded research projects and other initiatives aimed at casting a scientific eye on the role of religion and spirituality in American life.

10. Sherkat and Ellison (1999).

11. Wills (1990), p. 19.

12. For example, Delbancho (1999) and Kammen (1972).

13. Wills (1990), p. 131.

14. This quote, reportedly taken from Finney's memoirs, comes from a biography of Finney <http://xroads.virginia.edu/~HYPER/DETOC/religion/finney.html>.

15. On Finney and 19th century Protestantism, see Bush (1999), Kaminer (1992), Mathisen (1982), Wills (1990), and Wolfe (2000).

16. de Tocqueville (1835/1956), p. 47.

17. Ibid., p. 48.

18. Cushman (1995), Kaminer (1992), and Michaelsen (1975).

19. In an article entitled "Lord, Won't You Buy Me a Mercedes-Benz?" Judith Shulevitz (2001) comments on the prevalence of pro-prosperity messages in American religion today. She focuses on a pocket-sized self-help/spirituality book that sold 4 million copies in the United States in 2000. Written by an Atlanta-based evangelical minister named Bruce Wilkinson, *The Prayer of Jabez: Breaking Through to the Blessed Life* provides a four-step program for the good life and a promise that the reader should enjoy positive results within days. Following a prayer offered by an obscure Biblical figure named Jabez (I Chron.), the first step involves asking God to "enlarge your territory." "If Jabez worked on Wall Street," Wilkinson writes, "he might have prayed, 'Lord, increase the value of my investment portfolio.'" Wilkinson claims that God wants us to take entrepreneurial risks and to achieve worldly success. Shulevitz writes,

> The Jabez prayer grants the supplicant full access to the American cult of success, an adoration of power and material satisfaction untroubled by any sense that the enlargement of one's territory might leave others' diminished. That such upbeat theologies of convenience should have mass appeal is neither particular to our time—think of Norman Vincent Peale, whose 1952 best seller, *The Power of Positive Thinking,* was *The Prayer of Jabez* of its day—nor all that deplorable. It's useful to have these ideas spelled out, rather than at work in the culture but unexamined. Many readers clearly find Wilkinson's worldview to be similar to their own. Those who don't can indulge a voyeuristic fascination with the church of what the Protestant theologian Reinhold Nieburh, in 1950, called the American idolatry. (Shulevitz, 2001, p. 47)

20. For the role of religion in physical and mental health, see, especially, Dillon and Wink (2004); George, Ellison, and Larson (2002); Pargament (2002); Seybold and Hill (2001); and Sherkat and Ellison (1999).

21. Organized religion's role in augmenting social capital is a main theme in Robert Putnam's (2000) celebrated book, *Bowling Alone.* Putnam's main thesis, though, is that the decrease in religious participation among Americans between World War II and the 1990s contributed to a reduction in social capital and a fragmentation of American society. I will pick up on some of Putnam's ideas in chapter 9.

22. Pargament (2002).

23. Ibid., p. 172.

24. Dillon and Wink (2004); Hart, McAdams, Hirsch, and Bauer (2001).

25. Rossi (2001).

26. Sherkat and Ellison (1999).

27. Pargament (2002).

28. Putnam (2000); Rossi (2001); Sherkat and Ellison (1999).

29. In McAdams et al. (1997), my students and I coded specified sections of 70 life-narrative interviews for (a) depth, (b) clarity, and (c) continuity on corresponding 4-point rating scales, ranging from 0 (*very low*) to 3 (*very high*). For depth, we assessed the strength of a person's moral and political convictions and the extent to which the individual framed his or her life story in such a way as to suggest that his or her personal ideology was an especially significant factor or force. For clarity, we assessed the overall coherence, consistency, and articulateness of the person's expressed ideology. For continuity, we assessed the extent to which the individual's story suggested that beliefs and values endured over time. A high score on continuity was given for accounts in which the storyteller emphasized the extent to which his or her past and present beliefs were continuous with, connected to, or meaningfully related to each other. The three ratings were significantly intercorrelated (ranging from +.39 between depth and continuity to +.55 between depth and clarity). The results of the analysis showed that the mean scores on all three indices were statistically significantly higher ($p < .001$) for the 40 high-generativity individuals, compared to the 30 participants who were lower in generativity. The tendency for the high-generativity group to score higher on depth, clarity, and continuity of personal ideologies was not due to mean differences between the groups in length of protocols. If anything, the low-generativity participants tended to talk longer about their beliefs and values, perhaps because they perceived more change and discontinuity in them.

30. Coles (1993), p. xv.

31. M. Andrews (1991), p. 205.

32. Colby and Damon (1992).

33. Ibid., p. 16.

34. Ibid., p. xi.

35. Ibid., p. 6.

36. Long ago, I coined the term *ideological setting* in this overwrought passage:

We understand who we are in the context of what we believe to be real, to be true, and to be good. There is an ideological dimension to [narrative] identity which prods us, in late adolescence and throughout our adult years, to become lay philosophers in search of answers to questions of ultimate concern. As ontologists, we seek to comprehend the mysteries inherent in both ends of Hamlet's timeless question: to be (to exist, to be real) or not to be. As epistemologists, we seek to know what is true what it means to say that something is "true." As moral philosophers, we wish to distinguish between good and evil—what is virtuous and what is inimical. The stories we tell ourselves in order to live are grounded in certain ontological, epistemological, and ethical suppositions which situate the story within a particular ideological "time and space." I shall consider these suppositions to constitute an ideological setting for the individual's life story, a philosophical terrain of belief and value upon which the story's characters work, love, and play, and the plot unfolds. (McAdams, 1985, p. 215)

37. Colby and Damon (1992), p. 14. The concept of progressive social influence is also identified by Parks Daloz, Keen, Keen, and Daloz Parks (1996) in their study of 100 American adults who show "lives of commitment in a complex world." They write, "The single most important pattern we have found in the lives of people committed to the common good is what we have come to call a constructive, enlarging, engagement of the other" (p. 63). These authors suggest that adults with strong moral commitments continue to build on their beliefs and values through constructive social relationships with people who share their basic beliefs but from whom they can still learn new things. Like Colby and Damon, furthermore, these authors identify in their studies some of the same themes that I feature as central to the redemptive self—especially an early sensitivity to the suffering of others, the role of religion and spirituality in supporting unwavering conviction, and the tendency to transform negativity and suffering into positive growth (redemption).

38. A full description of the case of Daniel Kessinger appears in McAdams (1993), pp. 241–250.

39. Sherkat and Ellison (1999).

40. These figures come from a survey conducted by the Glemnary Home Missioners in 2000, reported by Goodstein (2002). The article reporting the study suggests, however, that the count for American Muslims may be low. Goodstein writes, "The estimate of Muslims was 1.5 million, derived by counting the members reported by a third of the nation's 1,200 mosques, which often do not maintain membership rolls. Because some Muslims are new immigrants and others are recent converts, reliable estimates are difficult. The study's number is far lower than the seven million claimed by most American Muslim groups."

41. Wills (1990).

42. C. Smith (2000).

43. "New Lights of the Spirit," *Time* (2000, December 11), p. 85.

44. Ibid., p. 91.

45. Dillon and Wink (2004); Roof (1999).

46. Wuthnow (1998).

47. Putnam (2000).

48. Dillon and Wink (2004). In this study, the researchers also discovered that dwelling and seeking patterns related to somewhat different aspects of generativity. As one might expect, the dwelling pattern tended to predict those aspects of generativity that relate to community involvement. By contrast, the seeking pattern connected more closely to the individualistic, self-expanding aspects of generativity. In general, dwellers tend to value interpersonal connection to a greater extent than seek-

ers. By contrast, seekers value self-growth to a greater extent than dwellers. Still, both patterns were positively associated with an overall concern for and commitment to promoting the well-being of future generations.

49. Roof (1999).

50. Erikson (1964), p. 151.

51. Ibid., p. 232. I owe these particular observations regarding Erikson's linking his concept of generativity and religious teachings to Dillon and Wink (2004).

Chapter 7

1. The final results of the 1967 mayoral election in Gary, Indiana, showed that the Democrat Richard Hatcher won by 1,865 votes out of 77,759 cast. A total of 96% of Blacks voted for Hatcher; 12% of Whites voted for Hatcher. Lane (1978).

2. Overt and virulent racism is less common today than it was in the 1950s and 1960s, when I grew up. It is also less commonly expressed in public. With notable exceptions, most people who do hold extreme racist beliefs keep these views to themselves today, knowing that mainstream society tends now to frown on them. In an authoritative review of the social psychology of bias and intergroup conflict, Susan Fiske (2002) has estimated that approximately 10% of Western democratic populations still profess strongly prejudiced views and blatant biases regarding race. These biases can readily lead to aggression, including hate crimes. Another 80%, however, express milder forms of bias, revealing themselves in subtle and even unconscious ways. Scores of studies, for example, show that White American college students and adults implicitly associate many negative traits with the category *Black,* or *African American.* These negative associations are automatically set into play in laboratory situations in which White participants are presented with stimuli such as photographs of Blacks' faces. The vast majority of Whites respond in subtle but negative ways to these stimuli. The responses are automatic and connected, research suggests, to activation of the amygdala—a portion of the brain linked to fear and anxiety conditioning. These automatic reactions matter in everyday behavior, Fiske suggests, "Awkward social interactions, embarrassing slips of the tongue, unchecked assumptions, stereotypic judgments, and spontaneous neglect all exemplify the mundane automaticity of bias, which creates a subtly hostile environment for out-group members" (p. 124). She adds, "Moderates [those with mildly biased views regarding out-group categories] rarely express open hostility toward out-groups, but they may withhold basic liking and respect; hence, their responses represent cool neglect" (p. 125).

3. Du Bois (1903/1989), p. 1.

4. Ibid., p. 5.

5. Sack and Elder (2000). Actual marriages between Blacks and Whites, however, are still rare (0.6% of all American marriages, tallied in 1998). Still, the increase in acceptance of interracial marriage and the slight increase in their incidence are seen as promising trends by at least one writer: see Kennedy (2003).

6. Sack and Elder (2000), p. A-1.

7. Shipler (1997), p. 18.

8. Although there is some disagreement on this, geneticists usually argue that "race" is not a meaningful biological category but is rather a social construction. Throughout the book, I use the term "race" in its colloquial and socially constructed sense. See, especially, the July 16, 2000, issue of the *New York Times Magazine,* "Talking About Race: How Race Is Lived in America."

9. Ellison (1947/1972), p. 3.

10. Du Bois (1903/1989), p. 215.

11. Ibid., pp. 11–12.

12. Details of the survey aspect of the study can be found in Hart, McAdams, Hirsch, and Bauer (2001).

13. Comparing the mean scores of generative concern, generative acts, generative goals, and generative themes in autobiographical memories showed no significant differences between the two groups—Black and White—so long as education and income were not taken into consideration. However, when education and income were employed as covariates, African Americans showed significantly higher scores on the Loyola Generativity Scale (generative concern) and on generative acts than White adults. In other words, the mean differences between African Americans and Whites on two generativity measures in this study arise only when statistical controls are used to partial out the effects of education and income. For the entire sample, there was a slight positive association between education and income variables, on the one hand, and generativity, on the other. When the variance in generativity associated with these variables was statistically accounted for first, the African Americans in this study—who tended also to show lower education and income levels—ended up showing significantly higher "corrected" generativity scores (corrected for education and income effects), compared to Whites. Though statistically significant, the mean difference in corrected scores between the two groups was relatively small.

14. See, for example, Anderson (1989); Schoen and Kluegel (1988).

15. See, for example, Bowman (1990); Cochran (1997); Cutrona, Russell, Murray, Hessling, and Brown (2000); R. B. Hill (1997).

16. Boyd-Franklin (1989); Cochran (1997); Frazier (1939); R. B. Hill (1997).

17. Beeghley, Van Velsor, and Brock (1981); Gallup (1984); Sherkat and Ellison (1999).

18. Johnson, Mare, and Ambrecht (1991); Malpass and Symonds (1974); Neff and Hoppe (1993).

19. P. Nelson (1989).

20. Aspects of the case of Jerome Johnson also appear in McAdams (2001b, pp. 618–620) and McAdams and Bowman (2001, pp. 3–10).

21. Gergen and Gergen (1986) describe three different general life-narrative forms: progressive, regressive, and stability narratives. Highly generative adults tend to tell progressive life stories. Regressive stories tell how a protagonist loses ground over time. It is not clear, however, how a stability narrative would work. It is difficult to tell stories in which nothing changes one way or the other.

22. Wills (1990, p. 217) writes, "The religious meaning Lincoln gave to the war was one of expiatory suffering."

23. Olney (1985) writes,

The writer of a slave narrative finds himself in an irresolvably tight bind as a result of the very intention and premise of his narrative, which is to give a picture of "slavery *as it is.*" Thus it is the writer's claim, it *must* be his claim, that he is not emplotting, he is not fictionalizing, and he is not performing an act of poiesis (shaping, making). To give a true picture of slavery as it really is, he must maintain that he exercises a clear-glass neutral memory that is neither creative nor faulty—indeed, if it were creative it would be *eo ipso* faulty for "creative" would be understood by skeptical readers as a synonym for "lying." (p. 150)

24. My description of the overall form of the typical slave narrative is taken largely from Olney (1985). Other important sources include W. L. Andrews (1986, 1998), Baker (1985), Davis and Gates (1985), M. Dixon (1985), Gates (1998), and Leibowitz (1989).

25. Gates (1998) writes,

What seems clear upon reading of the earliest texts by black writers in English—and the critical texts that respond to these black writings—is that the production of literature was taken to be the central arena in which persons of African descent could establish and redefine their status within the human community. Black people, the evidence suggests, had to represent themselves as "speaking subjects" before they could begin to destroy their status as objects, as commodities, within Western culture. For centuries, Europeans had questioned whether the African "species of men" could ever master the arts and sciences; that is, whether they could create literature. If they could, the argument ran, then the African variety of humanity and the European variety were fundamentally related. If not, then it seemed that the African was predestined by nature to be a slave. (p. 2)

Gates goes on to discuss a scene that appears in many slave narratives—what he calls the "talking book." In this dramatic episode, the slave picks up a book—typically the Bible—and desires that the book speak to him or her. But the book does not speak. The slave realizes that misery will always be the lot in life unless he or she can make the book speak. The slave resolves to learn to read.

26. Douglass (1845/1987), p. 255.

27. Ibid., pp. 255–256.

28. Ibid., p. 268.

29. Ibid., p. 274.

30. Ibid., p. 273.

31. Ibid., p. 293.

32. Ibid., p. 298.

33. Ibid., p. 299.

34. Ibid., p. 304.

35. Ibid., pp. 319–320.

36. See, especially, W. L. Andrews (1986); Davis and Gates (1985); Gates (1987, 2003); Gates and Andrews (1998); Glaude (2000); Leibowitz (1989).

37. Davis and Gates (1985), pp. xxxii–xxxiii.

38. Leibowitz (1989), p. 270.

39. Wills (1990). Other scholars have noted how the authors of the slave narratives needed to employ a rhetoric of virtue and moral indignation that would play well with the White Christian readership (W. L. Andrews, 1986; Baker, 1985; M. Dixon, 1985). The emphasis is clear in Frederick Douglass's narrative. For example, he writes at length about his own efforts to educate his fellow slaves and do good works aimed at "bettering the condition of my race" (Douglass, 1845/1987, p. 304). To awaken the moral indignation of his Victorian audience, furthermore, he highlights incidents in which White slave owners abused *women*. It is clear from his writing that White slave owners routinely seduced and raped Black female slaves, though Douglass does not provide graphic details. Details are provided, though, for the beatings of the women, and these accounts also intimate a sexual dynamic. The slave women are stripped and beaten across their bare shoulders and backs:

> Aunt Hester had not only disobeyed his [the master's] orders in going out, but had been found in the company of Lloyd's Ned [a male slave]; which circumstance, I found, from what he said while whipping her, was the chief offence. Had he [the master] been a man of pure morals himself, he might have been thought interested in protecting the innocence of my aunt; but those who knew him will not suspect him of any such virtue. Before he commenced whipping Aunt Hester, he took her into the kitchen, and stripped her from neck to waist, leaving her neck, shoulders, and back, entirely naked. He then told her to cross her hands, calling her at the same time a d———d b———h. After crossing her hands, he tied them with the strong rope, and led her to a stool under a large hook in the joist, put in for that purpose. He made her get upon the stool, and tied her hands to the hook. She now stood fair for his infernal purpose. Her arms were stretched up at their full length, so that she stood upon the ends of her toes. He then said to her, "Now you d———d b———h, I'll learn you how to disobey my orders!" and after rolling up his sleeves, he commenced to lay on the heavy cowskin, and soon the warm, red blood (amid heart-rending shrieks from her, and horrid oaths from him) came dripping to the floor. (pp. 258–259)

40. Martin Luther King, Jr., quoted in Wills (1990, p. 204).

41. Douglass (1845/1987), p. 273.

42. W. L. Andrews (1986).

43. Ibid., p. 11.

44. Glaude (2000), pp. 80–81.

45. Bruner (1986).

46. Abrahams (1985).

47. Mailer (1959/1987), p. 90.

48. This take on Malcolm X comes from Nichols (1985).

49. Eakin (2001), p. A15.

50. This contrasts with 30% among the White adults interviewed in this study. In this particular study, then, Blacks were about twice as likely as Whites to narrate an earliest memory that emphasized danger.

51. Bruner (1986); Mandler (1984).

52. W. L. Andrews (1986), p. 15.

53. Abrahams (1985), p. 39.

54. Quoted in "Talking About Race," *New York Times Magazine* (2000, July 16), p. 64.

55. Kennedy (2003).

56. Quoted in "Talking About Race," front cover.

57. Wynter (2002).

58. Akbar (1991); V. J. Dixon (1976); White and Parham (1990).

59. Shipler (1997), p. 80.

Chapter 8

1. The full case of Tanya Williams appears in McAdams and Bowman (2001, pp. 18–24).

2. Adults who score very low on generativity measures provide life stories that are in sharpest contrast to the redemptive narratives featured in this book. Most people, however, score neither extremely high nor extremely low in generativity. As is the case with many normally distributed psychological variables, most people fall somewhere in the middle. In McAdams, Diamond, de St. Aubin, and Mansfield (1997), we compared the life stories of adults who scored very high in generativity to those who scored pretty much in the middle range, showing that the key features of the redemptive self—for example, early advantage, suffering of others, moral steadfastness, redemption sequences, and prosocial goals for the future—appeared more often in the life narratives of highly generative adults than in those of their peers. In McAdams and Bowman (2001), however, we also looked at life stories of adults who scored extremely low in generativity. It is from this latter sample that the case of Tanya Williams is drawn.

3. McAdams and Bowman (2001); McAdams et al. (1997); McAdams, Reynolds, Lewis, Patten, and Bowman (2001).

4. McAdams et al. (1997); McAdams et al. (2001).

5. Lewis (2000). The quantitative results from this sample are also reported in McAdams et al. (2001). For her qualitative study, Lewis used a research strategy that is commonly employed in the fields of education, anthropology, and qualitative sociology. The approach is sometimes called *grounded theory* (Glaser & Strauss, 1967; Strauss & Corbin, 1990). In a grounded theory investigation, the researcher slowly pieces together a descriptive portrait of a given social phenomenon through a careful, step-by-step reading and rereading of all of the data at hand. The approach is exploratory and inductive. Not knowing ahead of time what he or she will find, the researcher aims to build a new theory that is "grounded" in the data. In Lewis's case, the "data" were the 34 life-story interviews she obtained from adults low in generativity. Her aim was to build a descriptive theory of the narrative identity of low-generativity adults. Because her findings are based on one relatively small sample, the results of the study are certainly not the last word on the life stories of adults low in generativity. More research needs to be done on the life stories of individuals who score at the low end of the generativity spectrum. Nonetheless, Lewis's descriptive findings make a great deal of psychological sense and are, therefore, worth our attention.

6. In a fascinating article, McColgan, Valentine, and Downs (2000) provide a narrative analysis of the obituaries written for a famous person who was stricken with the dementia of Alzheimer's—the British novelist Iris Murdoch. The authors argue that published obituaries provide a kind of official reckoning of a person's life just after that person has died: "In a culture still influenced, especially in death, by the Christian tradition, there is a strong belief that the final tally cannot be known until the life is ended" (p. 89). "Obituaries are concluding life stories told by living experts" (p. 90). In the case of Murdoch and other victims of dementia, the authors suggest, obituary writers draw upon society's common understanding of and fears about dementia. In a society that values so dearly the intellectual and cognitive dimensions of human life, Murdoch's loss of intellectual powers is seen as depriving her of her basic humanity. With the loss of these cognitive dimensions (drawn so acutely in Murdoch's case because of how sharp and clear-minded she was at the height of her powers), the person appears to have lost the self. Dementia is viewed as a tragic loss of the self—a regressive narrative that moves from the vitality and energy of true selfhood to selfhood's erasure. For the obituary writers, dementia provided an organizing frame for understanding not only Murdoch's illness but also the entire course of her life. A central part of this storytelling process, the authors suggest, is the depiction of the person in the late stages of dementia as being pure and simple—a "holy innocent" (p. 104). It is as if the person has regressed to the simplest state of pureness—as if we have now arrived at a point in the human life course that precedes all human agency and will, ontologically prior, as it were, to original sin.

7. Freud (1920/1955); also Bibring (1943). Schultz (1996) integrates Freud's idea of the repetition compulsion with other writings in the psychoanalytic tradition and in the humanities and social sciences more generally to describe an "Orpheus Complex" in the lives of some renowned authors—in particular, James Agee and Jack Kerouac. In the ancient story, Orpheus was a poet and musician who dedicated his life to the

memory of his bride, Eurydice, who died from a snakebite. Schultz argues that some authors similarly dedicate their creative lives to reliving and reworking traumatic events from the past, especially the early loss of loved ones. A tragic loss can become an animating life theme that provides a reservoir of images and ideas for subsequent creative work.

8. Tomkins (1979, 1987); also, Carlson (1981, 1988).

9. Although he did not identify himself as such, Tomkins may be viewed as one of the earliest narrative psychologists. His concept of *script* bears strong resemblance to my idea of a narrative identity. Furthermore, in his conception of a *commitment script,* Tomkins (1987) identified some of the main themes of what I have incorporated into my conception of the redemptive self. Tomkins argued, for example, that people whose lives follow a commitment script tend to focus unswervingly on clear goals for the future under the belief that bad things will typically turn good. Tomkins's writings have been very influential on my own thinking about personality more generally. One important difference between Tomkins's and my approaches, however, concerns development. Tomkins viewed the individual as a playwright from the earliest weeks of life onward. Scripts take form very early in human development, and they seem relatively resistant to change in later years. Early emotional scenes establish the basic parameters of the script. My viewpoint is informed more by Erikson's notion that identity issues first arise in late adolescence and young adulthood. It is at this later point in human development, I contend, that people living in modern societies find they need to integrate their lives into self-defining life narratives. The narratives they form through reconstructing childhood and imagining adulthood are strongly shaped by culture and subject to substantial revision over the adult life course. Similarities and differences between Tomkins's script theory and other narrative theories of personality are discussed in Barresi and Juckes (1997) and in McAdams (1999, 2001b).

10. Brooks (2000).

11. Ibid., p. 3.

12. Brooks (2000) explores the ambivalence and ambiguities surrounding the concept of confession. "We want confessions, yet we are suspicious of them," he writes (p. 3). "Western culture, most strikingly since the Romantic era to our day, has made confessional speech a prime mark of authenticity, par excellence the kind of speech in which the individual authenticates his inner truth. In a contemporary culture that celebrates the therapeutic value of getting it all out in public, confession has become nearly banal, the everyday business of talk shows, as if the ordinary person could claim individual identity only in the act of confessing. We appear today in a generalized demand for transparency that entails a kind of tyranny of the requirement to confess" (p. 4).

13. Quoted in Brooks (2000), p. 6.

14. Material on Katherine Ann Power comes mainly from Landman (2001). In this fascinating article, Landman compares Power's struggle with guilt, confession, and redemption to an analogous sequence portrayed in the life of Raskolnikov, the main character of Fyodor Dostoyevsky's great novel, *Crime and Punishment.*

15. Franks (1994), p. 44.

16. Landman (2001), p. 36.

17. Franks (1994), p. 54.

18. Landman (2001), p. 54.

19. Singer (1997, 2001).

20. Singer (1997), p. 215.

21. Jensen (2000). AA is not without its critics. Many behavioral scientists who study substance abuse object to the AA characterization of alcoholism as a "disease." Further, researchers object that AA is a closed organization that does not allow scientists to evaluate its methods in an empirical way. Many are skeptical about the relative efficacy of AA methods compared to other clinical treatment regimens for alcohol abuse. I am agnostic on these controversies. For the purpose of this book, AA illustrates a rather extraordinary cultural movement, begun in the United States but now expanded to many countries worldwide. I am especially interested in the kind of recovery narrative that AA promulgates and how that narrative connects to the concept of contamination and the central themes of the redemptive self.

22. Kurtz (1979), pp. 3–4.

23. On Bill Wilson (Bill W.) and the history of AA, see Hartigan (2000), Kurtz (1979), Makela et al. (1996), and Raphael (2000).

24. Quoted in Kurtz (1979), pp. 19–20. Bill Wilson's checking himself into the hospital is seen as the paradigmatic example of "hitting bottom" in AA. Denzin (1987) underscores the importance of hitting bottom—and the different meanings of this idea—in his thoughtful analysis of AA's approach to treating alcoholism.

25. Hartigan (2000); Makela et al. (1996).

26. Quoted in Hartigan (2000), p. 4.

27. Jensen (2000); Hanninen and Koski-Jannes (1999); O'Reilly (1997); Singer (1997). In *Sobering Tales: Narratives of Alcoholism and Recovery,* O'Reilly (1997) writes, "Telling the story—it may be said that, in some sense, there is only one story in AA—enables the speaker to reconstrue a chaotic, absurd, or violent past as a meaningful, indeed a necessary, prelude to the structured, purposeful, and comparatively serene present" (p. 24).

28. Frankl (1984), p. 137.

29. McGregor (1978).

30. The summary of McGregor's story is taken from Maruna (1997, pp. 59–60).

31. See Maruna (1997, 2001); Maruna and Ramsden (2004). Maruna's emphasis on the life stories of criminals and ex-convicts puts him in a long tradition of sociologists and criminologists who have employed life-history methods to understand social problems. In the 1920s and 1930s, the (University of) "Chicago School" of sociology published a number of famous case studies of deviance, such as Shaw's (1930) *The Jack-Roller.* Shaw (1929) wrote, "So far as we have been able to determine as yet, the best way to investigate the inner world of the person is through a study of himself through a life history" (p. 6). However, most of the life histories produced in this sociologically anchored tradition have been strong on describing the social condi-

tions of life but relatively weak on psychological analysis. Maruna is virtually unique in blending insights from psychology with the thick description of social phenomena characteristic of qualitative sociology.

32. In my theoretical writings, I define an *imago* as a personified and idealized image of the self that plays the main character in a segment of a person's life story (McAdams, 1985, 1993). Imagoes are one-dimensional, "stock" characters in the life story, and each integrates a host of different characteristics, roles, and experiences in a person's life. Imagoes are like little "me's" inside of a person's story who act and think in highly personalized ways. The concept of imago resembles the idea of a *possible self* as described by Markus and Nurius (1986), and it shares conceptual space with certain psychoanalytic ideas, such as *internalized objects* (Fairbairn, 1952), *inner states* (Berne, 1964), *internalized voices* (Hermans, 1996), and *personifications* (H. S. Sullivan, 1953). A person may see himself or herself as "the good boy (or girl) who never gets into trouble," "the sophisticated and intellectual professor," "the rough-around-the-edges working-class kid from the wrong side of town," "the corporate executive playing out the American dream," "the worldly traveler in search of all this is new and exotic," "the athlete," "the loyal friend," "the sage," "the soldier," "the teacher," "the clown," or "the peacemaker." Each of these capsule definitions might qualify as an imago. Each might exist within a particular life story as a carefully crafted part of the self that shows up as a main character in different parts of the narrative. A person's life story is likely to contain more than one imago. Each of the imagoes lays claim to a particular set of identity resources.

33. Quoted in Maruna (1997), pp. 73–74.

34. Quoted in Maruna (1997), pp. 74–75.

35. Maruna (1997), p. 76.

36. McGregor (1978), p. 369.

37. Quoted in Maruna (1997), pp. 75–76.

38. Quoted in Maruna (2001), p. 94.

39. McGregor (1978), pp. 94–95.

40. Maruna (1997), pp. 83–84.

41. Quoted in Maruna (1997), p. 83.

42. Quoted in Maruna (2001), pp. 98–99.

43. All three quotations in Maruna (1997), p. 86.

44. Although we routinely screen out participants in our life-narrative studies who have a history of mental illness or extreme psychological distress, it is clear that Tanya Williams was a depressed and anxious woman. Toward the end of the interview, she seemed to be asking the interviewer, who was a trained Ph.D. student in counseling psychology, for psychological assistance. Ethical standards for this research preclude our providing such assistance. In the rare instance that a research participant is in psychological distress during the interview, interviewers may provide the person with information regarding counseling or therapy possibilities in the community.

Chapter 9

1. Bakan (1966).
2. Mansfield and McAdams (1996); McAdams (1985, 1993); McAdams, Ruetzel, and Foley (1986).
3. Kammen (1972), p. 116.
4. de Tocqueville (1835/1956), p. 95.
5. Quoted in Putnam (2000), p. 24.
6. Lasch (1979).
7. Bellah, Madsen, Sullivan, Swidler, and Tipton (1985).
8. Ibid., p. 82.
9. Putnam (2000). For a more psychological take on some of the same issues, see Myers (2000). As a counterpoint to Putnam and Myers, however, see Rossi (2001). Wuthnow (1991) seems to take a middle position here, at least with respect to Americans' involvement in volunteer work and charitable activities. His research suggests that Americans are quite willing to help each other out and engage in voluntary "acts of compassion," but it also suggests that prosocial, altruistic behavior is most common in situations wherein the helper also benefits in some way.
10. Cushman (1995), p. 4.
11. Lynch (2002).
12. Kazin (1984).
13. de Tocqueville (1835/1956), p. 194.
14. Riesman (1949/1961).
15. See, especially, Adorno et al. (1950); Erikson (1950). After World War II, many social scientists sought to understand the social and psychological dynamics of conformity and the related idea of obedience to authority. What motivated these inquiries included curiosity over why so many Germans obeyed the Nazi regime before and during World War II and why so many postwar Americans now seemed so eager to conform to the corporate status quo. It was shortly after this time, as well, that social psychologists conducted their most famous experiments demonstrating surprisingly high levels of conformity (Asch, 1955) and obedience to authority (Milgram, 1965) in the laboratory.
16. Riesman (1949/1961), p. 139.
17. Ibid., p. 157.
18. Fromm (1941).
19. Riesman (1949/1961), p. 307.
20. Goode (2001).
21. S. Taylor (1983).
22. Diener and Diener (1995). See also Slater (2002), who writes,

Self-esteem, as a construct, as a quasi religion, is woven into a tradition that both defines and confines us as Americans. If we were to deconstruct self-esteem, to question its value, we would be, in a sense, questioning who we are, nationally and individually. We would be threatening our own self-esteem. . . . Imagine if you heard your child's teacher say, "Don't think so much of yourself." Imagine your spouse saying to you, "You know, you're really not so good at what you do." We have developed a discourse of affirmation, and to deviate from that would be to enter another arena, linguistically and grammatically, so that what came out of our mouths would be impolite at best, unintelligible at worst. Is there a way to talk about the self without measuring its worth? Why, as a culture, have we so conflated the two quite separate notions—(a) self and (b) worth? This may have as much to do with our entrepreneurial history as Americans, in which everything exists to be improved, as it does, again, with the power of language to shape beliefs. *How would we story the self if not triumphantly, redemptively, enhanced from the inside out?* (p. 46; emphasis added)

23. In a definitive review of the research literature, a team of social psychologists (Baumeister, Campbell, Krueger, & Vohs, 2003) asked four questions about high self-esteem: Does it cause better performance? Does it lead to interpersonal success? Does it make people happier? Does it lead to healthier lifestyles? Their answers were *no, no, probably,* and *sporadically,* respectively. Research shows that to the extent self-esteem is associated with good performance in work or school, the causal relation is reversed—in other words, doing well leads to higher levels of self-esteem, but high levels of self-esteem do not predict doing well: "The modest correlations between self-esteem and school performance do not indicate that high self-esteem leads to good performance. Instead, high self-esteem is partly the result of good school performance. Efforts to boost the self-esteem of pupils have not been shown to improve academic performance and may sometimes be counterproductive." With respect to the interpersonal realm, it is shown, "People high in self-esteem claim to be more likeable and attractive, to have better relationships, and to make better impressions on others than people with low self-esteem, but objective measures disconfirm most of these beliefs. Narcissists are charming at first but tend to alienate others eventually. Self-esteem has not been shown to predict the quality or duration of relationships." With respect to happiness, moreover, "Self-esteem has a strong relation to happiness. Although the research does not clearly establish causation, we are persuaded that high self-esteem does lead to greater happiness." However, the researchers write, "High self-esteem does not prevent children from smoking, drinking, taking drugs, or engaging in early sex. If anything, high self-esteem fosters experimentation, which may increase early sexual activity or drinking, but in general effects of self-esteem are negligible. One important exception is that high self-esteem reduces the chances of bulimia in females" (quotations at p. 1).

24. Gardner (1983).

25. Harrison (1998); Karr (1995).

26. Kaminer (1992), p. 17. The tendency to remember one's competence in the

past as slightly lower than it really was, in order to show how much one has improved over time, is a fairly common and probably unconscious strategy for autobiographical memory, according to A. Wilson and Ross (2001). We create stories about our lives that document the move from "chump" to "champ," these researchers suggest. The strategy helps to protect and enhance self-esteem.

27. Kaminer (1992), p. 152.

28. Jordan (2002), p. 25.

29. Cherry (1998); Kazin (1984); Tuveson (1968).

30. A. Sullivan (2001), p. 60. Following is another passage from Sullivan on the assault upon American innocence that was September 11:

> In this sense, what was done to America was also done to the collective consciousness of the world, to those future Americans not yet born on other parts of the globe, to those who have come to rely upon the United States as the last resort for a liberty long languishing in other somewheres. It was a place where the human past could, in dreams at least, be erased, eluded, relinquished, avenged by the sheer sight of millions of all types and creeds and races living well and freely, day in, day out. This was the dream, in the only country in which mere dreams were not derided as illusions. America's power, even when wielded across the globe, was therefore still a strangely innocent power—innocent of what true evil can bring, innocent of what real danger is. Even when we encountered it—in Flanders, in Normandy, in Auschwitz, in Moscow, in the Vietnam delta and the Iraqi desert—it was always someplace else. Never here. Not in this place. Not where freedom was reborn. This elsewhere would never just be somewhere. (p. 61)

31. Menand (2001), p. 61.

32. Lears (2003), p. A-20.

33. Quoted in Kazin (1984), p. 265. The self-righteousness of mainstream political rhetoric in the United States and the influence of that rhetoric on social policy are prominent themes in Schram and Neisser's (1997) collection of papers on the use of narrative in U.S. politics and policy.

34. Morone (2003).

35. Tuveson (1968), p. viii.

36. Quoted in Tuveson (1968), p. vii.

37. R. Kagan (2003). For a very different perspective on American power, see Purdy (2003).

38. Slotkin (1973), p. 5.

39. Quoted in Slotkin (1973), p. 17.

40. Slotkin (1973), p. 17.

41. Brock and Parker (2001).

42. Hermans and Hermans-Jansen (1995); Lieblich, McAdams, and Josselson (2004); White and Epston (1990).

43. Young (2000).

44. Greenspan (2003).

45. Ibid., p. 102.

46. Ibid., p. 106.

47. Ibid., p. 107.

48. Alon and Omer (2004).

49. My student and good colleague, Jonathan Adler, has a slightly different take on the question whether or not all bad things in life can be narrated in a redemptive way. As Adler sees it, the main flaw in the life stories of highly generative adults is their potential for shallowness or easy, unexamined conformity to conventional American narrative structure. Adler argues that it is a quality of the narrator and his or her story, not a quality of the actual event, which qualifies a story as redemptive; thus, any negative event might, in theory, be redeemable, even such extreme cases as living in a concentration camp. However, highly generative adults sometimes interpret or configure to-be-redeemed events in ways that fail to capture the full complexity of the experiences themselves. From this perspective, even the most horrific and random events in life could be narrated in a way to foster growth or positive change. But if this is to happen, the narrator must sometimes go beyond the conventional redemptive framework that is so common in American narratives to fashion an interpretation that is nuanced and deep. These kinds of interpretations usually require that the narrator remain open to the realities of profound, painful, and unexpected change in life, and sometimes to embrace life's ephemeral nature. As Adler sees it, too many redemptive narratives gloss over the complexities of human experience in the rush to achieve the "happy ending" that is called for by traditional American narrative structure. The redemptive self thus sometimes lacks complexity and depth, and it may, in some cases, prove indicative of what Erik Erikson called *identity foreclosure*.

Chapter 10

1. See, especially, Gay (1984).

2. Erikson (1968).

3. Kohut (1977); Lasch (1979).

4. Kardiner (1939).

5. Benedict (1934).

6. Shweder (1984) writes, "In 1934 Ruth Benedict's descriptions of 'Apollonian' and 'Dionysian' type cultures captured the imagination of culture theorists, and ever since then the idea of cultural integration or global thematic consistency has been assumed more than it has been tested. This is ironic, as Ruth Benedict herself [1934] emphasized that cultural integration is a *variable* and that she had *selected* for description some highly integrated cases" (p. 19).

7. Gorer and Rickman (1949).

8. LeVine (2001) traces the history of the culture and personality movement in

the social sciences. He argues that the movement reached its peak in the 1930s and 1940s, and that it faded dramatically after that. The negative reaction to Gorer and Rickman's book was one factor, LeVine argues, in the decline of culture and personality studies after 1950. Wrote one reviewer, "Gorer's hypothesis is too often supported by loose analogy, unwarranted assumption and not a few errors of fact" (Golden, 1952, pp. 415–416).

9. Geertz (1973); Shweder and LeVine (1984); Shweder and Sullivan (1993).

10. In Shweder (1984), p. 19.

11. LeVine (1982), p. 4.

12. Triandis (1997), p. 443.

13. See Holland (1997). Also, Markus, Kitayama, and Heiman (1998) write, "As constructors of experience, people are capable of selecting various imperatives, claiming, elaborating, and personalizing some of the available collective resources so that they are both individually and jointly held, while ignoring, resisting, contesting, and rearranging others" (p. 859).

14. The relative differences between individualist and collectivist cultures can be further spelled out in terms of four defining attributes (Triandis & Gelfand, 1998). The first attribute concerns goals. From an individualist standpoint, personal goals are more important than the goals of the in-group (e.g., family, community, state), whereas from a collectivist standpoint the in-group goals are more important. It is important to note in this regard that a collectivist perspective connects the person to a *particular* in-group rather than, say, to all humankind in general. From a collectivist standpoint, one is loyal to one's own group, and such loyalty may put one in strong opposition to other groups. A second attribute concerns relationships. From an individualist standpoint, rational exchange is the norm in relationships; separate and autonomous selves come together to "trade" resources (e.g., money, help, love), and social life resembles, in many ways, a marketplace. From a collectivist standpoint, people relate to one another more from the perspective of communal obligations and bonds of loyalty. A third attribute concerns the determinants of social behavior. From an individualist standpoint, the person's own attitudes take precedent over group norms in motivating and guiding behavior. Individualist cultures emphasize the ideas of "standing up for what you think is right" and "being true to your own convictions." By contrast, the collectivist meaning system elevates social norms above the opinions or attitudes of individuals. People are encouraged to act in accord with the standards of the in-group. Finally, individualist and collectivist cultures suggest rather different construals of the self. The individualist self is defined over and against others as an autonomous and independent agent. The collectivist self, by contrast, is viewed as highly interdependent within the community. For a review of recent research on individualist and collectivist cultures and their influences on personality, see Triandis and Suh (2002).

15. Markus and Kitayama (1991).

16. In an excellent review of the cross-cultural developmental literature, Patricia Greenfield and her colleagues (2003) assert that independence/individualism and

interdependence/collectivism are two idealized pathways through universal human ontogeny. Although human beings face many of the same developmental challenges worldwide, these two pathways can be seen to diverge sharply at particular points in the human life course, whereby individualistic and collectivist societies seem to prioritize very different approaches to parenting and education. Greenfield et al. highlight the tasks of early relationship formation (attachment), knowledge acquisition in childhood (schooling), and balancing autonomy and relatedness in adolescence as three developmental challenges wherein large cultural differences can be observed between those societies oriented toward the independent self and those oriented toward the interdependent self.

17. This tripartite framework for personality is described in McAdams (1994, 1995, 1996b, 2001b), and it is elaborated further in Hooker (2002) and Hooker and McAdams (2003).

18. In one of those "you could not pay me enough to do it" scenarios in psychological science, Allport and Odbert (1936) plowed through an unabridged dictionary of the English language, one containing 550,000 entries, to compile a list of all English words referring to individual differences in psychological functioning. They came up with about 18,000 words referring to psychological states, traits, and evaluations. Of these about 4,500 reflected, in their judgment, relatively stable and enduring personality traits.

19. In the 1960s and 1970s, many psychologists questioned the usefulness of the trait concept. They argued that traits were but labels in the heads of observers and that trait scores were poor predictors of what people actually do. The wisdom of the day held that people's behavior is much more strongly shaped by situational influences than by any internal personality traits (Mischel, 1968). Over the past 25 years, however, personality psychologists have amassed considerable research evidence to show that trait scores on well-validated scientific measures are good predictors of behavioral trends and important life outcomes, show long-term longitudinal stability, are at least moderately heritable, and are probably linked, though in complex ways, to fundamental brain processes. Among the most important sources for the reemergence of the trait concept in personality psychology are Epstein (1979), Funder (1995), Goldberg (1990), Hogan (1987), John and Srivastava (1999), McCrae and Costa (1990), Revelle (1995), and Tellegen et al. (1988). For a full and accessible discussion of the impressive evidence for the validity of personality traits, as well as the limitations of the trait concept, see McAdams (2001b, chaps. 5–7).

20. Caspi (1998); Costa and McCrae (1994); Helson and Moane (1987); Roberts and Friend-DelVecchio (2000); Schuerger, Zarella, and Hortz (1989).

21. Goldberg (1990); John and Srivastava (1999); McCrae and Costa (1990); Wiggins (1996).

22. Some researchers argue that a better name for the trait of neuroticism is *negative affectivity* (Watson & Clark, 1984).

23. Barrick and Mount (1991, 1993).

24. Correlations between O and IQ tests tend to be positive and often statistically

significant, but the correlations are not so high as to suggest that O is a valid measure of intelligence itself. Therefore, individuals high in intelligence tend as a group to score slightly higher on O than individuals low in intelligence, but there are many exceptions to this rule. Therefore, in a sample of bright college students, you will find substantial individual differences in scores on openness to experience.

25. Church and Katigbak (1989); DeRaad and Szirmak (1994); John and Srivastava (1999); McCrae and Costa (1997).

26. Heine, Lehman, Peng, and Greenholtz (2002) show that cross-cultural comparisons of personality that rely on self-report rating scales are severely compromised because members of different populations use different reference groups in responding to the scale items.

27. The distinction between dispositional traits (Level 1) and characteristic adaptations (Level 2) has been described by many personality psychologists. See, especially, Cantor (1990) and Winter, John, Stewart, Klohnen, and Duncan (1998). Among the most significant research programs in personality psychology today focused on characteristic adaptations are those examining intimacy and power motives (Woike, 1995), personal strivings (Emmons, 1999), goals (Freund & Baltes, 2002), personal projects (Little, 1999), values and personal ideologies (de St. Aubin, 1996), defense mechanisms (Cramer, 1991), relational schemas (Baldwin, 1992), and conditional patterns of situationally specific responses (Mischel & Shoda, 1995; Thorne, 1989).

28. The distinction between approach and avoidance goals has a long and venerable history in the study of motivation (see, especially, Atkinson, 1958; McClelland, 1985).

29. Elliot, Chirkov, Kim, and Sheldon (2001).

30. Personality constructs at different levels do not necessarily line up with each other in predictable ways, suggesting that personality is multifaceted, complex, and sometimes even self-contradictory. For example, many studies have shown that traits associated with achievement (e.g., conscientiousness, Level 1) do not correlate with motives and goals for achievement (Level 2; McClelland, 1985). Nonetheless, some links between some characteristic adaptations (Level 2) and life-story themes (Level 3) have been empirically documented in McAdams (1982, 1985); McAdams, Hoffman, Mansfield, and Day (1996); Woike (1995); and Woike, Gershkovich, Piorkowski, and Polo (1999). In general, these studies show that people who have strong motives and goals (Level 2) associated with power (what is called *power motivation*) tend to construct life narratives (Level 3) that emphasize scenes from the past in which they experienced personal strength or wisdom, enjoyed significant personal achievement, or had a powerful impact on others. In a recent study, my students and I have also documented statistically significant, though modest, relations between some Big Five traits (Level 1) and life-story (Level 3) themes (McAdams et al., 2004). We found that high scores on A were associated with themes of caring and dialogue in life narratives, that N was associated with negative story endings, and that people high in O tended to tell life stories that were more complex than those told by individuals low in O.

31. Caspi (1998); J. Kagan (1994).

Epilogue

1. See Josselson and Lieblich (1993); Josselson, Lieblich, and McAdams (2003).

2. Gergen (1991)

3. See Barglow (1994); Gergen (1991); Holstein and Gubrium (2000); Sampson (1989); Shotter and Gergen (1989); Turkle (1996). Shotter and Gergen (1989) write, "The primary medium within which identities are created and have their currency is not just linguistic but textual; persons are largely ascribed identities according to the manner of their embedding within a discourse—in their own or in the discourses of others" (p. ix). In a sense, each moment of discourse brings with it a new expression of self. Over time, expressions are collected and patched together, much like a montage or collage. The central problem for the postmodern self, then, is that of *unity*. Because all texts are indeterminate, no single life can really mean a single thing, no organizing pattern or identity can be validly discerned in any single human life. In *The Saturated Self,* Kenneth Gergen (1991) makes this point forcefully:

> The postmodern condition is marked more generally by a plurality of voices vying for the right to reality—to be accepted as legitimate expressions of the true and the good. As the voices expand in power and presence, all that seemed proper, right-minded, and well understood is subverted. In the postmodern world we become increasingly aware that the objects about which we speak are not so much "in the world" as they are products of perspective. Thus, processes such as emotion and reason cease to be real and significant essences of persons; rather, in the light of pluralism we perceive them to be imposters, the outcomes of our ways of conceptualizing them. Under postmodern conditions, persons exist in a state of continuous construction and reconstruction; it is a world where anything goes that can be negotiated. Each reality of self gives way to a reflexive questioning, irony, and ultimately the playful probing of yet another reality. The center fails to hold. (p. 7)

4. A. Wright (1994). I present a longer and more complicated discussion of Wright's novel and its relation to postmodern approaches to understanding selfhood in McAdams (1997).

5. A. Wright (1994), pp. 41–42.

6. Ibid., p. 263.

7. Ibid., p. 290 (emphasis added).

References

Abrahams, R. D. (Ed.). (1985). *African-American folktales: Stories from black traditions in the New World.* New York: Pantheon Books.

Abt, V., & Seesholtz, M. (1994). The shameless world of Sally and Oprah: Television talk shows and the deconstruction of society. *Journal of Popular Culture, 28.*

Ackerman, S., Zuroff, D., & Moscowitz, D. S. (2000). Generativity in midlife and young adults: Links to agency, communion, and well-being. *International Journal of Aging and Human Development, 50,* 17–41.

Adler, A. (1927). *The practice and theory of individual psychology.* New York: Harcourt Brace World.

Adorno, T. W., Frenkel-Brunswik, E., Levinson, D. J., & Sanford, R. N. (1950). *The authoritarian personality.* New York: Harper.

Affleck, G., & Tennen, H. (1996). Construing benefits from adversity: Adaptational significance and dispositional underpinnings. *Journal of Personality, 64,* 899–922.

Affleck, G., Tennen, H., Croog, S., & Levine, S. (1987). Causal attributions, perceived health benefits, and morbidity following a heart attack: An eight-year study. *Journal of Consulting and Clinical Psychology, 55,* 29–35.

Affleck, G., Tennen, H., & Gershman, K. (1985). Cognitive adaptations to high risk infants: The search for meaning, mastery, and protection from future harm. *American Journal of Mental Deficiency, 89,* 653–656.

Ainsworth, M. D. S. (1989). Attachments beyond infancy. *American Psychologist, 44,* 709–716.

Ainsworth, M. D. S., Blehar, M. C., Waters, E., & Wall, T. (1978). *Patterns of attachment.* Hillsdale, NJ: Erlbaum.

Akbar, N. (1991). The evolution of human psychology for African Americans. In R. L. Jones (Ed.), *Black psychology* (3rd ed., pp. 99–124). Berkeley, CA: Cobb & Henry.

Aldwin, C. M., Sutton, K. J., & Lachman, M. (1996). The development of coping resources in adulthood. *Journal of Personality, 64,* 837–871.

Allport, G. W. (1950). *The individual and his religion.* New York: Macmillan.

Allport, G. W., & Odbert, H. S. (1936). Trait-names, a psychological study. *Psychological Monographs, 47,* (1, Whole No. 211).

Alon, N., & Omer, H. (2004). Demonic and tragic narratives in psychotherapy. In A. Lieblich, D. P. McAdams, & R. Josselson (Eds.), *Healing plots: The narrative bases of psychotherapy* (pp. 29–48). Washington, DC: APA Books.

Anderson, E. (1989). Sex codes and family life among poor inner-city youths. *Annals of the American Academy of Political and Social Sciences, 501,* 59–78.

Andrews, M. (1991). *Lifetimes of commitment: Aging, politics, psychology.* Cambridge: Cambridge University Press.

Andrews, W. L. (1986). *To tell a free story: The first century of Afro-American autobiography, 1760–1865.* Urbana: University of Illinois Press.

Andrews, W. L. (1998). Preface. In H. L. Gates, Jr., & W. L. Andrews (Eds.), *Pioneers of the black Atlantic: Five slave narratives from the Enlightenment, 1772–1815.* Washington, DC: Civitas.

Angyal, A. (1941). *Foundations for a science of personality.* New York: Viking.

Anthony, R. (1991). *Doing what you love, loving what you do.* New York: Berkley Books.

Arnett, J. J. (2000). Emerging adulthood: A theory of development from the late teens through the twenties. *American Psychologist, 55,* 469–480.

Asch, S. E. (1955). Opinions and social pressure. *Scientific American, 193,* 31–35.

Atkinson, J. W. (Ed.). (1958). *Motives in fantasy, action, and society.* Princeton, NJ: Van Nostrand.

Bakan, D. (1966). *The duality of human existence: Isolation and communion in Western man.* Boston: Beacon Press.

Baker, H. A., Jr. (1985). Autobiographical acts and the voice of the Southern slave. In C. T. Davis & H. L. Gates, Jr. (Eds.), *The slave's narrative* (pp. 242–261). New York: Oxford University Press.

Baldwin, M. W. (1992). Relational schemas and the processing of social information. *Psychological Bulletin, 112,* 461–484.

Barclay, C. R. (1996). Autobiographical remembering: Narrative constraints on objectified selves. In D. Rubin (Ed.), *Remembering our past: Studies in autobiographical memory* (pp. 94–125). Cambridge: Cambridge University Press.

Barglow, R. (1994). *The crisis of self in the age of information: Computers, dolphins, and dreams.* London: Routledge.

Baron-Cohen, S. (1995). *Mindblindness: An essay on autism and theory of mind.* Cambridge, MA: MIT Press.

Barresi, J., & Juckes, T. J. (1997). Personology and the narrative interpretation of lives. *Journal of Personality, 65,* 693–719.

Barrick, M. R., & Mount, M. K. (1991). The Big Five personality dimensions and job performance: A meta-analysis. *Personnel Psychology, 44,* 1–26.

Barrick, M. R., & Mount, M. K. (1993). Autonomy as a moderator of the relationship between the Big Five personality dimensions and job performance. *Journal of Applied Psychology, 78,* 111–118.

Baumeister, R. F., Campbell, J. D., Krueger, J. I., & Vohs, E. D. (2003). Does high self-esteem cause better performance, interpersonal success, happiness, or healthier lifestyles? *Psychological Science in the Public Interest, 4*(1).

Beattie, M. (1992). *Co-dependent no more: How to stop controlling others and start caring for yourself.* Center City, MN: Hazelden.

Becker, E. (1973). *The denial of death.* New York: Free Press.

Beeghley, L., Van Velsor, E., & Brock, E. W. (1981). The correlates of religiosity among Black and White Americans. *Sociological Quarterly, 20,* 49–62.

Bellah, R. N., Madsen, R., Sullivan, W. M., Swidler, A., & Tipton, S. M. (1985). *Habits of the heart.* Berkeley: University of California Press.

Bellah, R. N., Madsen, R., Sullivan, W. M., Swidler, A., & Tipton, S. M. (1991). *The good society.* New York: Knopf.

Benedict, R. (1934). *Patterns of culture.* Boston: Houghton Mifflin.

Bennett, W. J. (Ed.). (1993). *The book of virtues: A treasury of great moral stories.* New York: Simon & Schuster.

Bercovitch, S. (1974). The American Puritan imagination: An introduction. In S. Bercovitch (Ed.), *The American Puritan imagination: Essays in revaluation* (pp. 1–16). London: Cambridge University Press.

Bercovitch, S. (1975). *The Puritan origins of the American self.* New Haven, CT: Yale University Press.

Berkow, I. (2002, November 5). Bob Love now speaks for himself: Former N.B.A. star goes from stuttering busboy to politician. *New York Times,* pp. C17–C18.

Berne, E. (1964). *Games people play.* New York: Grove.

Bibring, E. (1943). The conception of the repetition compulsion. *Psychoanalytic Quarterly, 12*(4), 486–519.

Block, J. (1971). *Lives through time.* Berkeley, CA: Bancroft Books.

Bluck, S., & Levine, L. J. (1998). Reminiscence as autobiographical memory: A catalyst for reminiscence theory development. *Ageing and Society, 18,* 185–208.

Bowlby, J. (1969). *Attachment.* New York: Basic Books.

Bowman, P. J. (1990). Coping with provider role strain: Adaptive cultural resources among Black husband-fathers. *Journal of Black Psychology, 16,* 1–21.

Boyd-Franklin, N. (1989). *Black families in therapy: A multisystems approach.* New York: Guilford Press.

Bradley, C. (1997). Generativity-stagnation: Development of a status model. *Developmental Review, 17,* 262–290.

Bradshaw, J. (1988). *Bradshaw on: The family.* Deerfield Beach, FL: Health Communications.

Breger, L. (1974). *From instinct to identity: The development of personality.* Englewood Cliffs, NJ: Prentice-Hall.

Brewer, W. F. (1986). What is autobiographical memory? In D. Rubin (Ed.), *Autobiographical memory* (pp. 25–49). New York: Cambridge University Press.

Brock, R. N., & Parker, R. A. (2001). *Proverbs of ashes: Violence, redemptive suffering, and the search for what saves us.* Boston: Beacon Press.

Brooks, P. (2000). *Troubling confessions: Speaking guilt in law and literature.* Chicago: University of Chicago Press.

Brown, N. O. (1959). *Life against death: The psychoanalytic meaning of history.* New York: Vintage Books.

Brown, R., & Kulik, J. (1977). Flashbulb memories. *Cognition, 5,* 73–99.

Browning, D. (2004). An ethical analysis of Erikson's concept of generativity. In E. de St. Aubin, D. P. McAdams, & T.-C. Kim (Eds.), *The generative society* (pp. 241–255). Washington, DC: APA Books.

Bruner, J. (1986). *Actual minds, possible worlds.* Cambridge, MA: Harvard University Press.

Bruner, J. (1990). *Acts of meaning.* Cambridge, MA: Harvard University Press.

Bush, H. K., Jr. (1999). *American declarations: Rebellion and repentance in American cultural history.* Urbana: University of Illinois Press.

Bush pushes plan for faith-based aid. (2002, April 12). *Chicago Tribune,* p. A-6.

Campbell, J. (1949). *The hero with a thousand faces.* New York: Bollingen Foundation.

Cantor, N. (1990). From thought to behavior: "Having" and "doing" in the study of personality and cognition. *American Psychologist, 45,* 735–750.

Carlson, R. (1981). Studies in script theory: I. Adult analogs of a childhood nuclear scene. *Journal of Personality and Social Psychology, 40,* 501–510.

Carlson, R. (1988). Exemplary lives: The uses of psychobiography for theory development. *Journal of Personality, 56,* 105–138.

Carnegie, D. (1936/1981). *How to win friends and influence people* (Rev. ed.). New York: Simon & Schuster.

Caspi, A. (1998). Personality development across the life course. In W. Damon (Ed.), *Handbook of child psychology, Vol. 3: Social, emotional, and personality development* (5th ed., pp. 311–388). New York: Wiley.

Cassidy, J., & Shaver, P. (Eds.). (1999). *Handbook of attachment: Theory, research, and clinical practice.* New York: Guilford Press.

Charme, S. T. (1984). *Meaning and myth in the study of lives: A Sartrean perspective.* Philadelphia: University of Pennsylvania Press.

Cherry, C. (Ed.). (1998). *God's new Israel: Religious interpretations of American destiny.* Chapel Hill: University of North Carolina Press.

Church, A. T., & Katigbak, M. S. (1989). Internal, external, and self-report structure of personality in a non-Western culture: An investigation of cross-language and cross-cultural generalizability. *Journal of Personality and Social Psychology, 57,* 857–872.

Clemetson, L. (2001, January 8). The age of Oprah: Oprah on Oprah. *Newsweek,* pp. 38–48.

Cloud, D. L. (1996). Hegemony or concordance? The rhetoric of tokenism in "Oprah" Winfrey's rags-to-riches biography. *Critical Studies in Mass Communication, 13,* 115–137.

Clymer, A. (2002, April 6). Rethinking Reagan: Was he a man of ideas after all? *New York Times,* pp. A17, A19.

Cochran, D. L. (1997). African American fathers: A decade review of the literature. *Families in Society: The Journal of Contemporary Human Services, 78,* 340–351.

Cohler, B. J. (1982). Personal narrative and the life course. In P. Baltes & O. G. Brim, Jr. (Eds.), *Life span development and behavior* (Vol. 4, pp. 205–241). New York: Academic Press.

Cohler, B. J., Hostetler, A. J., & Boxer, A. M. (1998). Generativity, social context, and lived experience: Narratives of gay men in middle adulthood. In D. P. McAdams & E. de St. Aubin (Eds.), *Generativity and adult development: How and why we care for the next generation* (pp. 265–309). Washington, DC: APA: Books.

Colby, A., & Damon, W. (1992). *Some do care: Contemporary lives of moral commitment.* New York: Free Press.

Cole, E. R., & Stewart, A. J. (1996). Meanings of political participation among Black and White women: Political identity and social responsibility. *Journal of Personality and Social Psychology, 71,* 130–140.

Cole, T. R. (1992). *The journey of life: A cultural history of aging in America.* New York: Cambridge University Press.

Coles, R. (1993). *The call to service: A witness to idealism.* Boston: Houghton Mifflin.

Conway, M. A., & Pleydell-Pearce, C. W. (2000). The construction of autobiographical memories in the self-memory system. *Psychological Review, 107,* 261–288.

Costa, P. T., Jr., & McCrae, R. R. (1994). Set like plaster? Evidence for the stability of adult personality. In T. F. Heatherton & J. L. Weinberger (Eds.), *Can personality change?* (pp. 21–40). Washington, DC: APA Books.

Covey, S. R. (1989). *The seven habits of highly effective people: Restoring the character ethic.* New York: Simon & Schuster.

Cramer, P. (1991). *The development of defense mechanisms.* New York: Springer-Verlag.

Crossley, M. (2000). *Introducing narrative psychology: Self, trauma, and the construction of meaning.* Buckingham, England: Open University Press.

Cushman, P. (1995). *Constructing the self, constructing America: A cultural history of psychotherapy.* Reading, MA: Addison-Wesley.

Cutrona, C. E., Russell, D. W., Murray, V., Hessling, R. M., & Brown, P. A. (2000). Direct and moderating effects of community context on the psychological well-being of African American women. *Journal of Personality and Social Psychology, 79,* 1088–1101.

Damasio, A. (1994). *Descartes' error: Emotion, reason, and the human brain.* New York: Avon Books.

Damasio, A. (1999). *The feeling of what happens: Body and emotion in the making of consciousness.* Orlando, FL: Harcourt.

Dannefer, D. (1984). Adult development and social theory: A paradigmatic reappraisal. *American Sociological Review, 49,* 100–116.

Davis, C. T., & Gates, H. L., Jr. (Eds.). (1985). *The slave's narrative.* New York: Oxford University Press.

Decker, J. L. (1997). *Made in America: Self-styled success from Horatio Alger to Oprah Winfrey.* Minneapolis: University of Minnesota Press.

Delbancho, A. (1999). *The real American dream: A meditation on hope.* Cambridge, MA: Harvard University Press.

Denzin, N. K. (1987). *Treating alcoholism: An Alcoholics Anonymous approach.* Newbury Park, CA: Sage.

Denzin, N. K. (1989). *Interpretive biography.* Newbury Park, CA: Sage.

DeRaad, B., & Szirmak, Z. (1994). The search for the "Big Five" in a non-Indo-European language: The Hungarian trait structure and its relationship to EPQ and PTS. *European Review of Applied Psychology, 44,* 17–24.

de St. Aubin, E. (1996). Personal ideology polarity: Its emotional foundation and its manifestation in individual value systems, religiosity, political orientation, and assumptions concerning human nature. *Journal of Personality and Social Psychology, 71,* 152–165.

de St. Aubin, E., & McAdams, D. P. (1995). The relations of generative concern and generative action to personality traits, satisfaction/happiness with life, and ego development. *Journal of Adult Development, 2,* 99–112.

de St. Aubin, E., McAdams, D. P., & Kim, T.-C. (Eds.). (2004). *The generative society.* Washington, DC: APA Books.

de Tocqueville, A. (1835/1956). *Democracy in America* (Rev. ed.). New York: New American Library.

de Waal, F. (1996). *Good-natured: The origins of right and wrong in humans and other animals.* Cambridge, MA: Harvard University Press.

Didion, J. (1979). *The white album.* New York: Simon & Schuster.

Diener, E., & Diener, M. (1995). Cross-cultural correlates of life satisfaction and self-esteem. *Journal of Personality and Social Psychology, 68,* 653–663.

Dillon, M., & Wink, P. (2004). American religion, generativity, and therapeutic culture. In E. de St. Aubin, D. P. McAdams, & T.-C. Kim (Eds.), *The generative society* (pp. 153–174). Washington, DC: APA Books.

Dixon, K. (2001). The dialogic genres of Oprah Winfrey's "Crying Shame." *Journal of Popular Culture, 35,* 171–193.

Dixon, M. (1985). Singing swords: The literary legacy of slavery. In C. T. Davis & H. L. Gates, Jr. (Eds.), *The slave's narrative* (pp. 298–315). New York: Oxford University Press.

Dixon, V. J. (1976). World views and research methodology. In L. King, V. J. Dixon, & W. Nobles (Eds.), *African philosophy: Assumptions and paradigms for research on Black persons.* Los Angeles: Fanon Center.

Douglass, F. (1845/1987). *Narrative of the life of Frederick Douglass, an American slave, written by himself.* In H. L. Gates, Jr. (Ed.), *The classic slave narratives* (pp. 243–331). New York: Penguin.

Du Bois, W. E. B. (1903/1989). *The souls of black folk.* New York: Penguin.

Dyer, W. W. (1976/1995). *Your erroneous zones.* New York: Harper Collins.

Eakin, E. (2001, May 5). Black captive in a white culture? Houston A. Baker Jr., a provocateur on matters of race, is required reading even for critics who find his pessimistic views too extreme. *New York Times,* pp. A-15, A-17.

Eisenberg, N., & Miller, P. A. (1987). The relation of empathy to prosocial and related behaviors. *Psychological Bulletin, 101,* 91–119.

Elder, G. H., Jr. (1995). The life course paradigm: Social change and individual development. In P. Moen, G. H. Elder, Jr., & K. Luscher (Eds.), *Examining lives in context: Perspectives on the ecology of human development* (pp. 101–139). Washington, DC: APA Books.

Elkind, D. (Ed.). (1981). *Children and adolescents* (2nd ed.). New York: Oxford University Press.

Elliot, A. J., Chirkov, V. I., Kim, Y., & Sheldon, K. M. (2001). A cross-cultural analysis of avoidance (relative to approach) personal goals. *Psychological Science, 12,* 505–510.

Ellison, R. (1947/1972). *Invisible man.* New York: Vintage Books.

Emerson, R. W. (1841/1993). *Self-reliance and other essays.* New York: Dover.

Emmons, R. A. (1986). Personal strivings: An approach to personality and subjective well-being. *Journal of Personality and Social Psychology, 51,* 1058–1068.

Emmons, R. A. (1999). *The psychology of ultimate concerns: Motivation and spirituality in personality.* New York: Guilford Press.

Emmons, R. A., & Paloutzian, R. F. (2003). The psychology of religion. In S.T. Fiske, D. L. Schacter, & C. Zahn-Waxler (Eds.), *Annual review of psychology* (Vol. 54, pp. 377–402). Palo Alto, CA: Annual Reviews.

Epstein, S. (1979). The stability of behavior: 1. On predicting most of the people much of the time. *Journal of Personality and Social Psychology, 37,* 1097–1126.

Erikson, E. H. (1950). *Childhood and society.* New York: Norton.

Erikson, E. H. (1958). *Young man Luther: A study in psychoanalysis and history.* New York: Norton.

Erikson, E. H. (1959). *Identity and the life cycle.* New York: Norton.

Erikson, E. H. (1963). *Childhood and society* (2nd ed.). New York: Norton.

Erikson, E. H. (1964). *Insight and responsibility.* New York: Norton.

Erikson, E. H. (1968). *Identity: Youth and crisis.* New York: Norton.

Erikson, K. (1966). *Wayward Puritans: A study in the sociology of deviance.* New York: Wiley.

Erikson, K. (2004). Reflections on generativity and society: A sociologist's perspective. In E. de St. Aubin, D. P. McAdams, & T.-C. Kim (Eds.), *The generative society* (pp. 51–61). Washington, DC: APA Books.

Fairbairn, W. R. D. (1952). *The object relations theory of personality.* London: Routledge and Kegan Paul.

Fineman, H. (2002, July 8). One nation, under . . . who? *Newsweek,* pp. 20–25.

Fiske, S. T. (2002). What we know now about bias and intergroup conflict, the problem of the century. *Current Directions in Psychological Science, 11,* 123–128.

Fivush, R. (1994). Constructing narrative, emotion, and self in parent-child conversations about the past. In U. Neisser & R. Fivush (Eds.), *The remembering self* (pp. 136–157). New York: Cambridge University Press.

Fivush, R., & Kuebli, J. (1997). Making everyday events emotional: The construal of emotion in parent-child conversations about the past. In N. L. Stein, P. A. Ornstein, B. Tversky, & C. Brainerd (Eds.), *Memory for everyday and emotional events* (pp. 239–266). Mahwah, NJ: Erlbaum.

Forward, S. (1989). *Toxic parents: Overcoming their hurtful legacy and reclaiming your life.* New York: Bantam Books.

Fowler, J. (1981). *Stages of faith: The psychology of human development and the quest for meaning.* New York: Harper & Row.

Francis, M. E., & Pennebaker, J. W. (1992). Putting stress into words: The impact of writing on physiological, absentee, and self-reported emotional well-being measures. *American Journal of Health Promotion, 6,* 280–287.

Frankl, V. E. (1984). *Man's search for meaning.* New York: Washington Square Press.

Franklin, B. (1961). *The autobiography and other writings.* New York: Signet.

Franks, L. (1994, June 13). The return of the fugitive. *The New Yorker,* pp. 40–59.

Franz, C., & Stewart, A. J. (Eds.). (1994). *Women creating lives: Identities, resilience, resistance.* Boulder, CO: Westview.

Frazier, E. F. (1939). *The Negro family in the United States.* Chicago: University of Chicago Press.

Freeman, M. (1993). *Rewriting the self: History, memory, narrative.* London: Routledge.

Freud, S. (1905/1953). *Three essays on the theory of sexuality.* In J. Strachey (Ed.), *The standard edition of the complete psychological works of Sigmund Freud* (Vol. 7). London: Hogarth.

Freud, S. (1920/1955). *Beyond the pleasure principle.* In J. Strachey (Ed.), *The standard edition of the complete psychological works of Sigmund Freud* (Vol. 18). London: Hogarth.

Freud, S. (1923/1961). *The ego and the id.* In J. Strachey (Ed.), *The standard edition of the complete psychological works of Sigmund Freud* (Vol. 19). London: Hogarth.

Freud, S. (1930/1961). *Civilization and its discontents.* In J. Strachey (Ed.), *The standard edition of the complete psychological works of Sigmund Freud* (Vol. 21). London: Hogarth.

Freund, A. M., & Baltes, P. B. (2002). The orchestration of selection, optimization, and compensation: An action-theoretical conceptualization of a theory of developmental regulation. In W. J. Perrig & A. Grob (Eds.), *Control of human behavior, mental processes, and consciousness* (pp. 35–58). Mahwah, NJ: Erlbaum.

Fromm, E. (1941). *Escape from freedom.* New York: Farrar & Rinehart.

Funder, D. C. (1995). On the accuracy of personality judgments: A realistic approach. *Psychological Review, 102,* 652–670.

Gallup, G., Jr. (1984). *The religion report: Religion in America.* Princeton, NJ: Gallup Report.

Gardner, H. (1983). *Frames of mind.* New York: Basic Books.

Gates, H. L., Jr. (Ed.). (1987). *The classic slave narratives.* New York: Penguin.

Gates, H. L., Jr. (1998). Introduction: The talking book. In H. L. Gates, Jr., & W. L. Andrews (Eds.), *Pioneers of the black Atlantic: Five slave narratives from the enlightenment, 1772–1815* (pp. 1–29). Washington, DC: Civitas.

Gates, H. L., Jr. (2003, February 9). Not gone with the wind: Voices of slavery. *New York Times,* pp. 2–1, 2–8.

Gates, H. L., Jr., & Andrews, W. L. (Eds.). (1998). *Pioneers of the black Atlantic: Five slave narratives from the enlightenment, 1772–1815.* Washington, DC: Civitas.

Gay, P. (1984). *The bourgeois experience: Victoria to Freud. Vol. 1: The education of the senses.* New York: Oxford University Press.

Geertz, C. (1973). *The interpretation of cultures.* New York: Basic Books.

George, L. K., Ellison, C. G., & Larson, D. B. (2002). Explaining the relationships between religious involvement and health. *Psychological Inquiry, 13,* 190–200.

Gergen, K. J. (1991). *The saturated self: Dilemmas of identity in contemporary life.* New York: Basic Books.

Gergen, K. J., & Gergen, M. M. (1986). Narrative form and the construction of psychological science. In T. R. Sarbin (Ed.), *Narrative psychology: The storied nature of human conduct* (pp. 22–44). New York: Praeger.

Gettleman, J. (2002, October 12). Nobel Peace Prize awarded to Carter, with jab at Bush. *New York Times,* pp. A-1, A-8.

Giddens, A. (1991). *Modernity and self-identity: Self and society in the late modern age.* Stanford, CA: Stanford University Press.

Glaser, B. G., & Strauss, A. L. (1967). *The discovery of grounded theory: Strategies for qualitative research.* New York: Aldine Press.

Glaude, E. S., Jr. (2000). *Exodus! Religion, race, and nation in early nineteenth-century black America.* Chicago: University of Chicago Press.

Goffman, E. (1959). *The presentation of self in everyday life.* Garden City, NY: Doubleday.

Goldberg, L. R. (1990). An alternative "description of personality": The Big-Five factor structure. *Journal of Personality and Social Psychology, 59,* 1216–1229.

Golden, J. (1952). Review of *The People of Great Russia. American Anthropologist, 54,* 415–416.

Goode, E. (2001, April 10). "A new improved me": Now appearing everywhere. *New York Times,* p. D-1.

Goodstein, L. (2001, November 26). As attacks' impact recedes, a return to religion as usual. *New York Times,* pp. A-1, B-6.

Goodstein, L. (2002, September 18). Conservative churches grew fastest in 1990s, report says. *New York Times,* p. A-17.

Gorer, G., & Rickman, J. (1949). *The people of great Russia.* London: Cresset Press.

Greenberg, M. A., & Stone, A. A. (1992). Writing about disclosed versus undisclosed traumas: Immediate and long-term effects on mood and health. *Journal of Personality and Social Psychology, 63,* 75–84.

Greenfield, P. M., Keller, H., Fuligni, A., & Maynard, A. (2003). Cultural pathways through universal development. In S. T. Fiske, D. L. Schacter, & C. Zahn-Waxler (Eds.), *Annual review of psychology* (pp. 461–490). Palo Alto, CA: Annual Reviews.

Greenspan, H. (2003). Listening to Holocaust survivors: Interpreting a repeated story. In R. Josselson, A. Lieblich, & D. P. McAdams (Eds.), *Up close and personal: The teaching and learning of narrative research* (pp. 101–111). Washington, DC: APA Books.

Gregg, G. (1991). *Self-representation: Life narrative studies in identity and ideology.* New York: Greenwood Press.

Grossbaum, M. G., & Bates, G. W. (2002). Correlates of psychological well-being at midlife: The role of generativity, agency and communion, and narrative themes. *International Journal of Behavioral Development, 26,* 120–127.

Guntrip, H. (1971). *Psychoanalytic theory, therapy, and the self.* New York: Basic Books.

Haag, L. L. (1993). Oprah Winfrey: The construction of intimacy in the talk show setting. *Journal of Popular Culture, 26,* 115–122.

Habermas, T., & Bluck, S. (2000). Getting a life: The emergence of the life story in adolescence. *Psychological Bulletin, 126,* 748–769.

Hamilton, W. D. (1964). The genetical evolution of social behaviour. *Journal of Theoretical Biology, 7,* 1–52.

Hanninen, V., & Koski-Jannes, A. (1999). Narratives of recovery from addictive behaviours. *Addictions, 94,* 1837–1848.

Harrison, K. (1998). *The kiss.* New York: Avon Books.

Hart, H., McAdams, D. P., Hirsch, B. J., & Bauer, J. J. (2001). Generativity and social involvements among African Americans and White adults. *Journal of Research in Personality, 35,* 208–230.

Hartigan, F. (2000). *Bill W.: A biography of Alcoholics Anonymous cofounder Bill Wilson.* New York: St. Martin's Press.

Hay, L. L. (1984). *You can heal your life.* Carlsbad, CA: Hay House.

Heine, S. J., Lehman, D. R., Peng, K., & Greenholtz, J. (2002). What's wrong with cross-cultural comparisons of subjective Likert scales? The reference-group effect. *Journal of Personality and Social Psychology, 82,* 903–918.

Helson, R., & Moane, G. (1987). Personality change in women from college to midlife. *Journal of Personality and Social Psychology, 53,* 176–186.

Hermans, H. J. M. (1996). Voicing the self: From information processing to dialogical interchange. *Psychological Bulletin, 119,* 31–50.

Hermans, H. J. M., & Hermans-Jansen, E. (1995). *Self-narratives: The construction of meaning in psychotherapy.* New York: Guilford Press.

Hermans, H. J. M., Kempen, H. J. G., & van Loon, R. J. P. (1992). The dialogical self: Beyond individualism and rationalism. *American Psychologist, 47,* 23–33.

Hill, J. R., & Zillman, D. (1999). The Oprahization of America: Sympathetic crime talk and leniency. *Journal of Broadcasting and Electronic Media, 43,* 67–80.

Hill, R. B. (1997). *The strengths of African-American families: Twenty-five years later.* Washington, DC: R & B.

Himsel, A. J., Hart, H., Diamond, A., & McAdams, D. P. (1997). Personality characteristics of highly generative adults as assessed in Q-sort ratings of life stories. *Journal of Adult Development, 4,* 149–161.

Hine, D. C. (1993). Harriet Tubman. In *Black women in America: An historical encyclopedia* (pp. 1176–1180). New York: Carlson.

Hochschild, A. (1995). *Facing up to the American dream: Race, class, and the soul of the nation.* Princeton, NJ: Princeton University Press.

Hoffman, M. L. (1981). Is altruism part of human nature? *Journal of Personality and Social Psychology, 40,* 121–137.

Hogan, R. (1982). A socioanalytic theory of personality. In M. Page (Ed.), *Nebraska symposium on motivation* (pp. 55–89). Lincoln: University of Nebraska Press.

Hogan, R. (1987). Personality psychology: Back to basics. In J. Aronoff, A. I. Rabin, & R. A. Zucker (Eds.), *The emergence of personality* (pp. 79–104). New York: Springer.

Hogan, R., Jones, W. H., & Cheek, J. M. (1985). Socioanalytic theory: An alternative to armadillo psychology. In B. R. Schlenker (Ed.), *The self and social life* (pp. 175–198). New York: McGraw-Hill.

Holland, D. (1997). Selves as cultured: As told by an anthropologist who lacks a soul. In R. D. Ashmore & L. Jussim (Eds.), *Self and identity: Fundamental issues* (pp. 160–190). New York: Oxford University Press.

Holstein, J. A., & Gubrium, J. F. (2000). *The self we live by: Narrative identity in a postmodern world.* New York: Oxford University Press.

Hooker, K. (2002). New directions for research in personality and aging: A comprehensive model for linking levels, structures, and processes. *Journal of Research in Personality, 36,* 318–334.

Hooker, K., & McAdams, D. P. (2003). New directions in aging research: Personality reconsidered. *Journal of Gerontology: Psychological Sciences, 58B,* 296–304.

Howe, M. L., & Courage, M. L. (1997). The emergence and early development of autobiographical memory. *Psychological Review, 104,* 499–523.

James, W. (1902/1958). *The varieties of religious experience.* New York: New American Library.

Jaynes, J. (1976). *The origin of consciousness in the breakdown of the bicameral mind.* Boston: Houghton Mifflin.

Jensen, G. H. (2000). *Storytelling in Alcoholics Anonymous: A rhetorical analysis.* Carbondale: Southern Illinois University Press.

John, O. P., & Srivastava, S. (1999). The Big Five trait taxonomy: History, measurement, and theoretical perspectives. In L. Pervin & O. P. John (Eds.), *Handbook of personality: Theory and research* (2nd ed., pp. 102–138). New York: Guilford Press.

Johnson, G. D., Mare, M., & Ambrecht, G. (1991). Race and religiosity: An empirical evaluation of a causal model. *Review of Religious Research, 32,* 252–266.

Jordan, P. (2002, July 28). Dysfunction for dollars. *New York Times Magazine,* pp. 22–25.

Josselson, R. (1995). Narrative and psychological understanding. *Psychiatry, 58,* 330–343.

Josselson, R. (1996). *Rewriting herself: The story of women's identity from college to midlife*. San Francisco: Jossey-Bass.

Josselson, R., & Lieblich, A. (Eds.). (1993). *The narrative study of lives*. Thousand Oaks, CA: Sage.

Josselson, R., Lieblich, A., & McAdams, D. P. (Eds.). (2003). *Up close and personal: Teaching and learning narrative research*. Washington, DC: APA Books.

Kagan, J. (1994). *Galen's prophecy*. New York: Basic Books.

Kagan, R. (2003). *Of paradise and power: America and Europe in the new world order*. New York: Knopf.

Kakutani, M. (2001, February 4). Faith base: As American as second acts and apple pie. *New York Times*, p. D-1.

Kaminer, W. (1992). *I'm dysfunctional, you're dysfunctional: The recovery movement and other self-help fashions*. Reading, MA: Addison-Wesley.

Kammen, M. (1972). *People of paradox: An inquiry concerning the origins of American civilization*. New York: Knopf.

Kammen, M. (1991). *Mystic chords of memory: The transformation of tradition in American culture*. New York: Knopf.

Kardiner, A. (1939). *The individual and his society*. New York: Columbia University Press.

Karr, M. (1995). *The liar's club*. New York: Penguin.

Kasser, T., & Ryan, R. M. (1993). A dark side of the American dream. *Journal of Personality and Social Psychology, 65*, 410–422.

Kazin, A. (1984). *An American procession*. New York: Knopf.

Kennedy, R. (2003). *Interracial intimacies: Sex, marriage, identity, and adoption*. New York: Pantheon.

Keyes, C. L. M., & Ryff, C. D. (1998). Generativity and adult lives: Social structural contours and quality of life consequences. In D. P. McAdams & E. de St. Aubin (Eds.), *Generativity and adult development: How and why we care for the next generation* (pp. 227–263). Washington, DC: APA Books.

Kim, G., & Youn, G. (2002). Role of education in generativity differences of employed and unemployed women in Korea. *Psychological Reports, 91*, 1205–1212.

King, L. A., & Miner, K. N. (2000). Writing about perceived benefits of traumatic events: Implications for physical health. *Personality and Social Psychology Bulletin, 26*, 220–230.

Klein, S. B., Cosmides, L., Costabile, K. A., & Mei, L. (2002). Is there something special about the self? A neuropsychological case study. *Journal of Research in Personality, 36*, 490–506.

Klinkenborg, V. (2002, October 11). Moral perfection and the incorrigible Franklin. *New York Times*, p. A-19.

Kohut, H. (1971). *The analysis of the self*. New York: International Universities Press.

Kohut, H. (1977). *The restoration of the self*. New York: International Universities Press.

Kotre, J. (1984). *Outliving the self: Generativity and the interpretation of lives*. Baltimore, MD: Johns Hopkins University Press.

Kotre, J., & Kotre, K. B. (1998). Intergenerational buffers: The damage stops here. In D. P. McAdams & E. de St. Aubin (Eds.), *Generativity and adult development: How and why we care for the next generation* (pp. 367–389). Washington, DC: APA Books.

Kurtz, E. (1979). *Not-God: A history of Alcoholics Anonymous.* Center City, MN: Hazelden Educational Services.

Lachman, M. (Ed.). (2001). *The handbook of midlife development.* New York: Wiley.

Landman, J. (2001). The crime, punishment, and ethical transformation of two radicals: Or how Katherine Ann Power improves on Dostoevsky. In D. P. McAdams, R. Josselson, & A. Lieblich (Eds.), *Turns in the road: Narrative studies of lives in transition* (pp. 35–66). Washington, DC: APA Books.

Lane, J. B. (1978). *City of the century: A history of Gary, Indiana.* Bloomington: Indiana University Press.

Langbaum, R. (1982). *The mysteries of identity: A theme in modern literature.* Chicago: University of Chicago Press.

Langewiesche, W. (2002, July/August). American ground: Unbuilding the World Trade Center. *Atlantic Monthly,* pp. 45–79.

Lapsley, D. K., & Power, F. C. (Eds.). (1988). *Self, ego, and identity: Integrative approaches.* New York: Springer-Verlag.

Lasch, C. (1979). *The culture of narcissism: American life in an age of diminishing expectations.* New York: Norton.

Lears, J. (2003, March 11). How a war became a crusade. *New York Times,* p. A-20.

LeDoux, J. (1996). *The emotional brain: The mysterious underpinnings of emotional life.* New York: Simon & Schuster.

Lee, F. R. (2002, August 24). The secular society gets religion. *New York Times,* pp. B-1, B-17.

Leibowitz, H. (1989). *Fabricating lives: Explorations in American autobiography.* New York: Knopf.

Levine, M. (2000). *The positive psychology of Buddhism and yoga.* Mahwah, NJ: Erlbaum.

LeVine, R. A. (1982). *Culture, behavior, and personality* (2nd ed.). New York: Aldine Press.

LeVine, R. A. (2001). Culture and personality studies, 1918–1960: Myth and history. *Journal of Personality, 69,* 803–818.

Lewis, M. S. (2000). *The life stories of less generative adults: Identifying narrative and psychological features.* Unpublished doctoral dissertation, Northwestern University, Evanston, IL.

Lieblich, A., McAdams, D. P., & Josselson, R. (Eds.). (2004). *Healing plots: The narrative basis of psychotherapy.* Washington, DC: APA Books.

Little, B. R. (1999). Personality and motivation: Personal action and the conative evolution. In L. Pervin & O. P. John (Eds.), *Handbook of personality: Theory and research* (2nd ed., pp. 501–524). New York: Guilford Press.

Loevinger, J. (1976). *Ego development.* San Francisco: Jossey-Bass.

Love, B. E., & Watkins, M. (1999). *The Bob Love story: If it's gonna be, it's up to me.* Chicago: NTC Publishing Group.

Lynch, J. J. (2002). *A cry unheard: New insights into the medical consequences of loneliness.* Chicago: University of Chicago Press.

MacDermid, S. M., Franz, C. E., & de Reus, L. A. (1998). Generativity: At the crossroads of social roles and personality. In D. P. McAdams & E. de St. Aubin (Eds.), *Generativity and adult development: How and why we care for the next generation* (pp. 181–226). Washington, DC: APA Books.

MacIntyre, A. (1984). *After virtue.* Notre Dame, IN: University of Notre Dame Press.

Mailer, N. (1959/1987). White Negro. In R. N. Bellah, R. Madsen, W. M. Sullivan, A. Swidler, & S. M. Tipton (Eds.), *Individualism and commitment in American life* (pp. 89–91). New York: Harper & Row.

Main, M., Kaplan, N., & Cassidy, J. (1985). Security in infancy, childhood, and adulthood: A move to the level of representation. *Monographs for the Society of Research in Child Development, 50*(1, 2), 66–104.

Makela, K., et al. (1996). *Alcoholics Anonymous as a mutual-help movement: A study in eight societies.* Madison: University of Wisconsin Press.

Malpass, R. S., & Symonds, J. D. (1974). Value preferences associated with social class, sex, and race. *Journal of Cross-Cultural Psychology, 5,* 282–300.

Mandler, J. M. (1984). *Stories, scripts, and scenes: Aspects of schema theory.* Hillsdale, NJ: Erlbaum.

Manheimer, R. J. (1989). The narrative quest in qualitative gerontology. *Journal of Aging Studies, 3,* 231–252.

Mansfield, E. D., & McAdams, D. P. (1996). Generativity and themes of agency and communion in adult autobiography. *Personality and Social Psychology Bulletin, 22,* 721–731.

Markus, H., & Kitayama, S. (1991). Culture and the self: Implications for cognition, emotion, and motivation. *Psychological Review, 98,* 224–253.

Markus, H., Kitayama, S., & Heiman, R. J. (1998). Culture and "basic" psychological principles. In E. T. Higgins & A. W. Kruglanski (Eds.), *Social psychology: Handbook of basic principles* (pp. 857–913). New York: Guilford Press.

Markus, H., & Nurius, P. (1986). Possible selves. *American Psychologist, 41,* 954–969.

Martin, D. (2002, September 15). Clement Stone dies at 100; built empire on optimism. *New York Times,* p. A-22.

Maruna, S. (1997). Going straight: Desistance from crime and life narratives of reform. In R. Josselson & A. Lieblich (Eds.), *The narrative study of lives* (Vol. 5, pp. 59–93). Thousand Oaks, CA: Sage.

Maruna, S. (2001). *Making good: How ex-convicts reform and rebuild their lives.* Washington, DC: APA Books.

Maruna, S., & Ramsden, D. (2004). Living to tell the tale: Redemption narratives, shame management and offender rehabilitation. In A. Lieblich, D. P. McAdams, & R. Josselson (Eds.), *Healing plots: The narrative basis of psychotherapy* (pp. 129–149). Washington, DC: APA Books.

Marx, A. W. (2003). *Faith in nation: Exclusionary origins of nationalism.* New York: Oxford University Press.

Maslow, A. (1968). *Toward a psychology of being.* New York: D. Van Nostrand.

Mathisen, R. (Ed.). (1982). *The role of religion in American life: An interpretive historical anthology.* Washington, DC: University Press of America.

McAdams, D. P. (1982). Experiences of intimacy and power: Relationships between social motives and autobiographical memory. *Journal of Personality and Social Psychology, 42,* 292–302.

McAdams, D. P. (1985). *Power, intimacy, and the life story: Personological inquiries into identity.* New York: Guilford Press.

McAdams, D. P. (1990). Unity and purpose in human lives: The emergence of identity as a life story. In A. I. Rubin, R. A. Zucker, R. A. Emmons, & S. Frank (Eds.), *Studying persons and lives* (pp. 148–200). New York: Springer.

McAdams, D. P. (1993). *The stories we live by: Personal myths and the making of the self.* New York: Morrow.

McAdams, D. P. (1994). Can personality change? Levels of stability and growth in personality across the life span. In T. F. Heatherton & J. F. Weinberger (Eds.), *Can personality change?* (pp. 299–313). Washington, DC: APA Books.

McAdams, D. P. (1995). What do we know when we know a person? *Journal of Personality, 63,* 365–396.

McAdams, D. P. (1996a). Narrating the self in adulthood. In J. Birren, G. Kenyon, J. E. Ruth, J. J. F. Shroots, & J. Svendson (Eds.), *Aging and biography: Explorations in adult development* (pp. 131–148). New York: Springer.

McAdams, D. P. (1996b). Personality, modernity, and the storied self: A contemporary framework for studying persons. *Psychological Inquiry, 7,* 295–321.

McAdams, D. P. (1997). The case for unity in the (post)modern self: A modest proposal. In R. Ashmore & L. Jussim (Eds.), *Self and identity: Fundamental issues* (pp. 46–78). New York: Oxford University Press.

McAdams, D. P. (1998). The role of defense in the life story. *Journal of Personality, 66,* 1125–1146.

McAdams, D. P. (1999). Personal narratives and the life story. In L. Pervin & O. John (Eds.), *Handbook of personality: Theory and research* (2nd ed., pp. 478–500). New York: Guilford Press.

McAdams, D. P. (2001a). Generativity in midlife. In M. Lachman (Ed.), *Handbook of midlife development* (pp. 395–443). New York: Wiley.

McAdams, D. P. (2001b). *The person: An integrated introduction to personality psychology* (3rd ed.). Fort Worth, TX: Harcourt.

McAdams, D. P. (2001c). The psychology of life stories. *Review of General Psychology, 5,* 100–122.

McAdams, D. P. (2004). Generativity and the narrative ecology of family life. In M. W. Pratt & B. H. Fiese (Eds.), *Family stories and the life course* (pp. 235–257). Mahwah, NJ: Erlbaum.

McAdams, D. P., Anyidoho, N. A., Brown, C., Huang, Y. T., Kaplan, B., & Machado,

M. A. (2004). Traits and stories: Links between dispositional and narrative features of personality. *Journal of Personality, 72,* 761–784.

McAdams, D. P., & Bowman, P. T. (2001). Narrating life's turning points: Redemption and contamination. In D. P. McAdams, R. Josselson, & A. Lieblich (Eds.), *Turns in the road: Narrative studies of lives in transition* (pp. 3–34). Washington, DC: APA Books.

McAdams, D. P., & de St. Aubin, E. (1992). A theory of generativity and its assessment through self-report, behavioral acts, and narrative themes in autobiography. *Journal of Personality and Social Psychology, 62,* 1003–1015.

McAdams, D. P., & de St. Aubin, E. (Eds.). (1998). *Generativity and adult development: How and why we care for the next generation.* Washington, DC: APA Books.

McAdams, D. P., de St. Aubin, E., & Logan, R. L. (1993). Generativity among young, midlife, and older adults. *Psychology and Aging, 8,* 221–230.

McAdams, D. P., Diamond, A., de St. Aubin, E., & Mansfield, E. D. (1997). Stories of commitment: The psychosocial construction of generative lives. *Journal of Personality and Social Psychology, 72,* 678–694.

McAdams, D. P., Hart, H. M., & Maruna, S. (1998). The anatomy of generativity. In D. P. McAdams & E. de St. Aubin (Eds.), *Generativity and adult development: How and why we care for the next generation* (pp. 7–43). Washington, DC: APA Books.

McAdams, D. P., Hoffman, B. J., Mansfield, E. D., & Day, R. (1996). Themes of agency and communion in significant autobiographical scenes. *Journal of Personality, 64,* 339–377.

McAdams, D. P., Josselson, R., & Lieblich, A. (Eds.). (2001). *Turns in the road: Narrative studies of lives in transition.* Washington, DC: APA Books.

McAdams, D. P., Reynolds, J., Lewis, M., Patten, A., & Bowman, P. J. (2001). When bad things turn good and good things turn bad: Sequences of redemption and contamination in life narrative, and their relation to psychosocial adaptation in midlife adults and in students. *Personality and Social Psychology Bulletin, 27,* 472–483.

McAdams, D. P., Ruetzel, K., & Foley, J. M. (1986). Complexity and generativity at midlife: Relations among social motives, ego development, and adults' plans for the future. *Journal of Personality and Social Psychology, 50,* 800–807.

McClelland, D. C. (1961). *The achieving society.* New York: Free Press.

McClelland, D. C. (1985). *Human motivation.* Glenview, IL: Scott Foresman.

McColgan, G., Valentine, J., & Downs, M. (2000). Concluding narratives of a career with dementia: Accounts of Iris Murdoch at her death. *Ageing and Society, 20,* 97–109.

McCrae, R. R., & Costa, P. T., Jr. (1987). Validation of the five-factor model of personality across instruments and observers. *Journal of Personality and Social Psychology, 52,* 81–90.

McCrae, R. R., & Costa, P. T., Jr. (1990). *Personality in adulthood.* New York: Guilford Press.

McCrae, R. R., & Costa, P. T., Jr. (1997). Personality trait structure as a human universal. *American Psychologist, 52,* 509–516.

McGregor, C. (1978). *Up from the walking dead: The Charles McGregor story.* Garden City, NY: Doubleday.

Mead, G. H. (1934). *Mind, self, and society.* Chicago: University of Chicago Press.

Melville, H. (1850/1892). *White-jacket, or the world in a man-of-war.* Boston: Page.

Menand, L. (2001). *The metaphysical club: A story of ideas in America.* New York: Farrar, Straus & Giroux.

Michaelsen, R. S. (1975). *The American search for soul.* Baton Rouge: Louisiana State University Press.

Milgram, S. (1965). Some conditions of obedience and disobedience to authority. *Human Relations, 18,* 57–76.

Miller, A. (2002). *The truth will set you free: Overcoming emotional blindness and finding your true adult self.* New York: Basic Books.

Mischel, W. (1968). *Personality and assessment.* New York: Wiley.

Mischel, W., & Shoda, Y. (1995). A cognitive-affective system theory of personality: Reconceptualizing situations, dispositions, dynamics, and invariance in personality structure. *Psychological Review, 102,* 246–268.

Moore, T. (1992). *Care of the soul: A guide for cultivating depth and sacredness in everyday life.* New York: Harper Collins.

Morone, J. A. (2003). *Hellfire nation: The politics of sin in American history.* New Haven, CT: Yale University Press.

Morris, E. (1999). *Dutch: A memoir of Ronald Reagan.* New York: Random House.

Murphy, F. (Ed.). (1977). *Whitman: The complete poems.* New York: Viking Press.

Myers, D. G. (2000). *The American paradox: Spiritual hunger in an age of plenty.* New Haven, CT: Yale University Press.

Nakagawa, K. (1991). *Explorations into the correlates of public school reform and parental involvement.* Unpublished doctoral dissertation, Northwestern University, Evanston, IL.

Nasby, W., & Read, N. (1997). The life voyage of a solo circumnavigator [Special issue]. *Journal of Personality, 65.*

Neff, J. A., & Hoppe, S. K. (1993). Race/ethnicity, acculturation, and psychological distress: Fatalism and religiosity as cultural resources. *Journal of Community Psychology, 31,* 3–20.

Neisser, U. (Ed.). (1982). *Memory observed: Remembering in natural contexts.* San Francisco: Freeman.

Nelson, K. (1988). The ontogeny of memory for real events. In U. Neissser & E. Winograd (Eds.), *Remembering reconsidered* (pp. 244–276). New York: Cambridge University Press.

Nelson, P. (1989). Ethnic differences in intrinsic/extrinsic religious orientation and depression in the elderly. *Archives of Psychiatric Nursing, 3,* 199–204.

New Encyclopaedia Britannica. (1997). (15th ed., Vol. 10, p. 369). Entry for "salvation." Chicago: Encyclopaedia Britannica.

New lights of the spirit. (2000, December 11). *Time,* pp. 84–91.

Nichols, C. H. (1985). The slave narratives and the picaresque mode: Archetypes for modern black personae. In C. T. Davis & H. L. Gates, Jr. (Eds.), *The slave's narrative* (pp. 283–298). New York: Oxford University Press.

Nielson, S. L., Johnson, W. B., & Ellis, A. (2001). *Counseling and psychotherapy with religious persons*. Mahwah, NJ: Erlbaum.

Olney, J. (1985). "I was born": Slave narratives, their status as autobiography and as literature. In C. T. Davis & H. L. Gates, Jr. (Eds.), *The slave's narrative* (pp. 148–175). New York: Oxford University Press.

O'Reilly, E. B. (1997). *Sobering tales: Narratives of alcoholism and recovery*. Amherst: University of Massachusetts Press.

Pargament, K. I. (2002). The bitter and the sweet: An evaluation of the costs and benefits of religiousness. *Psychological Inquiry, 13,* 168–181.

Park, C. L., Cohen, L. H., & Murch, R. L. (1996). Assessment and prediction of stress-related growth. *Journal of Personality, 64,* 71–105.

Parks Daloz, L. A., Keen, C. H., Keen, J. P., & Daloz Parks, S. (1996). *Common fire: Lives of commitment in a complex world*. Boston: Beacon Press.

Pasupathi, M. (2001). The social construction of the personal past and its implications for adult development. *Psychological Bulletin, 127,* 651–672.

Peale, N. V. (1952/1982). *The power of positive thinking*. New York: Fawcett Crest.

Peck, J. (1995). TV talk show as therapeutic discourse: The ideological labor of the televised talking cure. *Communications Theory, 5,* 170–189.

Peck, M. S. (1978). *The road less traveled*. New York: Simon & Schuster.

Pennebaker, J. W. (1989). Confession, inhibition, and disease. In L. Berkowitz (Ed.), *Advances in experimental social psychology* (Vol. 22, pp. 211–244). New York: Academic Press.

Pennebaker, J. W. (1997). Writing about emotional experiences as a therapeutic process. *Psychological Science, 8,* 162–166.

Pennebaker, J. W., Mehl, M. R., & Niederhoffer, K. G. (2003). Psychological aspects of natural language use: Our words, our selves. In S. T. Fiske, D. L. Schacter, & C. Zahn-Waxler (Eds.), *Annual review of psychology* (Vol. 54, pp. 547–577). Palo Alto, CA: Annual Reviews.

Peterson, B. E. (1998). Case studies in midlife generativity: Analyzing motivation and realization. In D. P. McAdams & E. de St. Aubin (Eds.), *Generativity and adult development: How and why we care for the next generation* (pp. 101–131). Washington, DC: APA Books.

Peterson, B. E. (2002). Longitudinal analysis of midlife generativity, intergenerational roles, and caregiving. *Psychology and Aging, 17,* 161–168.

Peterson, B. E., & Klohnen, E. C. (1995). Realization of generativity in two samples of women at midlife. *Psychology and Aging, 10,* 20–29.

Peterson, B. E., Smirles, K. A., & Wentworth, P. A. (1997). Generativity and authoritarianism: Implications for personality, political involvement, and parenting. *Journal of Personality and Social Psychology, 72,* 1202–1216.

Peterson, B. E., & Stewart, A. J. (1990). Using personal and fictional documents to assess psychosocial development: The case of Vera Brittain's generativity. *Psychology and Aging, 5,* 400–411.

Peterson, B. E., & Stewart, A. J. (1993). Generativity and social motives in young adults. *Journal of Personality and Social Psychology, 65,* 186–198.

Piaget, J. (1970). *Genetic epistemology.* New York: Columbia University Press.

Pillemer, D. B. (1998). *Momentous events, vivid memories.* Cambridge, MA: Harvard University Press.

Pinker, S. (1997). *How the mind works.* New York: Norton.

Polkinghorne, D. (1988). *Narrative knowing and the human sciences.* Albany: State University of New York Press.

Pratt, M. W., Danso, H. A., Arnold, M. L., Norris, J. E., & Filyer, R. (2001). Adult generativity and the socialization of adolescents: Relations to mothers' and fathers' parenting beliefs, styles, and practices. *Journal of Personality, 69,* 89–120.

Pratt, M. W., Norris, J. E., Arnold, M. L., & Filyer, R. (1999). Generativity and moral development as predictors of value-socialization narratives for young persons across the adult life span: From lessons learned to stories shared. *Psychology and Aging, 14,* 414–426.

Prochaska, J. O., Norcross, J. C., & DiClemente, C. C. (1994). *Changing for good: A revolutionary six-stage program for overcoming bad habits and moving your life positively forward.* New York: Avon Books.

Purdy, J. (2003). *Being America: Liberty, commerce, and violence in an American world.* New York: Knopf.

Putnam, R. D. (2000). *Bowling alone: The collapse and revival of American community.* New York: Simon & Schuster.

Rank, O. (1936/1978). *Truth versus reality.* New York: Norton.

Raphael, M. J. (2000). *Bill W. and Mr. Wilson: The legend and the life of A.A.'s cofounder.* Amherst: University of Massachusetts Press.

Reeves, R. (2001, October 1). Patriotism calls out the censor. *New York Times,* p. A-18.

Revelle, W. (1995). Personality processes. In L. W. Porter & M. R. Rosenzweig (Eds.), *Annual review of psychology* (Vol. 46, pp. 295–328). Palo Alto, CA: Annual Reviews.

Ricouer, P. (1984). *Time and narrative.* Chicago: University of Chicago Press.

Rieff, P. (1966). *The triumph of the therapeutic.* New York: Harper.

Riesman, D. (1949/1961). *The lonely crowd.* New Haven, CT: Yale University Press.

Ringer, R. J. (1977). *Looking out for number one.* New York: Fawcett Crest.

Roberts, B. W., & Friend-DelVecchio, W. (2000). The rank-order consistency of personality from childhood to old age: A quantitative review of longitudinal studies. *Psychological Bulletin, 126,* 3–25.

Rogers, C. (1951). *Client-centered therapy.* Boston: Houghton-Mifflin.

Roof, W. C. (1999). *Spiritual marketplace: Baby boomers and the remaking of American religion.* Princeton, NJ: Princeton University Press.

Rosenwald, G., & Ochberg, R. L. (Eds.). (1992). *Storied lives: The cultural politics of self-understanding.* New Haven, CT: Yale University Press.

Rossi, A. S. (Ed.). (2001). *Caring and doing for others: Social responsibility in the domains of family, work, and community.* Chicago: University of Chicago Press.

Sack, K., & Elder, J. (2000, July 11). Poll finds optimistic outlook but enduring racial division. *New York Times,* pp. A-1, A-23.

Sampson, E. E. (1989). The challenge of social change for psychology: Globalization and psychology's theory of the person. *American Psychologist, 44,* 914–921.

Sarbin, T. R. (Ed.). (1986). *Narrative psychology: The storied nature of human conduct.* New York: Praeger.

Schacter, D. L. (1996). *Searching for memory: The brain, the mind, and the past.* New York: Basic Books.

Scharnhorst, G. (1980). *Horatio Alger, Jr.* Boston: Twayne.

Schoen, R., & Kluegel, J. R. (1988). The widening gap in Black and White marriage rates: The impact of population composition and differential marriage propensities. *American Sociological Review, 53,* 895–907.

Schram, S. F., & Neisser, P. T. (Eds.). (1997). *Tales of the state: Narratives in contemporary U.S. politics and public policy.* Oxford, England: Rowman & Littlefield.

Schuerger, J. M., Zarella, K. L., & Hortz, A. S. (1989). Factors that influence temporal stability of personality by questionnaire. *Journal of Personality and Social Psychology, 56,* 777–783.

Schultz, T. (1996). An "Orpheus Complex" in two writers-of-loss. *Biography: An Interdisciplinary Quarterly, 19,* 371–393.

Second acts. (2002, September 30). *People,* pp. 123–129.

Seligman, M. E. P., & Csikszentmihalyi, M. (2000). Positive psychology: An introduction. *American Psychologist, 55,* 5–14.

Seybold, K. M., & Hill, P. C. (2001). The role of religion and spirituality in mental and physical health. *Current Directions in Psychological Science, 10,* 21–24.

Shaw, C. (1929). *Delinquency areas.* Chicago: University of Chicago Press.

Shaw, C. (1930). *The jack-roller: A delinquent boy's own story.* Chicago: University of Chicago Press.

Shea, D. B., Jr. (1968). *Spiritual autobiography in early America.* Princeton, NJ: Princeton University Press.

Sherkat, D. E., & Ellison, C. G. (1999). Recent developments and current controversies in the sociology of religion. *Annual Review of Sociology, 25,* 363–394.

Shipler, D. K. (1997). *A country of strangers: Blacks and Whites in America.* New York: Knopf.

Shotter, J., & Gergen, K. J. (Eds.). (1989). *Texts of identity.* London: Sage.

Shulevitz, J. (2001, May 20). Lord, won't you buy me a Mercedes-Benz? *New York Times Book Review,* p. 47.

Shweder, R. A. (1984). Preview: A colloquy of culture theorists. In R. A. Shweder & R. A. LeVine (Eds.), *Culture theory: Essays on mind, self, and emotion* (pp. 1–24). Cambridge: Cambridge University Press.

Shweder, R. A., & LeVine, R. A. (Eds.). (1984). *Culture theory: Essays on mind, self, and emotion.* Cambridge: Cambridge University Press.

Shweder, R. A., & Sullivan, M. A. (1993). Cultural psychology: Who needs it? *Annual Review of Psychology, 44,* 497–523.

Singer, J. A. (1995). Seeing one's self: Locating narrative memory in a framework of personality. *Journal of Personality, 63,* 429–457.

Singer, J. A. (1997). *Message in a bottle: Stories of men and addiction.* New York: Free Press.

Singer, J. A. (2001). Living in the amber cloud: A life story analysis of a heroin addict. In D. P. McAdams, R. Josselson, & A. Lieblich (Eds.), *Turns in the road: Narrative studies of lives in transition* (pp. 253–277). Washington, DC: APA Books.

Singer, J. A., & Salovey, P. (1993). *The remembered self.* New York: Free Press.

Slater, L. (2002, February 3). The trouble with self-esteem. *New York Times Magazine,* pp. 44–47.

Slotkin, R. (1973). *Regeneration through violence: The mythology of the American frontier, 1600–1860.* Middletown, CT: Wesleyan University Press.

Smith, C. (2000). *Christian America? What evangelicals really want.* Berkeley: University of California Press.

Smith, C. E. (2000). Content analysis and narrative analysis. In H. Reis & P. Shaver (Eds.), *Handbook of research methods in social and personality psychology* (pp. 313–335). New York: Academic Press.

Snarey, J. (1993). *How fathers care for the next generation: A four-decade study.* Cambridge, MA: Harvard University Press.

Sroufe, L. A., & Waters, E. (1977). Attachment as an organizational construct. *Child Development, 48,* 1184–1199.

Stein, N. L., Wade, E., & Liwag, M. C. (1997). A theoretical approach to understanding and remembering emotional events. In N. L. Stein, P. A. Ornstein, B. Tversky, & C. Brainerd (Eds.), *Memory for everyday and emotional events* (pp. 15–47). Mahwah, NJ: Erlbaum.

Stewart, A. J., & Ostrove, J. M. (1998). Women's personality at middle age: Gender, history, and midcourse corrections. *American Psychologist, 53,* 1185–1194.

Stewart, A. J., & Vandewater, E. (1998). The course of generativity. In D. P. McAdams & E. de St. Aubin (Eds.), *Generativity and adult development: How and why we care for the next generation* (pp. 75–100). Washington, DC: APA Books.

Strauss, A. L., & Corbin, J. (1990). *Basics of qualitative research: Grounded theory procedures and techniques.* Newbury Park, CA: Sage.

Sullivan, A. (2001, September 23). This is what a day means. *New York Times Magazine,* pp. 60–61.

Sullivan, H. S. (1953). *The interpersonal theory of psychiatry.* New York: Norton.

Tajfel, H., & Turner, H. (1979). An integrative theory of intergroup conflict. In W. G. Austin & S. Worchel (Eds.), *The social psychology of intergroup relations* (pp. 33–47). Monterey, CA: Brooks/Cole.

Talking about race: How race is lived in America: A special issue in pictures, dialogue, and memoir. (2000, July 16). *New York Times Magazine.*

Taylor, C. (1989). *Sources of the self: The making of the modern identity.* Cambridge, MA: Harvard University Press.

Taylor, S. (1983). Adjustment to threatening events: A theory of cognitive adaptation. *American Psychologist, 38,* 624–630.

Taylor, S., Lichtman, R. R., & Wood, J. V. (1984). Attributions, beliefs about control, and adjustment to breast cancer. *Journal of Personality and Social Psychology, 46,* 489–502.

Tebbel, J. (1963). *From rags to riches: Horatio Alger, Jr., and the American dream.* New York: Macmillan.

Tedeschi, R. G., & Calhoun, L. G. (1995). *Trauma and transformation: Growing in the aftermath of suffering.* Thousand Oaks, CA: Sage.

Tellegen, A., Lykken, D. J. Bouchard, T. J., Jr., Wilcox, K. J., Segal, N. L., & Rich, S. (1988). Personality similarity in twins reared apart and together. *Journal of Personality and Social Psychology, 54,* 1031–1039.

Thompson, C. P., Skowronski, J. J., Larsen, S. F., & Betz, A. L. (Eds.). (1996). *Autobiographical memory: Remembering what and remembering when.* Mahwah, NJ: Erlbaum.

Thorne, A. (1989). Conditional patterns, transference, and the coherence of personality across time. In D. M. Buss & N. Cantor (Eds.), *Personality psychology: Recent trends and emerging directions* (pp. 149–159). New York: Springer-Verlag.

Thorne, A. (2000). Personal memory telling and personality development. *Personality and Social Psychology Review, 4,* 45–56.

Thorne, A., & McLean, K. C. (2003). Telling traumatic events in adolescence: A study of master narrative positioning. In R. Fivush & C. Haden (Eds.), *Autobiographical memory and the construction of a narrative self* (pp. 169–185). Mahwah, NJ: Erlbaum.

Tomkins, S. S. (1979). Script theory: Differential magnification of affects. In H. E. Howe & R. A. Dienstbier (Eds.), *Nebraska symposium on motivation* (Vol. 26, pp. 201–236). Lincoln: University of Nebraska Press.

Tomkins, S. S. (1987). Script theory. In J. Aronoff, A. I. Rabin, & R. A. Zucker (Eds.), *The emergence of personality* (pp. 147–216). New York: Springer.

Tooby, J., & Cosmides, L. (1992). The psychological foundations of culture. In J. H. Barkow, L. Cosmides, & J. Tooby (Eds.), *The adapted mind* (pp. 19–136). New York: Oxford University Press.

Triandis, H. C. (1997). Cross-cultural perspectives on personality. In R. Hogan, J. Jones, & S. Briggs (Eds.), *Handbook of personality psychology* (pp. 439–464). San Diego, CA: Academic Press.

Triandis, H. C., & Gelfand, M. J. (1998). Converging measurement of horizontal and vertical individualism and collectivism. *Journal of Personality and Social Psychology, 74,* 118–128.

Triandis, H. C., & Suh, E. M. (2002). Cultural influences on personality. *Annual Review of Psychology, 53,* 133–160.

Trivers, R. L. (1971). The evolution of reciprocal altruism. *Quarterly Review of Biology, 46,* 35–57.

Tulving, E. (2002). Episodic memory: From mind to brain. In S. Fiske & D. Schacter

(Eds.), *Annual review of psychology* (Vol. 53, pp. 1–25). Stanford, CA: Annual Reviews.

Turkle, S. (1996). *Life on the screen: Identity in the age of the Internet.* New York: Simon & Schuster.

Tuveson, E. L. (1968). *Redeemer nation: The idea of America's millennial role.* Chicago: University of Chicago Press.

Vaillant, G. E. (1977). *Adaptation to life.* Boston: Little, Brown.

Vaillant, G. E., & Milofsky, E. (1980). The natural history of male psychological health: IX. Empirical evidence for Erikson's model of the life cycle. *American Journal of Psychiatry, 137,* 1348–1359.

Vandewater, E. A., Ostrove, J. M., & Stewart, A. J. (1997). Predicting women's well-being in midlife: The importance of personality development and social role involvements. *Journal of Personality and Social Psychology, 72,* 1147–1160.

Vanzant, I. (1998). *In the meantime: Finding yourself and the love you want.* New York: Simon & Schuster.

Wakefield, J. C. (1998). Immortality and the externalization of the self: Plato's unrecognized theory of generativity. In D. P. McAdams & E. de St. Aubin (Eds.), *Generativity and adult development* (pp. 133–179). Washington, DC: APA Press.

Watkins, M. (1986). *Invisible guests: The development of imaginal dialogues.* Hillsdale, NJ: Analytic Press.

Watson, D., & Clark, L. A. (1984). Negative affectivity: The disposition to experience aversive emotional states. *Psychological Bulletin, 96,* 465–490.

Weber, M. (1904/1976). *The Protestant ethic and the spirit of capitalism* (T. Parsons, Trans.). New York: Macmillan.

Wegner, D. M., Schneider, D. J., Carter, S. R., & White, T. L. (1987). Paradoxical effects of thought suppression. *Journal of Personality and Social Psychology, 53,* 5–13.

Welch-Ross, M. K. (1995). An integrative model of the development of autobiographical memory. *Developmental Review, 15,* 338–365.

Wellman, H. M. (1993). Early understanding of mind: The normal case. In S. Baron-Cohen, H. Tager-Flusberg, & D. J. Cohen (Eds.), *Understanding other minds: Perspectives from autism* (pp. 10–39). New York: Oxford University Press.

Wheatcroft, G. (2000, September 9). Politics without piety. *New York Times,* p. A-22.

Whitbourne, S. K., Zuschlag, M. K., Elliot, L. B., & Waterman, A. S. (1992). Psychosocial development in adulthood: A 22-year sequential study. *Journal of Personality and Social Psychology, 63,* 260–271.

White, J. L., & Parham, T. A. (1990). *The psychology of Blacks: An African-American perspective.* Englewood Cliffs, NJ: Prentice-Hall.

White, M., & Epston, D. (1990). *Narrative means to therapeutic ends.* New York: Norton.

Wiggins, J. S. (Ed.). (1996). *The five-factor model of personality: Theoretical perspectives.* New York: Guilford Press.

Williams, O. (Ed.). (1972). *The pocket book of modern verse* (3rd ed.). New York: Simon & Schuster.

Wills, G. (1990). *Under God: Religion and American politics.* New York: Simon & Schuster.

Wills, G. (1992). *Lincoln at Gettysburg: The words that remade America.* New York: Simon & Schuster.

Wilson, A. E., & Ross, M. (2001). From chump to champ: People's appraisals of their earlier and present selves. *Journal of Personality and Social Psychology, 80,* 572–584.

Wilson, E. O. (1975). *Sociobiology.* Cambridge, MA: Harvard University Press.

Wilson, E. O. (1978). *On human nature.* Cambridge, MA: Harvard University Press.

Winter, D. G., John, O. P., Stewart, A. J., Klohnen, E., & Duncan, L. E. (1998). Traits and motives: Toward an integration of two traditions in personality research. *Psychological Review, 105,* 230–250.

Winthrop, J. (1630/1985). A modell of Christian charity. In R. N. Bellah, R. Madsen, W. M. Sullivan, A. Swidler, & S. M. Tipton (Eds.), *Individualism and commitment in American life: Readings on the themes of* Habits of the Heart (pp. 22–27). New York: Harper & Row.

Woike, B. A. (1995). Most-memorable experiences: Evidence for a link between implicit and explicit motives and social cognitive processes in everyday life. *Journal of Personality and Social Psychology, 68,* 1081–1091.

Woike, B. A., Gershkovich, I., Piorkowski, R., & Polo, M. (1999). The role of motives in the content and structure of autobiography. *Journal of Personality and Social Psychology, 76,* 600–612.

Wolf, E. S. (1982). Comments on Heinz Kohut's conceptualization of a bipolar self. In B. Lee (Ed.), *Psychosocial theories of the self* (pp. 23–42). New York: Plenum Press.

Wolfe, A. (2000, October). The opening of the evangelical mind. *Atlantic Monthly,* pp. 55–76.

Wollman, C., & Felton, B. (1983). Social supports as stress buffers for adult cancer patients. *Psychosomatic Medicine, 45,* 322–331.

Wright, A. (1994). *After Gregory.* Dallas, TX: Baskerville.

Wright, R. (1994). *The moral animal.* New York: Pantheon.

Wuthnow, R. (1991). *Acts of compassion: Caring for others and helping ourselves.* Princeton, NJ: Princeton University Press.

Wuthnow, R. (1998). *After heaven: Spirituality in America since the 1950s.* Berkeley: University of California Press.

Wynter, L. E. (2002). *American skin: Pop culture, big business and the end of White America.* New York: Crown.

York, K. L., & John, O. P. (1992). The four faces of Eve: A typological analysis of women's personality at midlife. *Journal of Personality and Social Psychology, 63,* 494–508.

Young, J. E. (2000). Against redemption: The arts of countermemory in Germany today. In P. Homans (Ed.), *Symbolic loss: The ambiguity of mourning and memory at century's end* (pp. 126–144). Charlottesville: University of Virginia Press.

Index